On the Theory and History
of Ideological Production

Historical Materialism Book Series

The Historical Materialism Book Series is a major publishing initiative of the radical left. The capitalist crisis of the twenty-first century has been met by a resurgence of interest in critical Marxist theory. At the same time, the publishing institutions committed to Marxism have contracted markedly since the high point of the 1970s. The Historical Materialism Book Series is dedicated to addressing this situation by making available important works of Marxist theory. The aim of the series is to publish important theoretical contributions as the basis for vigorous intellectual debate and exchange on the left.

The peer-reviewed series publishes original monographs, translated texts, and reprints of classics across the bounds of academic disciplinary agendas and across the divisions of the left. The series is particularly concerned to encourage the internationalization of Marxist debate and aims to translate significant studies from beyond the English-speaking world.

For a full list of titles in the Historical Materialism Book Series available in paperback from Haymarket Books, visit: www.haymarketbooks.org/series_collections/1-historical-materialism.

On the Theory and History of Ideological Production

Juan Carlos Rodríguez and His Contemporaries

Malcolm K. Read

Haymarket Books
Chicago, IL

First published in 2023 by Brill Academic Publishers, The Netherlands
© 2023 Koninklijke Brill NV, Leiden, The Netherlands

Published in paperback in 2024 by
Haymarket Books
P.O. Box 180165
Chicago, IL 60618
773-583-7884
www.haymarketbooks.org

ISBN: 979-8-88890-320-9

Distributed to the trade in the US through Consortium Book Sales and
Distribution (www.cbsd.com) and internationally through Ingram
Publisher Services International (www.ingramcontent.com).

This book was published with the generous support of Lannan
Foundation, Wallace Action Fund, and the Marguerite Casey Foundation.

Special discounts are available for bulk purchases by organizations and
institutions. Please call 773-583-7884 or email info@haymarketbooks.org
for more information.

Cover art and design by David Mabb. Cover art is a detail from *Painting
55, Rhythm 69, (William Morris Block Printed Pattern Book, with Hans Richter
Storyboard, developed from Richter's Rhythmus 25 and Kazimir Malevich's
film script Artistic and Scientific Film – Painting and Architectural Concerns –
Approaching the New Plastic Architectural System)*. Paint and wallpaper on
canvas (2007).

Printed in the United States.

Library of Congress Cataloging-in-Publication data is available.

Contents

Preface

One grey, windswept afternoon, many years ago, the headmaster of the village primary school rang the bell that brought the pupils into line for entry into the afternoon classes. The playground, he announced, was untidy and part of the class was to be detailed to collect the litter. Then, silently, almost dramatically, he walked down the line, like a sergeant major reviewing his troops; and as he proceeded, he tapped on the chest those individuals who were to collect the litter. The remainder were led inside, and within a few minutes the school exploded to their distant, joyful cries. Those left in the cold stood and listened, exchanging worried glances; gradually, the significance of the occasion began to dawn: those inside were the ones who had 'passed' the 11-plus whereas those outside were the 'failures'. 'Mi mam 'n dad'll kill me', blubbered one. (Inside the cheers continued.) 'There goes mi brand new bike', mused another. A few affected not to give a damn. But for all of them it was a long walk home through the streets that day ...

And, so, it came to pass that I entered University at a slightly more advanced age than the average student, after a long, hard slog through the 'tech' and other institutions of further education. Statistically, I was only the second pupil in the history of my Secondary Modern school – in other words, one in hundreds, if not thousands – to have made it through to advanced education. And I bore the psychological scars to prove it: the Authorities did not take kindly to those 'failures' who refused to recognise their status. I arrived on the steps of Bristol University to study Spanish – the fact that it was Spanish and not, say, French or German was one more consequence of my irregular education. While I had read widely in the European literatures, I was, in fundamental respects, largely self-taught, with all the disadvantages that this implied, and this quickly began to manifest itself within a university context. Less expected were the advantages with which I was favoured. These included an incredible capacity for sustained and disciplined hard work. It was, I guess, the intellectual equivalent of the labour power of which working-class men boasted: 'get a gleg o'that, lad', my uncle would say, on inviting me to prod his firm, bulging biceps. My instinct, on finding myself at last in the academy, was to reapply this capacity mentally, and I did so, to telling effect.

I was further encouraged by the realisation that the upper- and middle-class students were burdened by their own disadvantages. Most of the former moved through the world 'as if they owned it', which, to all intents and purposes, some of them, or at least their fathers, did. One of the unforeseen and unfortunate side-effects of their proprietorial 'ease' was a fundamentally unquestioning attitude towards the world. The university was an extension of their social round, with all the privileges that this entailed, and which they had every reason to accept as it was. As for the students from grammar schools, university represented, in academic terms, a continuation of a familiar routine: the thrills came from escaping the reach of Authority, in its various guises, and from experimenting with adulthood. As in the case of the privately educated students, more than a few of them struck me as being intellectually quite mediocre. They had got where they had through every advantage that the grammar-school system could provide. In contrast, I found the academy to be a totally alien environment; and, compelled by the mere force of circumstance, I was determined to survive at any cost – to operate both *in* and *upon* the world.

As part of my upbringing, I had imbibed (from my father) what I would describe as a vaguely socialist culture and, understandably, in an attempt to find my bearings within the University, gravitated during the Freshers' Weekend towards the political clubs. Of course, I knew all about the practical effects of capitalist exploitation on working-class families – my grandfather had been made to work on the roofs at British Rail during the worst of weathers, as a punishment for his union activity. That said, my political awareness could only be described as embryonic, indicative of which was the confusion aroused in me by the existence of *two* Marxist clubs, one communist and one Trotskyist. What was the difference? Which was I going to join? In the event I joined neither, put off by the 'public school types' who, I realised immediately, were not from my background and who, I further intuited, were not to be trusted.

Beyond my prejudices, other, deeper pressures were at work – as I would subsequently learn, my situation was decidedly 'over-determined' – pressures that disposed me to distance myself from Left-wing politics. The message had been remorselessly hammered home, not least of all by my family: I was 'to get on and do well', which involved, in effect, severing the ties that bound me to my working-class background. Facilitating this disengagement was the fact that, within their respective spheres, my parents had themselves managed to haul themselves up by their bootstraps – after starting out as a bricklayer, then an assistant at the local Co-op, my father became a primary school headmaster, whereas my mother, initially an usherette at the local cinema, would eventually run her own stall in the town's Market Hall. We are, after all, talking about the 1950s and '60s, in which this kind of social mobility became feasible, even commonplace within certain social strata.

When I eventually came to react against this background, the ensuing wider family turmoil would prove all-engulfing, but that, as they say, is another story and, in any case, from the time I entered university the most important constraints upon the development of my political awareness were to be found within the academy. Hispanic scholarship at the time was dominated by a singularly obscure brand of Catholic orthodoxy, organised around the study of sixteenth- and seventeenth-century Spanish drama. Critical concerns centred accordingly on the difficulty of reconciling free-will with predestination, which for me constituted a mere academic exercise. Beyond this limited ambit, literary studies presupposed the student's possession of an appropriate 'sensibility', to which my peers appeared to have immediate access. My solution, by way of neutralising their advantage, was to transfer the focus of my attention to the study of language, as currently promoted by Noam Chomsky, whose work enabled me, in some degree, to re-engage with politics and broader intellectual issues.

My problematic situation notwithstanding, I managed to impress my examiners to the extent that I was eventually awarded a First-Class Honours degree. It was the only one in the country in Hispanic Studies that year, and I was much lauded as a consequence, not least of all in the local press in my hometown, Derby. Quite soon I was appointed to a position as assistant lecturer in the University of Wales and found myself giving classes on medieval Spanish literature, even as I pressed on with my research into linguistics. Of course, I continued to read widely – I recall being deeply influenced by Auerbach's *Mimesis* and Ernst Fischer's *The Necessity of Art: A Marxist Approach* – but professionally speaking I was confined to national traditions of – in their different ways – a singularly restricted kind. In the case of Spain, we are talking of a culture that was still under the heel of a Franco dictatorship. Students of English literature of a certain age will find it amazing that during these years I failed to engage the work of such a figure as Raymond Williams. But that in itself is symptomatic of their own confinement within a British tradition that, while less inward-looking than its Spanish counterpart, was also 'in contraflow', to borrow a term from Perry Anderson. The first of my intellectual 'breaks' only came when, in the mid-70s, I happened to read Norman Brown's *Life against Death: The Psychoanalytical Meaning of History* (1968) and Ernest Becker's *The Denial of Death* (1973). Then came the arrival of 'Theory' and, quite suddenly, everything was up for grabs, which brought about a second break.

It would have been in the early 1980s when I was first made aware of the work of the Spanish Althusserian Marxist Juan Carlos Rodríguez, via a footnote reference to *Teoría e historia de la producción ideológica* (1974) in *Historia social de la literatura española* (1978), edited by Carlos Blanco Aguinaga, Julio Rodríguez Puértolas and Iris Zavala. By this stage, Thatcherism had gone onto the offensive and, by way of reaction, I had begun, professionally, to refresh and deepen my understanding of Marxism. Coincidentally, many of the latter's petty-bourgeois adherents, including those who had run the relevant social clubs at university, were in the process of abandoning ship. Following up the lead, as one was accustomed to do, I ordered Rodríguez's text by inter-library loan and was somewhat taken aback to receive a copy from the Biblioteca Nacional in Madrid. (I was at the time lecturing in the University of Auckland, New Zealand, and our inter-library loans habitually arrived from Australia.)

I vividly recall perusing the introduction to the work, which, for security reasons, was restricted to use in the university library. First impressions were not encouraging: I could barely make any sense of what turned out to be a densely theoretical work. Was it a text, I wondered, that needed to be taken on board or could it be politely returned to the librarian? Gradually, I came to sense that the problem lay not with Rodríguez's text but could be traced to my own deficient knowledge of Marxist theory and, more specifically, of Althusserian theory.

So, in the event, I decided to press on … and on … and on. In the midst, also mists, of my confusion, I was hooked on the idea of an ideological unconscious. The bourgeois notion that 'we' are free subjects in control of 'our' destiny had increasingly struck me as a sick joke, not least when embraced by those academic Marxists who projected their own enhanced sense of agency onto the working class. I had only ever been aware of the structural barriers placed in my path and the ways in which, defenceless and powerless, I had been manipulated and pushed around by educational authorities. When, finally, I was able to gain access to the university, it had been through the tradesman's entrance, which, if nothing else, had given me a rather different 'take' on the 'freedom of the individual'. In Rodríguez I discerned a voice in common, emanating from a Spanish culture that, located on the margins of bourgeois society, was critical of, since exterior to, this same freedom. Now, I was coming to realise that structural forces determined my fate unconsciously at the level of ideology. Later that evening, I informed my rather perplexed wife that I feared I might have to jettison all my prior research, to the extent, by way of emulating Rodríguez, of literally having to 'throw it out of the window' …

Of what precisely did my break consist? Viewed retrospectively, I would suggest that, during the process of perusing *Teoría e historia*, I had begun to realise the need to *change terrain*, theoretically speaking, from a subject/object or individual/society paradigm to a problematic based on the social formation articulated on the basis of a mode of production. From the agonic conflict between the individual and society, in the case of the paradigm, the former was always destined to emerge victorious. The further temptation was to proceed to spin a narrative that, very much along the lines of my own, tells of how a subject possessed of unusual willpower had been able to make a success of himself;

or, alternatively, of how a whole culture had been able to slough off medieval darkness to embrace enlightenment. Of course, it could always be conceded that society 'influences' or even 'conditions' the individual. But, that said, ideological constraints would always favour the individual, in an ascending spiral that, at any level, always finds him or her located *outside* and, more importantly, *prior to* society. Again, with variations: this same individual might also raise him/herself *above* society, to view it from a transcendental vantage point. The effect was the same: the beautiful soul escapes the domain of material causality either into pre-history or into the realm of the supernatural/aesthetic; as indeed was the resultant epistemological paradox: existentially, I *experience* myself as a *free* subject, even while I *know* that, objectively, I am absolutely determined.

To locate oneself within the problematic based on the social formation was to realise that, to anticipate my conclusion, the understanding is no longer the act of an individual subject but of its structural conditions. Of course, one is never able to break entirely with ideology or, by the same token, with one's personal obsessions, hang-ups, prejudices, chips-on-the-shoulder and so forth, particularly after having negotiated the deadly minefield that was/is the British academy. But, that said, one can at least undertake a transformative displacement, which begins to operate in reverse and to pose questions, until, eventually, having traversed the social formation, in all its contradictory, microscopic and macroscopic density, it may be possible to 'find oneself'. But with a final proviso: the self that one finds may be barely recognisable and, for certain, will in no way resemble the beautiful soul that presides over the liberal narrative. There may be no subject *of* history but, emphatically, there *are* subjects *in* history ...

Several years later I stepped off the plane in Granada to meet the author of *Teoría e historia* in person for the first time. Our friendship was to be long and always comradely, although sometimes turbulent – while essentially a timid man, Rodríguez had managed to survive in a hostile academic environment only by being uncompromising in the defence of his positions. And I argued from the same standpoint. Our association came to an end only with his death in 2016. My last trip to Granada was to pay my respects to his mortal remains in the cemetery overlooking the city, in the company of his wife, the acclaimed poet Ángeles Mora. The ensuing chapters in many respects chart the course of our intellectual relationship.

Acknowledgements

Acknowledgements are gratefully made to the editors of the following books and journals, where these essays first appeared: *Journal of Critical Realism* for 'Educating the Educators: Critical Realism and the Ideological Unconscious' (*Journal of Critical Realism*, 12, 4 (2013), 443–78) and for 'On the Radical Historicity of Literature: Althusser versus Bhaskar' (*Journal of Critical Realism*, 15, 2 (2016), 142–69); *Journal of Medieval and Early Modern Studies* for 'Ideologies of the Spanish Transition Revisited: Juan Huarte de San Juan, Juan Carlos Rodríguez, and Noam Chomsky' (*Journal of Medieval and Early Modern Studies*, 34, 2 (2004), 309–43); Oxford University Press for 'Juan Carlos Rodríguez and Michel Foucault: Discourse, Ideology and the Unconscious' (*Oxford Encyclopedia of Communication and Critical Studies*, Oxford, 2018); and *Rethinking Marxism* for 'The Psychoanalytic Paradox and Capitalist Exploitation: Slavoj Žižek and Juan Carlos Rodríguez' (*Rethinking Marxism*, 31, 2 (2019), 194–221). 'Explorations of the Political/Ideological Unconscious: Fredric Jameson and Juan Carlos Rodríguez' first appeared in English in *Mediations* 32, 1 (2018), 71–94. This is a slightly adapted form of 'Exploraciones del inconsciente político/ideológico: Fredric Jameson y Juan Carlos Rodríguez', which appeared in *Pensar desde abajo*, 5 (2016), 193–224.

In gathering these articles together in a single volume, a certain amount of repetition has proved unavoidable. While the most obvious redundancies have been removed, I came to consider, after mature reflection, that a periodic restatement of theoretical positions contributed positively to the flow of the narrative. Accordingly, I have chosen to leave each contribution more or less as it stands, correcting only minor inaccuracies and stylistic infelicities.

Thanks must go to my good friend and colleague over many years, Professor Lou Charnon Deutsch, and to my wife, Susan Read, for their critical support and encouragement throughout my obsessive dedication to the present project. The moment is appropriate to acknowledge the influence upon me of Michael Sprinker, whose exemplary presence cast a bright light over my years at Stony Brook, New York.

Introduction

The present text was conceived, in project form, as a means of explaining a puzzle, namely why a research programme of the range and depth of Juan Carlos Rodríguez's should have been so restricted in its influence, both nationally and, to a much more notable extent, internationally. Like a good wine, it seems to have travelled badly. Some of the reasons are obvious. To begin with, Rodríguez's fortunes were tied in some measure to those of Althusser, with whom he studied in Paris in the mid-1970s, and which, precisely at the time when *Teoría e historia* appeared (1974), were poised to enter seemingly into terminal decline. Rodríguez was more adversely affected than most of Althusser's students insofar as he was located in a small, provincial university, in a country in the process of emerging from the grips of a fascist dictatorship, circumstances that translated, among other things, into a lack of material support, beginning with the kind of professional editorial assistance that many scholars in the First World take for granted. That said, I will be arguing throughout that, if *Teoría e historia* turned out to be a 'dog that didn't bark', the root cause of its silence is to be found in its attachment to the Althusserian notion of the social formation and to the ever-pregivenness of this formation's complex unity. To those who departed, unconsciously, from the standpoint of an empiricism of the subject and of a bourgeois humanism that made Man the axis of all social theory, Rodríguez's work remained a closed book.

Chapter 1 attempts to provide a useful roadmap for the journey ahead, with an eye to the major opposition between the two relevant paradigms or problematics. The first paradigm bases itself on the subject/object opposition, in conjunction with some version of the rise of the 'free subject'; the second presupposes the structure of a complex whole and gives rise to the notion of history without a subject, hence without a teleology. Each of these narratives will be shown readily to interpenetrate the other. The chapter's own narrative is organised along the lines of alternating sections, some of an overtly *applied* nature, focused on particular literary texts, others, of a more theoretical nature, targeted at the works of Althusser, Gramsci and Poulantzas.

Chapter 2 serves as a link between my preface and the body of the ensuing text, in which capacity it explores, from a personal standpoint, the connection between structural Marxism, exemplified by the work of Rodríguez, and the critical realism associated with Roy Bhaskar. It takes as its point of departure the tributes to Bhaskar published on the philosopher's death. Laudable and understandable though it was to prioritise the contributions of younger scholars, one of the tactic's unforeseen consequences, it is argued, was to marginalise the career trajectories of their mature colleagues. The latter perforce arrived upon the scene of critical realism already burdened with their own complex legacies, which demanded more in the way of negotiation. Taking my own career path as exemplary, I focus upon its 'Bhaskarian moment', upon the benefits accrued therefrom, but finally upon the difficulty in reconciling critical realism with structural Marxism, notably after the former's 'spiritual turn'.

Chapter 3 explores Noam Chomsky's interest in the early Spanish educational reformer Juan Huarte de San Juan (1575). Chomsky reads the Spaniard's 'creative wit' as an anticipation of the Cartesian subject, in a long tradition that will pass through Kant and Humboldt and eventuate in a transformational subject equipped with the linguistic means to make infinite use of finite means. To be contrasted with this liberal narrative is an alternative, Marxist narrative that, taking its cue from the brief references to Huarte in Rodríguez's *Theory and History* and from the critique of Chomsky mounted in *State, Stage, Language: The Production of the Subject*, will proceed to theorise Huarte's *Examen de ingenios* (*Examination of Men's Wits*) as the product of a clash between conflictual contemporary ideologies.

Fredric Jameson and Rodríguez both took Althusser as their point of departure to theorise respectively the 'political unconscious' and the 'ideological unconscious'. Superficially, they appear to have much in common: Jameson begins *The Political Unconscious* (1981) with the command to 'always historicise', whereas Rodríguez protests at the outset of *Theory and History* (1974) that 'literature has not always existed'. Such mutuality notwithstanding, their fortunes have been radically divergent. In contrast to Rodríguez, whose 'ideological unconscious' found little or no resonance in contemporary theory, at least outside of Spain, Jameson acquired universal acclaim through his 'political unconscious'. Chapter 4 explores the reasons for this discrepancy. It argues that the key to Jameson's success lies in his continuing allegiance to the subject/object opposition, albeit of Hegelian confection. In effect Jameson draws key Althusserian concepts back into an idealist framework through the simple process of ironing out the structural complexities internal to the social formation. The Hegelian Subject, we conclude, is admittedly a strange subject, but a subject nevertheless and hence amenable to bourgeois ideologues who refuse to surrender the primacy of a subject that is indispensable to the smooth functioning of capitalism.

Like Jameson, Terry Eagleton is an academic whose reputation as a Marxist in no way prevented him from acquiring star status within the global academy. Unlike Jameson's take on Althusserianism, however, Eagleton's *Criticism and Ideology* (1976) constitutes a far more faithful translation of the same into its national idiom. Among other things, it included a strong critique of Raymond

Williams, the doyen of the British Left, not to mention of prominent figures of the bourgeois establishment, for which reason the abruptness, almost brutality, with which Eagleton would subsequently cast Althusser to one side proves all the more arresting. Chapter 5 contextualises Eagleton's critical moves through a comparison with the work of Rodríguez. While, along with other members of the New Left, Eagleton will be quick to remind Williams of the extent to which historical processes transcend the level of 'experience', he will, like them, be gradually drawn back inexorably into the framework of the subject/object opposition, through the primacy accorded to the libidinal unconscious and an empiricist detour through the referent. Along with other Marxists from the same background, Eagleton cannot finally relinquish the notion that it suffices to open one's eyes in order to acquire knowledge. From such a standpoint, the Althusserian notion of an ideological unconsciousness would prove to be unthinkable, in every sense of the word.

Chapter 6 reviews the contrasting ways in which two of Althusser's students, namely Michel Foucault and Rodríguez, rose to meet the challenge posed by their former master's notion of ideological unconsciousness. In Foucault, Althusser's original insight underwent a radical transformation from which it emerged, stripped of its Marxist outworks, as a *discursive unconsciousness*, located in the rules that governed discourse and, subsequently, in social institutions and practices. Rodríguez, on the other hand, reworked the notion of ideological unconsciousness into that of an *ideological unconscious*. Understandably, Foucault's work found favour with a bourgeois academy that, throughout the 1980s and '90s, increasingly abandoned Marxism to embrace conservative forms of postmodernism and neo-liberalism. While, during the same period, Rodríguez struggled to make his presence felt from the margins of the global academy, his very location in a country that, by his own estimation, had failed historically to catch the capitalist train, paradoxically afforded an insight into the deeper workings of ideology, or so at least it will be argued.

Chapter 7 is in many ways a continuation of Chapter 1. While accepting the importance of Roy Bhaskar's contribution to Marxist theory, along recognisably Althusserian lines, it argues that the author of *A Realist Theory of Science* (1975) and subsequent texts was never able, finally, to liberate himself from the subject/object dichotomy. The corresponding priority that he accords to consciousness explains how he came to imagine that school pupils might shed the chains of unfreedom through a simple act of will and, by the same token, empty their minds of ideological baggage. For Rodríguez, by way of contrast, ideology originated not in the ideological apparatus of the school but in the relations of production. The school, he further argues, was charged with formalising and reinforcing the very notion of freedom that Bhaskar sought to promote and that was required to facilitate the smooth functioning of capitalist relations.

Chapter 8 compares the libidinal unconscious, as theorised by Slavoj Žižek, to Rodríguez's notion of the ideological unconscious. According to Žižek, the libidinal unconscious takes the form of a trans-historical 'real kernel', which returns as the force of desire, with subversive consequences for the discursive structure of language; individual praxis is cast accordingly as the genetic origin of social structures and the main dynamic in the transformation of society. In contrast, the ideological unconscious, as formulated by Juan Carlos Rodríguez, is 'secreted' by the social relations of production, 'before' being formally legitimised within the State Apparatus. Far from denigrating human subjectivity, Rodríguez devotes considerable attention to theorising its radically historical variants, also to exploring the contradictory structural forces of which this social subjectivity is deemed to be a condensation. The aim of the present chapter is to put both versions of the unconscious to the test of their objects through the close analysis of selected literary texts.

Chapter 9 is the most recently composed of all the pieces collected together in the present volume. It is principally concerned to trace the continuity between the assault upon Marxism orchestrated by Ernesto Laclau and Chantal Mouffe and the emergence in Spain of a new political party, Podemos. While seemingly originating in a critique of Althusserianism and, specifically, in its notion of the social formation, the post-Marxists actually reconstitute the 'matrix effect' of this formation within the endless fluidity of language. The ultimate horizon is a subjectivity cut adrift from its moorings in the infrastructure, hence free to re-constitute itself endlessly at the level of discourse. The chapter concludes with an assessment of Laclau and Mouffe's impact upon Podemos. To better stage the poverty of the post-Marxist tradition, its analyses will be contrasted throughout to those of Rodríguez.

One point needs to be clarified at the outset. The literary texts to be analysed during the ensuing discussion are not advanced as 'examples' to which 'theory' is *applied*, in accordance with the familiar empiricist command that 'speculation' be 'cashed in' pragmatically. Our intention, in other words, is not to offer a short course on Western or Spanish culture. Their purpose, rather, is strictly exponential; they serve to 'think through' problems posed at the level of theory. Other texts might well have been chosen and to the same or comparable effect. We ask the pardon and patience of those readers unfamiliar with the Spanish tradition from which the texts have been drawn. Every effort has been made, in their interests, adequately to locate the immediate conjunctural moments within the context of their appropriate social formations, themselves understood as unevenly developed and developing structures. That said, we make no apologies for breaking with the currently fashionable presentism that, we believe, masks a covert design to detach textual artefacts from their historical base with the further aim of elevating them into the transcendental space of 'Culture'.

CHAPTER 1

In the Shadow of Althusser

Althusser showed me a series of party documents and some articles from *L'Humanité*, with which I was familiar, more or less. He collapsed into an armchair while I leafed through the texts, which consisted of distilled venom directed against him. 'What do you think?' he asked. Even I was taken aback. 'They really hate you', I replied, dryly. And then something surprising happened. He spat out that, possibly, he also had begun to hate, to hate 'them'. I suggested that I believed him to be incapable of hating anyone. He began to smile: 'Perhaps it's because ...' We finished off the phrase in unison: 'because elephants are contagious'. And we both burst into guffaws of laughter. Because, as I forgot to explain, Althusser's laughter was as contagious as his intelligence. Although he lived in the Rue d'Ulm, the street where the sun never shone. (Juan Carlos Rodríguez)

1   Negotiating the 'Break'

The Althusserian notion of a 'break', to remind ourselves, was originally theorised with reference to the rupture that, allegedly, separated the early, humanist Marx, who prioritised the centrality of the subject, from the late Marx, who introduced a whole new battery of scientific concepts (mode of production, relations of production, surplus value, etc.) through which to facilitate the theorisation of a 'social formation'. The process involved was admittedly more complex and prolonged than the term 'break' itself would suggest, and doubtless forever incomplete, but the notion itself remained one that, for all his self-criticisms, Althusser would never relinquish, and with reason: any challenge to existing social conditions and the theorisation thereof necessarily connoted the possibility, developmentally, of novelty, newness, and innovation. Except that this possibility needed to be qualified in one important respect: any radical beginning should never be conceived along metaphysical, idealist lines, which is to say, as an absolute beginning.

Herein, to resume the details of Althusser's analysis, lies the danger of projecting Marx's later consciousness onto his youthful intelligence, along idealist lines: '*The contingency of Marx's beginnings was this enormous layer of ideology* beneath which he was born', Althusser warns, '*this crushing layer* which he succeeded in breaking through'.[1] 'Succeeded', but at what cost! A cost similarly to be borne by anyone who would try to emulate Marx's achievement! As try they must: 'To become "ideologists of the working class" (Lenin), "organic intellectuals" of the proletariat (Gramsci), intellectuals have to carry out a radical revolution in their ideas: a long, painful and difficult re-education. An endless external and *internal* struggle'.[2]

Struggles, external and internal, were the very stuff of daily existence for Juan Carlos Rodríguez under a Franco dictatorship, and their intellectual repercussions are visible from the very outset of his *Theory and History of Ideological Production* (2002 [1974]). No mercy was to be shown towards a critical tradition so ideologically complicit with the political order. Dispensed with are the notions of 'author', 'critic', 'reader' and – superordinate to these – the notion of the ('free', 'autonomous') 'subject', a list soon to be extended to include 'Reason', 'unreason', 'mind' and 'psychology', all of which are now placed under erasure. And that was only the beginning: also to be 'picked up with pincers' (to use Rodríguez's own turn of phrase) are the period concepts of the 'Middle Ages' and 'Renaissance', together with those of 'form' and 'content', and 'text' and 'context', in short, everything associated with the trans-historical notions of 'Man' and 'Literature'. In their place are concepts drawn from the heartland of Structural Marxism: the 'social formation' with its distinctive 'instances' (economic, political, and ideological), 'over-determination', 'dominance', 'determination in the last instance', and so on.

While, at this early stage, the obstacles to comprehension were not insurmountable, the introduction of concepts of Rodríguez's own confection,[3] such as 'productive logic of the text' and 'ideological matrix', could only prove highly destabilising, and those of 'ideological unconscious' and 'State Apparatus', a step too far, even for a reader possessed of an unusual amount of goodwill. As for the professional critics, they were left in effect with nothing to say about a text that had, confessedly, 'broken' with all their own taken-for-granted principles, leaving a somewhat bemused Rodríguez, in the 'postdata' to the second edition of *Theory and History*, to mull over the circumstances of 'the dog that didn't bark'.[4]

Objectively considered, the Spaniard should have been the last person to be surprised at his non-reception. After all, he himself had given prior warning in his own (belatedly published) doctoral thesis as to the radical change of theor-

---

1 Althusser 1990a, p. 74. Italics in quotations throughout are original, unless otherwise stated.
2 Althusser 1971, p. 12.
3 Rodríguez 2002a, p. 17 ff.
4 Ibid., pp. 32–3.

etical terrain that he himself was in the process of negotiating. This change, he further elaborated, required nothing less than the prior eradication of a subject/object opposition,[5] an opposition that, allegedly, had been incorporated into a generalised literary 'common sense',[6] and hence subsumed in a 'theory of knowledge'[7] that sustained the whole bourgeois edifice. Virtually insurmountable obstacles, then, were to be anticipated – had not Althusser himself spoken of the need for 'a long, painful and difficult re-education'? The stage seems set for an agon between, on the one hand, the prioritisation of the subject/object opposition and, on the other, the Althusserian notion of a social formation, understood as a structure in dominance; also between their corresponding narratives, namely, the liberal story of 'Freedom', on the one hand, and the notion of history as a process without a subject, on the other. And yet Rodríguez alludes to the radical incommensurability between these two problematics only, parenthetically, to obviate any direction confrontation between them: 'I have no intention at this point of replaying the notorious polemic over "humanism", which a few years ago surrounded the work of Althusser – a polemic that was boring for being so confused'.[8] This is surely very curious and calls for comment.

Undoubtedly, the conjunctural circumstances proved crucial. What appeared 'boring' at one moment, when Rodríguez was still assured of comradely support, would quickly prove to be less so when, following the relatively sudden eclipse of Althusserianism, an indifference to controversy would prove to be a luxury that the Spaniard could ill afford; confined to a marginalised status even within his national academy, he would exert little or no influence at the international level, notwithstanding the ongoing productivity of his work. But if the loss was his, it was also Marxism's, at a time when leftist traditions were under severe attack both from disenchanted members within and from capitalist ideologues without, under the standard of a resurgent liberalism.

That Althusserianism had its difficulties was, of course, undeniable – any theoretical problematic has them – but that they were not resolvable internally remained to be proved. There was something suspiciously opportunistic about the eagerness with which many so-called Marxists sought to bury the Althusserian project. If, as was frequently claimed, Althusser had comparatively little to say about the 'real concrete', that was because, as Michael Sprinker has suggested, he conceived concrete research to be the prerogative of the sciences,

---

5   Rodríguez 2015, p. 48.
6   Ibid., p. 58.
7   Ibid., p. 128.
8   Rodríguez 2002a, p. 20.

formulated along Althusserian lines.[9] Of these sciences, when it came to the theory and history of ideological production, Rodríguez's work was proving to be a richly productive, regional instance.

Given the recent resurgence of interest in Althusserianism, as evinced by the continued publication of Althusser's inedited works[10] and such texts as *Encountering Althusser*,[11] the moment seems ripe for a resumption of the relevant debates, with an eye to staging some of the encounters that failed to materialise the first time round. Attention will be directed specifically at the agon between the two narratives to which we referred above. To elaborate, the first narrative will ring the changes on the subject/object opposition: thus, individual/society, agency/structure, inside/outside, text/context, transcendental/empirical, form/matter, public/private, and so on, categories that are never taken apart or subjected to scrutiny. 'Liberals', our argument will run, always incline towards the individual, communitarians towards society. A third variant will seek the connections between both sides of the equation. Whatever the incidental form it takes, the same tale will be told, of an individual who, while s/he lives in society, also stands apart from, prior to and above the flow of history.

The second narrative consists of a succession of social formations, each formation embracing a totality of relatively autonomous instances (economic, political, and ideological) articulated on the basis of a mode of production. Contrary to what is commonly stated, the Structural Marxism that promotes these categories has always recognised the importance of subjectivity and dedicated considerable attention to theorising the 'interpellation' of the subject.[12] Nor is its concept of 'history as a process without a subject' in any way incompatible with the existence of subjects *in* history. On the contrary, in contrast to all forms of idealism, Structural Marxism theorises subjects as, at root, the historical product of social structures and relations.

Each of these narratives readily penetrates the other. Thus, bourgeois ideology, in the guise of the form/matter opposition, can masquerade as the Marxist distinction between the superstructure and the base; whereas dialectical materialism is not averse to sinking its roots into bourgeois positivism. Such is the extent of the interpenetration, particularly in its Marxian guise, that practitioners are easily deluded into believing that they have transcended the agency/structure opposition.

---

9   see Sprinker 1992, p. 130.
10   Althusser 2003, 2006, 2014.
11   Diefenbach et al 2013.
12   See Resch 1992, p. 27.

Our own text is organised along the lines of alternating sections, some of which are of an overtly theoretical nature, targeted at the works of Althusser, Antonio Gramsci and Nicos Poulantzas, while others, more concrete, address certain aspects of Rodríguez's work so as to illustrate its productivity; to indicate aporia and contradictions internal to it; and to suggest ways in which such difficulties might be resolved and the problematic developed. Of course, it does not follow, by any means, that the theoretical sections will remain at the level of abstraction or, conversely, that the concrete sections can be detached from the theoretical debate. On the contrary, the aim will be to play off one series against the other, dialectically speaking, on the understanding that, while theoretical concepts do not, in themselves, yield concrete knowledge of a concrete object, an investigation or an observation is only ever possible, in Althusser's own words, 'under the direction and control of theoretical concepts directly or indirectly active in it'.[13] This latter qualification needs to be stressed, given the widespread conviction, not least of all among Althusser's critics, that certain kinds of perceptual experience constitute an elementary form of knowledge in themselves. The possibility of a detour through the referent, which such a conviction implies, is feasible only to those in the grip of an ideological unconscious of empiricist extraction. And it is to the theorisation of this unconscious that we now turn.

2   The Ideological Unconscious

Rodríguez's *Theory and History of Ideological Production*, first published in the period of the transition in Spain from fascism to liberal democracy, implicitly takes as its starting point the famous passage in *Capital* in which Marx adumbrates the mechanisms of capitalist exploitation:

> The specific economic form in which unpaid surplus labour is pumped out of the direct producers determines the relationship of domination and servitude, as this grows directly out of production itself and reacts back on it in turn as a determinant. On this is based the entire configuration of the economic community arising from the actual relations of production, and hence also its specific political form.

---

13   Althusser 1990b, p. 48.

Marx elaborates:

> This does not prevent the same economic basis – the same in its major
> conditions – from displaying endless variations and gradations in its
> appearance, as the result of innumerable different empirical circum-
> stances, natural conditions, racial relations, historical influences acting
> from outside, etc.[14]

The historical influences that concern Rodríguez are those prevailing during
the transition from feudalism to capitalism in the case of Spain, which saw
the economic focus transferred from the relations between lord and serf to
those between Subject (employer) and subject (employee). The choice of topic,
Rodríguez explained retrospectively during a press interview, was dictated by
political considerations: '... in the Spain of the final years of Francoism, much
was said about the sixteenth and seventeenth centuries, because that was the
time of the Spanish empire; so I thought, I'm also going to write on the seventeenth century, except I'm going to write another history of what the century
was'.[15] His aim, in short, was to strike at the core narrative of the dominant ideology.

In the opening pages of *Theory and History* Rodríguez further specifies the
Althusserian version of Marxism that was to frame his own narrative. Briefly –
all too briefly, perhaps[16] – the reader is introduced to the principal concept of
a 'social formation', characterised in the case of the Spanish transition by the
co-existence of (at least) two modes of production, feudal and capitalist, and
by the dominance of the political instance with respect to its economic and
ideological counterparts, always on the understanding that, the rise of Absolutism notwithstanding, it is the economy that determines in the last instance.
Rodríguez's focus was upon ideology and specifically upon his newly formulated concept of the 'ideological unconscious', which he introduces, somewhat
obliquely, it has to be said, in the following terms: 'The notion of the subject
(and the whole problematic within which it is inscribed) is radically historical
because ... it derives directly (and exclusively) from the very matrix of the bourgeois ideological unconscious'.[17] The image of the subject, the argument runs, is
not 'for all seasons' but exists, rather, only within a bourgeois matrix; feudalism,
by way of contrast, turns on the opposition between serf and lord.

---

14   Marx 1981, p. 927.
15   Rodríguez 2016, p. 55. The translations throughout, unless otherwise stated, are my own.
16   See Read 2017.
17   Rodríguez 2002a, p. 21.

The 'subject/serf' coupling [...] does not suppose the transition from man-in-chains to man-in-himself, unencumbered and undetermined. On the contrary, such a coupling can only signify the transition from one set of social relations to another (*serf* is only a term that indicates the special – and necessary – inscription of individuals in class relations characteristic of feudalism; *subject* is only a term that indicates the special – and similarly necessary – inscription of individuals in class relations characteristic of capitalism, both in its early phase and in its later phases).[18]

A crucial distinction needs to be observed between the privileged *notions* of serf, lord, subject and so on and the *internal functioning* of the relevant ideologies, of which the notions are simply the visible, objectified expression.

Each ideological matrix, it further transpires, 'announces itself via certain key notions, to which it grants the status of essential and unalterable elements of reality'.[19] In this way, individuals inscribed under feudal relations come to conceive of themselves as 'servants of the Lord' by nature; those inscribed under bourgeois relations to conceive of themselves as 'subjects' by nature. Such are the imaginary relations through which individuals 'live' their respective social realities. An 'ideological matrix' is to be defined accordingly, as 'nothing other than the reproduction, at the level of ideology, of the basic class contradiction that constitutes each kind of social relations'.[20] The point to be emphasised is that the notions of serf and subject 'are not realities in themselves, either political or economic, nor even "eidetic" or "spiritual" realities, as some would argue. Such notions only exist as symptoms of a more underlying logic, that of the bourgeois ideological matrix that sustains them and that manifests itself in them'.[21]

Only one task remained to be performed by way of establishing the preeminence of the mode-of-production analysis over its bourgeois counterpart, the subject/object opposition, namely that of transferring the focus of attention from the Ideological State Apparatuses, in which ideology was consciously formulated, to the relations of production, through which ideology was 'originally' secreted into the social formation at large. The school system, to take Rodríguez's example, functions simply to formulate and legitimate an ideology that originates *elsewhere*: 'it is not the school that "creates" ideology, notwith-

18   Ibid., pp. 21–2.
19   Ibid., p. 22.
20   Ibid., p. 23.
21   Ibid.

standing its function as a State Apparatus; the school only materialises and reproduces this ideology'.[22] The 'elsewhere' in question consists of the relations of production that secrete the ideology that the state reproduces at a more elevated level: '... the dialectic inscribed in the literary texts (that which produces them as such, their internal logic) is what shapes an ideological unconscious. The latter is "born" not in the School, but in the interior of the social relations themselves, and derives directly from these relations'.[23] While secondary relations, at the level of the state, have the capacity to shape their primary counterpart retroactively, it is the despotism of capital that 'always already' determines, which is to say determines 'in the last instance'.

Such, in broad outline, were the grounds on which Rodríguez argued the superiority of the mode-of-production problematic over the subject/object paradigm. Our aim below will be to subject the Althusserian problematic to the test of empirical data through its application to localised conjunctures in the transition in Spain from feudalism to capitalism. That its explanatory capacity is considerable should already be evident. But equally evident are the theoretical ambiguities and inadequacies that remained to be resolved, and it is to get a better grip on these that we propose first to regress to their source in the Althusserian tradition.

3   Althusser: the Unconsciousness of Ideology

While Rodríguez was the first to formalise the 'ideological unconscious', the concept was unthinkable outside the Althusserian problematic and, indeed, outside Althusser's theorisation of the unconsciousness of ideology. This theorisation was conspicuous throughout the philosopher's early texts, notably *For Marx* (1965). 'In truth', Althusser will argue in this text, and at some length, 'ideology has very little to do with "consciousness", even supposing this term to have an unambiguous meaning. It is profoundly *unconscious*'.[24] And yet, as is also apparent from the same text, much of the detail remained to be worked out as regards the relevant determinations. In *Reading Capital* (1965) Althusser advances the notion of structural causality, according to which the social totality is nothing less than the reciprocal effectivities of its elements, at the same time as this totality, in the form of a matrix effect, reacts back upon the indi-

---

22   Ibid., p. 30.
23   Ibid.
24   Althusser 1990a, p. 233, original emphasis.

vidual elements.[25] All of which survives in *Philosophy and the Spontaneous Philosophy of the Scientists* (1967, 1974), as a consequence of which ideology 'may remain largely unconscious or, on the contrary, be more or less conscious and thought out'.[26] Except that still to be resolved is the exact relationship between the conscious and unconscious determinations, to which extent a closer look at *Philosophy and the Spontaneous Philosophy* proves rewarding.

By way of elaboration, Althusser turns to Marx's classic metaphor of the edifice, consisting of a relatively autonomous juridical-political *superstructure* atop an *infrastructure* of economic foundations. Within this edifice, Althusser explains, 'ideology must be accorded a very particular place', particularly insofar as, while situated within the superstructure, ideology also enjoys a 'general form of presence' and 'must be thought of as sliding into all the parts of the edifice, and considered as a distinctive kind of *cement* that assures the adjustment and cohesion of men in their roles, their functions and their social relations'.[27] The metaphor of 'cement', which, we will see below, is derived from Antonio Gramsci, captures the notion of a matrix effect that draws together into a totality the effectivity exercised by the social formation as a whole. Ideology, it is implied, exceeds all the forms in which it is subjectively lived by this or that individual; it exists in the form of an invisible structure that determines the individual's perception of things. Ideology's structure and the mechanisms that generate it are no more immediately visible to the people subjected to them than are the relations of production and mechanisms of economic life to the agents of production. To be inside ideology is to be unable to see it; it seemingly has no horizon.

So much is clear. But one point is not to be missed: located in the superstructure, ideology, by implication, works its way *downwards* from the upper floors of the edifice, the level at which *conscious* decisions are taken, to the base, in which it is secreted unconsciously. The primary production of ideology, it follows, takes place in the Ideological State Apparatuses, in contrast to its secondary reproduction that emanates from the relations of production. From the theoretical standpoint assumed in *For Marx*, which emphasised the matrix effect of the whole, this (re-)location represents a regressive step insofar as it invites a resumption of the subject/object dynamic and hence of ideological consciousness. (Rodríguez, to recall, saw ideology as secreted 'originally' by the relations of production.)

25   Althusser and Balibar 1970, pp. 182–9.
26   Althusser 1990b, p. 25.
27   Althusser 1990b, p. 25.

Philosophy and the Spontaneous Philosophy, we conclude, constitutes something of a transitional text from the early Althusser, who prioritises the social formation, to the later Althusser, who theorises the ideological interpellation of the individual within the confines of the Ideological State Apparatus. Ideology, it transpires in Althusser's famous essay on the topic, 'has no history' and is eternal 'exactly like the [Freudian] unconscious';[28] more importantly, the subject has been relocated at the centre of the social process: 'there is no ideology except by the subject and for subjects'.[29] This would be the aspect of Althusser's work that most attracted the attention of bourgeois scholars and predictably so insofar as it enabled them to view Althusserianism through the prism of the subject/object opposition that was central to their own ideology.

In sum, Althusser's shift towards the interpellation of the subject undoubtedly weakened the effectivity exercised by the social formation and, consequently, blocked the development of a theory of the ideological unconscious. Against this backdrop, the extent of Rodríguez's initiative stands out more clearly: his emphasis upon the primary production of ideologies within the relations of production inverts the argument to be found in the later Althusser, who prioritises the secondary reproduction of ideologies within and through the ISAs. But as Rodríguez was the first to admit,[30] his hypothesis of the primary production of ideologies within social relations left unresolved one vital question: what happens in those other modes of production in which the logic of the subject does not exist? Feudalism, by Rodríguez's own estimation, was one such mode and is, as a result, ideal territory in which to test out his concepts, empirically speaking.

4   Feudal Substantialism

The dominant ideology of feudalism, which Rodríguez labels alternatively *organicism* and *substantialism*, rested upon the serf/lord opposition. 'Organicism because [...] its key notion is the idea of the "organic body"; and substantialism because this image of the organic body immediately presupposes the idea of "substance" as what determines each body, whether it be social, human,

---

28   Althusser 1971, pp. 127–86.
29   Ibid., pp. 159, 161, 170.
30   Rodríguez 2002a, pp. 31–2.

mineral, vegetable or celestial'.[31] To begin to tease out the complexities of these concepts, let us turn to a classic text of feudal extraction, the thirteenth-century epic *Poema de Mio Cid (Poem of the Cid)*.

The section of the plot relevant to the present discussion may be briefly summarised. After having fallen out of favour with King Alfonso, the Cid is driven into exile. (We learn from the chronicles that he stands accused of having kept for himself part of the tribute collected from the kings of Cordoba and Seville.) Relations between the lord and his vassal are progressively restored against the backdrop of the Cid's successful conquest of Valencia. As a reward for his unswerving loyalty, the Cid is further honoured by the arranged marriage of his two daughters to the Infantes de Carrión. Following the nuptial celebrations, the Infantes, with their wives, return to Valencia, there to enjoy the fruits of the Cid's conquests and to participate in the defence of the city against the invading Mozarabs. At first all goes well, until, that is, the Infantes betray their cowardice before an escaped lion and are thereby put to shame. Their honour besmirched, the Infantes begin to plot their vengeance. The plan is to return to Carrión, bearing the wealth that they have accumulated during their stay in Valencia, stopping on the way to abuse and abandon their wives.

> sacar las hemos de Valencia,   de poder del Campeador,
> despues en la carrera   feremos nuestro sabor
> ante que nos trayan   lo que cuntio del leon.
> ¡Nos de natura somos   de condes de Carrion!
> Averes levaremos grandes   que valen grant valor;
> ¡escarniremos   las fijas del Canpeador!'
> 'D'aquestos averes sienpre   seremos ricos omnes,
> podremos casar con fijas   de reyes o de enperadores
> ¡ca de natura somos   de condes de Carrion!
> Assi las escarniremos   a las fijas del Campeador
> Antes que nos retrayan   lo que fue del leon.[32]

('we will remove them from Valencia, / from the power of the Cid, / later during the journey we will do as we please / before they raise the matter of the lion. / We are the Counts of Carrión by nature! / We will carry off all manner of wealth; / we will punish the daughters of the Cid!' / 'With all these possessions we will always be rich men, / we will be able to marry

---

31   Rodríguez 2002a, p. 93.
32   Smith 1977, lines 2546–56.

the daughters of kings and emperors / because we are Counts of Carrión by nature! / Thus will we punish the daughters of the Cid / before they raise the matter of the lion'.)

'Honour', 'dishonour', 'vengeance', 'insults', 'nature' – such are the ideologemes that constitute the core of the dominant feudal ideology. Above all 'nature' because the Infantes are defined, organically, by their substance, which is to say, by their 'lineage' or 'blood', to be contrasted favourably with that of a lesser lord, the Cid. But what precisely is one to make of the seemingly obsessive repetition? A modern reader would doubtless be tempted to discern in such notions evidence of a *'psychology'* or 'character structure', hence, the outlines of a 'case study'. The Infantes repeatedly protest their 'nature', also mull over the incident of the lion and their plan to abuse their wives. Repeatedly but also obsessively?

To construe the above passage psychologically may be tempting but, arguably, is to *mis*construe it by de-historicising it. Objectively considered, the semantics of the passage are those of a substantialist ideology whose supports, far from being internalised subjects, are individualities who are rigorously exteriorised. Exteriorised through the medium of language, which is why there must be *two* Infantes, just as there must be two Jews that preside over the Cid's exile. What is not verbalised does not exist; the elucubrations of the 'inner man' are never an issue. And what applies to the semantics of the passage similarly applies to its syntax: the repetitive paratactic structures are not those of a poorly organised narrative, otherwise the product of an unskilled 'author', but of a bard who reads the world, as inevitably he must, from the a-perspectival situation of his Lord; and also, incidentally, of a bard intent upon raising his audience's sense of outrage to fever pitch.

But let us press on with our reading. Midway through their journey back to Carrión, the Infantes pause to set up camp for the night and, as planned, to abuse their wives: 'Con sus mugieres en braços / demuestran les amor' (With their wives in their arms, / they make love to them). The next day, they proceed to wreak vengeance on the Cid's daughters. The brutality is palpable:

Alli les tuellen   los mantos e los pelliçones,
paran las en cuerpos   y en camisas y en çiclatones.
Espuelas tienen calçadas   los malos traidores,
En mano prenden las çinchas   fuertes e duradores.[33]

---

33   Ibid., lines 2720–3.

(There they remove their robes and furs, / they leave them stripped down to their under-garments. / Spurs they wore, the evil traitors, / in their hands they grasp straps rough and strong.)

The daughters beg the Infantes to take up their swords – both presents from the Cid – and kill them, thereby making them martyrs; beg furthermore not to be made 'malos enssienplos' (bad examples). But all in vain.

> Essora les conpieçan a dar   los ifantes de Carrion,
> con las çinchas corredizas   majan las tan sin sabor,
> con espuela agudas   don ellas an mal sabor
> ronpien las camisas e carnes   a ellas amas a dos;
> linpia salie la sangre   sobre los çiclatones.[34]

(Then they set about them the Infantes de Carrión, / with flying straps they beat them mercilessly, / with sharp spurs, to the girls' distress / they tear the garments and flesh of both; / clean ran the blood onto their under-garments.)

The exhibition of cruelty is overwhelming and seemingly cries out for a psycho-logistic reading. Each of the Infantes strives to surpass the other in his ferocity until the blood of their wives is literally splattered everywhere; finally, stripped down to their underwear, the wives are left for the birds and beasts to devour. Repeatedly, throughout this whole process, the chant rings out: 'De nuestros casamientos / agora somos vengados' (Of our marriages / we are now avenged).

    Yet, once again, the Structural Marxist would follow a radically different tack: the severity of the daughters' treatment, s/he would argue, is not to be traced to some inner turmoil on the part of the Infantes but, on the contrary, to the need, within the framework of a feudal semantics, for signs to be cashed out in terms of their substantial materiality. For the same reasons, it would be argued, to interpret the stripping of the daughters erotically is to commit an anachronism. The thrust of the episode of the Cid's daughters is strictly ideological: nudity signifies a loss of 'substance'. Even the reference to 'bad examples' needs to be decoded appropriately, which is to say, in substantialist terms: the Cid's daughters are already anticipating how their treatment will be *read*, not for the light that it sheds upon their interior, as opposed to exterior, worth, but for its exemplary value in terms of a substantialism inflected towards the allegorical.

---

34   Ibid., lines 2735–39.

To conclude: given that, under feudalism, the split between this world and the next was primary, the distinction between the private and public spheres could not help but be, at best, embryonic; pursuing the same logic, it would further follow that any undertaking to plumb the interior depths of a feudal individuality is theoretically misconceived. Rodríguez, it is no surprise to discover, has given psychoanalysis a relatively wide berth over the years, together with the notion of the libidinal unconscious. And yet, how far is it possible to press the anti-psychoanalytic argument? Is not the beating of the Cid's daughters just a little bit 'sadistic'? Is not the feudal lord's need to 'cleanse' his besmirched honour to some degree 'anal'? Is not the preoccupation with ritual, in evidence throughout the *Poem of the Cid*, clinically 'obsessive'? These are matters to which we will turn below, but before then let us consider some further aspects of Althusserian theory and Rodríguez's handling of them.

5   Althusser: Ontology, Epistemology, and Methodology

While something like a synthesis was emerging in *Theory and History*, within the localised theoretical region of ideology, certain pivotal issues were left unresolved. Particularly puzzling is the contrast drawn between, on the one hand, visible notions that do not really exist and, on the other, an internal functioning that, although invisible, is, allegedly, as real as economic and political processes. At this point, symptomatically, Rodríguez's text itself degenerates into a baroque structure consisting of parentheses contained within parentheses.

> When we say that the 'serf' or the 'subject' never actually exist, we do not mean 'only' at the economic level or at the political level, as the case may be. (Both of these are levels that a certain mechanistic tradition within Marxism considers to be the 'only real' and, by simply inverting the Hegelian dialectic, has commonly identified with the very essence of reality. As we know today, ideology constitutes an objective level of a particular social formation, is a reality as full as any other social level, and the fact that the economic instance is ultimately determinant does not mean that the other levels are not just as 'real'.) Rather we mean that the serf and subject do not actually exist as full values in themselves even within their respective ideological instances.[35]

---

35   Rodríguez 2002a, p. 22.

To begin to disentangle the syntactic chaos, let us draw out its constituent threads. The nub of Rodríguez's argument is clear enough: insofar as serf, subject, slave, and so on do not exist in the sense of being objectively real, individualities may be said to *live* their relation to their conditions of existence in imaginary terms, which is to say, through the mediation of their relevant ideological matrices. The task of the theoretician of ideology, Rodríguez will proceed to explain, is to expose the real mechanisms that secrete the ideological matrix, through the deployment of such abstract concepts as social formations, modes of production, instances, relations of production and so on. Complications arise when the Spaniard interrupts what is in essence a discussion about methodology to address, parenthetically, a related issue concerning the ontological status of real-world objects; and when, to be more precise, he undertakes to critique a species of vulgar materialism that would reduce everything, including the mind, to matter, even as he promotes the materiality of ideology along Althusserian lines.

As if all of this were not complicated enough, there remained the lurking presence of an epistemological problem. How precisely did the 'object of thought' relate to the 'real object'? Rodríguez does not address the question directly, but it presses for consideration. To have kept all these balls in play would have required considerable philosophical under-labouring. Perhaps understandably, given the nature of his professional focus upon literature and ideology, Rodríguez preferred, in every sense, to let the matter drop.[36] Having said which, materialism remains an ontological thesis about the nature of reality and not an act of blind faith. As David Hillel Ruben reminds us, '[i]t needs a theory of knowledge which underpins it and gives it plausibility, just as any ontological doctrine does'.[37] Arguably, by the same token, a materialist ontology demands a correspondence theory of knowledge, and any Marxist who believes it possible to do without one will always be in danger of deploying, implicitly, an ontology of a positivist or, alternatively, idealist kind.

To further unravel the threads of Rodríguez's argument, let us trace his preoccupations to their source in Marx's famous introduction to the *Grundrisse*.

> The concrete is concrete because it is the concentration of many determinations, hence unity of the diverse. It appears in the process of thinking, therefore, as a process of concentration, as a result, not as a point of

---

36   The above section of the Introduction to *Theory and History* was omitted when Rodríguez came to include the text in a volume of collected pieces, *De qué hablamos cuando hablamos de marxismo* (Rodríguez 2013, p. 77. See Read 2017).

37   Ruben 1977, p. 1.

departure, even though it is the point of departure in reality and hence also the point of departure for observation [*Anschauung*] and conception. Along the first path the full conception was evaporated to yield an abstract determination; along the second, the abstract determinations lead towards a reproduction of the concrete by way of thought. In this way Hegel fell into the illusion of conceiving the real as the product of thought concentrating itself, probing its own depths, and unfolding itself out of itself, by itself, whereas the method of rising from the abstract to the concrete is only the way in which thought appropriates the concrete, reproduces it as the concrete in the mind.[38]

As Ruben has effectively argued, Marx is not here raising the epistemological 'problem of knowledge' but the *methodological* question of the *production* of knowledge. Methodologically, one deploys abstract definitions in order to arrive at the concrete concept. 'But Marx is *not* saying that *epistemologically* the concrete reality that becomes an object of our knowledge is wholly a determination of thought (rather than of reality) since Marx holds that the abstract definitions are themselves derived from reality – although it is true that the reality from which they are derived is one of which we can, at first, have only a "chaotic" conception'.[39]

Althusser's commentary on Marx runs along much the same lines, as can be seen most clearly in *Philosophy and the Spontaneous Philosophy of Scientists*. Marx's 'synthesis of many determinations', according to this text, consists of *theoretical* concepts (in the strong sense) and *empirical* concepts. Theoretical concepts (in the strong sense) bear on abstract formal objects or objects of thought. 'Thus, we will say that the concept of *mode of production* is a theoretical concept which concerns the mode of production in general – an object which does not *exist* in the strong sense but is indispensable to the knowledge of any social formation'.[40] The same goes for 'productive forces', 'social relations', the 'ideological instance', and so on. These concepts do not give us concrete knowledge of concrete objects, but knowledge of abstract-formal objects. Only social formations – say, that of France in 1968 – can be said to exist in the concrete sense.

Empirical concepts, by way of contrast to their theoretical counterpart, 'bear upon' the determinations of the singularity of concrete objects, such as social

---

38   Marx 1973, p. 101.
39   Ruben 1977, p. 153.
40   Althusser 1990b, p. 47.

formations. Althusser explains: 'Empirical concepts thus add something essential to concepts that are theoretical in the strong sense: precisely the determinations of the existence (in the strong sense) of concrete objects'.[41] That said, these concepts are not to be confused with empirical objects: while observation, experiment and data are indispensable to concrete knowledge, empirical concepts are, at the same time, 'irreducible to the pure data of an immediate empirical investigation'.[42] Observational data, Althusser will insist, only furnish the *materials* that are then 'worked up into the *raw material* of a subsequent labour of transformation that is finally going to produce *empirical* concepts'.[43] Theoretical concepts are indispensable, implicitly or explicitly, to this transformation.

The message, then, appears clear enough: as in the case of Marx's original text, Althusser is here discussing the production of scientific knowledge, *not* the metaphysical question of whether thought is interpretive or reflective. Except that, perhaps unsurprisingly, it ultimately proves difficult to separate methodological and epistemological questions. Specifically, the distinction between the Marxist dialectic of realisation and its Hegelian counterpart, involving the speculative 'realisation' of the Idea, 'will obviously demand sustained clarification'.[44] Such clarification, it should be said, was never forthcoming, other than in the form of a vague reference to a 'very specific form of existence', attributed by Althusser to his formal-abstract objects. And quite suddenly epistemological considerations began to press for attention on all sides. 'It requires a real effort to resist the temptations of empiricism (for which only real-concrete objects exist), to adopt the critique of its ideological "facts", genuinely to criticise them, and to situate oneself at the level of *theory* – i.e., of its formal-abstract objects'.[45]

Warnings as to dangers posed by empiricism were lost upon those readers of Althusser who were rooted, unconsciously, in the tradition of British empiricism and who, accordingly, proceeded to conflate the logic of scientific analysis with the 'problem of knowledge'. Protestations of outrage were quick to follow. 'The emphasis falls with the monotony of a steam-hammer upon the unknowability of any objective historical process', protests E.P. Thompson.[46]

---

41 Ibid., p. 48.
42 Ibid.
43 Ibid., pp. 48–9.
44 Ibid., p. 49.
45 Ibid., p. 52.
46 Thompson 1995, p. 29.

Even more scandalously, '[t]he subject (or agent) of history disappears'.[47] For Terry Eagleton, Althusserianism constituted a species of neo-Kantianism that 'expung[ed] the role of evidence in theoretical debate'.[48] The ultimate paradox of structuralism, according to Ellen Meiksins Wood, works itself out when language is detached altogether from social reality, so as to give rise to a 'subjectivism without a subject'.[49] Wood's critique of Althusserianism, let us note parenthetically, like Thompson's, is sustained principally with references not to the work of Althusser but to that of Ernesto Laclau and Chantal Mouffe: as was often to be the case, Althussser would be held responsible for the sins of those who were to displace him.

6   The Libidinal Unconscious

A fact that has sometimes escaped his critics is that Althusser's 'anti-humanism' is to be traced less to any 'structuralist' bias, of recent vintage, than to Marx's own *impersonal* formulation in *Capital* of the relations between capitalist and landowner. '[I]ndividuals are dealt with here', Marx warns, 'only in so far as they are the personifications of economic categories, the bearers [*Träger*] of particular class-relations and interests. My standpoint, from which the development of the economic formation of society is viewed as a process of natural history, can less than any other make the individual responsible for relations whose creature he remains, socially speaking, however much he may subjectively raise himself above them'.[50] There is no reason, in principle, why this emphasis upon structure should work to block the development of a theory of social subjectivity. Indeed, as we have made clear, Structural Marxism is particularly attentive to the issue of subjectivity, which it views as a condensation of structural forces every bit as complex and laminated as the forces that constitute the mode of production. That said, in practice, psychoanalysis has usually been drafted in to provide the necessary analytic tools: Althusser set the precedent that his commentators have been only too willing to follow, with not altogether happy results.[51]

Specifically, the pillaging of psychoanalytic concepts has legitimated the incorporation into Structural Marxism of a trans-historical 'human nature', a

---

47   Ibid., p. 144.
48   Eagleton 1986, p. 3.
49   Wood 1986, p. 78.
50   Marx 1976, p. 92.
51   Althusser 1996; Resch 1992, pp. 210–12.

concept that may readily pass undetected when the focus of attention is upon capitalist societies, but which rears its ugly head when, as in the case of the *Poem of the Cid*, the Marxist scholar confronts ideologies that secrete individualities that are radically exteriorised, hence seemingly devoid of 'psychologies'. How, precisely, given the absence of 'subjects', is one to explain, without explaining away, those traces of oral, anal, and phallic perversions and obsessions that litter the feudal narrative? Two alternatives suggest themselves, both equally unpalatable from a Marxist standpoint: firstly, one can ignore the radical historicity of culture and inflate the traces into fully formed 'case studies'; or, secondly, one can simply minimise the traces so as better to efface them and thereby prioritise the radical historicity of relevant texts. This second approach certainly appears to be the one adopted by Rodríguez when called upon to explain the relation between the ideological and libidinal unconscious: 'It is not that the ego ['yo'] is not the owner of his/her face, as Freud would say, or that we are not owners of our faces. It is that the ego lacks a face, a place, a space'. He elaborates later: 'To try and analyse, then, how and why we dare to say "I" immediately locates us in the subsoil of a nothingness. A little smoke and a lot of vacuity'.[52]

As a way of resisting ideologically motivated attempts to universalise the bourgeois 'free subject', Rodríguez's tactic has much to recommend it: an anthropological Marxism that sets out to prioritise a trans-historical human nature ends up undercutting the foundations of a distinctively *historical* materialism. That said, the importance to be attached to the *organic* body, on Rodríguez's own reckoning, warns against closing down the debate prematurely. Any attempt to explain motivated behaviour, one supposes, must boast a psychology of some description, and those who attempt to do without one will, in the last instance, find themselves adopting an *implicit* psychology. At which point, obvious dangers present themselves. Given the workings of the ideological unconscious, an implicit psychology is likely to assume a trans-historical, bourgeois form, consisting of subjects that freely 'express' themselves. Nor do the readily available psychoanalytic models promise a solution: notoriously, Lacanian analysis 'returns psychoanalysis to a historical and political vacuum'.[53] One possible exception is Jean-Joseph Goux's *Symbolic Structures*. Let us briefly weigh certain relevant aspects of this work.

The individual's ontogenetic progression through the oral, anal, and phallic stages, Goux argues, reproduces, though in a compressed, abridged form,

---

52   Rodríguez 2001a, p. 393.
53   Dews 1987, p. 108.

the process of phylogenetic removal from a 'natural' economy. 'The infantile stages of libidinal maturation, the pregenital organisations, and better yet, the various neuroses that perpetuate them in disguise recall, respectively, the particular ideological syndromes (hysteria, obsession, paranoia) that are linked to corresponding modes of production in the sequence'.[54] 'Recall', but not – and the point needs to be stressed – as a mnemonic, phylogenetic trace, which leaves behind a knowledge of the past. The fact that feudalism follows a primitive mode of production, and capitalism supplants feudalism is inscribed in the successive modes in the form of a lack, a lacuna, a deficiency. The orality of a primitive mode is *not* represented in feudalism in the circulation and inscription of feudal 'symbols', just as the anality of feudalism is *not* represented in capitalist 'signs'. 'Filling the contours of this absence is neurosis, born as the effect of a *failure to translate into the social* a certain possible signifying formation. This deficiency of social translation is, in other words, repression, with the necessary substitution of private ideology (neurosis) for the dominant social ideology'.[55] The presence of multiple modes of production within a single social formation, together with the evidence of anticipations and hangovers, warns against the temptation to over-simplify and unduly emphasise the homogeneous, unilinear nature of the historical process: at any particular conjuncture, we should expect to find a social reality that is complex and contradictory.

Let us draw into the discussion Don Juan Manuel's *El Conde Lucanor* (1335), subtitled 'Book of the examples of Count Lucanor and Patronius'. Ideologically, the subtitle bears a heavy semantic load and confirms the work's rootedness in a substantialist subsoil. The medieval 'book', as Rodríguez reminds us, perforce took the form of a *dual* narrative, split along the lines of a division between the celestial and terrestrial worlds. On one level, it consisted of a *literal* text: 'What happened to a king and his adviser', in the case of one of Juan Manuel's short stories; on another level, it was to be interpreted as an allegorical, hence 'exemplary', text, which fittingly culminates in a 'maxim': 'Through the mercy of God and through good advice does a man extricate himself from difficulties and fulfil his desire'.[56] Along the same lines, Count Lucanor receives from his 'servant', Patronius, the kind of advice that was sorely required to survive amidst the fragmented, warring kingdoms of fourteenth-century Spain.

---

54   Goux 1990, p. 83.
55   Ibid., p. 85.
56   Manuel 1982, p. 80.

So much, then, is clear. But let us turn, more specifically, to *Count Lucanor*'s doctrinal fourth part, in which we find Christ's *incarnation* effectively foregrounded in organicist terms: 'He was the true body because, in order to save men, he wished to leave us his true body'.[57] While, according to Goux's schematisation, orality survives under feudalism as a lack or 'anthropophagic' residue from an earlier, primitive mode – hence the liturgical command in the Eucharist to eat of His body and drink of His blood – the dominant mode dictates the prevalence of the anal stage.[58] The same anality would explain the significance that Don Juan Manuel attaches to the baptismal ceremony as a *cleansing* ritual, from which, symptomatically, a feudal misogyny dictates that women are to be excluded: '[I]t is true that women, who are unable to participate in this sacrament, cannot be cleansed of original sin'.[59] Materiality, Goux reminds us, is 'always indexed by the maternal',[60] and its predominance under feudalism explains Don Juan Manuel's eagerness to liberate men, in the generic sense, from the proximity of the flesh and hence of anality, through the mediation of the phallic ritual of circumcision: '... for circumcision can only be performed on men; nobody can be saved from original sin other than through circumcision'.[61]

The obsessive anality characteristic of feudalism suggests an inconclusive triangulation of the mother-child relationship. Symptomatically, Don Juan Manuel shows himself to be much concerned with the Law of the Father and the shortcomings thereof. Particularly notable in this respect is his *Libro de los estados* (*The Book of Estates*), in which one of the characters, Julio, lectures the Infante Joas and his tutor, Turín, on the king's failure to impose his authority, before extrapolating to the dynamics of a typical family: 'And even in the case of the father and the mother and the children who live in a single dwelling, it often happens that not all of them live by the same law; that some believe in one law and others in another'.[62] Scandalised by Julio's revelations, the Infante calls upon Turín to justify his own complicity in such an unhappy state of affairs. After a prolonged exchange, all agree that, given man's possession of free will, a social law is always required to eke out its natural equivalent.

---

57   Manuel 1982, p. 338.
58   Goux 1990, pp. 78–9.
59   Manuel 1982, p. 339.
60   Goux 1990, p. 146.
61   Manuel 1982, p. 339.
62   Manuel 1974, pp. 42–3.

Read through the prism of Goux's exposition, the weakly imposed Law of the Father, in evidence in Don Manuel's texts, betrays a lingering, ever-repeated attachment to the matrilineal image of the father as a stranger to, or intruder upon, the mother-child nuclear couple. 'For the father's disjunction from the whole physiological fabric of procreation, his reduction to the pointillist speck of a biological link, and the contrasting reinforcement of his social connection, combine to constitute and enlarge the figure of the *pater* and his power, in proportion to the progress of culture'.[63] In Don Juan Manuel, that reduction is still being enacted within the context of the Immaculate Conception: Christ, Don Juan Manuel will never tire of insisting, 'was not engendered by a father that was a man but by the Holy Spirit'.[64] By the same token, cultural courtesies, not to mention Christian mythology, demand that any resemblance between son and father be recognised not in physiological but in spiritual terms: 'This resemblance that man has with God is of the soul'.[65] The result is a division of labour: material reproduction is the lot of the mother, social reproduction, the responsibility of the father. The implication is clear: a servant of the Lord the medieval sinner may be, but at a stage when energetic investment has yet to be displaced onto abstract structures – its fate under capitalism – he remains, in contrast to the future 'subject', attached to a maternal *jouissance*.

Given the weakness of paternal law, one surmises, only the proliferation of feudal ritual held at bay the spectral menace of the psychotic, and imperfectly, to judge at least by Don Juan Manuel's ruminations on the Oedipal dynamics of his family: '... when the Queen, Doña Beatriz, my grandmother, was pregnant with my father, she dreamed that through the child she was bearing, and through his lineage, the death of Christ was to be avenged', and so on.[66] On the face of it, there appears to be little to separate these and other such feudal fantasies from those of the modern psychotic; similarly, little to separate, on the one hand, Don Juan Manuel's version of Christian mytho-cosmology, which locates the servant of God, otherwise himself, in the grander scheme of things,[67] from, on the other, Daniel Paul Schreber's ambitious theology of the universe, which assigned its author a messianic mission within the context of the cosmic order.[68] But precisely for this reason, discriminations become

---

63   Goux 1990, p. 218.
64   Manuel 1974, p. 217.
65   Ibid., p. 149.
66   Manuel 1981, p. 122.
67   Manuel 1974, pp. 49–51.
68   Schreber's case was famously discussed by Freud in his essay 'Psycho-Analytic Notes on an Autobiographical Account of a Case of Paranoia (Dementia Paranoides)', see *Case*

important. The gist of Goux's argument, to remind ourselves, is that modern neurosis (and psychosis) is result of a failure to translate a signifying formulation into a social language. Now there is nothing 'private' about the feudal fantasies of Don Juan Manuel, nor could there be, given the nature of the feudal family and the radical exteriority promoted by feudal substantialism.

7   Antonio Gramsci and the Case for Historicism

When he came to explain the kind of effectivity that ideology exerted from its location within the superstructure, Althusser, to recall, had recourse to a metaphor derived from Antonio Gramsci, for whom 'ideology serves to *cement* and to unify' the entire social bloc.[69] Similarly, for Althusser in *Philosophy and the Spontaneous Philosophy*, ideology 'must be thought of as sliding into all parts of the edifice, and considered as a distinctive kind of *cement*',[70] but with a significant shift of emphasis: as deployed here, the metaphor serves to capture the process whereby an ideological unconsciousness comes to pervade the entire social formation. Thus, ideology 'can exist *in more or less diffuse or unthought forms, or, contrariwise, in more or less conscious, reflected, and explicitly systematised forms – theoretical forms*'.[71] In Gramsci's case, by way of contrast, theorisation of ideological unconsciousness would be held in check by a historicism that gravitates ineluctably towards a voluntarist, subjectivist notion of 'class consciousness'. Let us consider the details.

The crux of Gramsci's problem, in Althusser's view, was his failure to take on board what the French philosopher saw as a radical 'break' between the early and late Marx, in other words, between the radical liberal who continued to think in terms of the subject/object dichotomy and the Marxist who had transferred the discussion onto a totally new terrain, namely that of the social formation. A direct consequence of the Gramscian emphasis was the identification of Marxism, as a form of scientificity, with a 'conception of the world' or an 'ideology'.[72] But no less significant were the secondary effects of Gramsci's attachment to subjectivity: the Marxist conception of the complex social structure, replete with its distinctive instances or levels, is 'flattened out' into

---

      Studies 11, volume 9, The Pelican Freud Library (Harmondsworth: Penguin Books, 1979), pp. 131–223.
69   Gramsci 1971, p. 328, emphasis added.
70   Althusser 1990b, p. 25.
71   Ibid., p. 27.
72   Althusser and Balibar 1970, p. 131.

a variation of the Hegelian totality, which brings in its train the category of a human essence, located *outside* but to be realised *inside* history; and the rest follows: an irrealism that privileges social action over the structural conditions of its existence and that promotes epistemological relativism over scientific realism. His great respect for Gramsci notwithstanding, Althusser rejects such historicism in favour of a position 'that defends the primacy of realism over relativism in philosophy and the explanatory priority of social structure over human practice in history'.[73]

This Althusserian critique of Gramsci has given rise to a wide-ranging debate whose details do not concern us now.[74] Within the present context, attention must focus upon the Italian's allegiance to the Hegelian 'dialectic of consciousness' and specifically upon the slow-motion process, evidence of which abounds throughout the *Prison Notebooks*, whereby epistemology extends its boundaries so as to encompass ontology. 'Objective', we are informed, 'always means "humanly objective" which can be held to correspond exactly to "historically subjective": in other words, objective would mean "universally subjective"'.[75] The outcome is an epistemological *reductio ad absurdum*: to affirm that reality would exist, Gramsci insists, even if man did not, is either to speak metaphorically or to succumb to a form of mysticism.[76] Perforce, the performative contradictions begin to multiply: the outside world survives as a 'refractory reality' that refuses to be conjured away, and necessarily so: any kind of rational debate is simply not feasible without it. Nobody can alter the number of firms or their employees, Gramsci is forced to concede, or the number of cities or inhabitants of an urban population.[77] And by the same token, anyone who has plans for the transformation of society is advised to check them for their realism and practicality.[78]

Yet it is a measure of the grip that voluntarism exercises over Gramsci that he is finally prepared to sacrifice the notion of a scientific cause. Within the domain of the so-called human sciences, he insists, it is only possible to speak of general laws or 'tendencies', which may be accepted on practical grounds,

---

73   Resch 1992, p. 49.

74   The resurgence of interest in Althusser has led to a reconsideration of the relations
      between the two scholars. Peter Thomson offers a reading of Gramsci that emphasises
      the Italian's decentred conception of social formations, to be offset against Althusser's
      own early formulations but that finds resonances in Althusser's late 'philosophy of the
      encounter' (Thomas 2013).

75   Gramsci 1971, p. 445.

76   Ibid., p. 446.

77   Ibid., p. 181.

78   Ibid.

but which lack any objective status. Laws of tendency, to elaborate, are not laws in the naturalistic, which is to say, deterministic sense, but strictly in an 'historicist sense',[79] although at times Gramsci will even surrender this qualified notion to prioritise the uniqueness and unrepeatable nature of historical events, hence their resistance to concepts.[80] 'The so-called laws of sociology which are assumed as laws of causation [...] have no causal value: they are almost always tautologies and paralogisms. Usually they are no more than a duplicate of the observed fact itself'.[81] As for Marxism or a philosophy of praxis, as Gramsci terms it, it can live only in the concrete works of history.

Now it is important to grasp the exact nature of Gramsci's dilemma. At the most general level, the Italian is haunted by the spectre of a reductive Marxism that would collapse the realm of the subject into that of the object, haunted also by the inevitable side-effects of any such conflation, notably the acceptance of a regularity determinism, the feasibility of prediction and, by extension, the redundancy of the human will. And it was with an eye to exorcising such ghosts that Gramsci pointed to the presence within any social structure of *emergent* individualities, which, among other things, accounts for this same structure's *openness*. Once purposefulness and intentions were discarded as a causal factor, the voluntarist logic ran, a social formation would tend to cohere into an interplay of fixed and regular forces.

Its irrealist absurdities notwithstanding, there is much in Gramsci's argument that even a philosophical realist is bound to concede. The human sciences do indeed suffer from serious limitations in comparison to their hard counterparts. Principally, they are unable to isolate and trigger the generative mechanisms relevant to their disciplines in laboratory conditions. Social formations are, by any reckoning, characterised by open conditions in which causal powers operate conjointly and thereby generate complexly determined outcomes that are irreducible to a regularity determinism.[82] That said, this same realist would see no reason to deny the existence of real, trans-factual mechanisms within the human realm or, by the same token, to surrender the principle of a 'ubiquitous causality'. In social systems, his argument would run, structural mechanisms exist as powers or tendencies that are omnipresent, independently of whether they are empirically realised. The specifically Althusserian realist would wish to add that, while necessarily a non-predictive science, his-

---

79   Ibid., p. 401.
80   Ibid., p. 427.
81   Ibid., p. 430.
82   See Collier 1994, pp. 62, 128.

torical materialism is far from lacking explanatory power, to be assessed, as this power is, by the light that it sheds not on constant patterns of events but upon causal structures.[83]

8   The Eye/I That Sees the Thing

For the transition from the 'servant of the Lord', of substantialist extraction, to the *beautiful soul* of animist derivation, equally from the substantialist 'dispute' to the animist 'dialogue' (between mirror images), much needs to have happened in Spain. Notably, the existence of a new set of social relations, consolidated on the basis of a convergence of phenomena: the development of a market based upon the exchange of commodities, the emergence of salaried labour and consolidation of the first truly capitalist form of production, the development of banking and credit practices, the creation of the absolutist state (centralised territory as opposed to feudal fragmentation), the growth of cities as administrative centres, and so on. While he was the first to recognise the relative autonomy of such phenomena, Rodríguez was also more alert than most to their deep-seated inter-connections, hence to the existence of mediating mechanisms – for all its diversity, the social formation remained a totality. The most important of such mechanisms, he will argue, was the Absolutist State.

Viewed from the Althusserian perspective, the rise of Absolutism corresponds with a shift in dominance, under pressure from bourgeois relations, to an increasingly autonomous political instance. 'The *autonomous sphere of the political* will be constituted at the "public level", so as to preclude, at least in principle, any intervention in the private sphere, and, by the same token, to leave the latter relatively free and equally autonomous. This free, dual function is precisely the context that bourgeois relations need to achieve their full constitution'.[84] Feudalism, we have seen, recognises no such level, hence lacks a correspondingly *private* dimension: the feudal lord or serf may be split, but not internally so. The relevant partitions are cosmic: Man is the 'vinculum mundi'. In such terms are to be read those lines of the *Poem of the Cid* in which the feudal warrior promotes his aristocratic identity – 'I am Ruy Díaz, the Cid of Vivar' – and statements to the same effect emanate from a lord who coincides totally with his exterior being; substantially, *he is what he*

83   See Resch 1992, pp. 197–8.
84   Rodríguez 2002a, p. 36.

is. By way of contrast, the 'beautiful' soul is rigorously *privatised*, which is to say a proto-subject, split between an interior and an exterior or, in the language of contemporary poets, between 'lo de fuera' and 'lo de dentro'. The favoured literary genre through which to explore the new relation is the sonnet, soon to be joined by the 'dialogue' and the 'novel'. The centrality of the proto-subject, let us note in passing, is shared by the pictorial artist: the flat, vertical hierarchy of the feudal painter increasingly gives way to the perspectivism of the 'eye that sees the thing', with corresponding adjustments at the level of psychology: 'A shift from *obsessional religious ciphering*, which belongs to the feudal mode of signifying (every percept is a sign charged with meaning, but *I* am not its cause or its center; it is a "symbol" referring ultimately to transcendence), to something else, which cannot but recall a *paranoid egocentrism*'.[85]

Developmentally, Absolutism in Spain follows much the same pattern as in England and France: a nobility under siege by an emergent bourgeoisie will be obliged to 'live with' the split between the public and private spheres; a total regression to feudalism was out of the question. That said, even in England the bourgeoisie will be forced to allow for restorations that will effectively prolong the transition to capitalism. In Spain, more radically, a resurgence of feudalism at the political level from the third decade of the sixteenth century will constitute a major block upon economic development. Symptomatically, an Inquisition charged with unifying the nation will refuse to recognise the existence of a private space, hence will conduct a sustained campaign against those 'beautiful souls' assertive of their autonomous individuality; for many humanists, the choice will be between imprisonment and exile. Nor will the autonomy of the public sphere escape censure, and on precisely the same grounds: feudalising ideologues will be relentless in their denunciations of Machiavelli and of policies justified on the basis of 'reasons of state'. To elucidate further, let us turn to Juan Huarte de San Juan, a figure to whom Rodríguez only refers in passing[86] but whose treatise on educational psychology, the *Examen de ingenios* (*Examination of Men's Wits*) (1575, 1594), captures perfectly the central ideological tensions of the transition to capitalism in Spain.

Huarte's work is particularly striking for evidence of the tension between the different categories of human wit ('ingenio') or intelligence, which included a creative wit of manifestly animist descent, and the substantialist 'faculties of the soul', with which these categories are correlated. A brand of Aristotelian

---

85   Goux 1990, p. 175.
86   Rodríguez 2002a, p. 205.

materialism or, as Rodríguez preferred to call it,[87] 'non-organicist Aristotelian-ism' enabled such contemporary authors as Huarte to give expression, albeit somewhat obliquely, to a secularising impulse at a point when animism *per se* was being driven underground by a resurgent feudal organicism. Unfortunately for Huarte, the Inquisition was not easily deceived: the *Examination* appeared on the *Index librorum prohibitorum* in 1583/84 and would undergo a massive revision in the edition of 1594. Specifically of interest in the present context are the contents of chapter XIII, 'which explores the kind of ability relevant to military strategy'.

All kings, Huarte reminds his own monarch, on the authority of Aristotle, necessarily make war on other kings, or are themselves the object of others' aggression. The advice that follows is notable for its brutal, Machiavellian real-ism: the captain-general, tasked by his monarch with the defence of the realm, is advised to execute his duties in the name not of some 'supreme virtue' or abstract justice, but of practicality and utility. Huarte elaborates: 'It is worth noting that *malice* and *militia* are almost identical in form and also in mean-ing'.[88] The difference (in Spanish) is that of a letter, which is tantamount, in substantialist terms, to an essential equivalence, justifiable on the grounds that a captain-general, to be successful, needs to be skilled in every kind of deceit; in humoral terms, he needs to possess a strong imaginative faculty, which draws its sustenance from heat. A perfect example is to be found in Hannibal, 'who was naturally ferocious and inhumane; and who was reared in such a manner, from infancy, that he had learned not about laws or civil customs but about wars, deaths, and enemy betrayals. Hence, he turned out to be a cruel captain and very malicious when it came to deceiving men, and always on the alert as to how to deceive the enemy'.[89]

Whether Huarte was influenced directly or otherwise by Machiavelli is be-side the point, which is that he was rooted in the same ideology, hence argued along the same lines, in terms of the autonomy of the public sphere and of the basic opposition between Fortune and *Virtù* or, as Huarte will term it, 'Prudence'. From the perspective of the *Examination*, as from that of Ma-chiavelli's *The Prince* (1532), Fortune embodies the force of circumstance that human beings cannot control but that they are bound to resist; which explains why, according to the good doctor, a captain general must be, in Spanish, 'afor-tunado', in the etymological sense of being opposed to Fortune.[90] Fortune is an

---

87   Ibid., p. 276.
88   Huarte de San Juan 1977, p. 254.
89   Ibid., p. 259.
90   Ibid., p. 267.

indiscriminate goddess, the argument runs, when it comes to disposing of Her favours – the bad are just as liable to benefit from them as are the good – and needs to be outwitted at every turn by a human agency of equally mythical proportions. 'Good' and 'bad', it goes without saying, are not deployed here in any moral sense: Huarte is as emphatic as Machiavelli in repudiating received morality where the conduct of a captain-general is concerned, which explains why, for example, he is able to recommend Caesar as a model of prudence. Such is the logic of a new world order: 'the bad are very ingenious, and equipped with a strong imaginative faculty, hence are able to deceive when it comes to buying and selling and know how to acquire property and where to acquire it'.[91]

Such is the extent and nature of the 'break', enacted in the *Examination* between, on the one hand, a substantialist ideology based on the notion of *service* to a Lord/lord who determines the fate of His/his servant, and, on the other, an animist ideology that prioritises the initiative of a free proto-subject, possessed of the resources necessary to determine his or, as was soon to be the case, her own destiny. Huarte is arguing unambiguously in favour of the animist project: when an individual turns out to be 'fortunate', it is not because s/he just happens to have been blessed by Fortune, as ordinary people tend to believe, but because s/he has had the initiative to *outwit* Fortune; in warfare, as in a game of chess, victory goes to those who make the correct decisions, defeat to those who do not; it is not because of its good fortune that the pawn becomes a queen – in a game of chess, as in the game of social life, what counts is the freedom of the individual. The logic is unrelenting: 'When a man performs some heroic feat or unusual act of virtue or strange deed, then he is born anew and acquires other, better parents, and loses the being that he previously had; yesterday, he was called the son of Peter and the grandson of Sancho; now he is called the son of his works'.[92]

Sketched out, in sum, is the kind of individualism that was to grease the working of a 'new order', and, unsurprisingly, Huarte is quick to promote himself in such terms: in the preface to his text, he boasts of being the 'first inventor' of his 'art'.[93] It is a self-assessment with which many of his commentators have been only too willing to concur, as we will see later. Perforce, the Althusserian approach to originality is far more qualified. Specifically, in the case of the *Examination*, it is bound to emphasise those symptoms of a compromise

---

91   Ibid., p. 268.
92   Ibid., p. 274.
93   Ibid., p. 68.

formation of which its author is totally unaware. If Huarte's creative wit is a quintessentially animist concept, the Althusserian argument would run, his humoral materialism has yet to sever its ties to feudalism. And the rest follows: for all his burgeoning initiative, the new man as promoted by Huarte and other animist ideologues is modelled upon the sword-wielding feudal lord of yesteryear: 'My right hand and I are the only parentage that I recognise'.[94] A proto-bourgeois the good doctor may be, but of a suitably professional kind: '... nothing degrades a man more than the need to earn his bread through some mechanical craft'.[95]

We will be discussing Huarte in greater detail below (in Chapter 3). Yet even at this point, it is tempting to pronounce the Althusserian problematic irrefutably confirmed. What clearer evidence could one have of the clash between two class ideologies? Rodríguez, let us note, does not hesitate to advance the argument by projecting the relevant conflict onto the larger screen of the social formation. Attached to the Ptolemaic system, he reminds us, was the whole baggage of substantialist doctrine – the rigid feudal hierarchy of blood – just as the heliocentric system legitimated the animist doctrine of celestial harmony and a hierarchy of souls. Our only reservations relate to the relevant details, which are left unresolved. What, precisely, were the mechanisms of the dialectic and the causal processes involved? Was it a paradigmatic shift in science that generated the ideological conflict or was it the ideological break that opened up new intellectual possibilities? If the multiplicity of distinct practices existed always and only in the form of a 'complex unity', how exactly did the relevant transitive and intransitive processes of causality interlock and connect?

9   Nicos Poulantzas: the Matrix Effect

Few texts have been so deeply indebted to Althusser as Nicos Poulantzas's *Political Power and Social Classes* (1968), beginning with the 'break' highlighted by the French philosopher between the young and mature Marx, hence between a problematic based upon the individual/society opposition (and variations thereof) and the Althusserian concept of a social formation divided into its respective instances. Evident from the outset was the importance to be attached not simply to the effectivity of the separate instances of the social formation but to the reciprocal, contradictory effectivity of these instances,

---

94   Ibid., p. 276.
95   Ibid., p. 278.

understood as the 'matrix effect' of the whole. The Hegelian dialectic of consciousness, by way of contrast, functioned to deprive the subject of a place in the 'real', which led in turn to an over-politicisation of a voluntarist kind and the projection of class as the subject of history.[96]

Key to Poulantzas's formulation was the distinction to be drawn between 'economic class', otherwise the determination exercised by the economic instance, and 'social class', otherwise the global determination exerted indirectly through the ensemble of structures. 'More exactly', in Poulantzas's own words, *'social class is a concept which shows the effects of the ensemble of structures, of the matrix of the mode of production or of a social formation on the agents which constitute its supports: this concept reveals the effects of the global structure in the field of social relations'.*[97] Such a line of reasoning would prove to be a major, finally insurmountable, obstacle, to the absorption of Althusserianism within a dominantly empiricist milieu.

The logic of the Althusserian argument is pressed throughout *Political Power and Social Classes*: the danger, allegedly, lay in a brand of Marxism that promoted a problematic of the subject and that, furthermore, envisaged structures as the product of agents. The concept of interests, Poulantzas elaborates, does not mean that interests consist of behavioural motivations; and, indeed, the concept of interests can and must be stripped of all psychological connotations. Particular targets were the Hegelian model of *alienation* and the schema whereby a hegemonic class, in its capacity as the subject of history, is able to impose its worldview on a social formation and so bind the ensemble of social instances into an expressive totality of linear becoming. Ideologies so configured assume the status of 'products' of (class) consciousness. The classic exponent of the Hegelian positions, according to Poulantzas, was Gramsci (with the possible exception of Lukács), and it is upon this figure that the Greek Marxist comes to focus.

Poulantzas follows Althusser in viewing Gramsci as fundamentally voluntarist, hence the proponent of a view that theorises the hegemonic class as the source of ideology. Understood in this way, the ideological structure of society is reduced to the political organisation of a class, hence to class consciousness. That said, Poulantzas is more alert than Althusser to the possibility of conducting a symptomatic reading of Gramsci, specifically with regard to the Gramscian notion of ideology as a kind of 'cement'. To receive its appropriate, Althusserian weighting, this metaphor was in no way to be conflated

---

96   Poulantzas 1973, pp. 39–41.
97   Ibid., pp. 67–8.

with the notion of agency as the origin or subject of social structures. 'This is because the coherence (unity) specific to ideological discourse [...] does not cause but rather presupposes the decentration of the subject at the level of supports'.[98] The dominant ideology of a social formation encompasses the 'totality' of this formation not as a derivative of the 'class consciousness' of a subject but because it reflects the matrix effect of this formation.

Such a view of the social formation was in every respect unthinkable from within the parameters of British empiricism, and it was perhaps inevitable that a disagreement between the respective proponents should finally explode into the open in the form of the famous confrontation between Poulantzas and Ralph Miliband.[99] We will be considering the exchange in greater detail later in connection with Ernesto Laclau. Suffice it to note at this stage that the debate proved rather sterile in that, as Resch has argued,[100] Miliband's subject-oriented view of class power and Poulantzas's structure-oriented approach proved radically incommensurable. More crucial, from our perspective, is Poulantzas' contribution, through this debate, to Rodríguez's formulation of the ideological unconscious, which represented a decisive theoretical advance.

In *Political Power and Social Classes* Poulantzas seemed disposed systematically to unpack the logic of the matrix effect as it related to the ideological instance, hence poised to conceive of an ideological unconscious. 'As in the case of every other instance, the region of the ideological is fixed in its limits by the global structure of a mode of production and social formation'.[101] That said, his argument finally falters. Why? Presumably because he found the concept of the unconscious already occupied by a Freudian programme that prioritised the subject, hence was ill-suited to theorising a structural phenomenon. For his part, Rodríguez, observing the Miliband-Poulantzas confrontation from a distance, experienced no such reticence. 'The belief in a basic truth of the human subject, called "psychology", the corresponding blindness towards the existence of a determining, unconscious, ideological level, peculiar to each kind of class relations – here is what, in the last instance, always betrays the presence of empiricism, even in the case of discourses (economistic, progressive / mercantilist, etc.) which happen – as in the present case – to be frankly Leftist'.[102] The distance in question, we suggest, proved crucial: Spain's notably belated transition to capitalism left this country's national culture significantly detached

---

98   Ibid., p. 208.
99   Miliband 1970, 1973, Poulantzas 1976.
100   Resch 1992, p. 386n3.
101   Poulantzas 1973, p. 209.
102   Rodríguez 2002, pp. 303–4.

from a bourgeois subjectivity, hence serviceable as a perfect vantage point from which to view, objectively speaking, a British milieu that, at the level of its ideological unconscious, remained deeply imbued by empiricism.

Given that Poulantzas was so manifestly committed to Althusserianism, it may be wondered how certain of his early commentators, notably Martin Carnoy (1984) and Bob Jessop (1985), and, more recently, Peter Thomas (2011), were able to enlist Poulantzas's work to help bury the Althusserian legacy. The short answer, particularly apparent in the case of Thomas, is that they have transferred the focus of attention from *Political Power and Social Classes* to Poulantzas's subsequent *State, Power, Socialism* (1978), written shortly before its author's suicide. The long answer is that Poulantzas inherited from Althusser a somewhat tenuous ontological underpinning to his social analysis. The mode of production, Poulantzas agreed, constitutes an abstract-formal object, which does not exist in the strong sense of reality.[103] Such a view constituted an open invitation to proponents of the subject/object problematic to strip down the social formation to its bare, empirical foundations. On this basis, it proved only too easy to construct a bridge from Marxism to the various forms of post-Marxism, a bridge that some Marxists, not least of all the commentators on Poulantzas, were only too willing to cross.

In opposition to such a revisionist perspective, Resch has emphasised the (Althusserian) continuity in Poulantzas's work: '... there is no basis for claiming that he abandons his earlier problematic in his last work'.[104] While, admittedly, the focus of attention in *State, Power, Socialism* has been transferred from the social formation to the political instance, through which to emphasise the contradictions and popular struggles within the state apparatus, the ruling class continues in this later work to maintain its hegemony, or so at least Resch insists.[105] Resch has further argued that the attempt to present Althusser's influence on Poulantzas as constituting a mere transitional phase in the development of Poulantzas's thinking was part of an ongoing attempt to erase the name of Althusser from the living legacy of Marxism.[106]

Rodríguez, for his part, differs from both the above positions: while shunning revisionist interpretations of Poulantzas, as a final assessment, he targets *State, Power, Socialism* as an exception for its graduated concessions. '... it was symptomatic that, in his later work, the question of class exploitation, which had been the key to [Poulantzas's] earlier works, seems to disappear from

---

103   Poulantzas 1973, p. 15.
104   Resch 1990, p. 335.
105   Resch 1992, pp. 336–7.
106   Resch 1992, p. 385n1.

view'.[107] Particularly suspect was the tactical rejection of the notion of *dual power*, as theorised by Lenin and Gramsci: 'Such banal politicking – unusual in Poulantzas – was simply an attempt, of the moment, to underline the fact that the State was not a monolithic bloc but had its internal contradictions'.[108] Conveniently elided, through the emphasis upon factional differences, was the class dominance that continued to be exercised over the existing state apparatus, through the mediation of the social formation as a whole. Poulantzas was not alone in his failure to realise this: '... it is curious that almost all the theoreticians and politicians on the Left forgot the essential fact that in a capitalist system the ideological unconscious *en masse* is always capitalist'.[109]

Rodríguez discerns in Poulantzas, deep down, a *personal fear* of what the single party would do to *us*, were it ever to get into power. In view of what was currently taking place throughout the Stalinist world, such a fear was perfectly understandable. But the attempt to extend democracy through the parliamentary system presupposed a fundamental weakness, 'for if it was known only too well what a single party could do to us, too little attention was paid to what a single capitalism could do, in the context of globalisation, which is simply whatever it liked (as is now happening on a daily basis)'.[110] It was an oversight of which Rodríguez was never likely to be guilty: his was a research programme that prioritised the notions of class conflict and class exploitation; also, one that proved fully capable of generating a mass of empirical data in connection therewith. Incidentally, the Spaniard would give the lie to those critics, whose numbers multiplied in the late 1970s and '80s, who were eager to pronounce upon the demise of Althusserianism as a productive research programme.

---

107   Rodríguez 2013, pp. 32–3.
108   Ibid., pp. 33–4.
109   Ibid., p. 35.
110   Ibid., p. 36.

CHAPTER 2

On the Radical Historicity of Literature: Roy Bhaskar

The occasional pieces appearing under the rubric 'In Memoriam: Roy Bhaskar 1944–2014' and published in *Journal of Critical Realism*[1] admirably served their intended purpose: to celebrate the life and achievements of a major philosopher through the record of his impact, both personal and professional, upon an intellectually diverse and geographically dispersed group of aspiring young intellectuals. Cynical must be the reader who failed to be infected by the latter's enthusiasms; I confess myself to feeling slightly envious of their good fortune in making the acquaintance of such a deeply humane personality and such a rich philosophical tradition, and so early on in their careers to boot. By the same token, it is hard to argue with what, one would guess, was an editorial decision to focus attention specifically upon the young – obviously the future lies with them, not with the greying patriarchs who, all too frequently, dominate the conference scene and occupy the pages of prestigious journals with their dire warning about 'love at first sight' and claims to have 'seen it all before'.

And yet, and yet ... there are disadvantages to the focus upon youth. One important side effect of the celebratory pieces, it bears considering, is the stimulus that these provide for those of us whose careers ran parallel, chronologically speaking, to that of Bhaskar, the stimulus, specifically, to reprise and reassess, critically and objectively, the course of our own trajectories. The latter, perforce, are rather more complex than those of our younger colleagues: we arrived on the scene of critical realism already laden with an intellectual baggage acquired at considerable cost elsewhere. Of course, as we were the first to realise at the time, this baggage was not without its problems and shortcomings – an awareness of these, after all, was what had driven us initially to engage with critical realism; nobody was denying the need for assistance in eking out our limited resources. But still, we needed to be convinced that the investment of time and effort was going to be worthwhile, and nobody who has read Thomas Kuhn's work on the history of science would have expected anything less from us.

---

1 Groff et al 2015.

By way of illustration, I would like to offer in what follows a rough account of my own 'long trek' from its beginnings in the discipline of Hispanism (the study of Hispanic literature and culture) towards a final engagement with critical realism. Curious beginnings, to be sure: a backwater on the margins of what was, according to some,[2] a less than impressive British Academy. But then again, as Althusser reminds us, '*even philosophers* ... must be born somewhere, some time, and begin to think and write'.[3] Were there any advantages in beginning so far from the centre? Not, seemingly, my exposure to the curious brand of Catholic authoritarianism then prevalent within Hispanism; only the fact that, by virtue of my situation, I was forced upon a hard programme of self-education and training in abstract thought by way of freeing myself from the entanglements of an unconscious empiricism. And *unconscious* empiricism! Here, to anticipate, is the end to which the ensuing narrative will gravitate:

> An ideology ... can be regarded as characterised ... by the fact that *its own problematic is not conscious of itself*. When Marx tells us (and he continually repeats it) not to take an ideology's consciousness of itself for its essence, he also means that before it is unconscious of the real problems it is a response (or non-response) to, an ideology is already unconscious of its 'theoretical presuppositions', that is, the active but unavowed problematic which fixes for it the meaning and movement of *its problems* and thereby of their solutions. So a problematic cannot generally be read like an open book, it must be dragged up from the depths of the ideology in which it is buried but active, and usually despite the ideology itself, its own statements and proclamations.[4]

My starting point will be my early research – specifically on the Spanish sixteenth-century educationalist, Juan Huarte de San Juan – and the problems consequent upon its (unconscious) empiricist problematic. These proved to be insurmountable from *within* this problematic, which presupposed the subject/object opposition; and could only be postponed, not resolved, through recourse to an unconscious Hegelianism. The latter, while it promoted the valuable notion of history as a process without a subject, prioritised consciousness in the form of an unfolding Idea, as a prelude to establishing 'Man' as the immanent subject of all process. The break with consciousness could only

---

2 Anderson 1968.
3 Althusser 1990a, pp. 63–4.
4 Althusser 1990a, p. 69.

be engineered through a direct encounter with the Freudian unconscious, through which to explore an array of pre-modern and early modern Spanish texts. What was gained in terms of psychology, however, was lost in terms of History: the psychoanalytic unconscious, despite the best efforts of Norman Brown, upon whose *Life against Death* I drew, reduced to a trans-historical narrative that offered limited purchase on the social materiality, and therefore radical historicity, of literary texts. The solution, or so I imagined, lay in historical materialism and, specifically, the Althusserianism promoted, as it happened by a Spanish student of Althusser, Juan Carlos Rodríguez.

Rodríguez himself indicates one barrier to be negotiated: the legacy of an older tradition of British Marxists, who, their leftist discourse notwithstanding, were allegedly unable to break with the (unconsciously held) empiricist opposition between an interiorised 'psychology' and a material, economic 'outside'; unable, as a consequence, to take on board the Althusserian notion of history as a process without a subject. My intention on the present occasion will be to further explore the latter notion, through a more detailed appraisal of Rodríguez's rigorously historicising perspective on the sixteenth-century neo-Platonic or, to use the Spaniard's term, '*animist*' philosophy of love. The latter, if nothing else, should be of obvious interest to critical realists insofar as, in conformity with the late Bhaskar, it conceives love as a cosmic force, the Soul of the World, which pervades the whole of Creation. That said, the convergence between the Althusserian and the critical realist ends right there: for the Spaniard, animism is to be rigorously located as an emergent ideology, at a precise historical conjuncture, in a life-and-death struggle – only too literally so for some of its practitioners – with a dominant substantialism, a feudal ideology insistent on the cosmic division between this world and the next and the utter baseness of the flesh. I will put Rodríguez's ideas to the test through their application to the emergence of the 'free subject' in the context of an eighteenth-century novel by Pedro de Montengón.s

While the 'radical historicity of literature' was clearly a concept to be reckoned with – from the outset I took its widespread neglect, even among Marxist circles, to be nothing less than scandalous – important questions remained: what were the theoretical underpinnings to 'social formations', 'modes of production', the economic, political and ideological instances, and so on, and more specifically, with respect to Rodríguez, to the 'ideological unconscious' theorised in his work? To find the answers, I turned to the texts of Althusser himself and the commentaries thereon. Of the latter the most useful proved to be Robert Paul Resch's *Althusser and the Renewal of Marxist Theory* (1992), given its author's determination – of immediate and obvious relevance to Rodríguez – to begin with the concept of history and not, as was

invariably the case with other commentators, with epistemological considerations; or, more specifically, to begin with the Althusserian notion of structural causality, understood as the historical effectivity of the structured whole
upon its elements, whose distinct and unequal effectivities were simultaneously at work in a given conjuncture, to the extent of reacting back upon the
whole. Within this framework, the complexities of subject formation, explored
in depth by Althusser, defied any reduction to the 'freedom' of 'man' or to
a mechanistic reflection of the relations of production, or so at least Resch
argued.

This was the point at which Bhaskar entered upon the scene. The arguments set out in *Althusser and the Renewal of Marxist Social Theory* were,
Resch confessed, 'deeply influenced' by Bhaskar's *A Realist Theory of Science*
(1975) and *The Possibility of Naturalism* (1979). Specifically, Bhaskar's distinction between *ontological realism* and *epistemological relativism*, while manifestly indebted to Althusser's materialist theses – the primacy of the real over
thought about the real and the specificity of thought with respect to the real –
'expresses Althusser's position better than Althusser himself does'.[5] Better than
Althusser, but with qualifications: the Althusserian emphasis upon the effectivity of the social formation as a complex whole, we will argue, cannot be squared
with the priority Bhaskar accords in *The Possibility of Naturalism* to the indi-
vidual/society dichotomy. The latter is but a variation upon the subject/object
binary that, on Resch's own reckoning, the French philosopher consistently critiqued.

We will conclude with a brief examination of the work of several Marxist
or Marxian scholars who, while they have carefully measured their distance
from Bhaskar's spiritualist turn, have continued to waver in their allegiance
between a philosophical ideology that defends the 'freedom' of the individual,
raised to the level of a cosmic consciousness, and a Marxist science that departs
from the notion of a social formation, structured on the basis of a mode of
production. Our tactic, as should be obvious, is not to lecture critical realists
on topics of only marginal relevance to their own concerns, but constantly to
confront them with something that they themselves persistently attempt to
repress: historical products, in all their material density. History, we will conclude, is something that philosophical realists need to take on board if they are
to be serious about their self-appointed task of underlabouring for a materialist
science.

---

5 Resch 1992, p. 378n1.

1   **Who Walked a Crooked Mile**

Beginnings are never absolute, certainly not when it comes to the choice of
one's postgraduate research topic. Even at the time it was made, I was well
aware that my own choice was conditioned by many varied factors. That said, a
study of Juan Huarte de San Juan's *Examen de ingenios* (*Examination of Men's
Wits*) (1575) seemed, as a starting point, as potentially fruitful as any other, particularly after I discovered with some satisfaction that the sixteenth-century
Spanish educationalist had also attracted the attention of the leading theoretical linguist of the 1960s, Noam Chomsky.

Huarte's work can be briefly summarised. The author of the *Examination*
accepted as axiomatic that all souls are equal, but noted that, irrespective of
the teaching received and the *art* and willpower applied, some people are *by
nature* more skilled than others at particular tasks. He explains this in traditional terms as the result of a 'temperamental' imbalance in each individual,
resulting from the unequal combination of bodily 'humours', which led, in turn,
through a causal (material) process, to corresponding imbalances at the level of
the faculties of the soul, and, finally, to the reality that individuals excel or fail in
different ways. Having established this much, Huarte proceeded to categorise
certain kinds of wit. The details need not concern us here. Suffice it to note his
description of individuals possessing the second kind of wit – 'those capable
of inventing and uttering things they have never heard from their teachers' –
to be measured alongside those possessing the third, truly creative kind, who
'utter – without study or guidance – things so delicate, so true and prodigious,
that they have never occurred to men before, or been seen, heard, or written
down'.[6]

The affinity between Huarte's views on creative generation and Chomsky's
brand of 'transformational grammar' should be immediately obvious. The business of such grammar, the linguist insists, is to discover the generative mechanisms underlying actual speech. He elaborates: 'Huarte's framework is useful
for discussing "psychological theory" in the ensuing period. Typical of later
thought is his reference to the use of language as an index of human intelligence, of what distinguishes man from animals, and, specifically, his emphasis
on the creative capacity of normal intelligence'.[7] The emphasis upon human
creativity allegedly ran from Huarte through Cartesian thought, the Cambridge
Platonic School and, in opposition to its dominant empiricist, positivist coun-

---

6   Huarte 1977, pp. 432–3.
7   Chomsky 1968, p. 9.

terpart, Kantian metaphysics, before flowing into, we would add, the school of critical realism itself, which has never hesitated to list Chomsky among its fellow-travellers and supporters.

The mediated connection between Huarte and critical realists is not one I intend to pursue: it is made simply to forestall a premature disengagement, on the part of the latter, from what may seem, at first blush, rather obscure goings-on in sixteenth-century Spain. My immediate concern is to highlight my own inability at this stage to address the obvious problems with Chomsky's position.[8] Principal among these was the omission of any reference to what was arguably the most salient feature of the *Examination*, namely its rootedness in what appears to be a species of anatomical materialism curiously reminiscent of the Skinnerian behaviourism that Chomsky was otherwise concerned to critique. The Spanish Inquisition, let us note parenthetically, was more discerning of the threat posed by Huarte's materialism and quickly moved to place the *Examination* on its index of forbidden texts.

As for myself, while I was certainly aware that Huarte's work had been subjected to diametrically opposed readings, so imprisoned was I within my own brand of empiricism that I simply lacked the theoretical resources to *explain* as opposed to *describe* the conflicts involved. One needed to be *outside* empiricism to ask the relevant questions: namely how do we explain the contradictions within Huarte's text; and what, precisely, had Chomsky's Cartesian rationalism to do with a text seemingly mired in the crosscurrents of feudal science and pre-modern ideologies? Absent from both my own and Chomsky's work was, in the last instance, the elephant in the room, namely History. But if that much was clear, less clear was how to incorporate this History into my scheme of things, as I discovered in my next book, *The Birth and Death of Language*.[9]

2   A Hegelian Turn

The Birth and Death of Language! The very title tells it all: it was to the Hegelian tradition that I turned for an early escape from the confines of a strictly empiricist tradition. Not that I was poring over the pages of *The Phenomenology of Mind*: we are still at the level of an ideology that imposes itself unconsciously. Still, there was no denying the gains: gone was the assumption of an empirical subject that *sees* its object. The story has now become that of a Subject

---

8   Read 1981.
9   Read 1983.

that unfolds over the course of the ages, from early 'medieval' texts, through the 'Renaissance', and into the 'Baroque', a Subject that constantly finds itself ill at ease in the circumstances of the moment and that struggles to overcome its limitations. We do not have the space to explore the argument in detail but, again, nor is it strictly necessary to do so. Suffice it to focus upon the ideological constraints that continued to determine my own writing, albeit in a Hegelian guise, with an eye to which, let us adduce one of the historical products analysed.

> De los sos ojos   tan fuertemientre lorando
> tornava la cabeça   y estaba los catando.
> Vio puertas abiertas   e uços sin cañados,
> alcandaras vazias   sin pielles e sin mantos.[10]

(From his eyes, so strongly crying, / he turned his head and beheld them, / saw open doors and doors without locks, / empty perches, without furs or blankets.)

In these opening lines of the anonymous thirteenth-century feudal epic, *Poema de Mio Cid* (*Poem of the Cid*), the Cid expresses his sorrow on being driven into exile. The occasion is marked by an omen.

> A la exida de Bivar   ovieron la corneja diestra
> y entrando a Burgos   ovieron la siniestra.
> Meçio mio Cid los ombros   y engrameo la tiesta:
> '¡Albriçia, Albar Ffañez,   ca echados somos de tierra!'[11]

(At the exit from Vivar, they had the crow on the right, / and on entering into Burgos, on the left. / The Cid jerked his shoulders and shook his head: / 'Rejoice, Albar Fáñez, that we are driven into exile!')

On the surface, everything seems straightforward enough. So much so that it is easy to miss the text's peculiarities. It is one thing to cry, but why the tautological insistence upon 'from his eyes'? The detail registers an important fact about the Cid, namely the requirement that he *exteriorise* his emotions, if, that is, these are to mean anything at all, or so at least I argued, outrageously tak-

---

10   *Poema*, lines 1–4.
11   Ibid., lines 11–14.

ing my cue from an essay by Roland Barthes on the semantics of professional wrestling.[12] And as the Spirit or Subject unfolds – the argument proceeded – it finds material expression in a particular (cultural) form, until, that is, through a process of progressive *interiorisation*, it manages finally to coincide with its essence. The plan of *The Birth and Death of Language* followed naturally from such basic premises: each chapter would chart a moment in the Subject's development.

Well, of course, it all seems rather strange now, looking back at it. But the alleged inability of a Subject to find expression did have its virtues. Specifically, it explained a rather curious fact about the *Poema*, namely the halting, spasmodic, juxtapositive, pro- and retrogressive movement of its paratactic syntax, which, while certainly typical of the epic genre, seems to defy all logic. Clearly at this stage we were still dealing with a Subject of History 'in itself' but not 'for itself'. But again these are not matters that need detain us at the present moment: I am more concerned to foreground the critical narrative that takes for granted the existence of a 'subject' that is imprisoned within its feudal constraints, but that will be subsequently 'reborn' – during the course of the 'Renaissance' and 'Enlightenment' – before finding its full expression in something called modernity and even post-modernity. Of course, it was never necessary to embrace the civilising process in full: for reasons not immediately apparent, my own version ends with the great writers of the seventeenth century, notably Miguel de Cervantes, whose Don Quixote would, single-handedly, undertake his own reforming project in defence of individual freedoms. But in whichever form it came, the ensuing narrative proved tenacious in the extreme.

Proved and continues to prove. Nobody, it appears, is immune to the charms of the Moving Spirit, and certainly not critical realists, specifically when called upon to chart the development of 'Western Philosophy', from its humble beginnings in Antiquity to a triumphant Modernity, crucially by-passing the darkness of the Middle Ages. In the words of Colin Wight: 'As a historically located mode of thought ... [Enlightenment thinking] emerges in an era that was attempting both to throw off the shackles of dogma and fanaticism, whilst at the same time trying to come to grips with a new political order where power was concentrated in the form of the modern state'.[13] A historically located mode of thought or an ideologically inflected, even rampantly idealist 'history of ideas', concerned to foreground the triumph of the bourgeoisie, now dominant over a residual nobility? Whatever else it is, one thing is for sure: this kind of

---

12   Read 1983, pp. 8–9.
13   Dean et al. 2006, p. 39.

historical analysis has lost its way in the heady realms of an all-consuming *consciousness*. And that, unfortunately for the literary critic, is where the Hegelian project runs aground: so many of his or her objects, in their material density, are grounded not in the realm of the Spirit or consciousness but in that of the *unconscious*.

3   Visions in Exile

Hispanism, I have said, with its claustrophobic, neo-Catholic orthodoxies, was not the best of places to begin. Perforce one turned increasingly to 'theory', as it began to take shape within literary studies in the wake of 1968. Crucial in terms of my own development was one of the classic texts of the period, Norman Brown's *Life against Death*. Unsurprisingly, Brown chose to defend his psychoanalytic conception of history against its only serious competitor, once the liberal narrative of 'enlightenment' had been discarded, namely that of Marx. Brown's objection to the latter had nothing to do with the importance Marx attributes to the 'economic factor' in history; indeed, the dialectical materialist is explicitly praised for the clarity of his insight in this respect. It is, rather, that, from the Marxist perspective, economic necessity is contained within the realm of the reality-principle, whereas 'the essence of man lies not in the reality-principle but in repressed unconscious desires'.[14] Brown is insistent: 'No matter how stringently economic necessities press down on him ... man does not live by bread alone'.[15] There is thus a vacuum, the argument concludes, in the Marxist utopia: '... beyond labor there is love. And if beyond labor at the end of history there is love, love must have always been there from the beginning of history, and it must have been the hidden force supplying the energy devoted to labor and to making history'.[16] History, it follows, consists of a process of sublimation, whereby the different stages of the individual's ontogenetic development are reproduced in the phylogenetic development of culture, crucially with respect to 'anality': Swift, Brown pointedly reminds us, 'lost his wits because Celia shits'.

It proved relatively easy to transfer the 'excremental vision' to Spanish literature, principally to the texts of Francisco de Quevedo (1580–1645). Here was matter aplenty.

---

14   Brown 1968, p. 26.
15   Ibid.
16   Ibid., p. 27.

Para quien sabe examinarte, eres
lo solamente vil, el asco, el lodo.[17]

(For whoever knows how to examine you, / you are the strictly vile, puke,
mud.)

Quevedo felt compelled to accept that the beloved has a body like any other,
that her divine face registers the passing of time, that she has an anus and
that, in sum, she dies, flushed away in a heap of dust: 'Look at the envy that
is your hair, that however splendid it may seem, is not excused from being
excrement'.[18] What are the cosmetics with which Woman daubs herself but a
sickening stickiness, whose application effectively 'manures the heavens'? The
conclusion is unavoidable: the Queen of heaven, proclaimed to be all soul, is in
reality a mass of stench and decay, in which respect she simply condenses the
truth of the human condition:

Puto es el hombre que de putas fía,
y puto el que sus gustos apetece,
puto es el estipendio que se ofrece
en pago de su puta compañía.[19]

(A faggot is the man who in whores trusts, / and a faggot whoever desires
what he desires / whorish is the stipend that is offered / in payment of his
whorish company.)

So that when the layers of civilisation are stripped away, what we find is not a
soul but the original dirt from which the cultural edifice was constructed:

La mierda es mierda, y su orina, orina;
sólo que ésta es verdad y esotra enredo,
y estánme encareciendo la letrina.[20]

(Shit is shit, and piss, piss; / except that the former is truth and the latter,
mere obfuscation. / [In effect] they are exalting the latrine.)

---

17   Quoted from Read 1990, p. 66.
18   Ibid.
19   Ibid., p. 79.
20   Ibid.

Now while there was much to admire about Brown's *Life against Death* – even after four decades the psychoanalytic vision therein outlined can prove quite overwhelming – I became convinced that its 'desire' flowed outside of history, understood as a social reality, and that, while breaching consciousness, it remained resolutely individualised, which is to say, rather *trans*-historical than historical, and attached in secret to the autonomous subject of bourgeois thinking. To what extent was it legitimate to argue the priority of love over the economic? Individuals are, after all, born into a social formation that lies in wait for them and in which their 'psychology' is formed and takes shape. Such a reality doubtless explained the existence under feudalism of individuals who lacked the kind of interiorised 'psychology' that was the common stuff of the fully-fledged individual of subsequent historical formations, and who indeed were not individuals in the strictest sense of the term or at least 'non-self-conscious' individuals. An unconscious, there may well be in feudal culture, but the form it takes is that of an inscrutable God, located at the cosmic level.

Timely, then, was my acquaintance with the Althusserian tradition and its notion of 'history without a subject', which took place through one of Althusser's most distinguished pupils and his chief theoretician of ideology, the Spaniard Juan Carlos Rodríguez. Rodríguez was not, to be sure, well known to British Hispanism; in fact, he was not known at all – the discipline was fiercely resistant to Marxism in any form – but that only served to incite my curiosity. Love, in the Spaniard's seminal *Theory and History of Ideological Production*, certainly figured prominently as a thematic but now within the radically transformed framework of the 'radical historicity of literature'.

4   History without a Subject

The benefits to be derived from Rodríguez's work, within the context of my own trajectory, were immediate. History was no longer imagined as the transcendental development of the Spirit or as a sublimatory process but, in the case of sixteenth- and seventeenth-century Spain, as a struggle between (at least) two conflicting modes of production, more specifically, at the level of ideology, between a dominant feudal *substantialism* and its mercantilist counterpart, *animism*. Allegedly, substantialism did not have a subject or Subject at all but rested upon the opposition between lord and serf/servant; nor for that matter did animism, whose 'beautiful soul' aspired only to the status of a proto-subject, prior to the subject's classic formulation, extending to many variations upon the theme, under a finally dominant bourgeoisie. The Cid, within this new problematic, was not a subject, exteriorised or otherwise, but a *lord*, who happened himself to be a *servant* of a secular lord, King Alfonso, and of a celestial Lord. The problem was not that sorrow – to return to the example of the tears – did not exist unless embodied in visible form, as I had formerly argued, but that substantialism did not recognise the division between an *inside* and an *outside* or, alternatively, between a *private* and a *public* sphere; even less did it recognise these oppositions' derivates, the 'individual' and 'society', and consciousness and the unconscious. Its own favoured dichotomy was that between *this* world and the *next*. Predictably enough, 'love' between men and women was, in such circumstances, unthinkable.

And that was the least of it. The Cid's future is prefigured in the opening stanzas of the Epic – through an omen – for the simple reason that the feudal narrative is structured on the assumption that the epic hero must, in the end, return to his *natural* place, alongside his lord/Lord, from whom he has been temporarily absented; in this feudal world, stasis is the normal order of things and movement a temporary disturbance of it, symptomatically the same principle to be deduced from Ptolemaic physics, which sought legitimation in substantialism, even as this ideology served to support feudal science. Moreover, in the absence of a subject, the notion of an authorial subjectivity is unimaginable, as is that of a 'third-person' capable of organising his or her narrative along transcendental lines. The limits of the bard's world were those of his paratactic syntax; his only conceivable perspective is that of his lord/Lord. 'Authors' only become feasible under the shelter of *animism* where, in their capacity as free proto-subjects, they can begin to conceive of a hero exposed to the hazards of *contingency*, equipped with the *freedom* to make his or (subsequently) her own destiny.[21]

By the same token, it finally became possible to theorise Huarte's *Examination* in the light of its actual historical provenance, as enacting a clash between two conflicting ideologies, one of which, the substantialist, prioritised the organic inter-mixture of body and soul, while the other, the animist, promoted a vision of the creative ingenuity of a proto-subject, whose body was capable of spiritual transformation.[22] The difference is that encapsulated in the contrast between two bodies, one envisaged as rotten with sin, which a seigneurial class hastens to *dress* in its (always substantialised) finery; the other as a spiritualised expression of carnal beauty, whose ideal form is that of the nude. Understood within this problematic, Huarte's text had little to do with the transcendental Kantian subject that Chomsky sought to project back onto it, and

---

21   See Read 2010, pp. 163 ff.
22   See Read 2004a.

even less with transformational grammar under whose auspices the bourgeois subject, now stuffed with all manner of deep structures, had swelled to consume what properly belonged to socio-historical structures.

At this juncture, we will consider in greater detail Rodríguez's theorisation of the secular branch of animism, as this emerged in Spain in the early sixteenth century, with an eye to the theoretical principles on which this theorisation rests and the problems to which it gives rise. To this end let us return to the literary text in all its historical density.

5   On the Radical Historicity of 'Love'

A Dafne ya los brazos le crecían
y en luengos ramos vueltos se mostraban;
en verdes hojas vi que se tornaban
los cabellos qu'el oro escurecían;
    de áspera corteza se cubrían
los tiernos miembros que aun bullendo 'staban;
los blancos pies en tierra se hincaban
en torcidas raíces se volvían.
    Aquel que fue la causa de tal daño,
que a fuerza de llorar, crecer hacía
este árbol, que con lágrimas regaba.
    ¡Oh miserable estado, o mal tamaño,
que con llorarlas crezca cada día
la causa y la razón por que lloraba![23]

(Daphne's arms were already growing / and showing themselves as branches; / into green leaves I saw that they were transforming / the strands of hair that eclipsed gold; / in coarse bark were covering themselves / the soft limbs that still wriggled away; / the white feet into the earth were sinking / and into twisted roots changing. / He who was the cause of such devastation, / who, by dint of crying caused to grow / this tree that with tears he watered. / Oh, miserable state, oh great misfortune, / whereby his very tears should cause to grow each day / the cause and reason for his crying!)

---

23   Vega 1989, pp. 58–9.

Confronted by such a text, the traditional critic deploys the only concepts s/he is equipped to think with, namely those of a 'subject' and an 'object', otherwise an 'author' who 'expresses' his or her 'ideas', 'thoughts', 'intentions', 'sentiments' and so on in an exterior form. The effect is to pitch the analysis at the level of universalised 'human nature'. Thus, for Alexander Parker, 'Garcilaso communicates to us not a personal sorrow but the sadness inherent in life'. People, by the same token, are born, live, love, and die in much the same way: '[A]nyone who has suffered from love', according to Elias Rivers, the leading North American authority on Garcilaso, 'will recognise that this poetry has deep roots in the universal human experience'.[24]

The fundamental presupposition, assumed unthinkingly, is that of a 'textual transparency', the site of a coming together of author and reader, which renders further commentary unnecessary, except by way of elaboration. 'What is left to us', continues Fernández-Morera, 'is to discover new levels of meaning, to see myth as a general representation of the subconscious of the human race; or as a poetic expression of religious beliefs or eternal human predicaments'.[25] At most, it falls to the professional critic to strip away the historical debris through stilts of footnotes and so expose the bare body of the text to the gaze of the reader.

Understandably enough, such a problematic raises its own, idiosyncratic set of questions. Did Garcilaso truly love Isabel Freyre? Were his feelings, as expressed in his lyrics, merely *rhetorical* or truly *authentic*? The same set of questions that can be asked of the Romantic or modern poet. For how otherwise is it possible to speak of the universality of literature? Their effect, necessarily, is to transfer attention from the materiality of the text to what *preceded* it.

In approaching the frustrated encounter between Daphne and Apollo, the Althusserian takes a radically different tack. His point of departure is not that of some fantasised transcendental subject but the history that a bourgeois criticism wishes to dispel or, more specifically, the social formation taking shape at a particular historical conjuncture, that of the opening decades of the sixteenth century.

It is a question, then, in the last instance, of knowing the unconscious ideological matrix (produced, as always, by a specific *historical* 'social formation') which is secreted by the internal logic that rules the text,

---

24   Quoted from Read 1992, p. 31.
25   Ibid.

that determines its textual configuration, its global sense and the specific meaning of each one of the elements that enter to form part of such a structural articulation.[26]

By what ideological matrix, then, is Garcilaso's sonnet determined? To begin with, its narrative structure is organised in terms of a beautiful soul, the proto-subject who, from his uniquely perspectival position, no longer *reads* the world as a book, in substantialist terms – remember the Cid and the crow – but who *sees* the 'thing', in all its material density. But that is only the beginning of what is, in effect, the continuation of an ideological struggle whereby animism, in contrast to substantialism, for which forms are essential and unchanging, acknowledges the possibility of a radical metamorphosis. Daphne readily mutates into a tree because, in an animist context, her skin is 'the same as' bark, her hair 'the same as' leaves, her feet 'the same as' roots, and so on. Daphne drowns her own life in the 'Soul of the World' as in a kind of cosmic ground-state, in defiance of Apollo. The latter, in his capacity as an individualised soul, secretly fears such a merger and is accordingly frustrated in his attempt to enter *into* Daphne, even as Daphne, pressed beyond his reach, continues to grow, ironically watered by the tears that Apollo sheds over her: within the new Copernican cosmos, legitimated ideologically in animist terms, movement is of the essence.

Let us leave the textual details for a moment to focus upon what is implied theoretically by the shift from the subject/object opposition to that of the social formation. From the standpoint of the latter, the sonnet should not be seen as the 'expression' of something anterior to it; its key notions, although 'lived' unconsciously, 'are never given beforehand, are never simply *there*, solid and within reach, in the form of a block that can be directly transposed or transferred into the text'.[27] The same applied to the notion of the *soul*: this also must be *produced* but with an important proviso: 'production' is to be understood not in the 'technicist' sense. The difference is more than a nuance: Rodríguez takes care to measure his distance from fellow Althusserian and theoretician of ideology, Pierre Macherey, who, in his concern to resist the 'spiritualist' strains in bourgeois thinking, allegedly re-installs the bourgeois subject. Stripped of its Kantian content, the latter simply deploys technical means through which to express itself:

---

26   Rodríguez 2002a, p. 140.
27   Rodríguez 2002a, p. 122.

In other words, 'technicism' simply presupposes that the subject, failing to be invaded by any 'poetic raptus', needs to polish, nurture, elaborate, etc. the expressive vehicle that it uses. It is assumed beforehand that the 'poet' already possesses the idea, the experience, the sentiment, etc. that is to be expressed.[28]

The nub of the Spaniard's argument is clear: his is a problematic in which the poetic process is understood as perfectly *objective*, in the sense of secreted by a certain set of ideological relations, as opposed, say, to being *inspired* by one's muse. Such, after all, is what is meant by 'history as a process without a subject'.

6   Ideology as 'Productivity'

It is important, I believe, that we understand exactly the nature of the contrast between the traditional, empiricist approach to literature and the Spaniard's. My own understanding is that we are dealing with two radically opposed problematics, one of which departs from the position of a (free) subjectivity, otherwise a 'psychology', which confronts an exterior objectivity that imprints itself on it; and another that departs from the notion of a social formation, consisting of ideological, political, and economic instances, the economic being determinant in the last instance. The first problematic, to elaborate, presupposes the existence of a subject or agent replete with ideas, intentions, and so on and characterised by an essential freedom – constitutive of a 'human nature' – which is liable to find itself alienated in a society with uneven distributions of power; the second prioritises the concept of an ideological matrix, originating in a specific set of social relations, between master and slave under slavery; lord and serf under feudalism; and Subject and subject under capitalism, each of which has its own definition as to what constitutes 'human nature'.

The difference between the two problematics may be alternatively posed as follows: the first wishes to start from the notion of 'Garcilaso' as a 'unique', individualised subjectivity or agent; the second, from the historical structures and relations that produce individualities at a particular conjuncture, the assumption being that one might eventually arrive at 'Garcilaso', just as the sociologist might eventually arrive at 'Man', but only after having traversed the totality of

---

28   Ibid., p. 123.

the social matrix. But to elaborate on this second, Althusserian problematic, let us turn to a text not considered by Rodríguez, *El scholástico* (c. 1550) of Cristóbal de Villalón.

The very dialogic form of *El scholástico* betrays its animist affiliation at the outset. Such an 'exchange' reproduces, at the relatively autonomous level of ideology, the mercantilist exchanges taking place at the economic level in an increasingly 'free' market; predictably enough, issues of freedom will figure prominently throughout, with respect to slaves, women, and the beautiful soul. Just as predictably, debate centres upon 'love', understood as the privileged force that, in defiance of substantialism, reconstitutes the Creation as an infinitely extended *cosmos*, pervaded by the spiritualising force of the sun's rays. As Francisco de Bobadilla, one of the dialogists, protests to another:

> This celestial love has as its object and basis the beauty of the soul, which is the radiance of the divine form that God infused in it at the dawn of its creation, as if such objects were His own children. And this beauty is the inclination of love to act virtuously, which, although imprinted on all creatures that are capable of love, God infuses to greater perfection in souls, and particularly in angels, insofar as they are created to rejoice in God and are made in His image. And although it can be said that plants are beautiful, along with herbs and stones, stars, planets and the sun and many other material things, yet they are not said to be beautiful in the sense of expressing this divine beauty; but the more they share in this beauty, and the greater their resemblance to it, the more they will participate in His celestial love and be capable of it. Someone will ask me how something that has no soul can be said to have this beauty, since in my view the latter is an inclination to do good. This can best be understood through examples: the plants that produce nothing but flowers, such as wallflowers, white lilies, [common] lilies and jasmines, delight us with their perfume. Who could possibly suggest, in view of this albeit small service, that we should not love them and desire them?[29]

Love it is that, in the form of friendship, binds together Villalón's group of beautiful souls in the seclusion of their private (e)state. What is significant about animist love, as Bobadilla's description of it perfectly demonstrates, is its transformative capacity, not least of all with respect to the human body.

---

29   Villalón 1966, p. 204.

And in this way human bodies are capable of [beauty] on account of the soul that they carry within them; because the soul fills the body with beauty, transfers [this beauty] to the body's outward form, revealing it, with gracious piety, to our eyes, in the face's good complexion, in the elegance and refinement of gesture; as a result of which the body shows on the outside all the goodness taken together that the soul has within; and thus we come to love both.[30]

How exactly this philosophy is elaborated across a whole social spectrum need not detain us further. The important point to be grasped in the present context is that even here, in philosophical guise, the animist notion of the soul must never be understood as *pre-existent*, at the moment of its textualisation, but rather as secreted dialectically, together with its cognate elements – the 'eyes', 'ice', 'tears', 'fire', 'sun', 'water', and so on – at the level of the ideological matrix. The trap to avoid, to reiterate, is to imagine, in accordance with a bourgeois dynamic, that these notions *originate* in a 'psychology', in a subjectivity where they simply await their expression, whether the latter be grounded in Kantian 'intentions' or in empiricist 'impressions'. For the Althusserian, ideological notions are, in contrast to their empirical counterpart, perfectly objective, in the sense of being ultimately determined by the social matrix:

> Moreover, the *objectivity* of the poetic process is deduced from the fact that ideological relations, at the same time as they are determining with respect to (discursive) production, also need to be 'produced' (to assume a concrete 'body') throughout the text that they determine, insofar as they do not already exist prior to the text, in any solid or tangible form. Only those people who want to ignore this fact will find it at all abstruse.[31]

What the Althusserian is trying to get at, if I understand him correctly, is the notion of a social formation as a contradictory and uneven complex of elements *in process*, within one historic mode of production; of a mobile system of relations that constitute, nay, construct individualities as, say, masters, slaves, lords, serfs and, yes, even as subjects, and there is the rub. For while everyone can readily accept the 'otherness' of the 'medieval' epic and even of the 'Renaissance' sonnet, bourgeois ideologues always run the risk of promoting a subject 'for all seasons', embodying a 'human essence' which somehow tran-

---

30   Ibid., p. 205.
31   Rodríguez 2002a, p. 123.

scends and operates (indeed causes) the social system. Not even Althusser himself was immune to its charms: all ideology, he averred, exists through and for the subject. Rodríguez's argument, by way of contrast, stands or falls on its capacity to ground the subject-form in a radical historicity, which is why, by way of substantiating this argument and at the risk of irreversibly alienating my non-Hispanist readers, I propose to drill one more time into the bedrock of my primary sources, but this time with my sights trained on the historical origins of the free bourgeois subject in its classic form.

7   The Historical Origins of the Free Subject

I will be exploring Rodríguez's concept of the ideological unconscious for the benefit of critical realists in Chapter 7 and do not intend to anticipate my conclusions here. Suffice it to remind ourselves of its relevance to the 'free subject':

> The notion of the subject (and the whole problematic within which it is inscribed) is radically historical because [...] it derives directly (and exclusively) from the very matrix of the bourgeois ideological unconscious: the 'serf' can never be a 'subject', etc. But for that very reason also the theoretical perspectives originating in the same bourgeois ideology will never be able to accept that their own unconscious is at root an ideological (that is to say, historical) issue, but will always believe that the elements and logic peculiar to such an 'unconscious' constitute the truth about the human condition, in all its clarity.[32]

The singular relevance of Rodríguez's comment will be immediately apparent from even the most casual perusal of Pedro de Montengón's *Eusebio* (1786–7), the text that I have selected to explore the production of the subject-form.[33]

The details of the novel's plot need not concern us. In broad outline, it begins with a shipwreck off the coast of New England, survived by a lone child, the novel's eponymous hero, Eusebio, who is taken in by a Quaker community and adopted by two of its members, the commercial artisan Enrique Myden and his wife Susana. The good fortune is not simply Eusebio's: until his arrival, Enrique and Susana had lacked the heir for whom they desperately craved. Responsibility for Eusebio's education, it transpires, will be surrendered to a private tutor,

---

32   Rodríguez 2002a, p. 21.
33   It almost goes without saying that Montengón wrote in exile and that his novel would quickly appear on the Inquisition's list of prohibited texts.

Hardyl, who, through a technique of micro-management, will instil in Eusebio the requisite virtues of the free subject, pre-eminent among which is the capacity for self-control. The paradox – of a freedom achieved through subjection – takes us to the very heart of the relevant ideological unconscious. Let us consider the following passage, in which, having made an unwise purchase from the butcher, Eusebio is sent off to make amends:

> [Hardyl] let him go alone in order that he might learn from experience, confident in his pupil's capacity for circumspection that is the product of finer feelings, and so that Eusebio should also continue to perform acts of virtue without the slightest admixture of subjection and dependence upon his master; constraints that will never restrain the will of the young as long as the latter feel the impulse to indulge their unrestrained inclinations, the reason being that their proper behaviour is purely superficial and enforced only by fear of the master, from which it follows that, as soon as they find themselves to be owners of their own actions, their teaching becomes an irrelevance and, like a hateful yoke, is readily shaken off.[34]

To have become the 'owner of one's actions' or, alternatively, to be 'in possession of oneself'[35] is to have internalised not simply a certain set of moral values but a whole 'habitus', to borrow a concept from Bourdieu, that extends to such matters as dress and even table manners. In the case of Eusebio, it is also to avoid 'spending' or 'squandering' one's assets, sexual and otherwise, during a long betrothal. An instinctive asceticism, part of the same habitus, protects Eusebio from the temptations of consumerism when he confronts them during his European tour, under the watchful eye of his tutor: 'He felt a thousand impulses to buy whatever took his fancy in every shop. Hardyl, always at his side, let him give vent to his curiosity, without saying anything, so as to see if he was able to contain his desires and only to warn him whenever he was in danger of buying superfluous things'.[36] Needless to say, once the marriage contract is signed, Eusebio will prove to be the perfect patriarch, well equipped to control the sexuality of his wife and, by extension, to prevent her 'spoiling' his infant son through her indulgence.

And so on and on, page after page. We are, of course, a thousand miles away, or more correctly, seven centuries away from the *Poem of the Cid*. 'Love', it bears repeating, found no place in that text: Jimena, the noble's wife, gets down on her

---

34   Montengón 1984, p. 174.
35   Ibid., p. 329.
36   Ibid., p. 502.

knees in the presence of her husband, who is also her *lord*; and her daughters will be subjected to marital violence of a brutally feudal kind. All of which is nothing more than we would expect from an epic genre whose semantics cater for the *external* display of emotion. The dynamics of animist love, it is true, ease the transition, through the familiar distinction between an 'inside' and an 'outside', unsurprisingly insofar as Garcilaso's proto-subject is the recognizable forerunner of Montengón's free subject. But three centuries and an ideological rift separate the 'sensibility' of the 'beautiful soul' from the 'finer feelings' of the full-blooded liberal subject, the latter characterised not simply by a love that finds no outlet but by the dark 'folds of the heart'.[37]

The isolation of key ideologemes, for example, seigneurial 'honour' as opposed to bourgeois 'conscience', is only the first step towards tracing the contours of the relevant ideological unconscious. An analysis truly responsive to the material density of *Eusebio* would need, among other things, to engage the novel's syntax. What greater contrast could one imagine than that between the rigid pro- and regressive parataxis of the epic and the convoluted hypotaxis of the bourgeois novel, with its complex of embedded and subordinate clauses, interwoven by a third-person narrator who views and organises the unfolding narrative of events from his own perspective. The relevant questions, as it happens, are internalised within the context of *Eusebio* when a catastrophe – the theft of their coach – strikes Eusebio and Hardyl, soon after their arrival in England. Symptomatically, Gil Altano, their Spanish servant, once separated from his masters, reverts to type, and turns to beggary, whereas his masters put their artisanal skills to immediate practical use to resolve their financial difficulties. More significantly, when called upon to give an account of his experiences, Gil Altano proves unable to construct an appropriately succinct, fluid narrative, to the obvious impatience of his bourgeois audience. The sharp contrast between the residually feudal servant and the emergent subject will be further thrown into relief when the tourists move on to Catholic Spain.[38]

But let us call a halt to the analysis to draw the relevant theoretical conclusions, principal among which is the importance of framing analysis not in terms of authorial *intentions* but of the appropriate ideological unconscious. To adopt the former strategy, following the logic of Rodríguez, would be to take one's cue from a capitalism that requires 'free' (intending) subjects to provide labour for its equally 'free' enterprises; to adopt the latter is to emphasise the materiality

---

37   Ibid., p. 210.
38   For an extended analysis, see Read 1998, pp. 146–60.

of ideology, envisaged as the force that greases a mode of production, through the production of a certain kind of individuality. Ideological relations, it follows from the materialist standpoint, need to be *produced*, in the same way that, on a different level, the economic process is charged with 'producing' (as opposed to 'expressing') the relevant social relations.

In one important respect at least the Althusserian is mistaken. Far from being abstruse only to those who wilfully refuse it, as we saw him claim above, the objectivity of the poetic process, as a concept, surely borders on incomprehensible to anyone located within an idealist problematic of 'freedom', and one might have expected a greater awareness of this fact from a theoretician of ideology. For is not ideology, in the last instance, the desire 'not to know' and is not this desire precisely what motivates ideologues when they are driven up against the limits of their ideology? Indeed, the very evidence of Rodríguez's own text can be marshalled against him in this regard. Such is the reach and influence of the ideological unconscious, on his own estimate, that it is ridiculous to imagine that it can be conveniently cast aside. And again, by the same estimate, the shift from an ideology of the subject to a materialist science of the social formation requires a veritable *change of terrain* – no small undertaking.

The Spaniard's line of reasoning further falters when he proceeds to insist that traditional and Althusserian literary criticisms are, in effect, dealing with different 'real objects', just as, allegedly, bourgeois economists and Marx deal with two different 'real objects'.[39] If the relevant literary critics are dealing with different real objects, one is bound to ask, what precisely is the point of comparing the one with the other, and ditto with respect to the economists? Clearly, the theoretician of ideology stood in desperate need of some philosophical underlabouring, which is where, speaking personally, Bhaskar entered upon the scene.

8   The Closet Althusserian

I reprised earlier, in my prefatory remarks, the moment (in the mid-1980s) when, having received a copy of the Spanish original of *Theory and History* via inter-library loan, I tossed up whether to engage with a work that appeared to call into question all my previous labours. The predicament was one that I found myself in earlier, with respect to the psychoanalytic work of Brown, and

---

39   Rodríguez 2002a, pp. 126–7.

on that occasion, I had decided to risk all. There seemed little point now in losing my nerve and turning back, and so I read on. And fairly soon, my initial fears were confirmed: I needed to break out of 'literary studies' *per se* and take on another whole body of work; more specifically, I needed to educate myself, as best I could, as to the philosophical basis of the Althusserianism that underscored *Theory and History*.

Althusser's works, it transpired, constituted a highly complex corpus, which, for help in deciphering, I turned to his commentators. Among these, I was drawn to Resch's *Althusser and the Renewal of Marxist Social Theory* (1992). My reasoning was simple: Rodríguez, I recalled, had critiqued British Marxists for their inability to break with an unconscious empiricism; Resch, similarly, critiqued the same Marxists for the 'scurrilous' distortions to which they had subjected Althusser's work[40] and, more importantly, undertook to correct these by taking as his starting point in his assessment of Althusser not epistemology but 'structural causality'. The latter notion, I decided, was crucial to understanding what Rodríguez meant by the 'objectivity' of ideology.

'Structural causality', Resch proceeded to elaborate, commences with the concept of the social formation, conceived as a parallelogram of economic, political, and ideological forces manifested in determinate social structures and relations. While the economic function is primary, political and ideological functions have their own distinct character and effectivities, respectively secondary and tertiary (in the case of capitalism); all determinate structures and relations are simultaneously, if unequally, at work as a structured whole. 'The social formation, in other words, constitutes the historical matrix or intransitive condition of existence of individual structures, yet it exists only as the "complex unity" of their present or transitive effectivities'.[41] The question of subjectivity is treated accordingly: 'Far from denigrating human subjectivity, as is so often claimed, Structural Marxism has always recognised its significance and devoted considerable attention to developing concepts of both subjectivity and practice'.[42]

Had he been familiar with Rodríguez's work, Resch might have added that Althusserianism had also developed *historical* concepts of both subjectivity and practice, but still the essential point is well made:

> The difference between Structural Marxism and its postmodern and neoliberal rivals is that for the latter, human subjectivity is accepted as the

---

40   Resch 1992, pp. 4–5.
41   Ibid., p. 24.
42   Ibid., p. 27.

basis of social theory, while for Althusser and Structural Marxists, the social structures and relations that produce social subjects are primary. Structural Marxists wish to explain first the structures and processes by which social subjects are created and second the relationships between social subjectivity, power and practice.[43]

From this, everything else followed: Althusser's philosophical defence of science foregrounds issues relating to the production of knowledge as a historical process, rather than obsessing over the epistemological quest for 'guarantees' of knowledge. The latter, it was further argued, is always an ideological quest, organised around the central categories of subject and object, that accounts for the collapse of the process of knowledge into an ontology of experience and a 'fascination with the object', otherwise the purely objective given that is open to the possessive gaze of the individual.

Althusser, I further gathered from Resch, criticises the empiricist view on two grounds: first, it takes the initial object or raw material of theoretical practice to be reality itself; second, it takes the product of theoretical practice, knowledge, to be a part of the real object to be known. The French philosopher operates on a totally different terrain, within a radically different problematic.

> [B]y conceptualising the social world in terms of distinct structural relationships (ontologically real if only empirically observable in their effects) that are articulated and over-determined yet possess distinct and hierarchically stratified effectivities, Althusser is able to explain social phenomena causally (in terms of intransitive mechanisms and powers) not simply descriptively (in terms of transitive patters of events).[44]

This was the moment at which I first made the acquaintance of the work of Roy Bhaskar, to whom, paradoxically, Resch was confessedly indebted for his formulation of the Althusserian problematic, or perhaps not so paradoxically since, by Resch's account, Bhaskar was something of a 'closet Althusserian', in the sense that, while he did not mention Althusser explicitly, the British philosopher based his defence of realism and critiques of empiricism and phenomenology on the work of the Frenchman.

---

43   Ibid.
44   Ibid., pp. 197–8.

I know of no better philosophical elaboration of the strengths of Althusser's philosophical position than the one implicit in Bhaskar's *Possibility of Naturalism* (1979). Since he expresses Althusser's position better than Althusser himself does, I have applied Bhaskar's term *ontological realism* and *epistemological relativism* to Althusser's materialist theses (which are obviously the source of Bhaskar's original inspiration anyway).[45]

9　　　Methodology versus Epistemology

It was, then, on the strength of Resch's work that I proceeded to engage critical realism, at a relatively late stage in my career. This involved a process of catch-up, mediated to some extent through the work of my colleague at Stony Brook, Michael Sprinker (1992). A career in Hispanism and its version of literary studies, I quickly realised, was the worst of all positions from which to undertake such a project. My one advantage, or so it seemed to me, was that the work of Rodríguez had furnished me with two seminal notions: that of the ideological unconscious, for which Althusser was the original source, and that of the radical historicity of literature, from which to evaluate the free-wheeling speculation of the philosophers. And from this perspective, it was clear at the outset, my enthusiasm for Bhaskar's work was always going to be more qualified than Resch's.[46]

To begin with, the charge made by Bhaskar that the concept of structural causality is never clearly articulated is,[47] as Sprinker himself avers,[48] very odd, since much of *Reading Capital* is devoted precisely to defining the concept. But that was the least of the difficulties with Bhaskar. There was also the question of Althusser's alleged 'failure to give any apodictic status to the real object',[49] which will subsequently lead the critical realist to charge Althusser, along with Derrida and Habermas, with being guilty of a 'super-idealism'.[50] I confess that, at first, I found the argument persuasive. After all, had not Rodríguez tellingly referred to the 'real object' with scare quotes? Nor could I totally ignore a whole

---

45　Ibid., p. 378n1.
46　Although in all fairness, it should be noted that Resch himself was less than totally committed: 'I dissent from the stronger claims made by Bhaskar for his "transcendental realism"' (Resch 1992, p. 378n1).
47　Bhaskar 1989b, p. 143.
48　Sprinker 1992, p. 133.
49　Bhaskar 1989b, p. 188.
50　Bhaskar 2002b, p. 63.

host of British Marxists who commonly accused Althusser of having lapsed into a species of neo-Kantianism, 'which risked pressing the "real" to a vanishing point beyond discourse';[51] even Sprinker, whose work I deeply respected, conceded that Bhaskar 'is perhaps correct to chastise Althusser for undertheorising the intransitive dimension in knowledge production'.[52]

And yet, I was not entirely persuaded. The fact remained that nothing in the Althusserian account of knowledge was at odds with the ontological priority of relatively enduring real structures or mechanism, nor, emphatically, was *Theory and History*, whose every page proclaimed the enduring ontological density of history.

Matters came to a head in Althusser, it seemed to me, during his commentary upon the famous passage of the *Grundrisse* in which Marx expatiates on the process of abstraction through which science appropriates the real. Althusser, for his part, is emphatic as to how the section is to be read and, more importantly, how it is *not* to be read. Marx, we are informed, is not concerned with the 'problem of knowledge', as traditionally understood, which is to say with the relation between thought and reality; from which it follows that, 'he is not for one second falling into an idealism of consciousness, mind or thought'. To elaborate: 'the "*thought*" we are discussing here is not a faculty of a transcendental subject or absolute consciousness confronted by the real world as *matter*; nor is this thought a faculty of a psychological subject, although human individuals are its agents'.[53] Marx, then, is concerned with how the scientist comes to have a theory, the point being that 'theoretical practice constitutes a process that takes place *entirely in thought*';[54] from which it follows that, contrary to what empiricism claims, knowledge never confronts a *real object*, only ever an 'object of knowledge', which is not to say, by any means, that we *produce* the reality we contemplate. By the same token, it could be argued, Rodríguez's primary objective was to emphasise the specificity of thought with respect to the real, as a methodological principle, and therefore to steer clear of an *epistemological* Marxism that would return social scientists to a concern with the subject/object relation and see them entangled in the 'problem of knowledge'.

I am not persuaded that this lets the Althusserian entirely off the hook: even as he otherwise interprets the same passage of the *Grundrisse* along the same lines as Althusser, David Hillel Ruben acknowledges that the methodo-

---

51   Eagleton 1986, p. 3.
52   Sprinker 1992, p. 129.
53   Althusser and Balibar 1970, p. 41.
54   Ibid., p. 42.

logical and epistemological considerations cannot ultimately be separated.[55] And Rodríguez, we saw above, somewhat confused the issue by fudging the crucial distinction between 'real objects' and 'objects of thought', although perhaps understandably so, given Althusser's own slippage in the same regard.[56] But these are minor considerations. I remain convinced that, at root, what we are observing is the clash, adumbrated above, between two alternative problematics and their supporting philosophies.

I leave the task of further elucidating these issues to the philosophers. My only concern is the threat posed to *historical* materialism by Bhaskar's prioritisation of consciousness, not to mention his speculative freewheeling. *Dialectic: The Pulse of Freedom*, to take a case in point, seems to have left scientific analysis far behind to pursue an abstract, universal notion of praxis, and, at the same time, to have dispensed entirely with the historical, ideological complexities of material production. And while Bhaskar certainly cannot be held responsible for the sins of his followers, the latter have been quick to turn his critique of Althusser to account and, echoing the denunciations of an earlier generation, to declare the 'demise' of Althusserianism. 'The lesson Marxism can learn from critical realism', Andrew Brown further elaborates, 'is the need to articulate Marxist and hence real-world concepts at the level of generality of philosophy, i.e. at the trans-historical level'.[57] Structural Marxists, of course, are the first to concede the need for general scientific concepts, applicable across the broad spectrum of time and space, but that said, Brown's conclusion scarcely augurs well for those of us convinced of the radical historicity of literature. Perhaps there are those, even among Anglophone scholars, who have a different tale to tell, in the hope of which we turn to the exchange reproduced in *Realism, Philosophy and Social Science* and,[58] specifically, to Dean's essay on 'Agency and Dialectics: What Critical Realism can learn from Althusser's Marxism'.

10   **Critical Realism and Althusserianism**

First impressions of the volume in question are not encouraging: the specialities of those contributing extend to anthropology, sociology, politics, and inter-

---

55   Ruben 1977, p. 153.
56   For a discussion of the subtle terminological developments in Althusser from *For Marx* to *Reading Capital*, see Geras 1986, p. 102.
57   Brown et al. 2002, p. 19.
58   Dean et al. 2006.

national relations, but not, seemingly, to history (although historical judgements are freely expressed and litter the text). Equally disconcerting is the focus of Dean's essay upon 'agency' and 'emancipation', concepts that, within the context of Althusserianism, needed (one might say) to be 'picked up with pincers', insofar as redolent of an essential 'human nature', the latter susceptible to 'alienation'. Both thematics – of human nature and alienation – it should be unnecessary to point out, are entirely alien to the Althusserian problematic, from the standpoint of which they lack the specificity demanded of scientific concepts. Our suspicions that, in the hands of Dean, the Althusserian legacy is going to be reconfigured are quickly confirmed when Bhaskar is taken to task for allegedly *violating* 'the nature of human nature'.[59]

The nature of human nature! A decidedly tautological, even oxymoronic phrase and, insofar as it hints ineluctably at the existence of trans-historical phenomena, one for the historian to treat with suspicion. As if sensing the dangers, Dean hastens to elucidate: following Marx, we are assured, human nature is to be understood as historically determinate and variable. But still, if we are talking about Althusser, then at the very least we need to take on board the 'break' that this philosopher believed to exist between the early and late Marx. The former, it will be recalled, allegedly promoted the still metaphysical notion of alienation, and hence of a primal lack behind capitalist social relations, while the latter emphasised the constitutive role of social relations. Whatever the merits or demerits of such a distinction – and needless to say, its validity has been much contested – one thing must surely be conceded, namely that, historically speaking, 'human nature' in the guise of the 'natural slave', 'lineage', 'blood', 'stock', and so on, habitually served as an ideological prop to dominant classes, in their hour of need, to justify their dominance transhistorically. If Dean is seriously interested in taking the *historicity* of human societies into account – and her critique of Bhaskar's highly abstract model of master-slave relations suggests she is[60] – then 'human nature', one anticipates, is likely to prove something of an obstacle. And so, it comes as no surprise when history is gradually relinquished for a 'philosophical anthropology'.[61]

Of course, Dean is perfectly entitled to base her defence of Marx upon his anthropology, 'however poorly the latter is developed'.[62] But what she is not entitled to do is to project her opinions onto Althusser, the letter of whose texts is completely unambiguous:

---

59   Dean et al. 2006, p. 124.
60   Ibid., p. 125.
61   Ibid., p. 126.
62   Ibid., p. 152.

> Marx rejected the problematic of [his] earlier philosophy and adopted
> a new problematic in one and the same act. The earlier idealist ('bour-
> geois') philosophy depended in all its domains and arguments (its 'theory
> of knowledge', its conception of history, its political economy, its ethics,
> its aesthetics, etc.) on a problematic of *human nature* (or the essence of
> man).[63]

Althusser's claims at least have the virtue of being based on a close reading
of *Capital*, from which it followed that, notwithstanding the 'mirage of a theoretical anthropology', also the 'obviousness' of a 'naïve anthropology', the true
'subjects' of the social process are the relations of production (and political and
ideological social relations).[64]

But leaving aside Althusser and his concerns, let us resume the thread of
Dean's own argument. Of what does her 'human nature' consist? Among other
things, of the human potentials of 'love' and 'creativity',[65] as these are actual-
ised under 'culture', the latter 'as much part of humanity as is our biology'.[66]
Once again, the alarm bells sound. Whatever happened to 'modes of production', 'surplus value', 'exploitation' and so on? Dean, it is true, begins to feel her
way towards a cultural unconscious or, as she would have it, 'unselfconscious
learning'. All cultures, we are informed, 'teach' in a way that does not require
conscious co-operation.[67] This is encouraging, until Dean takes a step too far:
'Here Althusser's work on the materialist dialectic and on ideology has been a
necessary corrective to the a-historical abstractions of historical materialism
itself'.[68] The effect is to draw attention to a slippage in Dean's essay that might
otherwise have passed unnoticed: from 'ideology' to 'culture'.

Reasons for the semantic shift are not hard to find: Dean is able to talk about
culture as being 'open', and thence to continue to focus upon the question of
'freedom'; whereas to mention 'openness' and 'freedom' in the same breath as
'ideology' is rather more problematic, at least from the standpoint of Althusserianism. The differences between the two terms are quite radical: culture is
drawn from the heartland of bourgeois discourse and arrives laden with every
kind of benign resonance; whereas 'ideology' unavoidably connotes Marxism

---

63   Althusser 1990a, p. 227.
64   Althusser and Balibar 1970, p. 180.
65   Dean et al. 2006, pp. 128–30.
66   Ibid., p. 133.
67   Ibid.
68   Ibid., p. 134.

and is viewed with unease by a liberal audience.[69] Of course, Dean secretly knows all this and hopes to sneak 'culture' by the reader unnoticed, under the cover of a somewhat incoherent footnote reference which regrets Althusser's use of 'ideology' to advance his theory.[70] A footnote reference of Althusser's own is further adduced to legitimate Dean's conflation of ideology with culture, 'without doing violence to his theory'. In fact, it is hard to imagine what greater violence could have been done to Althusser.

11 Conclusion

Confirmed by the above discussion is the reality of a clash between two seemingly incommensurable problematics: on the one hand, a problematic that posits the ever pre-givenness of social structure as its ultimate horizon, a pre-givenness whose functioning is, in essence, unconscious, in the sense that it transcends the consciousness of each will, that it constitutes a force without a subject; on the other hand, a problematic that prioritises the relation between individual and society, alternatively, between agency and structures, understood as universal, ontological, therefore trans-historical, categories. Both problematics have been reworked: the Althusserian by Rodríguez, who foregrounds, after the late Marx, the direct relationship between the owners of the conditions of production and the direction producers, be these master-slaves, lords/serfs, or Subject/subjects; and the second by critical realists, for whom intentionality takes precedence, along with ideas, agency, 'emergence', and the transcendental efficacy of love.

Perforce, little love has been shown between the latter-day exponents of the two problematics, on the rare occasions when they have come into contact. In a recent work, Rodríguez has been predictably scathing of Bhaskar's attempt, in *The Possibility of Naturalism*, to couch a discussion of Marx in terms of the individual/society opposition.[71] In point of fact, the Spaniard gets some of the details wrong: Bhaskar emphatically does not see the individual as *preceding* society. But from the standpoint of a theoretician of ideological production,

---

69 In the words of Fred Jameson, 'ideology' functions as a 'declaration of adherence' to the Marxist problematic (Jameson 2010, p. 316). Having said which, as we will see later, Jameson himself will negotiate a similar shift in the direction of 'culture'.

70 Ibid., p. 182n29.

71 Rodríguez 2013, pp. 46–51. I confess to having been instrumental, at the personal level, in recommending Bhaskar's work to Rodríguez, who, in the absence of Spanish translations, wrestled valiantly with the English original.

for whom 'subject' and 'individual' are in any event historical constructs of a determinate set of social relations, questions of prioritisation could seem only a minor detail. Critical realism amounts to a 'micky-take', also to 'one more caricature of Marxism'; 'To insert Marxism there is to sink it, to not understand anything',[72] and so on. The Althusserian is insistent: the dichotomy between individual and society 'is completely diluted in Marx', and to think otherwise is to remain captive, *at the level of the ideological unconscious*, to bourgeois categories that are mistakenly taken for ontological realities.[73]

At first blush, critical realism has been far more welcoming to Rodríguez, graciously agreeing to publish a recent article of mine in which I undertook to introduce the Spaniard's work to a broader Anglophone audience (see Chapter 7). That said, reaction has been (to the best of my knowledge) muted; symptomatically, the editorial committee dismissed a subsequent offering of mine.[74] My guess is that the notion of an ideological unconscious has proved radically uncongenial to a philosophical group attuned to the alternative notion of ideology as a system of false *ideas* and in consequence to the companion concept of *consciousness*, the latter seen as ingredient at all levels, individual and cosmic. My own position is clear: the move away from the analysis of social and material conditions towards the new spiritualism has rendered critical realism increasingly unserviceable to a social science concerned with the theory and history of ideological production. Somewhat more tentatively, I would also suggest that a philosophical tradition that was at one time concerned to underlabour for the sciences has become increasingly inclined to *exploit* the sciences for its own ideological purposes. Already in 1992, Sprinker ominously warned that 'Bhaskar's own comparative slighting of the ways in which ideology permeates the transitive dimension risks the charge of metaphysical dogmatism'.[75]

Those Marxists closely attached to critical realism have themselves found no place for the 'unconscious' in either its libidinal or ideological form, which doubtless accounts for the bemusement of some before the unwillingness of many immediately to sign up to their political cause. Unsurprisingly, they continue to parody when they do not totally misrepresent what Althusser actually says. Thus, paraphrasing the relevant section of Althusser's *For Marx*, Sean Creaven, perhaps the leading exponent of an 'emergentist Marxism' of Bhas-

---

72   Ibid., pp. 148–9.
73   Ibid., p. 149.
74   'We don't find your structural super-determinism coherent or convincing either in itself
      or in relation to Althusser.'
75   Sprinker 1992, p. 129.

karian inspiration, writes: 'From this perspective, humans necessarily have an imaginary relationship to the world, and an ideological *consciousness* of reality, in order that they perform their function of reproducing the structure of society through their actions'.[76] As even a perfunctory perusal of the relevant sections reveals, Althusser is saying something very different, indeed something that is diametrically opposed to what Creaven is claiming: 'In truth, ideology has very little to do with "consciousness", even supposing this term to have an unambiguous meaning. It is profoundly *unconscious*'.[77] Nor do the surprises cease: in *Emergentist Marxism* we find Creaven arguing that 'pre-capitalist societies generally did not have "dominant ideologies" that sought to legitimate class domination in the eyes of the downtrodden or which functioned to bind the subordinate classes to their oppressors and exploiters'.[78] He references in support of his claim the work of a number of other British Marxists, confirmation, if confirmation is required, of the dire poverty of British Marxism over matters relating to the theory and history of ideological production.

---

76   Creaven 2015, p. 23, italics added.
77   Althusser 1990, p. 233.
78   Creaven 2007, p. 361n209.

CHAPTER 3

Ideologies of the Transition: Noam Chomsky

The availability of the English translation of Juan Carlos Rodríguez's *Teoría e historia de la producción ideológica* (1974, 1990),[1] together with that of *La norma literaria* (1984, 2001)[2] offers the Anglo-American academy another opportunity, which to date it has declined, to engage a research programme that, after four decades of continuous productivity, shows no signs of exhaustion. *Theory and History*, which remains in fundamental respects Rodríguez's seminal text, charts the transition from feudalism to capitalism between the fourteenth and sixteenth centuries. While the narrative is a familiar one, standard accounts, with respect to Spain, have proceeded by 'ignoring the life-and-death struggle between two coexistent modes of production and ignoring the social and class struggles within each mode of production and between their respective relations'.[3] One effect of these productive relations, Rodríguez argues, was to generate a series of material practices, made up of ideas, mentalities, ethical and moral values, habits, modes of behaviour, and so on, which were assumed 'unconsciously' by the mass of the population. *Language, State, Subject* consolidated these original insights by extending the concept of radical historicity to include more recent social formations. Class ideologies, it goes without saying, are not experienced as such by individual men, women, and children but 'as the very truth of nature, as being as natural as their own skin'.[4] Such, in broad outline, are the mechanisms of the *ideological unconscious*, as Rodríguez understands them.

Our first task must be to facilitate an engagement with Rodríguez's ideas within the tradition of Althusserianism out of which they grew, a tradition that in turn needs to be referred, retrospectively, to the historical epistemology associated with Gaston Bachelard. We will then proceed to examine those aspects of Rodríguez's research programme related specifically to Juan Huarte's *Examen de ingenios* (*Examination of Men's Wits*), a work on educational psychology undertaken to show that certain kinds of mind are 'naturally' predisposed to

---

1 *Theory and History of Ideological Production: The First Bourgeois Literatures: (The 16th Century)* (2002).
2 Under the title of *State, Stage, Language: The Production of the Subject* (2008).
3 Rodríguez 2002a, p. 12.
4 Rodríguez 2008b, p. 11.

certain disciplines.[5] Huarte's work is renowned on several accounts. To begin with, it functioned as a kind of compendium of knowledge about psychology in the sixteenth century, encapsulating the 'state of the art', one might say, as is indicated by the fact that it was translated into all the major European languages.[6] Cervantes, in all likelihood, was familiar with the work at first hand, and if not, was certainly steeped in the concepts and ideas to which Huarte gave general currency. Rodríguez's obvious fascination with the *Examination* lay in the fact that it illustrated the enduring reach of feudal ideology upon texts of the transition (from feudalism to capitalism), while these same texts were also impacted by changing social relations within the new world 'disorder' of the sixteenth century. In the 1970s and '80s, Huarte's work achieved a certain notoriety after figuring prominently in several studies by Noam Chomsky on the history of linguistics. Which brings us to the third and final topic to be considered.

It will be our claim that both Chomsky and his critics are guilty of reading sixteenth-century scholarship through a post-Kantian lens and, consequently, of finally succumbing to a species of ahistoricism. At the root of the problem, we suggest, is a lingering attachment to an ideological individualism that, among other things, explains Chomsky's aversion not only to revolutionary Marxist organisations but to the theoretical basis that has sustained them: 'I find much of the Marxist literature rather boring, frankly, and I am far from a Marxist scholar ... I have read Marx selectively. I don't try to keep up with the current literature, with Marxology'.[7] We will not engage such comments here, except to observe that, ironically, they betray the kind of intellectual carelessness and irresponsibility that has characterised conservative reviews of Chomsky's own work. They certainly presuppose a lack of preparation that Chomsky has never permitted himself in his critiques of neo-liberalism, where he always had to be much more vigilant and informed. Our more immediate concern is to point to the price that Chomsky paid, intellectually, for turning his back on Marxism and the theories of ideology that it has refined. In the present con-

---

5 Little is known for certain about Huarte's life. Born in San Juan de Pie de Puerto, Navarre, in about 1526, he emigrated to Andalusia with his family in his early years. He studied at the University of Baeza and subsequently at Alcalá. We know that he held the post of municipal doctor in Baeza between 1571 and 1573. The *Examen de ingenios para las ciencias* achieved an immediate success following its publication in 1575. After it was placed on the Spanish Index in 1584, an expurgated version was prepared and appeared in 1594. For a general treatment of Huarte, see Read 1981.

6 Huarte's work was first translated into English by Richard Carew, from the Italian translation by Camillo Camilli, in 1594. A second English translation by Edward Bellamy followed in 1698.

7 Chomsky 1987, p. 29.

text, at least, we will be looking to Rodríguez's work to provide a corrective to Chomsky's anachronistic procedures. Further to which, we will suggest ways in which the Althusserian paradigm or, more accurately, problematic, may itself be refined and extended.

1   Chomsky and Huarte

One of the more unexpected aspects of Chomsky's work on the history of linguistics, produced in the late 1960s and early '70s, is the prominence he accords two Spanish scholars of the second half of the sixteenth century, Juan Huarte de San Juan and Francisco Sánchez de las Brozas or, as he was also called, el Brocense. Francisco Sánchez was the author of *Minerva*, a Latin grammar, whose chief claim to fame was the importance that it attached to *ellipsis*, as a figurative means through which lexical elements were inserted into grammatical syntagms in order to bring them into line, structurally speaking, with allegedly more orthodox constructions. Chomsky was attracted by the obvious parallels between this and his own distinction between deep and surface structure.[8] However, it was the work of Huarte that most attracted the attention of the modern linguist.

Chomsky drew attention to Huarte's work in a long footnote in his *Cartesian Linguistics*, where he credits the Spanish doctor with emphasising the innate generative power of the human mind, for which he is heralded as a forerunner of seventeenth-century French scholars, notably Descartes.[9] According to Chomsky, Huarte distinguishes between three major *wits* or *'ingenios'*. Certain 'docile wits' lack any kind of creative capacity, leading Aristotle to envisage the mind in general as a *tabula rasa*. A second kind of wit exhibits, in its ideal cases, true creativity, 'inventing and saying such things as they never heard from their Masters, nor any Mouth'.[10] And finally a third wit is disposed to exceptional creativity, of the kind found in the arts. These three kinds of wit involved the memory, understanding, and imagination respectively. Chomsky quotes Huarte's subsequent remarks about eloquence, to the effect that man 'distinguishes himself from the Brutes, and approaches near to God'; he also notes Huarte's reference to those wits that are so uneducable as to be incapable of creativity and so 'differ not at all from Brute Beasts'.

---

8   For a detailed study of El Brocense, see Claramonte 1983.
9   Chomsky 1966, pp. 78–9.
10   Chomsky is here quoting from the English translation by Bellamy.

In *Language and Mind*, Chomsky rehearses his arguments for a distinctively Cartesian linguistics: 'The Cartesians tried to show that when the theory of corporeal body is sharpened and clarified and extended to its limits, it is still incapable of accounting for facts that are obvious to introspection and that are also confirmed by our observation of the actions of other humans'.[11] He continues: 'Consequently, it becomes necessary to invoke an entirely new principle – in Cartesian terms, to postulate a second substance whose essence is thought, alongside of body, with its essential properties of extension and motion'.[12] It is at this point, when attention focuses on the 'generative' capacity of normal human intelligence, that Chomsky again turns to Huarte.

Of particular interest is Huarte's distinction between docile wit, which meets the empiricist maxim, and normal intelligence, with its full generative capacities; upon such a distinction, Chomsky paraphrases, rests that between beast and man.[13] The Spaniard's generative wit, the argument proceeds, is the springboard for a discussion of 'psychological theory' in the ensuing period. 'Typical of later thought is his reference to use of language as an index of human intelligence, of what distinguishes man from animals, and, specifically, his emphasis on the creative capacity of normal intelligence'.[14] Huarte's second type of wit is described as 'the generative ability that is revealed in the normal human use of language as a free instrument of thought'.[15] Chomsky concludes: 'The properties of human thought and human language emphasised by the Cartesians are real enough; they were then, as they are now, beyond the bounds of any well-understood kind of physical explanation. Neither physics nor biology nor psychology gives us any clue as to how to deal with these matters'.[16]

This interest shown by Chomsky in Spanish scholarship was unexpected but very welcome to Hispanists long accustomed to seeing Spain's national tradition disparaged for its 'backwardness' by exponents of high European culture. Predictably, it was from among these same Hispanists that so-called 'Cartesian linguistics' recruited some particularly fervent adherents. Emboldened by Chomsky's ground-breaking research, they were soon championing Huarte as a Descartes 'avant la lettre', as a basis from which to celebrate, as opposed to excuse, Spain's notorious 'difference'.[17] Just as predictably, however, Chomsky's

---

11   Chomsky 1968, p. 5.
12   Ibid., pp. 5–6.
13   Ibid., p. 8.
14   Ibid., p. 9.
15   Ibid.
16   Ibid., p. 11.
17   Otero 1970, pp. 22–31. See also Torre 1977.

attempt to rewrite history in a light favourable to Transformational Grammar was subjected to a number of (sometimes hostile) critiques, in which the discussion of Huarte did not escape censure. In empirical terms, it was relatively easy to pick up the descriptive inadequacies of Chomsky's view of Huarte. For while it was true that Huarte attached considerable importance to the faculty of language and to the creative wit, the fact remained that the Spanish physician did not associate creativity with language per se, a subject that he discusses separately.[18]

There were other troubling aspects of Chomsky's interpretation of Huarte that amounted to a veritable misreading. First, the details of Chomsky's account of the first and second kinds of wit are not quite accurate, in that Huarte associates the *tabula rasa* theory unambiguously with the second kind of wit.[19] Secondly, while Huarte certainly emphasises the importance of man's generative capacity, it is misleading to say, as Chomsky does, that the different kinds of wit are simply 'involved' with the existence of three faculties of the mind. In point of fact, the *Examination's* faculty psychology is the basis of a doctrine of rigorous determinism, which aims to demonstrate that man's freedom is, if not illusory, at least severely circumscribed. Further analysis of the work confirmed that even seemingly creative acts are deemed to correspond to shifts in humoral states.[20] Huarte was prepared to press his arguments to the extreme of implicitly questioning the immortality of the soul, or so at least the Inquisition believed. The obvious conclusion was that his work lent itself to both 'behaviourist' and 'mentalist' interpretations.

It is a sobering experience to review the major texts involved in all these intellectual exchanges. For while some of them undoubtedly enriched our understanding of the Western linguistic tradition and generated scholarship of considerable descriptive and empirical value, it is impossible to avoid the conclusion, with the benefit of hindsight, that they fall seriously short of 'explanatory adequacy'. Conspicuously absent, for example, was any serious attempt to theorise the relationship between science and ideology or to analyse science as a social process. Moreover, while it was certainly important to offset Huarte's emphasis on the issue of creativity, upon which Chomsky insisted, against his deterministic biologism, important questions remained unanswered. Indeed, even more symptomatically, they were not even posed. For example, how was one to explain the existence of such rampantly contradictory discourses as those contained in Huarte's *Examination*? What were the relevant factors

---

18   See Read 1981, pp. 90–2.
19   Huarte 1976, p. 130.
20   See Read 1981, pp. 67–70, 127.

involved – personal, ideological, political, or economic? Whence did these discourses derive, historically speaking? It was not simply an understanding of Huarte's work that was at issue. As a powerful misreading, Chomsky's work itself seemed to elude the interpretive grasp of both its supporters and opponents. The one research programme to throw light on such issues, that directed by Juan Carlos Rodríguez, went unobserved, at least within the Anglophone academy.

2 Ideologies of the Absolutist State

The transition (from feudalism to capitalism), we have seen Rodríguez argue, is characterised by a class struggle between the nobility, the dominant class under feudalism, and the emergent bourgeoisie that was ultimately to displace it. This struggle is conducted principally at the political level, which exerts a dominant influence during the absolutist stage upon other levels. *Theory and History* does not spell out the details, but they are implicit throughout. State administrators had an interest in the continuation of feudalism: after all, part of their own income originated in the feudal exploitation of peasants on monarchical lands. But they also had an interest in the further development of trade and of capitalist forms of exploitation, which provided them with an expanding urban tax base. Finally, they had an interest in maintaining a balance between the two modes. This explains the Janus face of merchant capital. The quickest way to make wealth was to identify with the anti-feudal forces, but the best way to preserve it was to reinvest it in land. The clash – at this point Rodríguez intervenes – is to be understood not in terms of the individuals involved, but of the relevant social relations:

> However 'automated' the function of the state may appear at a given moment, we must not forget that, in the last instance, this state always subsumes certain social relations; and that in the case of the transition these social relations consist of 'two' sets. While such a 'double' representation is not double to the same extent – it is rather born of the impact of bourgeois social relations on feudal organisation – the Absolutist State tends unavoidably – by its mere existence – to 'serve' both sets of relations infrastructurally, although 'super-structurally' its apparatuses may be seen to be dominated by the nobility.[21]

---

21   Rodríguez 2002a, p. 116.

While there is no gainsaying the importance of the political battles, not least those literally waged between the absolutist state and the *Comuneros*, every bit as material were those waged on the level of ideology.[22] And it is with these that Rodríguez is principally concerned. His basic debt, in this respect, is to Althusser and, through the French Marxist, to the Bachelardian tradition. To begin with, let us consider the term *substantialism*, which Rodríguez took from Bachelard but defined in a crucially far narrower sense. As he explains:

> [I]n contrast, according to our usage, 'substantialism' belongs to a system of categorisation that can only refer to a specific historical conjuncture. That is to say, it has only existed and can only develop in certain determinate social relations, namely those corresponding to a feudal – or feudalising, in the broad sense – ideology.[23]

Fundamental to substantialist ideology is the notion of a 'substantial form', together with that of a 'natural place', towards which a thing naturally tends, in conjunction with the idea of a hierarchy. There are diverse souls that inform diverse matters – vegetable, animal, and human. The demoniacal represents the fall of form into the 'monstrous'. Rodríguez comments:

> On this basis, the organicist adaptation of the Galenic doctrine of humors suggests a *pulchritudo* or bodily perfection (health) which depends upon the harmonic proportion of the four organicist elements, whose disequilibrium (or 'distemper') provokes an alteration (disorder) in the body as a 'whole'. A disorder (illness) that can only be restored via the restoration of the harmonic proportion of the parts impacting upon the 'whole', that is, through bleeding.[24]

---

22   The significance that Rodríguez attaches to the rebellion of the *Comuneros* in 1520–1 is to be explained by the extent to which its outcome, a defeat for the cities in their struggle against the emperor, Charles I, determined the route that Spain was to follow out of feudalism. It had a choice between two options: the cities, on the one hand, and the absolutist state, on the other. The consequences for Spain of selecting the second option were considerable, for while it counted on the strength of bourgeois relations, it depended far more on the strength of seigneurial relations that, under absolutism, continued to be hegemonic (pp. 108–13).
23   Ibid., p. 93.
24   Ibid., p. 81.

The notion of blood and bleeding are thus key concepts and go along with those of vengeance and the cleansing of honour. The image of the organic body is central to substantialism.

In Bachelard, substantialism stands diametrically opposed to another trans-historical category: *animism*. Again, Rodríguez will borrow the concept but reapply it in a radically historical sense. The crucial 'break', he will argue, occurs between the feudal problematic and that of a Renaissance animism:

> There are now ... two ideological systems, each struggling to impose itself on the transition, at the expense of the other: hence, the term *animism* cannot be accepted, in the Bachelardian sense, as something identical, although inverted, with respect to substantialism. (Such an identity/inversion corresponds, we insist, to a situation that is present only within the feudal matrix.) What we are speaking of here is a battle between two systems that are completely different to the extent that their social relations and their ideological contradictions are also radically distinct and opposed.[25]

The bourgeois matrix is always characterised by the continuous production of the 'subject'[26] or, as it exists during this first phase of bourgeois development, of the proto-subject or beautiful soul, 'bared' through the Petrarchan discourse of lyric poetry and fed by the philosophical tradition of neo-Platonism. This beautiful soul will permeate a hierarchy of forms that is based not on blood but on sensibility and the capacity to love.

Rodríguez recognises the existence of a feudal animism, associated notably with Augustinianism and the tradition of medieval magic, alchemy, and astrology.[27] But while the transition from the manipulation of the universal spirit to scientific control over nature may seem at times imperceptible, the Spanish scholar insists on the reality of the 'break' that separates the two. Substantialism treats the world allegorically, by reading it as a book. Fundamental in this respect is the generic form of the 'Speculum', which hinges on the reflection between the book of nature and the Bible, and between the 'divine order' and the 'earthly order' – man made in the image of God. (Linguists will be familiar with this dichotomy from the medieval concept of the 'speculative grammar'.) Animism, by way of contrast, inculcates the virtues of the literal gaze, at first spiritualised through the force of love but increasingly materialised through

---

25   Ibid., p. 94.
26   Ibid., p. 54 ff.
27   Ibid., p. 76.

the pressures of, among other things, hunger. For if lyric poetry dramatises a direct encounter or 'dialogue' between two beautiful souls, the picaresque novel will explore the trajectory of the poor subject, which must justify itself publicly.[28]

Key distinctions emerge in matters pertaining to the body, including to the body of language. For substantialism, clothing is substantial – it defines one's status – which explains why the nobility invested so much of its wealth in it. Linguistically, the same attitude manifests itself in the attachment to etymological spelling, which registers the lineage of words, and to styles that are highly ornate and elaborate. The body itself was unfavourably considered insofar as it is associated with sin and decay. Animism, in contrast, discovers the body beautiful, otherwise the nude, whose flesh is transformed by the radiating force of the spirit. Clothing, within this context, represents a barrier to the union of beautiful souls, a union that is facilitated, at the linguistic level, by a 'plain style' and by phonetic spelling, both of which permit a more direct access to the pure form of the Idea: 'Doing what comes naturally, then, at this particular juncture, simply means expressing oneself without intermediaries'.[29]

In sum, then, while Rodríguez draws upon Bachelard in key respects, his borrowings are redefined in very specific and crucially important ways. Much the same can be said regarding his relation to Althusser – although here the departures from the French tradition are less clearly marked – and again it is the Spaniard's more rigorously historicising impulse that accounts for the innovation. Attention should be drawn to three areas: ideology, science, and philosophy. For Althusser, ideology in general is the discourse of the subject, in which respect it stands opposed to scientific discourse, which is impersonal and objective. In contrast Rodríguez will insist on the dangers of universalising particular categories. Substantialism, to take the example that most concerns him (and us), is an ideology that operates not through the subject but, as suggested above, through the concept of the world as a book. Ironically, not to say catastrophically, Althusser takes it upon himself to illustrate ideological (Subject/subject) discourse through reference to the biblical encounter between Yahweh and Moses, a classic instance, if ever there was one, of the Lord/servant dichotomy.[30] For Rodríguez, it is only with animism that the subject becomes prominent as an ideological category.

---

28   Although *Lazarillo de Tormes*, it is worth recalling, is also technically a 'dialogue'.
29   Ibid., p. 217. For further details on the conflict between linguistic ideologies, see Read 1990, pp. 1–16; 1992, pp. 47–53.
30   Althusser 1971, pp. 171–9.

In the same way, Rodríguez departs from Althusser's concept of science. For the Spaniard, there are only ever 'sciences', for the simple reason that science is always related to a particular mode of production, which defines the nature of its problematic. In this respect – and taking Rodríguez's own example – a crucial distinction needs to be drawn between Ptolemaic science, with its key notions of stasis and inertia, and the new Copernican science, which works on the assumption that movement is natural. Let us note in passing the affinities between Ptolemaic science and substantialism, and between Copernican science and animism.

Finally, Rodríguez critiques Althusser's notion of philosophy. He objects particularly to Althusser's assumption that philosophy is the 'same' thing for Plato and Husserl, which he sees as the result of a professional academic prejudice.[31] Always lurking behind such ahistoricism – or so, at least, Rodríguez claims – is some notion of human reason, as a trans-historical category. As a corrective to this tendency, he continues, it is important to insist upon the constraints imposed by a problematic. Otherwise, we will be led astray, for example, by the question of 'sources' and 'influences'. 'In reality there is no "source" or "influence" more direct than that which is exercised from a shared, common, ideological problematic, as opposed to an alien ideological problematic'.[32]

While opposing substantialism to animism, Rodríguez takes care to allow for the existence of blends between both ideologies at the level of individual texts. I have already spoken of medieval forms of animism. Comparable discourses can also be found in the sixteenth century, notably in the mystical tradition. Animism itself, it is worth repeating, is in essence a transitional discourse that facilitates the coexistence of residual with emergent social relations. Cartesian rationalism and Galilean mechanism represent developmentally more advanced forms of bourgeois ideology, but these forms will not take root in Spain. In this country, animism is gradually rolled back during the Reformation, leaving mercantile relations to be thematised in the second half of the sixteenth century by 'Aristotelian rationalism', a discourse more suited to conditions of retrenchment. At this point, nuances become crucial, at least if we are going to capture the complexities of the transition. For although something of a reversal, Aristotelian rationalism should not be identified with its feudal, substantialist predecessor:

---

31   Rodríguez 2002a, p. 63n36.
32   Ibid., p. 63n36.

This rationalism, Erasmianism, etc. would then be fully understood in the context of a particular conjuncture, in which, given the virtual disappearance of animism (as an accepted and legitimate structure), a non-organicist Aristotelianism was the only viable oppositional form vis-à-vis feudal organicism. (It was made possible through the break opened up by Cartesianism and by its own relatively well-established brand of 'rationality', and through the latter's capacity to assume Aristotelian expressions on behalf of another matrix, the feudalising one. This feudalising matrix was also bolstered – considerably – by Aristotelian elements passing through the scholastic sieve).[33]

Such was the ideological, discursive labyrinth into which Huarte's *Examination* was born.

3   Rodríguez and the *Examination*

Obvious points of departure in my analysis of Juan Huarte's *Examination*, given the importance I attach to Rodríguez's work, are those passages in *Theory and History* that engage Huarte's text directly. The most extended reference hinges on Huarte's refusal of any kind of miraculous explanation applied to the 'natural sciences'. By way of contextualising Rodríguez's discussion, let us return briefly to Huarte's actual text. According to the latter, it is a sign of an individual's incapacity for the study of the natural sciences that he should wish to 'attribute everything to miracles'.[34] The same applied to an individual's poetic creativity, which Huarte refused to attribute to the operations of divine influence or inspiration, on very sound *substantialist* grounds: 'Because each of the faculties that govern man – whether natural, vital, animal, or rational – correspond with a particular temperament'.[35] In other words, all *spiritual* souls, including rational souls, are to be grounded in matter. In terms of substantialist ideology, each thing is identified with its own material form, to the extent that its transformation requires a force of supernatural proportions.

Huarte's association with substantialism, Rodríguez argues, is totally at odds with the traditional, liberal approach to the *Examination*, epitomised by Américo Castro in his famous work *El pensamiento de Cervantes*. Castro simply

---

33   Ibid., pp. 276–7.
34   Huarte 1976, p. 84.
35   Huarte 1977, p. 433.

does not realise that Huarte's *Examination* is actually a materialist text, within an Aristotelian tradition that places severe restrictions upon the role of divine intervention. The internal logic of this tradition, according to Rodríguez, is unforgiving: the greatest miracle will always be the Incarnation, in itself and as it is re-enacted ritualistically through the Eucharist. By way of contrast – and following closely Rodríguez's line of argument – animism can accept the reality of metamorphosis relatively easily, which allows an individual to assume radically different identities.[36] From this mobile 'beautiful soul', the royal road to the 'free', self-creative, liberal subject stands open.

Now all of this is perfectly clear and, in my view, difficult to fault in its general outlines. But the case of the *Examination*, as Rodríguez himself concedes, is far from being straightforward: rather, it 'is a delicate one, because of its atheistic or, at least, excessively naturalist, ramifications'.[37] Such ramifications are played out in accordance with a very specific dynamic: once a scholar engages in 'learned' commentary, he feels compelled to deploy a rationalist discourse of pre-eminently Aristotelian extraction. The result is a text such as Huarte's, in which a residual substantialism constantly threatens to overwhelm concepts of unmistakably animist derivation. As Rodríguez elaborates later:

> The imprecise limits of the age are perhaps best captured by the work of Huarte de San Juan, which, by carrying the 'medico-organicist' component to an extreme, issues into a practically 'atheistic' 'naturalism'. But perhaps not even Huarte saw any problem here. 'Organicist-Aristotelian' scholasticism was, after all, the global discourse of orthodoxy, and 'organicist galenism' its specifically medical counterpart, to which extent expressing organicist arguments could not but seem other than 'normal' to a 'learned, orthodox theoretician'.[38]

Extrapolating from these disparate comments and viewing them within the general context of *Theory and History*, it is possible to construct a fairly coherent picture of the *Examination*. Huarte was an ideologue engaged in that pre-eminently absolutist project of restructuring the state system of education along *national* lines. His goal was to turn this system into the ideological equivalent of the repressive apparatus, which was similarly undergoing reconstruction through the constitution of a 'national' army. To this end, he naturally engaged the concept of the *'ingenio'* or proto-subject, the means

---

36 Rodríguez 2002a, pp. 262–3.
37 Ibid., p. 205.
38 Ibid., pp. 264–5.

through which, among other things, the absolutist state could *interpellate* (to use Althusser's own term) and thereby control a population that was becoming geographically much more mobile. Within such a context, feudal relations were never going to pass unchallenged:

> True, there are some so ignorant and lacking in consideration that they refuse to believe that their nobility had any origin at all, claiming, rather, on the basis of their blood, that it is eternal. They believe, in other words, that it is a supernatural, divine creation, and not the result of some king's fiat.[39]

What Huarte's promotion of the principle of social mobility amounts to is an attack upon 'lineage', the key substantialist concept, as opposed to the 'deed'. The good doctor is not slow to draw the obvious conclusions with respect to the educational apparatus. We would be deceived, he argues, if we thought that diplomas purchased at great expense by the students at Salamanca make them any superior, academically speaking, to those poor students who are forced to graduate through Alcalá, 'on the basis that ability and letters derive not from the title that we are awarded but from study and application'.[40] Expressed more succinctly, we are each the off-spring of our deeds.[41]

Now all this would be perfectly logical and consistent, at least from the standpoint of animist ideology, had not Huarte also been advocating throughout, with respect to all disciplines, the idea that what actually determines ability is not individual effort or will-power but the force of a natural faculty. In the case of military strategy, we saw, the faculty involved is the imagination, 'because when it comes to the powers that depend on heat, speed is of the essence; and for this reason, men of great understanding are not suited to warfare'.[42] As throughout the *Examination*, anatomy determines a destiny, which makes something of a mockery out of the whole business of rewarding individuals for their achievements, educational or otherwise: 'And then along come the judges, who give first prize to the person whose ability is the product of nature, not of hard work, while the wooden spoon goes to the person who was born without wit but who never stopped studying, as if the one had acquired letters by reading books and the other had lost them through sleeping'.[43] On

---

39   Huarte 1976, p. 272.
40   Ibid., pp. 272–3.
41   Ibid., pp. 276.
42   Ibid., p. 257.
43   Ibid., p. 282.

this basis, to reward individual excellence, as Huarte himself concedes, is like rewarding an athlete for winning a race against the person with one leg.

It would be very easy to read a late bourgeois ideology, of a 'behaviourist' variety, back into Aristotelian rationalism, but the temptation must be resisted. In Huarte's discourse, the weight of determinism is borne by a substantialist, not by a positivist science: 'And the worst thing of all is that the will, being free, grows restless and shows a tendency to descend to the level of the lowest appetites'.[44] The difference may sometimes seem like a nuance but is absolutely fundamental. The inequalities characteristic of bourgeois societies, while real enough, will be promoted on the basis of 'talent', not of 'blood' or 'tempera-ment' (understood in the substantialist sense). In the *Examination*, the relevant scenario is man conceived as a sinner, in *this* world: 'Just how disinclined to virtue man is by nature is obvious if we consider the make-up of the first man, who, although the most perfect in the history of the human species, found it impossible, because of the nature of his constitution, not to be drawn towards evil'.[45] On the basis of which, Huarte will proceed to unpack all the traditional Christian doctrine of man's primal fall and the need for God's grace.[46]

In sum, no matter how daring the *Examination* may seem, in the context of its day, which was that of the Reformation, it is important to understand it for what it is, namely, an expression of the impact on animism of a domin-ant feudal matrix. And once drawn into this orbit, animism will need to make the necessary ideological accommodations. The causal dynamics involved are those already outlined, whereby an ideological unconscious secretes certain discourses that radically constrain what can be thought and said. Through this process, emergent animist concepts are adapted to the requirements of an Aris-totelian or Galenic rationalism, in the context of a resurgent feudalism. The end result was that the nobility was able to block capitalist development at the economic level and effectively to prolong the transition from feudalism to cap-italism.

4   The Literal Gaze

There is one textual level, within the *Examination*, at which substantialist and animist dimensions of the text are so deeply interwoven as to be virtually inex-tricable. I have in mind the manner in which substantialist ideology is implic-

---

44   Ibid., p. 295.
45   Ibid., p. 296.
46   Ibid., p. 298.

ated within a perspectivism that presupposes the presence of the I/eye. To illustrate this point, consider the following passage, selected more or less at random, in which Huarte attempts to prove that fire is the lightest of the elements:

> The first reason I have for believing this is seeing, through experience, that any flame has two natural movements, without which it cannot live for a moment: one is upwards, whereby it expels from itself the excrements that result from its being fed; and the second, downwards, so as to feed upon the material that it needs to survive. And this second movement no natural philosopher can deny, because if we take two candles, one dead and smoking and the other lit and placed above it, we will clearly see that the flame from the lit candle descends along the path of the smoke to attach itself to the wick of the dead candle.[47]

Substantialism, we recall, was less concerned to look at the world in any literal sense, than to *read* it, as a book. Contrast in this regard the sheer literalness with which Huarte views the world, and which is clearly demonstrated in the above passage. It was not just literary works, such as *Lazarillo de Tormes*, that were discovering the virtues of what Rodríguez calls 'the eye that sees the thing',[48] but also learned texts otherwise steeped in the ideology of substantialism. To this extent, Huarte's boast about having initiated a radically new science was not entirely idle, however much it was belied by his theoretical dependence upon feudal science. The coincidence between the new science and the modern novel is no accident, nor is the fact that the *Quixote* appears to be directly indebted to the *Examination* for its model of psychology.

Of course, we are not talking here of a classic bourgeois science, just as, with respect to literature, we are not talking of the classic bourgeois novel. Indeed, if one is struck by the novelty of its literalism, the above quotation from the *Examination* reveals its author's continuing debt to the substantialist view of *natural* movements. This is the world of Ptolemaic physics, in which inertia and repose are the norm. Movement is natural only to the extent that things show a tendency to gravitate towards their natural place: a horse towards its stable, fire, being more 'spiritual', upwards, and more material objects downwards; although even fire does not escape bodily matter, with which it must, like all earthly things, be mixed or 'fed'. By the same token, even Huarte's trenchant

---

47   Ibid., p. 400.
48   Rodríguez 2001b, pp. 121–2.

reliance upon the senses, as opposed to the intellect, betrays its origins in an Aristotelian materialism: 'This is what Aristotle began to prove, that the senses are always true, whereas the understanding, for the most part, reasons badly'.[49] Always true because, as Huarte proceeds to explain (still paraphrasing Aristotle), the mental impressions left by things are always real, firm and stable.

Yet, for all that, Huarte still *sees* the thing, nay, sometimes contravenes Aristotle on the evidence of his senses. And it is at such moments that empiricism of a substantialist variety folds over into something that closely resembles its bourgeois counterpart. Emphatically, truth now rests not with God but with the informed gaze, which is invariably that of Huarte himself. Consider, for example, the disparities he observed between himself and two fellow students when it came to studying Latin: 'In my amazement, I began to ponder the fact and to philosophise, and discovered on my own account that each science requires an appropriate wit, which is suited to it'.[50] Likewise, it is not so much the authority of Plato that confirms in Huarte's own mind the existence of a creative wit as his own personal experience ('I can testify to it as an eyewitness').[51] The cumulative effect of such statements is to impart to the subject a new legitimising function, which in turn concedes to the material senses an importance that they did not possess under Aristotelian organicism. All of which confirms our view that Aristotelian rationalism was, in the last instance, a compromise discourse, that could be bent to any kind of ideological purpose in the conditions of the transition.

5   The Letter of the Law

The nature of Aristotelian rationalism, as a compromise discourse, is particularly in evidence, and predictably so, in those sections of the *Examination* that are directly concerned with language. Consider the manner in which Huarte frames the Aristotelian view of language as the production of convention: 'From the fact that languages are strictly the result of men's will and fancy, it follows that the sciences can be taught in any one of them, and any one of them can say and declare what was said in another'.[52] From this conventionalism, Huarte moves quickly to the quintessentially animist promotion of the virtues of the vulgar tongue. Reduced to pure transparency, the latter can be used to

---

49   Huarte 1976, p. 217.
50   Ibid., p. 72.
51   Ibid., p. 433.
52   Ibid., pp. 165–6.

critique substantialist Aristotelianism, as embodied in the elaborate terminology of scholastic philosophers. One consequence is that, for the first time
in Western culture, a wedge is being driven between philosophy and science,
between metaphysics and physics: 'Nothing damages man's knowledge more
than mixing the sciences, using metaphysics to deal with natural philosophy,
and natural philosophy to deal with metaphysics'.[53] From such a standpoint,
Huarte does not hesitate to qualify the 'naturalist' thesis, of Platonic extraction, that regards words as tied *essentially* to the things they name. Names are
imposed, he suggests, in accordance with a 'rational will'.[54] Having said which,
the kind of 'rationality' involved is manifestly of a non-organicist Aristotelian-
ism, resting upon the substantialist notion that words are tied to the material
'nature' of things, preserved quintessentially in Latin.

It is perilously difficult, then, to get the balance right, to avoid, say, exagger-
ating Huarte's conservatism at the expense of his modernity, and vice versa, not
least of all when the concept of a 'rational will' is deployed in the sphere of law:

> The law, properly considered, is nothing more than the rational will of the
> legislator, through which the latter wishes each case to be decided, of the
> kind that happens in his republic on a daily basis, with the aim of keep-
> ing the peace among his subjects and teaching them how to live and what
> to avoid. I said *rational* will because it is not sufficient that the king or
> emperor, who is the efficient cause of the law, explain his will in any way
> he pleases for it to become the law, nor is it, just as someone who lacked a
> rational soul would not be a man. And so, it is agreed that monarchs make
> their laws in consultation with the learned and the wise, so that these laws
> are proper, equitable, and good, and that subjects willingly accept them
> and are duty bound to keep them and abide by them.[55]

In his insistence that laws are made by men and, as such, are subject to change,
Huarte is but a stone's throw from the Enlightenment notion of the social 'contract', entered into by 'free subjects': 'because when all is said and done, [the
law] was established by following human advice, and the latter does not have
the power to determine everything that lies in the future' (pp. 212–13). Yet, at
the same time, to talk in terms of a cultural secularisation, in the case of Spain,
would be fatally misleading. Huarte remains, in an important sense, a theoretician of the absolutist state, whose presiding concept is not the subject or

---

53   Ibid., p. 139.
54   Ibid., p. 177.
55   Ibid., pp. 208–9.

'*sujeto*', otherwise the free subject, but the '*súbdito*', in the political sense of sub-jected to the authority of the monarch, who in turn derived his authority from God. Hence the equation in the *Examination* between the interpretation of the law and biblical exegesis, with an emphasis upon multiple levels of meaning. Hence also Huarte's repeated warnings as to the deleterious consequences of following the letter of the law.

The importance of emphasising Huarte's conservatism is reinforced once we continue the quotation cited above as proof of Huarte's literalism:

> If God were to place a lighted candle that reached from the concave of the moon to the centre of the earth, its flame would descend over this whole distance, without any problem whatsoever. Galen and the natural philosophers are quite mistaken in their view that upward movement is the most natural, because the pyramidal shape is actually caused by the smoke, to which the flame, as the lighter element, is attached. This is eas-ily proved: look how, as the smoke gradually dissipates, the flame shrinks and is consumed.[56]

Obviously, Huarte is substituting work in the head for the closed conditions of laboratory experimentation. What is less obvious is why. One's immediate response is to suggest that at this stage science just did not dispose of the experimental instruments necessary for controlling events in closed condi-tions. However, I believe this view to be misguided in that it projects back upon Huarte's fundamental scholastic science the assumptions of modern empiri-cism. Huarte, it is true, and as I have been at pains to insist, was not unaffected by the earliest forms of bourgeois ideology, and specifically by the literalism of animism. But it is anachronistic in the extreme to expect him to behave in accordance with the norms of classical empiricism. 'Verification' and 'falsifica-tion' are simply not part of his conceptual arsenal, sustained as they are by the empiricist notions of 'subject' and 'object'.

6   The Subsequent History of Animism

Such, then, was the historical, ideological substratum of Juan Huarte's *Exam-ination*. But history and ideology, in this objective sense, were the last thing on Chomsky's mind. His immediate concern was the need to break with the

---

56   Ibid., p. 400.

empiricist, positivist problematic characteristic of the classic bourgeoisie and, more specifically, with the way in which it conceived of the relation between 'subject' and 'system'. Irrespective of whether it assumed 'mentalist' or 'materialist' positions, empiricism promotes an 'interior' subject that infuses life into an 'exterior' system, identified with the technical means of expression. One effect was to relegate syntax to the 'freedom' of 'speech', as opposed to the constraints of 'language'. Chomsky's solution, by way of transcending this problematic, was to identify or fuse the 'subject' with the 'system', so as produce a 'subject-system'.[57] Every 'performative' action, the linguist argued, presupposed the existence of a 'competence', otherwise a human nature, replete with principles, rules, and faculties, which constituted a syntactic base from which the deep structures of language could be generated.

Chomsky's immediate target was the behaviourism of Bloomfieldian linguistics, but this linguistic tradition was itself an outgrowth of William James' pragmatism and Dewey's instrumentalism, which were in turn rooted in the classic tradition of Hume. Thus, when he came to legitimate his own position, in terms of its historical lineage, it was perhaps inevitable that Chomsky should align himself unambiguously with, and attempt to recuperate, the tradition that had always been the historical counterpart to pragmatic empiricism, namely, an innatist tradition originating in Renaissance Petrarchism, of neo-Platonic vintage. Platonic innatism has several attractions from Chomsky's standpoint. First, its beautiful soul recognises itself ('remembers' its origins) in data received, just as, according to the linguist, the same data awakens an innate linguistic faculty. Moreover, it drew no distinction between subject and system, a characteristic that was given even greater prominence in Cartesianism, with respect to 'I' and 'Reason', which explains why Chomsky finally grounds transformational grammar in 'Cartesian linguistics'. While this innatist tradition sometimes shows a tendency to revert to a specifically feudalising ideology, at other times it assumes secular forms, in which it is cleansed of 'divine' elements. But whatever form it takes, its role is that of a *transitional ideology* between feudalism and capitalism. Rodríguez explains:

> Such, then, is the animist/innatist ideology, articulated, to repeat, in neo-Platonic or rationalist terms, such as correspond to the formative phase of the bourgeoisie. It always begins with a 'subject', but one that is 'full' and ontologised, as expressed in the notions of the 'soul' and 'cogito'. While both are specifically 'adapted' to co-exist with feudal organisation, they

---

57   See Rodríguez 2008b, p. 73.

obviously stand in opposition to it, constitute a clear 'rupture' with it, through the very fact of being a 'subject'.[58]

In the latter part of *Theory and History* and again in *State, Stage, Language*, Rodríguez returned to the history of animism, this time with an eye to its subsequent development and to its significance for Chomskyian linguistics. On his reckoning, animism survives in a latent form in the baroque in Spain, Italy, and France, notably in the spiritualism of Pascal and Jansenism in general. It will persist in England during the eighteenth century, in the tradition from Donne to Blake, 'passing through the Cambridge School (vindicated by Chomsky and analyzed in depth by Cassirer)'.[59] Moreover, while animism as such disappears from other European traditions, the legacy of its 'full' proto-subject does not. Indeed, it is given one of its classic formulations by Kant, in whom the 'beautiful soul' matures into a transcendental subject.[60] Even the 'double experience' of liberalism could be given a transcendental twist, notably through Locke, who argues that experiences received from the outside are worked upon by reason.

According to Rodríguez's reading, while Chomsky clings to Locke's second source of determination, that is, to the interior reason of the subject,[61] he remains sufficiently attached to the empiricist tradition not to stop at the transcendental subject but to take an interest in its 'affective' counterpart. The latter had surfaced towards the end of the eighteenth century, within those countries in which the bourgeois revolution had yet to be carried through, such as Germany – Wilhelm von Humboldt's contribution is crucial – or as a reaction that was occurring *against* the bourgeois revolution, as in French Romanticism. By this point, however, animism has become the specialised ideology of the petty bourgeoisie, in other words, of that social fraction which will resist the technicist impulse of the bourgeoisie proper.

The conclusions that Chomsky arrived at with respect to language, notably the identity between subject and system, are carried over into his discussion of literature. Perforce, he envisages freedom of expression as the other face of necessity. Rejected are all absolutist conceptions of 'freedom', of Romantic origin, on the grounds that rules are precisely what enable creativity.[62] Poetic 'abandonment' is governed by its own normativity, albeit of a flexible kind.

---

58   Ibid., p. 72.
59   Rodríguez 2002a, p. 299.
60   Rodríguez 2008b, p. 74.
61   Ibid., p. 97.
62   Rodríguez 2008b, pp. 98–9.

What this suggests, among other things, is that the deep/surface relation, beyond its effective presence in particular languages and specific texts, is inherent in human nature; and that, to be more specific, there is an organic connection between the transformative capacity of the syntactic system, on the one hand, and sexual generation and poetic potency, on the other. The existence of a parallel was certainly not lost upon the organicist Juan Huarte de San Juan 'as Chomsky specifically recalls'.[63] All of which, as Rodríguez proceeds to explain, would account for Chomsky's preference for Huarte over Sánchez el Brocense, who, by way of contrast, is simply concerned with the operations of ellipsis at the level of textual exegesis.

7   Conclusion

Far from breaking with bourgeois ideology, Chomsky simply re-inscribes linguistics under 'psychology', a discipline that hinges upon the eminently bourgeois category of a trans-historical subject, together with the familiar Kantian distinction between the transcendental and empirical. From which, according to Rodríguez, everything else follows, including Chomsky's gravitation, through Paul Goodman and others, towards communitarian anarchism, existential humanism and the New Left: 'Not exactly promising from a genuinely materialist theoretical perspective'.[64] Now, while there are obvious dangers to extrapolating from such a narrow frame of reference, important connections are certainly there to be found, notably between Chomsky's principled opposition to the instrumentalism of so-called 'experts' (the 'New Mandarins', etc.) and the human creativity promoted through recourse to the *Examination*. Such creativity, from Rodríguez's standpoint, is contaminated at its core through its association with the bourgeois 'freedom', to exploit and to be exploited. The position thereby assumed, understandably enough, has found little favour with the liberal academy. Symptomatically, a series of studies devoted to subjectivity in early modern Spain[65] failed to record a single reference to the Althusserian. Then came the events of 11 September 2001, when the ideology of 'service' (to the Lord), theorised in depth in *Theory and History*, suddenly reared its ugly head, to the bewilderment of Western intellectuals. Rodríguez ruefully diagnosed liberalism's dilemma: 'to forget the reality of exploitation is to be

---

63   Rodríguez 2008b, p. 85.
64   Rodríguez 2008b, p. 106.
65   Pereira Zazo 1994.

led, in one way or another, into an ideological cul-de-sac or dead-end'.[66] A cul-de-sac from which, we might add, the Left is only now beginning to re-emerge.

---

66   Rodríguez 2002a, p. 15.

CHAPTER 4

Explorations of the Political/Ideological Unconscious: Fredric Jameson

We will be exploring below the definition and determination of two theoretical concepts, namely the *'ideological unconscious'* and the *'political unconscious'*, both rooted in Althusser's understanding of Marx and his relation to Hegel but developed along very different, even contrasting lines in, respectively, the work of Juan Carlos Rodríguez and that of Fredric Jameson. Before entering into detail, let us broadly locate the relevant texts and their authors in their social and intellectual contexts.

While Jameson's *The Political Unconscious* appears in 1981, some seven years *after* the publication of Rodríguez's *Theory and History of Ideological Production*, it has its origins in an earlier period – by his own reckoning, Jameson was a product of the late 1950s, otherwise the age of McCarthyism, and of an academy lacking not only any sense of affinity with the Soviet Union but also anything resembling the tradition of Western Marxism.[1] To have matured, intellectually, during that decade meant for many on the Left, including Jameson, to have imbibed the existential philosophy of Sartre, together with its Hegelian brand of Marxism; and while certainly the latter was conspicuous by its absence from the American's early research, it was perhaps inevitable that, following in the wake of Sartre, his theorisation of the unconscious, when eventually undertaken, should take a distinctively 'political form', inflected along the lines of an Hegelianised Marxism. Such political allegiances notwithstanding, Jameson would look to rest his political unconscious upon a reading of the resolutely anti-Hegelian work of Althusser. Other key ingredients would be provided by Lacanian psychoanalysis. The final result, although undoubtedly provocative, was destined to enjoy a wide currency and to be widely debated.[2]

Even at this introductory stage, it is impossible not to pose the obvious question: how does Jameson manage to reconcile such contradictory attachments? The answer, as we will see, is that the matrix effect of a social formation, as

---

1 Buchanan 2006, pp. 120–1.
2 For example, Roberts 2000; Helmling 2001.

theorised by Althusser, will be systematically reworked to eliminate its internal structural levels and thereby to bring it into line with the Hegelian notion of the Absolute Spirit. Eliminated also is the alleged 'break' between the early and late Marx, upon which Althusser otherwise insists, and the consequent displacement of focus from a Moving Spirit to a structure in dominance. In sum, with the Althusserian threat attenuated if not entirely removed, the Hegelian can freely continue to prioritise the subject/object opposition fundamental to bourgeois ideology – which doubtless helps explain Jameson's widespread appeal in the US academy and elsewhere – and, correspondingly, to prioritise a subjective *consciousness*. To the latter, the Jamesonian 'political unconscious' will always remain mortgaged.

The 'ideological unconscious' is systematically theorised for the first time by Rodríguez in his *Theory and History of Ideological Production* (1974), wherein it is envisaged as consisting of an ideological matrix or nucleus, the effects of which are felt throughout the entire social formation. This matrix further takes the form of certain binary pairings, the master/slave, in the case of slavery; the lord/serf, in the case of feudalism; and the Subject/subject in the case of capitalism. While Rodríguez will continue to deploy the key Althusserian concepts of 'social formation', 'mode of production', economic, political, and ideological 'instances', and so on, his 'ideological unconscious' will require some significant reconfigurations of the Althusserian legacy. For example, ideology will not necessarily exist through and for the 'subject' – the dominant ideology of feudalism, it will transpire from the Spaniard's work, knows no such category – and to assume otherwise, whether from a bourgeois or Marxist standpoint, is, arguably, to think ahistorically. Nor, contrary to what Althusser sometimes implies (when he regresses unconsciously to bourgeois orthodoxy), does the subject pre-exist its social formation or, to use Althusser's own terminology, its social 'interpellation', other than as a bundle of genes. The existence of a libidinal unconscious is recognised but does not enter into the Spaniard's theoretical equations.

How is one to account for such radical innovations? Undoubtedly, much was owed to the direct influence of Althusser at the *Rue d'Ulm* where Rodríguez studied in the mid 1970s. But other circumstantial factors must have been relevant, beginning with the Spaniard's prior and equally direct exposure to fascism. Strange to say, the exposure came with its advantages. What better starting point could anyone have had, when it came to theorising the ideological unconscious, than the personal experience of being smothered by layers of feudal ideology in a Francoist guise? Perhaps more importantly, Spain's belated incorporation into capitalism – the indispensable condition for the rise of fascism – meant that Rodríguez was able to observe liberal ideology objectively, from *without*, or at least from its margins.[3] Such benefits, it should be said, came at a price, namely professional isolation on the outer circuits of the global academy: symptomatically, Rodríguez's work has been the subject of only one monograph.[4] But while such factors undoubtedly explain in part the contrast with Jameson's fortunes, the root cause of the peculiar 'silence' that has dogged the Spaniard's work must undoubtedly be found elsewhere, namely in the nature of its object, a social formation structured on the basis of a mode of production, and its seeming incompatibility with the subject/object paradigm prioritised by the dominant ideology, or so at least we will be arguing.

Our first task, by way of assessing the contributions of both scholars, must be to return to Marx and Althusser and to consider those aspects of these predecessors' work that are relevant to the notion of the unconscious, both ideological and political.

1   From Marx to Althusser

Even as he redefined the original, Enlightenment concept of ideology, so that it ceased to refer to an individual's distorted ideas and came instead to correspond to supra-individual systems of beliefs, the young Marx continued to think within the horizons of a problematic centred on the subject and, by the same token, to detach ideology from the base and locate it as a differentiated block of consciously held, although false, ideas within the superstructure. The shift, it follows, from 'Man' to the 'economic law of motion', in evidence in the mature Marx, is undeniably qualitative and far from being the private fantasy of Althusser, as it is sometimes portrayed. The text of *Capital* is perfectly explicit: 'individuals are dealt with here only in so far as they are the personifications of economic categories, the bearers [*Träger*] of particular class-relations and interests'[5] – and it is undoubtedly significant that, more or less contemporaneously, we glimpse the first intimations of ideological processes operative at the infrastructural level, as when, in the *Grundrisse*, for example, Marx describes in suggestive terms how a specific kind of production can predominate over the rest: 'It is a general illumination which bathes all the other colours and modifies

---

3 Rodríguez's doctoral thesis, based on research conducted in the late 1960s and early '70s, has been published belatedly, in an updated form (Rodríguez 2015). In it, the Althusserian ranges over the totality of Western 'theory'.
4 See Caamaño 2008.
5 Marx 1976, p. 92.

their particularity. It is a particular ether which determines the specific gravity of every being which has materialised within it'.[6] Even so, powerful factors militated against any theoretical advancement: to begin with, the concept of the unconscious necessarily remained embryonic in what was, after all, a pre-Freudian age; moreover, within the limited context of Marxism, it was never a question of simply inverting Hegel – after all, even within the context of *Capital*, economic activity necessarily retained an ideational component. In other words, much remained to be done if the unconsciousness of ideology was to be detached conceptually from 'consciousness' and developed to its full potential. At which point, enter Althusser.

Whether or not the mature Marx himself subscribed to the criticism of humanism that Althusser attributed to him need not concern us here. There is no gainsaying the fact of the philosopher's own point of departure, namely the 'ever-pre-givenness of a structured complex unity',[7] nor of its consequences for his view of ideology: human societies allegedly 'secrete ideology as the very element and atmosphere indispensable to their historical respiration and life',[8] in the form of structures, of images, myths, ideas and concepts, impersonally imposed upon their subjects. The latter, we should know, 'live' their ideologies '*not at all as a form of consciousness, but as an object of their "world"* – as their *"world"* itself';[9] and that lived relation, between individuals and their world, 'only appears as "conscious" on condition that it is *unconscious*, in the same way only seems to be simple on condition that it is complex'.[10] In essence, therefore, we are talking about an *imaginary* relation. 'Just as a people that exploits another cannot be free, so a class that *uses* an ideology is its captive too' (p. 235).

Given such emphasis upon the unconsciousness of ideology, one is bound to ask what prevented Althusser from arriving at the notion of an ideological unconscious. The answer, seemingly, was that he found the 'unconscious' inescapably rooted in psychology, to judge at least from a private letter to René Diakine in which the philosopher takes his psychoanalyst to task for sparing psychology in his theoretical critique of empiricism:

> In my telling you that, you will see that I too *interpret* what one might be tempted to call your ideologic-theoretical *unconscious*. I would have many reservations to make on those *terms*, since I believe that [it] is not

6   Marx 1973, p. 107.
7   Althusser 1990a, p. 199.
8   Ibid., p. 232.
9   Ibid., p. 233.
10   Ibid.

possible to speak of an ideological unconscious. In the event, that 'unconscious' (which I would call by a different name, but never mind) exists,
and *it should not be confused with the psychoanalytic unconscious*.[11]

The ideological unconscious, then, remained a concept to be explored, as did
Althusser's complex web of transitive and intransitive causalities. But there was
one question that, even at this early stage, clamoured for consideration, namely
the displacement of the subject and its relevance to the science/ideology relation.

2   **Science and Ideology**

Bourgeois ideology, to remind ourselves, in any of its variants, takes the same
subject/object paradigm for granted. In the words of Althusser: 'The subject
and object, which are given and hence pre-date the process of knowledge,
already define a certain fundamental theoretical field'.[12] The philosopher's
solution, after Marx, was to transfer the whole debate onto a different terrain by
accepting from the outset, as basic theses, the priority of the real over thought
about the real, and the specificity of thought and the thought process.[13] In other
words, he does not answer the philosophical question of the validity of knowledge; rather he bypasses it.
     As indicated earlier (in Chapter 1), matters have come to a head in the con-
text of a famous passage of the *Grundrisse* in which Marx expatiates on the
contrast between, on the one hand, traditional attempts to depart from the
concrete in order to reach the abstract and, on the other, the (in his view) scientifically correct method that begins with abstract definitions and, by way of
them, 'rises' to the concrete during the course of reasoning.[14] Althusser, for his
part, is emphatic in *Reading Capital* as to how the section is to be read and,
more importantly, how it is *not* to be read. Marx, we are informed, is not concerned with the 'problem of knowledge', as traditionally understood, which is
to say with the relation between thought and reality; from which it follows that,
'he is not for one second falling into an idealism of consciousness, mind or
thought'.[15] Marx, then, is concerned with how the scientist comes to have a the-

11   Althusser 1996, p. 52.
12   Althusser and Balibar 1970, p. 35.
13   Althusser 1976, pp. 191–93.
14   Marx 1973, p. 101.
15   Althusser and Balibar 1970, p. 41.

ory, the point being that 'theoretical practice constitutes a process that takes place *entirely in thought*';[16] from which it follows that, contrary to what empiricism claims, knowledge never confronts a *real object*, only ever an 'object of knowledge', which is not to say, by any means, that we *produce* the reality we contemplate.[17]

The case is convincingly argued: the underlying tenor of Marx's work is undoubtedly one of both epistemological and ontological realism. But in focusing on the specificity of thought, one is bound to wonder whether Althusser is not letting slip the primacy he otherwise accords to the real. The immediate signs are not encouraging: he leaves unexamined the specific modes – experimentation in the hard sciences and abstraction in the human sciences – through which science appropriates the real world; new knowledge, we learn, simply 'concerns' the real object, without necessarily corresponding with it.[18] The effect is to drain ontology into epistemology, such that while knowledge itself is progressively 'deepened', vertically, and 'extended', horizontally or, to use Althusser's own term, geographically, as new continents are revealed, the '*labour of theoretical transformation ...* necessarily affects the *object of knowledge*, since it is only applied to the latter'.[19] What is missing is any sense of a correspondingly deep ontology.

Once set in motion, the weakening or, more strictly, flattening out of ontology rolls inexorably onwards, to the extent that we find Marx himself castigated for failing to situate the opposition between *essence* and *appearance* where it properly belongs, in the 'inner site of its concept'.[20] But with unfortunate consequences: Althusser opens himself up to the charge that he undertheorises the intransitive dimension of knowledge production and, specifically, that, in his hands, the theoretical constructs of science serve simply 'to ease our mental labour'.[21]

---

16   Ibid., p. 42.
17   For a discussion of the subtle terminological developments in Althusser from *For Marx* to *Reading Capital*, see Geras 1986, p. 102. The details of Althusser's argument have not saved him from being charged, along with Derrida and Habermas and other such philosophers, with underplaying ontology. Bhaskar explains: 'What happens in the case of these authors is that they implicitly inherit an implicit ontology, which is the positivist ontology, the epistemology of which they reject, so that you get a super-idealism' (Bhaskar 2002b, p. 63). We will be discussing Bhaskar's position in more detail in Chapter 7.
18   Althusser and Balibar 1970, p. 156.
19   Ibid.
20   Althusser and Balibar 1970, p. 189.
21   Collier 1994, p. 68.

3   Althusser Reconfigured: from Kant to Hegel

Like so many of his Leftist contemporaries in literary studies, Jameson's focus in the research he conducted in the 1950s was upon the work of Sartre, the defining features of which were a radical splitting of the world into two parts, subject and object, and, in a characteristically Hegelian manner, the collapsing of the latter into the former. Thus, in Jameson's own words: 'The reflection of subjectivity on the thing, the manner in which a subjectivity betrays its secrets through an apparently objective perceiving of a thing outside it, is possible because this facticity can never be directly apprehended, because it must be *assumed* by consciousness and thus immediately compromises the viewer and reflects him back'.[22] The priority thereby accorded to consciousness will prove to be a lasting legacy: in a retrospective afterword, his youthful first book still strikes Jameson as 'plausible',[23] requiring nothing more than some terminological tinkering. Nor, it will transpire, would the Hegelian dialectic he proceeded to enthusiastically embrace require any 'break', of the kind that distinguished the work of Althusser, insofar as the Spirit that allegedly unfolds during the course of human history is nothing less than a Subject.

The continuity in Jameson's thought is in evidence from the early *Marxism and Form* (1971), which continues to foreground subjectivity. Dialectical thought, as a result, takes the form, not of a dialectics of nature, of the real world, with its suffering, exploitation and violence, but of *thought*, which is to say, 'nothing more or less than the elaboration of dialectical sentences',[24] an argument that would be pressed to the extreme through a detailed appraisal of the work of Theodor Adorno. It is difficult to imagine, at first, how, in such circumstances, anything like an *unconscious*, and a political one to boot, could possibly emerge from such divagations. Unsurprisingly, Jameson's *Marxism and Form* (1971) continues to take its cue from a brand of Lukácsian Marxism in which 'the act of consciousness overthrows the objective form of its object'.[25] That said, the concept of a class consciousness spontaneously generates its opposite, a class-conditioned *unconsciousness*, and, as even Althusser was the first to admit, the Hegelian tradition adds one crucial ingredient to any Marxism worthy of the name, and certainly to any Marxist formulation of an

22   Jameson 1984 [1961], p. 87.
23   Ibid., p. 205.
24   Jameson 1971, p. xii.
25   Lukács 1973, p. 18.

unconscious, namely the concept of a 'process without a subject'. Jameson elaborates: 'The former subject no longer thinks, he "is thought", and his conscious experience, which used to correspond to the concept of *reason* in middle-class philosophy, becomes little more than a matter of registering signals from zones outside itself, either those that come from within and "below", as in the drives and bodily and psychic automatisms, or from the outer circles of interlocking social institutions of all kinds'.[26] All of which would be very encouraging, from a Marxist standpoint, were it not for the fact that, the references to 'social institutions' notwithstanding, the emphasis remains firmly fixed upon the world of thought: what happens is that 'the mind is able, momentarily, to glimpse a concrete totality'.[27] It is not that the material world is absent: dialectics is emphatically *about* the empirical world; simply that the *aboutness* constantly slips from view. The result is a *de-ontologicisation* that deprives the world of any material depth.[28]

Given such a formation, within the womb of Hegelian thought, it might well be wondered how Jameson, notwithstanding his capacity to accommodate all-comers, is going to find room for a thinker as resolutely *anti*-Hegelian as Althusser, who consistently argued against 'an idealism of consciousness' and emphatically asserted the primacy of the real over thought about the real. And yet, perhaps, the room for manoeuvre was greater than initially appeared to be the case. For, as was conceded above, the Althusserian insistence upon the specificity of thought was conducive to a correspondingly flat ontology, along idealist lines. Inconsistencies, then, there were, and Jameson would be quick to seize upon them. Thus, in *The Prison House of Language* (1972) he set out systematically to (mis)construe the relevant Althusserian texts along Kantian lines. Althusser's originality, we learn, was to have 'reversed the terms of the old materialistic epistemology, for which reality is "outside the mind"'.[29] Willy-nilly, the philosopher is re-located within the familiar epistemological scenario of the subject/object opposition, where a theory of theoretical practice is reconfigured as a *psychology* and thence transposed into a theory of knowledge. 'For Althusser, in a sense, we never really get outside our own minds',[30] which is to say that theoretical praxis runs its course 'in the sealed chamber of the mind'.[31]

---

26   Jameson 1971, p. 28.
27   Ibid., p. 41.
28   For this emphasis upon de-ontologicisation in Jameson, I am indebted to Norrie 2012.
29   Jameson 1972, p. 106.
30   Ibid.
31   Ibid.

Given such premises, 'the basic terms of the problem have now become recognizable: it is essentially a replay of the Kantian dilemma of the unknowability of the thing-in-itself'.[32]

Still, if Althusser was always vulnerable to an epistemological, as opposed to methodological, reading of his notion of theoretical production, he might have seemed well equipped to resist attempts to draw him into the field of Hegelian Marxism. For the French philosopher, we recall, a world of difference separated the Marxist whole – a complex structure in dominance – from the Hegelian view of society as pervaded expressively by a single spirit. Conflation of the twin totalities seemed an impossibility. And yet the letter of his texts would, in practice, offer Althusser little protection against Jameson's homogenising enthusiasms. Nor would it deter the American critic from taking full advantage of Althusser's failure to coherently thematise ontology.

Thus, things begin rather ominously in Jameson's next work, *The Political Unconscious*: economic determination 'in the last instance' – the scare quotes deployed unambiguously signal an Althusserian provenance – is replaced with its political equivalent, to arrive at the view that 'everything is "in the last instance" political'.[33] And even before we have been able to assess the full import of this manoeuvre, the American critic is already busily dismantling the Althusserian 'structure in dominance', on the alleged basis that, for its originator, 'the more narrowly economic [...] is, however privileged, not identical with the mode of production as a whole, which assigns to this narrowly "economic" level its particular function and efficiency as it does all the others'.[34] Conveniently but, from the Althusserian standpoint, deceptively elided are the causal complexities of the social process and, specifically, of the intransitive effectivity exercised by the economy through the matrix effect of the whole. The elision proves crucial: through it, Jameson ensures that we are left with only one structure, that of the mode of production, which simply awaits correlation with the Hegelian Spirit. 'Such momentary reunification would remain purely symbolic, a mere methodological fiction, were it not understood that social life is in its fundamental reality one and indivisible, a seamless web, a single inconceivable and transindividual process, in which there is no need to invent ways of linking language events and social upheavals or economic contradictions because on that level they were never separate from one another'.[35]

32   Ibid., pp. 108–9.
33   Jameson 1981, p. 20.
34   Ibid., p. 36.
35   Ibid., p. 40.

Althusser, the arch-anti-Hegelian, drawn within the horizon of Hegelian Marxism! One has to marvel at Jameson's audacity and what is tantamount to a conjuring trick. In effect, Althusser has been re-written in terms of the very 'expressive causality' that it was his prime concern to critique. Gone are the contradictions internal to each instance; gone those between the various instances of the social formation; gone also, the action of the social formation on each practice and each contradiction; gone, in sum, the irreducible presence of multiple levels, the structure of structures, to be displaced by a concept of continuity across a homogeneous theoretical space.[36] The Hegelian process without a subject, it follows, is less the explanation of a process than the transitory expression of a process. None of which augurs well for the ensuing theorisation of a political unconscious.

4   Theorising the Ideological Unconscious

Petty-bourgeois intellectuals, Althusser himself insisted, 'have to carry out a radical revolution in their ideas' if they are to think from a Marxist standpoint.[37] Rodríguez would agree, except with one important qualification: it is not with their *consciousness* that these intellectuals must break, as the philosopher implies, but with their ideological *unconscious* and, specifically, with their attachment to the subject, as a trans-historical category. Specifically, this was something that Jameson had failed to do, to the extent that he had become 'a totaliser of the spirit of the age, a "Geist" from which nobody could escape'.[38] Rodríguez elaborates later: 'Although the contradictions continue impassively, under the surface, it is clear that such a Spirit, in its capacity as the Whole, will always overwhelm any single instance, ... even in the progressive criticism

---

36   As even some of Jameson's more sympathetic commentators have felt obliged to conclude, this simply will not do, and fully justifies the complaint that such Hegelian synthesising 'threatens to homogenise the antitheses [Jameson] brings together' (Helmling 2001, p. 143). His Marxist critics have been correspondingly more severe, taking the position that Jameson is in fact not terribly interested in Althusser's work in itself but more concerned to resolve problems internal to his brand of Hegelian Marxism. Callinicos, for example, argues that Jameson's attempt to enlist the support of Althusser in his Hegelian project, if successful, would have been a 'remarkable feat', since Lukács' analysis of reification was a prime example of the kind of expressive totality that the French philosopher was most concerned to critique (Callinicos 1989, p. 131). Eagleton similarly argues that Jameson never seriously took on board the Althusserian critique of Marxist historicism (Eagleton 1986, p. 73).

37   Althusser 1971, p. 12.

38   Rodríguez 2002b, p. 110.

of Jameson'.[39] The Althusserian's first task, it followed, was to do something that, for all his emphasis upon the forms of existence of historical individuality, Althusser himself had never dared to do, namely to historicise the notion of the 'subject'. Hence, the calculated shock of his point of departure: 'Literature has not always existed'.[40] Not at least in the traditional sense of the term, namely as 'a series of discourses that are above all the *works* of a single *author*'. Defined thus, its existence coincides with the beginnings, in the fifteenth century, of bourgeois ideology itself, one of whose unquestioned assumptions will be that, while the 'subject' may not be *unique* to literary discourse – it is shared by its equivalents in science, politics, etc. – literary discourse certainly *expresses* better than any other the *inner truth* of the subject or, in Rodríguez's own words, 'the true intimacy of the "subject/author of a work"'.[41]

Ominously, the problematising of the subject was only the beginning. Historicised, by the same token, would be all those categories that constitute what the Spaniard calls the 'productive logic of the text',[42] namely 'author', 'expression', 'mind', 'reason' and so on, in other words, the very conceptual tools that the bourgeois critic *thinks with*. This logic, it further transpired, is rooted in a bourgeois ideological matrix,[43] consisting of the Subject/subject opposition and functional to a specific mode of production. The latter's class articulation requires that 'its' individuals think of themselves as 'subjects', each possessed of their own interior truth and, more fundamentally, possessed of their own labour power, which they are 'free' to sell to a Subject, otherwise the owner of the means of production. Without individuals who imagine themselves to be free, the capitalist system quite simply cannot function, or so at least Rodríguez wished to argue.

The historically limited nature of the bourgeois matrix is clear if we compare it with that of the preceding mode, namely the lord (Lord)/serf (servant) matrix characteristic of feudalism, and similarly functional to the re-production of feudal relations. Under feudalism, the last thing that the serf imagined him/herself to be was 'free', other than (in special cases) free to serve this as opposed to that lord, to whom s/he was otherwise 'bonded'. But a word of warning: it is wrong to think of a dominating class as 'consciously' exploiting the dominated. In reality, people are collectively convinced of the truth, as it appears to them, of the human condition, are caught up in social relations that,

39   Ibid., p. 217.
40   Rodríguez 2002a, p. 17.
41   Ibid.
42   Ibid., p. 18.
43   Ibid., p. 19.

however 'imaginary', are objectively 'secreted'; even the lord *really* believes he is a lord, just as the free subject *really* believes s/he is a free subject. The contrast with, and the threat to, critical orthodoxy could not be clearer. Gone is the truth of nature, displaced by an ideological secretion, to be formalised as a distinctively *ideological unconscious*: 'The notion of the subject (and the whole problematic within which it is inscribed) is radically historical because ... it derives directly (and exclusively) from the very matrix of the bourgeois ideological unconscious: the "serf" can never be a "subject"'.[44]

To drive home this extension of Althusserian thought, Rodríguez has to rethink the functioning of the social formation and the role of ideology within it. Althusser, to recall, tied ideology to the Ideological State Apparatus, conceding only parenthetically the fact that ideology was 'originally' secreted in the social infrastructure. The Spaniard, by way of contrast, aims to locate ideology unambiguously in the relations of production: '... the dialectic inscribed in the literary texts (that which produces them as such, their internal logic) is what shapes an ideological unconscious. The latter is "born" not in the School, but in the interior of the social relations themselves, and derives directly from these relations'.[45] In effect, Althusser's original model has been turned on its head: ideology now originates not in the super-structural State Apparatus but in the base component, whence it is circulated through the social formation: '... it seems clear that the functionality of literary discourse and its real meaning for our societies are issues that need to be sought more in the interior of the ideological level proper than in the apparatuses that materialise and reproduce them'.[46] Turned on its head or, more accurately, totally reconfigured and dialecticised.

In his second seminal work, *State, Stage, Language*, Rodríguez provided more of an overview of the ideological dialectic, which allegedly takes the form of a double articulation: the elements secreted by the ideological unconscious are reproduced within the ISA, where they are formalised, thematised and theorised by philosophers, critics, and writers 'situated within the horizon of a class';[47] once processed, ideology is then fed back into a generalised unconscious that pervades the whole of society and is accepted by everyone as 'the very truth of nature, as being as natural as their own skin'[48] or, alternatively, in the form of a 'humus'. Certain details call for clarification. Firstly,

---

44   Ibid., p. 21.
45   Ibid, p. 30.
46   Ibid., p. 31.
47   Rodríguez 2008b [1984], p. 11.
48   Ibid.

while it registers the fact that the base determines the super-structure asymmetrically ('in the last instance'), Rodríguez's schema specifically allows for the reciprocal effectivity of the superstructure upon the base; this is important, given the lurking presence of versions of vulgar Marxism. Secondly, it is strictly misleading to talk in terms of a causal *sequence*, involving a 'before' and an 'after', as opposed to a circular process that is 'always already' in action. Thirdly, while the 'humus' metaphor captures the matrix effect of the social whole more effectively than 'cement', its Althusserian equivalent, it is not without dangers of its own, as Rodríguez was the first to realise. Crucially, unless qualified, it overloads the notion of continuity across a homogeneous theoretical space, after the fashion of a Hegelian spirit. What needs to be asserted, by way of a counterbalance, is the restless dialectical interplay within and between structures and, above all, the essentially conflictual nature of class relations, even within the relatively autonomous, class-dominated realm of the literary norm:

> ... because it is *unconscious* and therefore *latent*, ideology never coincides exactly with itself; and also, because it is *objective*, this same ideology has cracks and crevices everywhere (which need to be filled in endlessly, which is what gives rise to the norm). Literature, then, because it is conscious / unconscious, and because it takes an objective form, as a productive process, can be at odds with its growing medium and its own intentions. I speak, in short, of writing qua ideological struggle, as it is conducted inside the hegemonic ideology proper.[49]

Such, then, was the ideological unconscious, as formulated by Rodríguez. The contrast with Jameson's political equivalent cannot be emphasised enough.

5   The Political Unconscious

In the discussion of Conrad's *Lord Jim*, in the concluding chapter of *The Political Unconscious*, entitled 'Romance and Reification', Jameson takes time to consider the role of the sea in Conrad's fiction, as a non-space of life and work that 'is also the space of the degraded language of romance and daydream, of narrative commodity and the sheer distraction of "light literature"'.[50]

---

49   Ibid., p. 22.
50   Jameson 1981, p. 213.

A long quote follows, by way of illustration, in which Conrad draws a contrast between the passengers, otherwise the 'mass of sleepers', and the workers labouring in the engine-room, both contained within the bounds of the same steamer, as it ploughs its way through the ocean. Jameson himself then picks up the refrain, rehearsing the contrast between these 'sleepers' and the workers in existential terms, before proceeding to explore the deeper level of the consumable commodity, at which realities are transformed into style.[51] Next comes a reference to Berkeleyan idealism, followed in turn by a long quote from Marx's *The German Ideology*, which Jameson expands along the following lines:

> So this ground base of material production continues underneath the new formal structures of the modernist text, as indeed it could not but continue to do, yet conveniently muffled and intermittent, easy to ignore (or to rewrite in terms of the aesthetic, of sense perception, as here of the sounds and sonorous inscription of a reality you prefer not to conceptualise), its permanencies ultimately detectable only to the elaborate hermeneutic geiger counters of the political unconscious and the ideology of form.[52]

At first blush, one scarcely knows what to make of it all: at one moment we confront a text that teeters upon paraphrase; at the next, an active and autonomous critique whose aim, seemingly, is to formulate the concepts or laws of the text's production. An intriguing ambivalence, to be sure, but deployed to what effect? To disguise theoretical practice, one ventures to suggest, in the case of a critic who is struggling to *theorise* within the confines of an academic culture deeply suspicious, if not antagonistic, to abstraction. Alternatively, to remain attached to an object that, true to his instincts, the Hegelian theoretician is reluctant to relinquish. These, certainly, are part of the truth, but not the whole truth. The always insightful Terry Eagleton discerns, more precisely, the operations of a dialectical criticism that 'both evokes and displaces its object'[53] by drawing this object onto its own critical terrain; and that, furthermore, eradicates the object's existence 'as a mere fiction of the subject's power and desire'.[54] Such, we recall from above, are the dynamics of Hegelianism: subject and object pass into one another, to the advantage of the former, insofar as the object must itself

---

51   Ibid., p. 214.
52   Ibid., p. 215.
53   Eagleton 1986, p. 70.
54   Ibid., p. 76.

be a creation of the subject. A creation or, possibly, as Jameson himself seems to be implying, a *re*-creation, through which the aesthetic strips the commodified object of its reified crust and so returns it to something like its pristine form.

Our suspicions are confirmed in what follows: for all his references to the world, society, and so on, Jameson is committed to extending the bounds of epistemology at the expense of ontology, through a process whereby thinking is transformed into an independent subject (the idea), as the demiurge of an empirical world. Thrown into relief by the same token is a rather curious paradox: a body of work rooted in the command 'always to historicise' finds real history pressed beyond conceptualisation, relegated to the status of an 'absent cause' that is inaccessible other than in a textual form.[55] The consequences are severe: with all outlets to the Real blocked, the critic is left little option but to seek compensation in a style of writing that can leave even his more sympathetic readers 'engulfed by the threatened onset of an ideational congestion, a cerebral meltdown or synaptic overload, a sense of argumentative threads and suggestions, themes and variations, multiplying beyond any hope of keeping track of them'.[56] If this is the example of the political unconscious at work, one is bound to conclude, the concept is ill-defined, except upon the basis of a most radical re-definition of the term 'political'.

So beguiling is Jameson's style that one crucial aspect of his criticism easily passes unnoticed, namely that it selects its texts very carefully. Typically, in the present instance, he focuses upon Conrad's brand of 'schizophrenic' writing. To blend with its object, the subject prefers a text deeply embedded in a Romantic 'sensibility', that positively cries out for readerly communion, as, to some degree, does any text that is inscribed within the bourgeois ideological horizon: 'literature', by definition, is the medium through which an author 'expresses' his or her inner truth to a similarly sensitised reader – hence the need for any 'scientific' conceptualisation to be smuggled into the critical commentary *obliquely*. Jameson's treatment of the *chanson de geste*, by way of contrast, is brief and starkly objective: here, any intimacy between the bard and his audience is precluded from the outset, even as a convenient slippage from the Lacanian real to 'reality' enables the modern critic to discourse at relative length upon the social circumstances of the late Carolingian period, and even upon the niceties of the agon between good and evil. What precisely is the obstacle to the lovers' tryst? The answer is surprising: nothing less than His-

---

55   Jameson 1981, p. 35.
56   Helmling 2001, p. 122.

tory itself, in the form of the radical alterity of the bard, who, in his capacity as a servant of his lord/Lord, as opposed to an interiorised subject of modernity, must remain austerely aloof.

6   From Substantialist to Animist Tears

To illustrate how the ideological unconscious works in practice, let us consider the thematic of 'tears' and its treatment in a number of historically disparate works, beginning with the *Poem of the Cid*.

'De los sos ojos tan fuerte mientre lorando' (From his eyes so strongly crying),[57] we read of the Cid as he sadly departs into exile. Modern readers may well protest that such a typically feminine expression of grief ill becomes a warrior knight. Except that by doing so, they betray habits of modern readers who are suffused by the prevailing ideological unconscious, which dictate that the Cid's tears be construed along petty-bourgeois lines, as the expression of a privatised 'sensibility'. A reading attentive to the historicity of ideological artefacts will interpret the tears alternatively, along *organicist* lines, which is to say as the 'substantial', 'exteriorised' display of a 'public' grief. As Rodríguez explains: 'Strictly speaking, for feudal organicism the *interior/exterior* relation is never posed as a problem'.[58] The Cid must therefore cry because it is important that his sadness be raised above the level of the constituent ambiguity of *this world* and seen, as God might see it, in all its purity. And that of course is only the beginning. What must be further understood is that the absence of an interior, therefore, private sphere is dependent upon the substantial nature of feudal signs or, to be more exact – for here it is vitally important to make the necessary distinctions – of *signatures*, understood as traced by the voice of the Lord: '... within the feudal horizon everyone "knew" who was a noble and who was not, who was a serf and who was not'.[59]

Perforce, the ideological role of 'tears' underwent a transformation under the impact of animism, the ideology of the emerging bourgeoisie. Evidence to that effect has already emerged with respect to Garcilaso's eighth sonnet, which we analysed above. To recall, in his sadness and frustration, Apollo continues to water with his tears the vegetable spirit, otherwise the laurel tree, into which the interiorised spirit of Daphne has been transformed.

---

57   *Poema* 1972, line 1.
58   Rodríguez 2002, p. 159.
59   Ibid., p. 159.

Aquel que fue la causa de tal daño
a fuerza de llorar, crecer hacía
este árbol, que con lágrimas regaba.
    ¡Oh miserable estado, oh mal tamaño
que con llorarla crezca cada día
la causa y la razón por que lloraba![60]

(He who was the cause of such harm, / by dint of crying, caused to grow /
this tree, that he watered with his tears. / Oh, miserable state! How great
the misfortune / that the tears spilt on its account each day should com-
pound / the cause of and reason for the crying.)

The key to the workings of such a sonnet is the 'dialectic of tears' – Rodríguez's
phrase – enacted in the soul's failed attempt to unite with the loved object;
tears that, in radical contrast to their substantial, organicist counterpart, are
constructed 'as pure, direct secretions of the inner spirit'.[61] But a word of warning: the modern reader who too readily identifies with the erotic dynamic being
enacted in the sonnet is much deceived. In fact, the dangers of misrecognition
are far greater here than was the case with the epic text. Let it be emphasised:
these are not the tears of the sensitive subject of Romantic, petty-bourgeois
extraction, but of the animist sensible soul, through whose transparency the
Soul of the World finds expression. Together with 'sighs', tears so configured
externalise the frustration of the soul, whose love finds no exit from a newly
created but still embryonic interior realm.[62] Consider another example.

Si quejas y lamentos pueden tanto
que enfrenaron el curso de los ríos,
y en los diversos montes y sombríos
los árboles movieron con su canto;
    Si convirtieron a escuchar su llanto
los fieros tigres y peñascos fríos;
si, en fin, con menos casos que los míos
bajaron a los reinos del espanto:
    ¿por qué no ablandará mi trabajosa
vida en miseria y lágrimas pasada,
un corazón comigo endurecido?

60   Garcilaso 1989, pp. 58–9.
61   Rodríguez 2002a, p. 148.
62   Ibid., p. 196.

Con más piedad debria ser escuchada
la voz del que se llora por perdido
que la del que perdió y llora otra cosa.[63]

(If keens and laments are able / to halt the flow of rivers, / and if the different mountains and shady trees / are moved by his song; / if are gathered
to listen to his crying / the wild tigers and cold rocks; / if, finally, with less
motive than mine / he descended into the kingdoms of fear: / why will not
my laborious / life passed in misery and tears / soften a heart hardened
against me? / With greater pity should be listened to / a voice that cries
for being lost / than one that lost and cries for another.)

The tears, in this case those of Orpheus, are thwarted in their attempt to flow:
movement is of their essence – hence the reference to rivers, hence also the
frustration which is experienced when tears 'freeze' or when, as in the present
case, they are blocked by the 'hardness' of another's heart and fail to find
expression. Ideally, they would mingle and fuse with the 'Soul of the World' that
manifests itself in the mountains, trees, and wild creatures. The cosmological
dimensions are not to be missed: gone is the static hierarchy of lineages and
'blood' – rungs in a vertical Chain of Being that accords to each object its natural niche in the Creation – in favour of a new ideology, which arrives to grease
the workings of an emergent capitalist mercantilism, against the backdrop of a
heliocentric system in which all things are bound together by the all-pervasive
spiritual force of the Sun's rays.

We now begin to grasp *in practice* the importance of the theoretical concepts
constitutive of the Althusserian problematic. For as Rodríguez had argued at
length, even before entering upon the detailed analysis of the Petrarchan lyric,
it was the conflict between the feudal and capitalist modes that explains the
dominance of the political level during the transition and, just as importantly,
its *autonomy*, materialised in the Absolutist State and *determined* in the last
instance by the economy: 'In both cases, the constitution of the political level
as autonomous and dominant is symptomatic of the tendency, within social
relations, for bourgeois relations to dominate feudal ones'.[64] The existence of
a *public* space, the Spaniard goes on to argue, implies, as a corollary, that of
its *private* equivalent, otherwise the interiorised realm of the beautiful soul. At
which point, distinctions become of the greatest importance: the claim is not

---

63   Vega 1989, pp. 60–1.
64   Rodríguez 2002a, p. 6.

that social transformations of a generalised kind *directly* caused the birth of lyric poetry; still less that there are no connections between the general and the particular; Rodríguez is rather arguing for the existence of *structural mediations* between the political instance and the otherwise remote realm of lyric poetry, even as he recognises the relative autonomy of the respective levels. Thus: '... although it "believes" absolutely in the division between private and public, animism presupposes, through its own internal logic, the existence of a special transparency between the "inside" and "outside" of signs only in those cases in which the soul is able truly to express itself in each thing'.[65]

7   Postmodernism and the End of Ideology

The Political Unconscious carries through several important theoretical displacements. The first we have already had occasion to consider, namely that from economics in the last instance – a concept of classically Althusserian extraction – to that of politics in the last instance. But, in the present context, it is a second displacement that is of more interest, namely that from ideology to politics. Interestingly, in this case, Jameson feels called upon to 'explain himself'. Many of the findings of *The Political Unconscious*, he confesses, could well have been expressed more forcefully in a Marxist 'manual', that 'would have as its object *ideological analysis*'[66] and that would thereby require that he 'settle its accounts with rival methods in a far more polemic spirit'.[67] Such a prospect clearly does not appeal to Jameson in the slightest, notwithstanding his artful appeal to Althusser's lemma of 'class struggle within theory'.[68]

The more cynically minded might argue that the substitution of an etiolated 'politics' for the marked category of 'ideology' could only have served one purpose: to avoid a term whose use, within the precincts of a conservative academy, could only have signalled a damaging allegiance to Marxism.[69] Even so, as the political tide began to turn decisively against the Left in the 1980s, Jameson was forced to make a further reformist concession by actively disowning 'ideology' altogether. The latter, we are informed, in *Postmodernism* (1991),

---

65   Ibid., p. 161.
66   Jameson 1981, p. 12.
67   Ibid.
68   Ibid.
69   An early review of *The Political Unconscious*, by Jerry Aline Flieger (Flieger 1982), symptomatically carries the title 'The Prison-House of Ideology'. The implication, surely, is that Jameson has misnamed his work.

no longer provides the key social function it formerly exercised; indeed, it may now be legitimate to speak of the 'end of ideology', understood in the sense of '*conscious* ideologies and political opinions', which is to say, more strictly, understood as constitutive of 'thought systems' or official philosophical ideologies. Jameson elaborates: '... the whole realm of *consciousness*, argument, and the very appearance of persuasion itself (or reasoned dissent) – has ceased to be functional in perpetuating and reproducing the system'.[70]

The convenience of limiting ideology to *consciously held ideas* should be obvious: such reductionism leaves a space open, that of the unconscious, to be occupied by a less provocative concept: no longer politics but 'culture', sometimes to be celebrated in its postmodern guise, sometimes to be critiqued, but which, in either instance, now permeates the entire social fabric in the familiar guise of a Hegelian Spirit. Ideology, to be sure, will make an occasional appearance as an unconscious force, as when, in *The Seeds of Time*, in its postmodern guise, it is portrayed as a 'symptom of the deeper structural changes in our society', rooted in the dominant mode of production.[71] But for the most part, it remains an eminently conscious phenomenon and therefore surplus to explanatory requirements, replaced by a culture that, among other things, serves as a convenient bridge over which to pass from Hegel to Marx. The cultural forces involved are those that relate to commercialised practices and habits, in other words, to commodification, through the latter's capacity to 'colonise' the libidinal unconscious.[72] The reference, note, is to the distinctively *libidinal* unconscious: once the complex intervening layers of the Althusserian structure in dominance have been stripped away, little remains but for the Hegelian Moving Spirit to impregnate this unconscious directly, through the operations of an expressive causality.

The psychical effects of commodification are, it must be conceded, only too real and their pertinence to any Americanised culture undeniable, except that, as Terry Eagleton observed apropos Jameson's work, the focus upon reification redirects attention away from class conflict and the material realities of the process of production towards consumption, notably of literary texts, and the quality of *lived experience* under capitalism.[73] This emphasis upon 'lived experience', it will transpire, is the key to Jameson's notion of the unconscious. With the Real pressed, in Lacanian terms, beyond the bounds of language, confined within the realm of the unknowable, it becomes difficult, if not impossible, to

---

70   Jameson 1991, p. 398, emphasis added.
71   Jameson 1994, p. xii.
72   Jameson 2002, p. 12.
73   Eagleton 1986, p. 63.

pass from the study of commodified forms to infrastructural dynamics.[74] With one unavoidable consequence: cut off from the material base, notably from the relations of production, Marxism, as a science dedicated to the analysis of class conflict, is a dead letter.

A hasty reading of Jameson's more recent texts might lead one to conclude that the critic has finally relieved himself of the burden of the Marxist hermeneutic. But not so: the relevant conceptual framework is equipped for all weathers, and when, following the global crisis of 2008, the wind began to blow from a different quarter, Jameson was quick to respond with *Representing Capital*, a work that significantly qualifies some of his earlier claims. While capitalism, in its complexity, continues to be *unrepresentable*, theoretically speaking, it was never Jameson's intention, or so he now assures us, to imply that it was *ineffable*, like some kind of mystery located beyond language and thought. And unsurprisingly, after having consistently dismissed Althusserianism as 'somewhat outmoded',[75] with its 'extinguished' canon,[76] Jameson now wishes to emphasise 'what is still stimulating, suggestive, and even urgent about this unfinished theoretical business';[77] and so, quite soon, is discovering, after a close reading of *Capital*, that Marx's text 'seems retroactively to confirm Althusser's insistence on system rather than subject'.[78] The effect of such vacillations and contradictions, habitual throughout Jameson's texts, is to prohibit conclusions of any kind: no tidal waters can be found to compare to these shifting sands.

8   The Melodrama of Tears: Jorge Isaacs's 'María'

Animist ideology was driven underground in the seventeenth century, only to re-emerge in a petty-bourgeois guise in the following, in which form it functioned, and would continue to function, as the underside to the classic form of bourgeois ideology. The latter found its most forceful expression in the sensualism of Lock and Hume, the characteristic feature of which was its emphasis upon the strictly physical, to the exclusion of the moral. The petty-bourgeois tradition takes its cue from the philosophies of Rousseau and Kant, which, in contrast to those of their empirical counterparts, are full of spiritual and moral content. According to Rodríguez and Álvaro Salvador, in their *Introduc-*

---

74   Jameson 2009, p. 334.
75   Jameson 1991, p. 345.
76   Jameson 1994, p. 167.
77   Jameson 2009, p. 337.
78   Jameson 2012, p. 40.

ción al estudio de la literatura hispanoamericana, this characteristically 'melo-dramatic' tradition serves as a 'transmission belt' along which are conveyed the values of the dominant classes to the dominated, values that – and this is the crucial point – are lived *unconsciously* by the dominated, 'as something opposed to their real, material conditions of existence'.[79] The goodness, the idealised love, the fraternity, the filial love, the beauty, the religious sentiment, are human qualities that can freely cross social barriers and so mould the pro-letarians, peasants, indigenous elements and other marginal groups into the category of 'the people'. As the same authors elaborate:

> The dominating classes have a vested interest in speaking of the 'people' because this term shrouds them in a curtain of equality, but they do so indirectly, so as to make the curtain appear more credible, through the mediation of petty-bourgeois ideologues. The latter do sincerely believe in the existence of the 'people', precisely through being where they are, namely perched between one class and another; perched insofar as not identifying fully with either class but with both simultaneously.[80]

In Latin America, the result of such 'populism' was a social 'utopianism', the most immediate symptom of which was a 'lachrymose' thematic that found expression in the 'sentimental novel'. The classic of the genre is Jorge Isaacs' *María* (1867). By way of illustration, let us consider the following passage, in which its protagonist, Efraín, agonises over his love for his beloved.

> I went to bed when it struck two in the same clothes I was wearing. María's handkerchief, still fragrant with the perfume that she always used, crumpled and wet with her tears, received on the pillow the tears that rolled from my eyes as from a fountain that would never run dry.
> If those that I still spill, on recalling the days that preceded my journey, serve to moisten this pen that records them; if it were possible once more, even for a single moment, for my mind to discover in my heart the extent of my secret pain, so as to reveal it, the lines that I am going to trace would be beautiful for those who have cried, but perhaps terrible for me.[81]

The plot of the novel is as follows. Efraín, the son of a rich, learned landowner, also poet, and María, cousin of Efraín, live an intensely idealised, chaste rela-

---

79   Rodríguez and Salvador 1987, p. 136.
80   Ibid., p. 137.
81   Isaacs 1988, p. 284.

tionship amid an idyllic setting in Colombia, until María, of Jewish extraction, is stricken with a fatal, inherited illness and dies before Efraín is able to return from his studies in Europe. The social order that functions as the backdrop to events consists of a variety of levels, each disposed in their allotted place, the whole pervaded by the paternalism of Efraín's family and redolent of a regime that is at the same time neo-colonial and pre-capitalist. The novel is pervaded by a lachrymose sensibility that finds its most condensed expression in Efraín, the poet, and María, the sublimated personification of Poetry. 'The tears are transformed into an archetypal value in the context of a petty-bourgeois mentality, of the kind that manifests itself even in daily life'.[82] While, externally, literary activity had begun to be devalued – insofar as non-serious and non-productive – internally, at the level of sensibility, 'the poetic condition is the most elevated because it constitutes the maximum realisation of the spirit'.[83] The refinement of the protagonists and their immediate family is further enhanced through the contrast drawn between it and the vulgarity and shallowness of another well-to-do family, namely that of the frivolous Carlos, who plays the role of the anti-Efraín.

Below the level of the aristocracy are to be found the white peasants and mountain folk, exemplified by José, Braulio and Tránsito, who are the recipients of Efraín's paternalism; and below these the 'mulatos', followed in turn by the blacks. Such is the make-up of a transitional social order that, its discrete elements notwithstanding, is promoted as a totality, without fissures, without breaks, without discontent, in which everything occupies its divinely appointed place. Efraín 'treats María with all the clichés typical of an aristocratic, gallant culture, typical of the "animism" that begins with Petrarch, at the same time that the text itself intensifies the purely abstract, ideological values of the idolatry of which his beloved is the object'.[84] The tragedy of María's premature death further serves, masochistically, to display Efraín's sensibility to its full potential. There can be no catharsis, no heart-rending *furore*; only the sublimated release of emotional tension through the medium of tears.

9   Conclusion

Through the figures of Jameson and Rodríguez, we have been able to compare and contrast two cognate concepts: the political unconscious and the

---

82   Rodríguez and Salvador 1987, p. 133.
83   Ibid., p. 141.
84   Rodríguez and Salvador 1987, p. 146.

ideological unconscious, both indebted to the work of Althusser but otherwise framed by two very different problematics, namely those of Hegelian Marxism and its Structural counterpart. Doubtless, important aspects of both writers remain to be considered.[85]

But, for our present purposes, the dichotomous nature of their relationship should by now be clear: on one side, the Hegelian variant, which takes as its point of departure the subject/object or agency/structure binary; on the other, the Structural variant that prioritises the social formation, structured on the basis of a mode of production.

The major problem to confront Jameson, when it came to theorising the political unconscious, was the centrality accorded to *consciousness* within the Hegelian paradigm. This centrality, predictably enough, encouraged him to gravitate towards the early Marx and the notion of alienation, in other words, towards 'Man', as explored in various major figures of Western Marxism. At the same time, he registered the strong sense in Marx of how structures of social relations shape human consciousness, which found him having constantly to negotiate the gulf that separated Marxism from Hegelianism. The resultant concentration on the fetishism of commodities, whatever its limitations, proved to be experientially amenable to the American academy and doubtless explains the continuing appeal of what was, by any standards, a dense and difficult body of work.

Rodríguez, by way of contrast, took as his point of departure the unconscious understood as the secretion of an ideological matrix, the latter determined in the last instance by the economy, which is to say mediated through the matrix effect of the social formation functioning as a whole. This encouraged him, predictably, to gravitate towards the late Marx and, specifically, towards *Capital*, which, like Althusser, he insisted on viewing as the authentic expression of Marxism. If the Spaniard did not begin with the concept 'Man', it was in order to break with the subject-centred ideology of which it constituted the nucleus. Like Althusser and, allegedly, Marx, he preferred to focus instead on the structural causes that maintains the illusion of the centrality of Man. For this displacement of the free subject from its position of eminence, the author of *Theory and History* was to pay a heavy price, namely the non-reception of his work within the academy and elsewhere; at which point his ideological unconscious finally connects with its libidinal equivalent: in both cases there are certain things that people just do not want to know.

---

85   See Caamaño for some insights into their respective treatments of Brecht (Caamaño 2008, pp. 142–56).

CHAPTER 5

Continuities and Discontinuities: Terry Eagleton

When I put the final period to this text that is now being re-edited, I understood that something decisive had begun in my work. The *alea jacta* was henceforth irreversible. So was my break with all earlier approaches: I literally threw them out into the street. (Juan Carlos Rodríguez)

A lot of my concerns run back to very early days and simply get rearticulated. There are shifts in my work but no dramatic breaks. (Terry Eagleton)

Far from minimising the role of the human subject, as is often claimed, Structural Marxism has always recognised this subject's internal, contradictory complexity. To Rodríguez, the task fell to trace its historical production, from its origins in the bosom of an otherwise 'subjectless' *substantialism*, the dominant ideology of feudalism, through its constitution as a 'beautiful soul' – the lynchpin of bourgeois ideology in its first, transitional stage – and thence to the classic (empiricist, Kantian, and Hegelian) formulations of the Enlightenment and beyond. The difference between Structural Marxism, on the one hand, and neo-liberalism and postmodernism, on the other, is that for the latter, human subjectivity is accepted as the basis of social theory, while for the former, the social structures and relations that produce social subject are primary. A Marxism that fails to 'break' with the priority accorded to the subject always runs the risk of regressing to bourgeois ideology and thence to a *libidinal unconscious* of Freudian/Lacanian provenance, the only form of the unconscious readily available within the limits of this ideology. Or so at least we will be arguing below.

Their fundamental differences notwithstanding, the ideological unconscious and libidinal unconscious, as varieties of the same species, exhibit a comparable paradoxical structure. In the case of the ideological unconscious, ideology, when viewed from within, lacks an *outside*, even as it determines our every action; like the air that surrounds us, it is at the same time invisible yet essential to our survival. In the case of the libidinal unconscious, the paradox lies in the fact that we are denied conscious knowledge of a repressed maternal object that unconsciously continues to condition our behaviour. There is one further feature shared by both forms of the unconscious: both Marxist science and psychoanalytic science pride themselves on being able to acquire knowledge of their respective subject matters, namely of the structural forces that determine our social practice, on the one hand, and of our personalised, individual development, on the other. But that is the last of the resemblances: to start from the notion of the social formation is to reject the existence of a 'human nature' that is prior to social being, other than in the form of a minimal genetic package; to start from the subject/object dichotomy, by way of contrast, is to assume the existence of a 'species being' that, its historic variations notwithstanding, precedes and transcends socialisation. Rodríguez is an exponent of the first position, Terry Eagleton, of the second, with radical consequences for their understanding, respectively, of the notion of the unconscious. We will be reviewing those consequences below. But our first task is to obtain some clarity regarding Althusser's position on the unconsciousness of ideology and the role within it played by the libidinal unconscious.

1   **Servants of the Lord**

The key to the 'break' executed by Althusser was the latter's insistence on the need to take as one's starting point for investigation not the subject/object opposition beloved of bourgeois ideology but the 'social formation', understood as a 'complex unity' of relatively autonomous instances – economic, political, and economic – each one of which exerts its own form of effectivity. In this light must be understood Rodríguez's break with his earliest theoretical formulations: 'I literally threw them out into the street'.[1] Doubtless his social circumstances favoured such radical measures: from his perspective, within a Fascist dictatorship, the layers of Catholic ideology under which he was buried were never conceivable as a solution to Spain's problems, only as part of them. Quite simply, one did not linger in social democracy, in whatever guise, but, rather, cut straight through to a revolutionary Marxism. Hence, *Theory and History* takes as its starting point not 'authors' and 'readers', conceptualised as 'subjects', confronting each other through the medium of the 'text', but the Althusserian social formation, as defined.

The focus in *Theory and History* will be upon the transition between feudalism and capitalism, with specific reference to Spain. Transitional formations exhibit their special peculiarities, as Rodríguez explains:

---

1   Rodríguez 2002a, pp. 32–3.

The forms of transition are characterised by a co-existence of modes of production, at the structural level, and consequently by a 'mixture', and therefore inevitably by a struggle, between the different types of social relations that co-exist in them. It is through this struggle that the dominance of the political level is imposed on the remaining elements of the absolutist social formation, so that the political level not only emerges as dominant, but at the same time ... constitutes itself as autonomous. Its material forms are either the Absolutist State or the various 'signorias', principalities, etc. of the Italian cities.[2]

The effectivity exerted ('in the last instance') by the economic instance on the social formation, according to standard Althusserian theory, determines, among other things, which of the instances, whether economic, political, or ideological, is dominant. Arguably, in the Middle Ages, it had been ideology; the transition, by way of contrast, involved a battle between two conflicting classes, a dominant nobility and an emergent bourgeoisie, which will be fought out within the framework of the Absolutist State, and hence will witness the dominance of the political. Rodríguez will further construe this battle, as it relates to Spain, as a struggle between two ideologies, *substantialism* or, as the Spaniard alternatively refers to it, *organicism*, the dominant ideology of feudalism, and *animism*, the emergent ideology of the bourgeoisie. We will be considering the nature of the latter below. Let us first turn our attention to substantialism.

The key to substantialism is its notion of the *organic body*, which in turn rests upon the notions of *substantial form* and *natural place*. Rodríguez explains: 'Throughout the whole history of feudalism, it was imagined – in accordance with the concept of substantial forms or qualities – that the world was composed of *organic signs*, such that the substance of the king was a reflection of the divine spirit and society could be conceived as an organic body and the estates or organisations as substantial bodies (like "corporations")'.[3] Under the feudal regime, the question of freedom never arises: to be a serf/servant is to be *bound* to a lord, hence to gravitate towards one's natural place, at the side of one's lord. To be an object is, similarly, to be traced by the presence or voice of the lord. Both serf and object function as 'signatures', integrated as ciphers into the World conceived along the lines of a Book. And books are there to be *read*, through the process of allegorical exegesis. To illustrate the finer details of this argument, let us return to the *Poem of the Cid*.

---

2   Ibid., pp. 35–6.
3   Ibid., p. 55.

In his capacity as a feudal lord, the Cid defines himself in terms of his noble *lineage*, understood as a direct reflection of the divine spirit. The repeated assertions as to his identity – 'Mio Çid', 'Ruy Diaz of Vivar', 'el Campeón' (Supreme Warrior), 'en buen hora çinxiestes espada' (who in the good hour girded his sword), etc. – are, accordingly, to be understood not as those of an internalised, privatised *'subject'* or *'individual'* – substantialism knows no such thing – but as those of a lord or noble, whose identity corresponds to his public persona: quite simply, the Cid *is* what he is, to the extent that even his clothing is to be understood 'substantially'. And the rest follows: the Cid's fate, for example, can be read, allegorically, in the flight of the crow that crosses his path as he rides into exile; like all destinies, his is pre-ordained, figurally speaking, insofar as, in the last instance, 'blood will out'.

> Blood, from its use to support the claims of lineage (in other words, the currently disputed legitimacy of the nobility) to its use in medical practice (the *bleedings* of which our literary works are full), a practice that leads, via the thematisation of seigneurial honor/blood, to that equally bloody inundation of the theatre and, in turn, to the need for vengeance (in the organicist sense of the *cleansing* of honor) by means that include bleeding.[4]

The Althusserian critic, then, sets off not from the 'subject' and 'object', assumed as universal, trans-historical categories, but from the opposition between the 'lord' and his 'vassal' or 'serf/servant', notions secreted by the historically localised set of social relations characteristic of feudalism. The *Poem of the Cid* is perfectly explicit in this respect: ¡Dios, que buen vassalo! ¡Si oviesse buen señor!'[5] [God! What a fine vassal! Would that he had such a good lord!]. These relations, we learn from the chronicle versions of the epic, were disturbed at an initial stage by a squabble over the collection of the King's tribute. Accused of having kept part of the tribute for himself, instead of surrendering it to his lord, the Cid is driven into exile. Doors are closed against him and provisions denied, on the orders of the king. As a nine-year old girl explains:

> ... anoch del entro su carta
> con grant recabdo   e fuerte mientre sellada.
> Non vos osariemos abrir   nin coger por nada;

---

4   Ibid.
5   *Poema* 1977, line 20.

si non, perderiemos   los averes e las casas
e demas   los ojos de las caras.[6]

(... last night a missive from him arrived / elaborately and safely sealed. / We should not dare to open our doors or receive you in any way; / otherwise, we would forfeit our belongings and homes / not to mention our eyes out of our faces.)

When first approached, the episode may seem to turn upon an opposition between the 'inside' of the homes of Burgos's inhabitants and their 'outside'. But in fact, appearances prove deceptive. As we have argued throughout, the only dichotomy that matters to substantialism is that which opposes the celestial to the terrestrial world. The contrast that the bard draws between the street and the house is not that between the private and public spheres. Modern writers, it is true, have been drawn to the elegiac possibilities of the exchange between the patriarchal warrior and the defenceless young girl, but for the twelfth-century bard, the richly interiorised realm of the privatised subject has still to be produced. The same goes for what might seem at first sight to be a fundamental distinction between the form and content of the King's message: perforce, the emphasis must fall upon the former, almost to the total exclusion of the latter: 'con grant recabdo e fuerte mientre sellada' (elaborately and safely sealed). The temptation to explain the King's threats in psychologistic terms is to be resisted – we warned earlier of the dangers of interpreting along sadistic lines what are in fact symptoms of a feudal demand that signs be raised, semantically, to the level of an Adamic purity.

Before it is challenged directly by a *lay* animism, of bourgeois provenance, feudal organicism is challenged *from within* by a *feudal* variation of the same, in the form of an Augustinian spiritualism. We do not have the space here to enter into the multiple forms this spiritualism would take.[7] Suffice it to signal the importance that they attach to an 'inner moral virtue', in the light of which it is no longer sufficient, if one is to be properly 'valorised', to be a good vassal, to possess a good lineage, to be brave in battle, and so on; the servant of his lady also needs to exhibit the chivalrous qualities associated with 'love'. Beyond this, Augustinianism runs up against the limits imposed by feudal relations. A distinctively *bourgeois* ideology will only take shape following a complete 'break' with the seigneurial notions of 'blood', 'nobility', etc. and the secretion of a new 'ideological matrix', that is to say, of an ideological field 'in which is

---

6 *Poema de Mio* Cid, lines 42–9.
7 For the details, see Rodríguez 2002a, p. 59 ff.

expressed the class conflict between the bourgeoisie and the nobility as the struggle between a "hierarchy of souls" and a "hierarchy of blood".[8] The souls in question constitute the proto-forms of the free, interiorised 'subjects' or 'individuals' of a liberal capitalism.

2   The Legacy of Catholicism

A casual perusal of *For Marx* should be enough to persuade anyone of the importance that its author attaches to locating ideology within the social formation, viewed as a complex totality, hence within the domain of unconsciousness. Yet, even as he stood poised on the brink of theorising the existence of an *ideological unconscious*, Althusser faltered. 'I believe that it is not possible to speak of an ideological unconscious', we saw him write above in a 'Letter to D',[9] even as, strange to say, he conceded the existence of the unconscious in question: 'In any event, that "unconscious" (which I would call by a different names, but never mind) exists, and *it should not be confused with the psychoanalytic unconscious*' (original italics). Whatever the reasons for such mystification, Rodríguez did not share them. Confronted by the reality of fascist ideology, in which 'servants' of the Lord continued to exist, ideologically, alongside bourgeois 'subjects', the Spaniard was ideally situated to theorise the radical historicity of ideology, and thence to arrive at a substantive notion of the 'ideological unconscious'. 'The notion of the subject (and the whole problematic within which it is inscribed)', he writes, 'is radically historical because … it derives directly (and exclusively) from the very matrix of the bourgeois ideological unconscious: the 'serf' can never be a "subject", etc.'[10] Each mode of production, according to this argument, secretes its own ideological matrix, within the context of which 'serfs', 'lords' and 'subjects' are *lived* as ontological realities. Fundamental to the feudal matrix was the opposition between this world and the next. Let us pause to tease out further the details of the argument.

Sustaining the dialectic between the perfect truth of the celestial sphere and imperfect truth of its terrestrial counterpart is the whole edifice of Aristotelian Scholastic philosophy. Medieval Scholasticism presupposes a direct union or reflexion between both spheres, along traditional lines, but with radical innovations. Thus, whereas all Christian thinkers before him had sought to explain

---

8   Rodríguez 2002a, p. 69.
9   Althusser 1996, p. 52.
10   Rodríguez 2002a, p. 10.

the effect by the cause, St Thomas Aquinas (1226–74) started with the effect; that is, instead of trying to explain God in transcendent terms, he began with what could be known from His creatures and the creation. The consequences merit close attention: '*appearances*' are not to be construed as a *lie*; a 'dream' they may well be, but a *real* dream. Hence the importance attributed under substantialism to 'saving appearances', as the means to gaining access to a veiled world; hence also the predominance of medieval hermeneutics, whose task it was to gloss the *signatures* or symbols of this world for their hidden meaning.[11]

The logic throughout was the same: just as objects were substantially embedded in the words that referred to them, so bodies were implicated in souls, hence were to be assumed as an irremediable necessity; indeed, even further, the Church itself and society in general were envisaged as an organic body, with its corresponding corporate, hierarchical structure.[12] Except that such an intellectual edifice was not without its problems. How was it possible to square the notion of the soul as a '*substantial form*' with the possibility of its *trans-substantiation*? Equally, to square the fusion of form and matter with the possibility of trans-formation, upon which the mystery of the Incarnation and the ritual of the Eucharist rested? How, in other words, was it possible for a substance that was impure and earthly to intermingle with one that was pure and divine? To these questions there could be only one answer, at least from the standpoint of substantialism: the Eucharist was the supreme miracle, the exception that proved the rule, through which the seemingly impossible was achieved.[13] The reformist movements, it goes without saying, had a different tale to tell.

To turn from Rodríguez to Terry Eagleton is to turn from a scholar who has already distanced himself, professionally speaking, from his Catholic heritage – existential enigmas did not fall within his Althusserian remit – to one who enlists Marxism with an eye to bolstering his Catholic faith and resolving problems internal to the latter, crucially those surrounding transubstantiation and the Eucharist. True, the author of *The Body as Language: Outline of a 'New Left' Theology* (1970) will sometimes address the dynamics of late capitalism, but his historical perspective is, overall, of the *figural* kind, which is to say trans-historical. Unsurprisingly, the distinctively *social* relations that, historically, secrete Catholic ideology never figure as part of *his* remit.

Somewhat predictably, the Marxist tradition upon which Eagleton draws is of the Hegelian variety, which prioritises the notion of *species being* as opposed

---

11   For a good overview of Scholasticism, see Leff 1958.
12   Rodríguez 2002a, p. 54 ff.
13   Rodríguez 2002a, p. 205.

to historically based modes of production. Herein is to be found the source of another fundamental difference between the two writers in question, and a far more significant one in the present context; for whereas Rodríguez, we have seen, takes the Althusserian notion of a social formation as his starting point, from which to theorise, among other things, the radical historicity of the subject/object opposition, Eagleton assumes the latter as an ontological reality, hence speaks unconsciously from a position internal to bourgeois ideology.

To such a perspective on Eagleton there may well appear to be an obvious objection. What about the notion of 'community' that the author of *The Body as Language* consistently promotes? Is this not directly opposed to the notion of bourgeois individualism? Well, yes, of course, it is, but that is precisely the point! Eagleton's 'community' is simply a variation upon 'society' and, as such, stands opposed to the promotion of the 'individual'. That he happens to prioritise 'community' is of merely localised interest, localised in the sense of internal to bourgeois ideology. The difference between a 'society' made up of 'individuals' and a social formation articulated along the feudal lines of an 'organic body' could not be greater: Eagleton focuses unremittingly upon a *public* sphere, as opposed to its *private* equivalent; substantialism, we saw above, knows no such distinction.

Perforce, Eagleton's approach to the Eucharist will prove to be conflictive. On the one hand, given the soul's irremediable attachment to a body rotten with sin, he must be able to account for the transubstantial process through which, as traditionally conceived, 'the substance of bread and wine becomes the substance of the body of Christ'.[14] On the other hand, for doctrinal reasons, he is alert to the threat posed to Catholicism by the advent of the nominalist *sign*, which, given its capacity to detach itself from its material body or, as Eagleton would have it, from its 'thwarting "facticity"',[15] is disposed to flaunt its conventional nature and hence to risk inflecting the Eucharist in the direction of Protestant reformism.

Homologous to the rise of nominalism is a process that is equally troubling to an organicist Catholicism whereby, under capitalism, exchange values have been progressively cut adrift from their use values.[16] Here also Eagleton is alert to the dangers of co-option by the 'liberal era of late capitalism', whose controlling assumptions, he concedes, are more deceptive for being invisible. Under their seemingly benign influence, theology readily assumes the guise of a flexible, open-ended progressivism that, carefully considered, 'reproduces

---

14   Ibid., p. 36.
15   Ibid, p. 39.
16   Ibid., pp. 21–2.

precisely the civilised yet impotent conscience of a conservative society'.[17] But it is one thing to advert to such complicities and quite another to resist their insidious, unconscious attraction: *The Body as Language* cannot finally 'break' with bourgeois ideology and the individual/society opposition upon which it rests because, like theological progressivism, it is always already complicit with this opposition and with activities, notably those relating to usury, that it would otherwise critique.

3   Radical Historicity: the Case of the Theatre

Throughout the late 1960s and early '70s, Eagleton struggled to reconcile the conflicting traditions of Catholicism, Lukácsian Marxism, and Raymond Williams's 'Culture and Society', while also being concerned to meet the graduate requirements of a conservative British academy.[18] Over the same period, on the evidence of *Theory and History* and his own doctoral thesis, Rodríguez was busy steeping himself in the works of Kant, Hegel, the British empiricists and their phenomenological and positivist successors, while familiarising himself with the basic principles of Althusserian Marxism.[19] The respective positions of the two scholars and the differences between them are best appreciated by comparing their work on the theatre. Let us begin by considering Rodríguez's contribution.

To describe the Cid as coinciding with his *public* persona, we suggested above, is deceptive insofar as, in the absence of a private sphere, as typically under feudalism, it is impossible to speak of a distinctively *'public'* domain. From which it follows, among other things, that there can be no such thing as a medieval theatre. The mystery plays that appear in the literary anthologies so categorised are, strictly speaking, a species of religious ritual; to charge a fee for the privilege of entry would have been as unthinkable as charging for participation in mass. But more is required for the appearance of the theatre than the mere existence of a public realm. As Rodríguez warns: 'The stage is ... the representation of the public as such, for which reason it illustrates the systematics and the actual problematisation of this sphere: its values, its struc-

---

17   Ibid., p. 95.
18   He confesses to treating his Ph.D. 'purely instrumentally, as an academic exercise' (Eagleton and Beaumont 2009, p. 68).
19   See *Theory and History* (2002a, pp. 125 ff.) and *Para una teoría de la literatura* (2015). The latter is, confessedly, a reconstituted version of Rodríguez's doctoral thesis.

ture, its conflicts'.[20] We are talking, in other words, about the 'representation of the public', which is to say of *politics*, conceived as an autonomous realm. And to talk of politics, in the case of the transition from feudalism to capitalism, is to talk of the rise of the Absolutist State.

The tendency of British Marxist historians has been to attribute the rise of absolutism to an extension of feudalism. Hence Perry Anderson speaks of a *'redeployed and recharged apparatus of feudal domination*, designed to clamp the peasant masses back into their traditional social position'.[21] The result is a curious *non sequitur*, for while feudalism, we are assured, was itself an effect of the 'catastrophic collision of two dissolving anterior modes of production – primitive and ancient',[22] the same cannot be said of the rise of absolutism, which was 'never an arbiter between the aristocracy and the bourgeoisie, still less an instrument of the nascent bourgeoisie against the aristocracy'.[23] To what, then, does it owe its existence? Only, it seems, to the defensive instincts of a threatened nobility. Rodríguez begs to disagree: 'That the nobility should dominate "in" the functioning of this state is, in fact, what is least important. The vital thing is that such functioning actually *exists* and that the nobility cannot *control* it, cannot make it change'.[24] True, the dominant thematics of the state, therefore of the Spanish *comedia* as of Elizabethan drama, turn upon the seigneurial, therefore eminently feudal, preoccupations of 'honour' and 'blood'. But while the nobility dominates the public sphere, 'it dominates in "molds" that *are not its own*, in the strictest sense: it dominates the theatrical thematic but it does not control the basic epistemology (just as in the same way it dominates politics, but cannot avoid the existence of the Absolutist State in its private/public function)'.[25] And crucial to the latter function was the emergence of the 'beautiful soul', otherwise the proto-form of the bourgeois subject. To elaborate further, we must resume the thread of our earlier discussion.

A distinctively *feudal* animism, it will be recalled, was superimposed upon the feudal dynamic of 'blood', to generate a religion of 'love', based on the notion of an *inner moral* virtue. This blend of eroticism and chivalrous honour will in turn receive the impress of the Platonic notion of the soul, with transformative consequences. In the words of Rodríguez, whose argument we are following

---

20   Rodríguez 2002a, p. 46.
21   Anderson 1974, p. 18.
22   Anderson 2013, p. 128.
23   Anderson 1974, p. 18.
24   Rodríguez 2002a, p. 47.
25   Ibid., p. 48.

closely: '... the privileged soul was stripped of any organicity and therefore ceased to be bound to any particular state'.[26] The same process is registered within the strictly religious ambit, but with a difference: Christian animism continues to abhor the flesh and, hence, to think in terms of a 'leap', from this world to the next, through which to fuse with the Absolute. The distinctively *secular* brand of Platonism, by way of contrast, rests upon the notion of the 'Soul of the World', the beauty of which pervades the totality of the creation, including *this* world. We are talking here of a distinctive 'break': gone is the notion of the corrupt body; installed in its place is the spiritualised body, in evidence in the 'Renaissance' cult of nudity. What is the nude but a body that is no longer tied to its substantial form? Cosmically, the same spiritualisation takes the form of a Copernican cult of numbers and ciphers.

The rise of this lay brand of animism, Rodríguez insists, is symptomatic of fundamental shifts at the level of social relations, shifts that it is perilously easy to ignore, given the primacy of the nobility within the public sphere. The theatre is exemplary in this respect. The thematic obsession with 'blood', 'vengeance' and 'honour' notwithstanding, the fact remains that for the public, therefore theatrical, space to come into being, the servile, vassalic relations of the feudal mode of production must have given way to the 'free' relations characteristic of the new mercantilism.[27] The same applies with respect to professional *actors*: their very existence is proof in itself of the extent to which the notion of substantial identities, in which body and soul are inextricably conjoined, has ceded ground to the animist notion of a body that can be detached from matter.

The ramifications of Rodríguez's argument are not to be missed, as regards, for example, the wearing of masks and disguises. Under feudal jurisdiction, it will be recalled, both were only permissible on the day of the Carnival, this being the only occasion on which signs were deemed to be non-substantial. Compare, by way of contrast, the sheer malleability permitted to characters in such Shakespearean plays as *As You Like It* and *A Midsummer Night's Dream*. What greater confirmation could one have of the extent to which animist attitudes to transvestism had been able to subvert the prevailing substantial notions of the organic body? What greater evidence of the 'sympathy' that, allegedly, bound together the things of this world, of a Platonic desire that could cancel out the differences between things and restore them to their original unity in the Soul of the World?

---

26   Ibid., p. 61.
27   Rodríguez 2002a, pp. 85–7.

Of course, animism itself was obliged to make concessions of its own. We are dealing, it should never be forgotten, with the co-existence of two mutually conflicting modes of production, more specifically, with a dominant feudalism and an emergent mercantile capitalism. The nobility, we have emphasised, control the 'content' of the theatre. But that by no means marks the limit of its dominance: substantialism also imposes its norms on the functioning of the theatre as a material ideological state apparatus; norms that, for example, prohibited the wearing of theatrical attire off the stage. The substantial logic is unforgiving: clothing was deemed to be substantial; hence to be dressed as the King was, potentially, to lay claim to *being* the King, in other words, to court an accusation of treason.

The same reasoning lies behind the prohibition of the use of female actors on the Elizabethan stage. In this case, the determining factor is the nobility's refusal to recognise the existence of an independent, relatively autonomous public sphere, other than in the guise of *this world*, with its unavoidable connotations of corruption. Hence the pall of suspicion attached to all *mundane* professions. Of the latter, acting was the original prototype, just as the stage was the prototype of the public space. And so, the logic unfolds: any woman who appeared on the public stage was *ipso facto* to be classified as a *public* woman, which is to say, as a prostitute.[28]

Important concessions, then, that testify to the nobility's continuing dominance of the Absolutist State, yet mere concessions, for all that, to be acknowledged with a proviso: in laying down its rules and regulations, organicist ideology is already conceding defeat over the only thing that matters, namely the very existence of a public/private distinction.[29]

4   The Individual and Society

In a recent interview, Matthew Beaumont criticises Eagleton's *Shakespeare and Society* (1967) for its ahistoricity and quizzes its author as to why he failed to 'ground' his work in the 'origins of capitalism'. Eagleton confesses, by way of

---

28   We are talking here, it is important to emphasise, about the Elizabethan stage. The Spanish theatre, by way of contrast, permitted women actors, although, contrary to what is sometimes claimed, for anything but progressive reasons. Rodríguez explains: 'Organicism [...], which views substantiality and honor as fundamental, is relatively indifferent to "sex"' (Rodríguez 2002a, p. 85).

29   For an application of Rodríguez's concepts to the figure of Don Juan, see Read 1998, pp. 51–90.

response, to 'not having enough historical knowledge'.[30] In truth, a good deal more was required than historical grounding before Eagleton could break with the 'Culture and Society' tradition that, as Beaumont further suggests, framed Eagleton's first contribution to 'lit crit'. Of course, all of us have to begin somewhere, and Eagleton is certainly not to be blamed for beginning where he did. In the absence of a British sociology, as a recognised discipline, and given the singularly effete state of British philosophy, he perforce gravitated, along with many other students, towards one of the few sites within the British academy where, at the time, theoretical research of the relevant kind could be conducted. Moreover, given his prior attachment to a radical Catholicism, it should come as no surprise that the young post-graduate student should attach himself to its secular equivalent, namely the Left-Leavisite criticism associated with the name of Raymond Williams.

To remind ourselves, Williams was at the time attempting to steer a mid-course between a 'good deal of history' that prioritised the 'base' components of society, namely economics and politics, and its idealistic inversion, in the form of a free-floating literature, art, philosophy, etc. His aim, more positively, was to work his way towards a cultural analysis that restored 'activities' to a 'genuine parity'.[31] He concludes: 'I would then define the theory of culture as the study of the relationship between elements in a whole way of life'.[32] What might seem, at first sight, to be a formulation not too far removed from the 'complex unity' of the Althusserian social formation turns out, on closer inspection, to be nothing of the kind. The key to their difference lies in the importance that *The Long Revolution* attaches to the opposition between the 'subject' and 'object', inflected in the direction of the former; hence also in the direction of specific 'activities' and a sense of the ways in which these activities 'combined into a way of thinking and living'.[33] In the last analysis, everything depends upon the centrality of individual 'experience'.

The transition from his youthful Catholicism to 'Culture and Society', it follows, committed Eagleton to nothing as radical as a 'break'; only to a relatively minor re-adjustment or, more exactly, a shift of emphasis from the 'organic

---

30   Eagleton and Beaumont 2009, p. 68. In his subsequent discussion of Eagleton's *William Shakespeare* (1986), Beaumont will again accuse its author of neglecting 'the important task of providing a historical and materialist reading of the plays' (Eagleton and Beaumont 2009, p. 201). Eagleton concedes that the charge was 'pretty just' and again confesses to lacking the 'necessary grounding'.

31   Williams 1965, pp. 61–3.

32   Ibid., p. 63.

33   Ibid.

body' of society to a secular materialism. The continuity lies in the relevant the-oretical categories: Shakespeare's plays are to be approached from the stand-point of the 'individual and society', with an eye to their 'contemporary signi-ficance', as this relates to 'our own experience'.[34] The effect is to cast History into a Neverland, in which the personal, spontaneous life of the individual is stunted by oppressive structures of society or, alternatively, in which a sense of community is undermined by an assertive individualism. Eagleton, it is true, will be searching from the outset for a 'new way of looking at both individual and society, a new kind of synthesis',[35] but strictly as this relates to contempor-ary, twentieth-century social dilemmas.

The critical undertaking to project the public/private distinction onto a Greek society, as portrayed in *Troilus and Cressida*, was always likely to strain credulity – historically speaking, after all, this society prioritised the (public) forum over the domestic space of slaves and women. The same could not be said of those plays of Shakespeare that deal with contemporary themes. Seventeenth-century society, we have seen, witnessed the materialisation of a private sphere, as the objective correlate to its public equivalent. Eagleton, it follows, experiences relatively little difficulty in re-drawing a fundamental distinction between those characters who define themselves in terms of social service and others who are motivated by individual concerns, between, say, in the case of *Hamlet*, the likes of Osric, whose primary allegiance is to 'your lord-ship', and Hamlet himself, who attends primarily to his 'innermost part' and his private love for Ophelia.[36] That said, what is lost here, as throughout Eagleton's analysis, is the fact that the 'service' rendered by Osric is that of a serf/servant to his Lord/lord, and that Hamlet's love for Ophelia is that of a newly emergent interiorised beautiful soul or proto-subject.

Eagleton is too intelligent a critic and, we would concede, too aware of the claims of historical materialism, not to sense the dangers posed by his focus upon the seemingly trans-historical tension between the spontaneous life of the individual and the communitarian demands of society. History makes its demands, and these are to be respected: it could never be a ques-tion of a *mechanical* updating of Shakespeare, the author of *Shakespeare and Society* concedes, or of *reducing* his plays to an abstraction.[37] But what will never be contested is the act of updating itself, as if historical differences were obstacles to be removed, so as to allow the subject/reader *immediate* access to

---

34   Eagleton 1967, pp. 9–10.
35   Ibid., p. 11.
36   Ibid., pp. 39 ff.
37   Ibid., p. 177.

the object/text. Similarly, key concepts such as 'individual' and 'society' must be sufficiently abstract to bestride the centuries. And here, finally, is the crunch: to aim at achieving a 'new kind of synthesis' between the 'individual' and 'society' is one thing; to break with, even to problematise, the dichotomy itself, is something else entirely, something inconceivable within the boundaries of bourgeois ideology and, one might add, British Marxism.

5   Transitional Ideologies

A conceptual abyss separates Eagleton's theoretical model from the terms in which Rodríguez frames his notion of the ideological unconscious. Crucially, as we have seen, the Spaniard's formulation pitches the ideological unconscious at the trans-individual level of the social formation and, by the same token, relocates the notion of the subject in its historical matrix. Hence, in the case of the *Poem of the Cid*, we posed the existence of a work in which the private sector is functionally embryonic insofar as limited to the domestic space of women and children: the Cid's wife and his daughters figure only marginally in the military world of the knight. To move from this eminently feudal work to a transitional text is to be struck immediately by the radical distinction in evidence in the latter between the 'house' and the 'street'. I propose to follow Rodríguez in focusing, by way of illustration, upon the picaresque novel, *Lazarillo de Tormes* (1554) and, more specifically, upon the episode of the *escudero* or squire.

The nub of the Althusserian argument is as follows: to assume, as bourgeois critics are wont to do, that the relevant characters are psychological 'individuals' seeking to negotiate their way through 'society' is to take a false step at the outset; objectively considered, Lazarillo is a servant to a master, the latter a member of the lesser nobility, both struggling to survive in the new transitional (dis)order of sixteenth-century Spain. To take the case, firstly, of the squire: although obliged to operate in terms of the division, imposed by the bourgeoisie, between the public and private spheres, as a feudal relic of an aristocratic caste he is at ease in neither. The house he rents – the market is now a reality to be reckoned with – is as an empty space, literally devoid of all the trappings of domesticity, including tables and chairs. Rodríguez elaborates: '... the "walls" are the sign of privacy, and privacy is the sign of the specific realm of bourgeois "economic" relations: mercantile, family, etc.'[38] This is neither the

---

38   Rodríguez 2001b, p. 158.

domain of the feudal master nor the private space of a bourgeois individual. Perforce, the squire must cling to the public sphere, except that the street in which he struggles to keep up appearances can only be 'assumed' as 'this world', in which, on substantialist grounds, the 'saving of appearances' is vital: hence, the squire's obsessions about his dress and, above all, with 'the black thing that they call honour'[39]

While, like the squire, Lazarillo is a marginalised figure, he is, unlike the squire, perfectly equipped to survive in the 'modern' world and, moreover, to flourish in it. His is an eye that *sees the thing* in all its literalness – the squire, for example, as a 'rich' man – at least, for the most part. The qualification is important: given his dependency upon his lord, the servant is also drawn into the substantial ideology of feudalism, as demonstrated by the incident of the funeral procession: on overhearing it suggested that the corpse was to be taken to 'the sad, unhappy house, to the gloomy, dark house, to the house in which nobody eats or drinks',[40] Lazarillo assumes the destination to be his master's abode, and rushes home to inform him of such. Traditional critics have, of course, cut straight through to analyse the *picaro* in 'psychological' terms, as a case study. But Rodríguez is emphatic:

> It should be a question rather of seeking an angle that might reveal the objective determination of the episode within the productive dialectic peculiar to the text. That is, the 'schematic' unconscious through which Lazarillo 'lives' the dominant situations in general and, in this specific case, the 'schematic unconscious' with which he assumes the latent 'organicism' of the squire, the organicism to which the lad has decided to surrender so totally after his initial doubts.[41]

Given his social situation, we are given to understand, Lazarillo is ideologically bilingual, in the sense that he can slip, unconsciously, from animism to substantialism without too much difficulty.

Similarly, from Rodríguez's standpoint, we would commit an error of judgement if we were to approach the question of the authorship of *Lazarillo* from a *psychological* standpoint. To emphasise: while the dominant animism is mediated through the 'author', the author is not its source. Rodríguez explains: 'The claim is not that there exists a "neutral" kind of narrative information; rather

39   *Lazarillo de Tormes* 1987, p. 159.
40   Ibid., p. 170.
41   Rodríguez 2001b, p. 171.

that the work possesses an objective structure, based on animist logic, irrespective of the degree of consciousness/unconsciousness, of intentionality or lack of intentionality, that, in this particular case, the author displays with respect to the animist logic that suffuses him'.[42] More to the point is the narrative's mediation through the figure of the narrator, Lazarillo, who performs a double function, firstly, that of exposing the tangible presence of a new world order, as *seen* from the perspective of animism, and, secondly, that of demonstrating what it *feels* like to *live* this presence, crucially, what it is to feel *free* and to be in charge of one's own destiny. For its part, substantialism manages to persist – Lazarillo's master is its living embodiment – but precariously so: it dissipates at the slightest touch of the new real; significantly, when his creditors appear on the scene and demand a payment of twelve or thirteen *reales*, the squire is nowhere to be found.

6   Power versus Exploitation

Eagleton is perfectly explicit as to the source of his own key notion of a 'possible consciousness', as deployed in *Myths of Power* (1975):

> I take the phrase from Lukács and Goldmann, to suggest those restrictions set on the consciousness of a historical period which only a transformation of real social relations could abolish – the point at which the most enterprising imagination presses against boundaries which signify not mere failures of personal perception but the limits of what can be historically said.[43]

The social emphasis undeniably raises the spectre of an ideological unconsciousness: Lukács, to remind ourselves, talks revealingly of a class-consciousness that, 'on the objective side', is tantamount to a 'class-conditioned *unconsciousness*'.[44] Moreover, when, in Eagleton, the social emphasis is enhanced still further, the limit on what is ideologically feasible or imaginable threatens to assume the proportions of an Althusserian 'break'. But only briefly: the dialectic of consciousness binds Eagleton to Williams's 'structure of feeling' like some umbilical cord, which at this point the budding Marxist is still in no position to cut. Not quite.

---

42   Ibid., p. 162.
43   Regan 1998, p. 58.
44   Lukács 1971, p. 52.

That Eagleton's Marxist turn should take a distinctively Lukácsian form should come as no surprise, given the importance attached to the Hungarian Marxist within the British tradition. Not that this tradition lacked for variations: thus, for example, whereas Perry Anderson and Tom Nairn promoted the notion of a collective 'self-consciousness', of a manifestly Hegelian-Lukácsian kind, E.P. Thompson, understood ideology in empiricist terms as simply a combination of 'ideas', whether political, religious, or scientific. Except that, by definition, these were but variations upon a common theme, namely the centrality of the subject. Anything else, within the parameters of the British social formation, was unthinkable, or so at least Rodríguez was arguing in *Theory and History*.[45] To remain within such parameters, the Althusserian further elaborated, however 'Marxist' one imagines oneself to be, was to fail to break with bourgeois ideology.

> The whole debate, it follows, needs a very different focus; and its questions have to be formulated within a different conceptual horizon. More concretely, it is important to recognise the *objectivity* of relations of production and of capitalist social relations (of production), and, by the same token, to recognise the latter's objectively bourgeois nature. This, in turn, will foreground the *objectivity* of the (unconscious) ideological level corresponding to these same bourgeois social relations.[46]

To illustrate briefly what form such a theoretical reconfiguration might take, let us focus upon the following passage from *Wuthering Heights*.

> 'A good heart will help you to a bonny face, my lad', I continued, 'if you were a regular black; and a bad one will turn the bonniest into something worse than ugly. And now that we've done washing, and combing, and sulking – tell me whether you don't think yourself rather handsome? I'll tell you, I do. You're fit for a prince in disguise. Who knows but your father was Emperor of China, and your mother an Indian queen, each of them able to buy up, with one week's income, Wuthering Heights and Thrushcross Grange together? And you were kidnapped by wicked sailors and brought to England. Were I in your place, I would frame high notions of my birth; and the thoughts of what I was should give me courage and dignity to support the oppressions of a little farmer'.[47]

---

45   Rodríguez 2002a, pp. 298–9.
46   Rodríguez 2002a, p. 301.
47   Brontë 2003, p. 84.

Eagleton's analysis takes the form of a running commentary that, although a perceptive example of its kind, clings to the literalness of the text, in the tradition of the 'lit crit' prevalent within the English-speaking academy. Heathcliff is a waif and orphan, who is inserted into a close-knit family unit 'as an alien'.[48] He appears out of an 'ambivalent domain of darkness', ambivalent because it is both 'fearful and fertilising'.[49] 'Stripped of determinate social relations', his is an intruding presence within the family, a presence that yet offers Cathy, as an individual, an opportunity of liberty from the constraining effect of society. 'He is, of course, proletarian in appearance, but the obscurity of his origins also frees him of any exact social role; as Nelly Dean muses later, he might equally be a prince',[50] etc. etc.

Of course, Eagleton will subsequently pull back from the immediacy of the text to elaborate upon its 'determinate social relations'. Heathcliff's rise to power, we are told, 'symbolises at once the triumph of the oppressed over capitalism and the triumph of capitalism over the oppressed';[51] even as the socially mobile outcast remains committed to an out-dated, mythologised past, he will be annihilated by the same capitalist forces that he otherwise embodies, etc. Critical discourse of this kind, we suggest, is symptomatic of the problems confronting any critic responsive to Marxism but constrained, by mere force of circumstance, to work within the Anglophone academy. The principal obstacle to be negotiated is how to *theorise* the production of the literary text, while at the same time 'living with' the tenets of an empirical tradition that is deeply hostile to abstraction. It proves to be insurmountable: 'capitalist social relations', 'agrarian capitalism', 'capitalist aggression', 'class conflict between the bourgeoisie and landed gentry', etc. are simply providing the exterior, objective 'context' or historical setting to the subjective intimacy of the 'text'. The ideological distinction between an 'inside' and an 'outside' remains firmly in place.

When the same Marxist concepts are interspersed with others, of bourgeois origin, such as 'naturalness and civilised life', 'culture and nature', 'bondage and freedom', 'nature and artifice', etc. the confusion is complete and a sense of eclectic chaos unavoidable. The only congealing element is a thinly disguised, liberal narrative, which tells of an ascent out of (medieval) unconsciousness

---

48   Regan 1998, p. 52.
49   Ibid., pp. 52–3.
50   Ibid., p. 53.
51   Ibid., p. 60.

and barbarity towards the summit of rational and enlightened consciousness. One's final impression is of a tentative foray into theory that falls some way short.[52]

How would an Althusserian approach to *Wuthering Heights*, conducted on the basis of *Theory and History*, differ from Eagleton's brand of Marxian eclecticism? Its broad outlines can be deduced from studies of comparable nineteenth-century works.[53] Perforce, its point of departure would be precisely the one shunned by Eagleton, namely the historical layering of the distinctive modes of production and their associated ideologies. This, manifestly, would require a willingness not only to break with the opposition between a textual *inside/outside*, but also to dig deep beneath the surface conflict between the bourgeoisie and the landed gentry, which Eagleton's text foregrounds. To give an idea, albeit rather schematic, let us return to the passage of *Wuthering Heights* cited above.

We would miss a key aspect of the narrative structure of Nelly Dean's portrayal of Heathcliff if we failed to notice the similarity between the trajectory of the feudal knight, epitomised by that of the Cid, and the vagabond boy. For if the Cid greets the sight of the black crow, crossing his path from left to right, with cries of joy, it is because he treats it as a signature, predictive of his future return from exile and, hence, of his future triumph. In this sense, we suggested, feudal exegesis is committed to a distinctly figural view of history: the commentator *reads* the future in contemporary events. Circumstances may dictate that the feudal protagonist is, temporarily, evicted from his or her *natural place* in the scheme of things, also that s/he may be unaware of his or her true nature – archetypically, the princess or prince reared by a peasant family is unaware of their true status – but, that said, within the context of feudal organicism, *blood will out* for the simple reason that bodies are '*substantial*'. Such is the reasoning behind Nelly Dean's reading of Heathcliff's body. We should not be surprised, therefore, if her prophecy proves correct: Heathcliff's ascent is *written*.

By the time of *Wuthering Heights*, feudal organicism survives only as a residual element – notably in the form of Linton's sense of 'duty', 'charity' and 'humanity' towards his servants, qualities that Heathcliff so contemns.[54] Predictably, moreover, such organicism is buried under the accumulated rubble of successive modes, of 'Renaissance', 'Romantic' and Darwinian extraction. An

---

52   Juan Caamaño criticises Eagleton along the same lines (Caamaño 2008, pp. 91–119).
53   We refer the reader to Rodríguez's 'Reflexiones sobre Tolstoi' (Rodríguez 2011a, pp. 101–34) and Read 2004b.
54   Brontë 2003, p. 189.

awareness of such historical stratification remains largely absent from Eagleton, and exposes his arguments, even in his most recent texts, to the charge of being 'oddly disembodied' and 'oddly dehistoricised'.[55] To which there can be only one possible response: 'The historical dimension needs more shading in'.

7   The 'Break' That Never Was

It was Althusser's conviction, to remind ourselves, that the true subjects of history are not 'concrete individuals' or 'real men' but the relations of production. With the crucial qualification: 'But since these are "relations", they cannot be thought within the category *subject*. And if by chance anyone proposes to reduce these relations of production to relations between men, i.e., *"human relations"*, he is violating Marx's thought'.[56] Such claims are in no way contradicted by the importance that Althusser attaches to *practices*, whether economic, political, or ideological: these, their status as human activity notwithstanding, never cease to be concrete actualisations of social structures. This position is one from which Rodríguez will never shrink and that he will never cease to contrast to its bourgeois counterpart. Even as he talks of the poetic horizon opened up by 'Garcilaso de la Vega', the Althusserian focuses attention not upon some putative subjectivity, which expresses itself through the technical means at its disposal, but upon the 'productive dialectic of animism', secreted by bourgeois-mercantilist relations and 'lived', *unconsciously* and, above all, *objectively*, at the everyday level.

> Our assumption is that all poetic processes (and literary processes in general) are perfectly *objective* insofar as they are always determined in the last instance by ideological relations (by which they are secreted and to which they belong). In turn these relations are determined by a specific matrix. ... Moreover, the *objectivity* of the poetic process is deduced from the fact that ideological relations, at the same time as they are determining with respect to (discursive) production, also need to be 'produced' (to assume a concrete 'body') throughout the text that they determine, insofar as they do not already exist prior to the text, in any solid or tangible form.[57]

---

55   Eagleton and Beaumont 2009, p. 300.
56   Althusser and Balibar 1970, p. 180.
57   Rodríguez 2002a, p. 123.

For better or for worse, we conclude, Rodríguez's break with bourgeois criticism was absolute and, by his own estimation, irreversible. How would Eagleton fare, by way of comparison, when, in his next major work, he undertook to critique his own native tradition, from what appears, at least at first sight, to be a resolutely Althusserian perspective?

The author of *Criticism and Ideology* (1976) is in no doubt, retrospectively, as to the significance of this text and the moment of its appearance: 'I had a strong sense that somebody was going to write this book. There were several possible authors; it just happened by some statistical law that I authored it'.[58] And, certainly, notwithstanding his comments elsewhere as to the 'extraordinary consistency' of his oeuvre overall, there is no gainsaying the radical nature of this new departure. 'So if *Criticism and Ideology* is the work of the "break", in Althusserian parlance, the other books are hanging about in some kind of antechamber'.[59] Except that doubts clearly remain, and Eagleton himself has been the first to raise them, consistently over the years: his work, he will typically reflect, was too quickly labelled Althusserianism.[60] Are such uncertainties justified?

Initially, at least, *Criticism and Ideology* looks every bit like a radical departure from its author's earlier attachments, specifically to Williams's brand of cultural materialism that, the argument now runs, collapses the distinct levels of the social formation into the 'anthropological abstraction' of 'culture'. Eagleton elaborates: 'Such a collapsing not only abolishes any hierarchy of actual priorities, reducing the social formation to a "circular" Hegelian totality and striking political strategy dead at birth, but inevitably *over-subjectivises* that formation'.[61] The litany of Williams's limitations includes the Welshman's emphasis upon individual experience – a disguised form of anti-intellectualism – and the importance attached to dialogue – judged to be 'politically sterile'. Such, then, is the setting for Eagleton's next move, which is to outline the 'Categories for a Materialist Criticism'.

58   Eagleton and Beaumont 2009, p. 105. Given the insularity of the British academy, Eagleton was perhaps to be excused for not knowing that the book had already been written. His continued silence on the existence of *Theory and History* is less excusable. Rodríguez, by way of contrast, has followed Eagleton's work closely. His view of *Criticism and Ideology* is damning in the extreme: 'Terry Eagleton understood very little about the Althusserian problematic'. Nor is his view of Eagleton's *On Ideology: An Introduction* particularly flattering: 'I do not deny Eagleton's intelligence, but his empiricism continues to be ... inane' (Rodríguez 2013, p. 175n12).

59   Ibid., p. 105.

60   See, for example, Eagleton and Beaumont 2009, p. 133.

61   Eagleton 2006, p. 26.

At this stage, things look decidedly promising from the Althusserian stand-point. Symptomatically, the second chapter breaks with the subject/object dichotomy beloved of bourgeois ideology: 'Every work is the work of many things besides the author', runs its epigraph (taken from Valéry); and, with the 'General Mode of Production' looming large over proceedings, the course is set towards a 'Science of the Text', to be articulated along Althusserian lines.

Yet, strange to say, almost immediately, hopes for a radical departure are dashed when the theorisation of the social formation is condensed into a matter of several lines.[62] And that proves to be only the beginning: as the list of 'categories' unfolds, one category after another, through the 'literary mode of production', 'general ideology', 'authorial ideology', etc. the realisa-tion slowly dawns that, far from breaking with the subject/object dichotomy, Eagleton is simply inverting it. So that, whereas Williams 'oversubjectivised' literature, Eagleton will 'overobjectivise' it. The result is a system closed in upon itself, whose changes are strictly endogenous. From the Kantian 'thing-in-itself' we pass to the immanent essence of the thing, which is both tran-scendental and empirical at the same time. 'History', as the argument unfolds, is reduced to the status of a discourse, somewhat tenuously attached to its materialist roots: 'History, one might say, is the *ultimate* signifier of literature, as it is the ultimate signified';[63] soon language itself, of an everyday kind, rap-idly retreats over the horizon, displaced by an ideology 'raised to the second power'.

True, enough of the revolutionary legacy of Althusserianism remains to cause confusion. Pivotally, a text does not originate in a subject; nor does ideology precede its expression. 'The particular production of ideology which we may term the "ideology of the text" has no pre-existence: it is identical with the text itself'.[64] And Eagleton will subsequently hint at the existence of a matrix effect of a social formation whereby every phrase, every image of the text, is determined by and exerts a determination upon the whole. 'We may say, then, that the text in this sense "produces itself" – but pro-duces itself in constant relation to the ideology which permits it such rel-ative autonomy'.[65] At this stage, seemingly, everything points in the direc-tion of an ideological unconscious, and sure enough, the task of criticism, it transpires, is precisely that of speaking or completing what the text neces-

---

62   Ibid., p. 45.
63   Ibid., p. 72.
64   Ibid., p. 80.
65   Ibid., p. 89.

sarily leaves unsaid. 'Its object is the *unconsciousness* of the work – that of which it is not, and cannot be, aware'.[66] But exactly what kind of unconsciousness?

While Althusser originally theorised his ideological unconsciousness in the context of the Marxist social formation, he also appealed to Freud, by way of legitimating certain aspects of his own work.[67] This Freudian connection will be picked up and elaborated still further by Althusser's pupil, Pierre Macherey. And it is from Macherey's *Theory of Literary Production*, already a lurking presence in *Myths of Power*, that *Criticism and Ideology* suddenly begins to take its cue. Only now the debt is explicit: 'It is worth noting here that these formulations of Macherey suggest the possibility of an encounter between Marxist criticism and the great scientist who has so often figured within such criticism merely as an eloquent silence: Freud'.[68] With the entry of Freud into the debate, attention can shift from the social formation back to the subject. And so, instead of the contradictions of a 'complex unity' or 'structure in difference', we are treated to those that are characteristic of 'dream-work'. The displacement of focus will prove to be permanent: the Freudian axis will be the one upon which the rest of Eagleton's discussion will turn.

The moment is opportune to recall Rodríguez's caveats on Macherey's work. The latter's emphasis upon *objectivity* with respect to textual *production*, the Spaniard was already warning in *Theory and History*, is qualitatively distinct from his own. As deployed in *Theory of Literary Production*, he argues, the term 'production' simply enables the French Althusserian to take his distance from the irrationalist, romantic emphasis upon 'literary creation'. Such 'technicism', allegedly, continues to fall within the empiricist or Kantian ambit, which thinks unconsciously in terms of the expression (by the subject) of 'ideas', 'sentiments'.[69] This position is one that Rodríguez will consistently maintain. Thus, in his recently published *De qué hablamos*, he will again insist upon the difference between his own position and that of Macherey: 'It is a simple nuance, but, I believe, an important one nevertheless'.[70]

66   Ibid.
67   Notably, in *Reading Capital* (Althusser and Balibar 1970, pp. 16n1, 241–7) and *Lenin and Philosophy* (Althusser 1971, pp. 189–219).
68   Eagleton and Beaumont 2009, p. 90.
69   Rodríguez 2002a, p. 123.
70   Rodríguez 2013, p. 193n28.

8   Conclusion

Rodríguez's location, on the margins of Europe, furnished him with a singular advantage, given the exposure that it entailed to what was, in effect,
a double transition: firstly, to his nation's long transition from feudalism to
capitalism, from the fifteenth to the twentieth century, and secondly, to the
condensed transition from fascism to social democracy in the three decisive
years from 1976 to 1979. Clearly, an experience of the latter proved crucial to
Rodríguez's personal and theoretical development. 'And, in fact, that's where
the whole problem lies', he was subsequently to reflect, 'liberty, yes, but nothing
about anti-capitalism'.[71] A better laboratory for the discovery and refinement
of the notion of the ideological unconscious could scarcely be imagined: '... all
had the same libidinal/ideological unconscious, totally configured in capitalist
terms: the capitalist ideological unconscious inscribed itself in every interstice,
collective or personal, beginning with the conviction that "I-born-free" and
impregnating the magical words of Freedom and Democracy'.[72] All that seemingly remained to be done, after the moment of *Theory and History*, was the
necessary 'mopping up' (Kuhn), an undertaking from which Rodríguez would
not flinch.

The result, by any standards, was an impressive research programme, extending over four decades, during which Rodríguez has never ceased to lend
critical support to the Althusserian legacy, nor to alert Marxists to the dangers
of 'society and the individual', understood as ontological categories. 'We are
then (our bourgeois common sense, our capitalist unconscious) those who
continue to think from the standpoint of such categories, as if they were truths
in themselves. And this is what lacks any sense for thinking that starts from a
Marxist problematic'.[73] The position is one totally uncongenial to the Anglophone academy, which helps explain, in part, why the Spaniard's work has
failed to travel. Not everyone, including so-called Marxists, care to be reminded
that capitalism is a social system based upon the individual's right to exploit
and to be exploited.

Eagleton's development followed a very different trajectory. If the Spaniard continued to embrace structural Marxism, Eagleton's sortie into Althusserian theory, by his own estimation, was a 'moment' that quickly 'faded', for
reasons that leave the author of *Criticism and Ideology* himself a little non-

---

71   Rodríguez 2013, p. 31.
72   Ibid., p. 34.
73   Rodríguez 2013, pp. 49–50.

plussed.[74] And in this way, one moment will quickly follow upon another – post-structuralist, psychoanalytic and feminist – so as to form a new eclecticism. Eagleton, it should be said, will continue to speak from a Marxist standpoint, but a standpoint that rekindles his earlier predilection for an 'anthropological' Marxism, in other words, a Marxism based on 'species being' and the 'continuity of human history'.[75] Althusser remains a haunting presence, and needs periodically to be exorcised, notably on account of his 'rather drooping' subject.

Eagleton's trouble with the subject is not to be attributed primarily to him but rather to his location within a social formation of a very distinctive kind. Distinctive in that, within this formation, the strata intermediary between feudalism and capitalism were capitalised early on, hence overlain, as in a geological formation, by subsequent accretions, culminating, ideologically, in empiricism. Perforce, the latter came to form the ultimate and only horizon of possibility, with fatal consequences: historiography, as a discipline, was inflected in the direction of the subject *that makes or is made*; whereas the theorisation of unconsciousness took the only form of the unconscious compatible with this subject, namely the libidinal unconscious. Symptomatically, in his *Ideology: An Introduction*, Eagleton will channel discussion away from Althusser towards Lacan, hence from ideology towards the individual libido.[76] Just as symptomatically, the complex unity of the structure in dominance finds itself relegated to an addendum.[77]

Curiously, or perhaps not so curiously, the image of an ideological unconscious, of a vaguely structural kind, lingers on, as when Eagleton warns against the perils of anthropomorphising the work and of psychoanalyzing the author.

> The text has an unconscious because, like any piece of language or any human subject, it is by virtue of its performative statements inevitably caught up in a network of significations that exceeds and sometimes subverts that performance, and which it can't fully control. And this unconscious is not just some more-than-text that is beyond the work's control; it's a lack of control, a way in which the text evades itself and is non-identical with itself, which is inscribed within the text itself and without which it would be able to say nothing at all.[78]

74　Eagleton and Beaumont 2009, p. 137.

75　Caamaño arrives at the same conclusion (Caamaño 2008, p. 101).

76　Eagleton 1991, pp. 142–46.

77　Ibid., p. 153.

78　Eagleton and Beaumont 2009, p. 127.

A network, to be sure, that, at the unconscious level, subverts the activity of the subject, but a network of *significations*, note, integral to a discursive as opposed to a social formation, integral, in other words, to a subjective individuality. Which sets the scene for the completion of what was, it transpires, but a long detour, through Marxism, towards an updated version of Eagleton's origins: 'The hardest form of emancipation is self-emancipation, as feminists, psychoanalytic theorists and theologians know, but a lot of Marxists (even after Gramsci) don't appear to'.[79]

---

79   Ibid., p. 281.

CHAPTER 6

Discourse and Ideology: Michel Foucault

Juan Carlos Rodríguez and Michel Foucault have several things in common. To begin with, both were former students of Louis Althusser, to whose work their respective research programmes constituted calculated responses; more importantly, these responses took the form of projects to explore unconsciousness or the unconscious, not in the Freudian sense of a region located within the psyche, but in the form of a primary social network that *produces* individuals. That said, the fanfare that greeted the appearance of Foucault's *Les mots et les choses* (1966) contrasts strikingly with the muted reaction to Rodríguez's *Teoría e historia de la producción ideológica* (1974). Reprints of Foucault's text, to remind ourselves, quickly ran into their thousands and catapulted Foucault nationally into the academic stratosphere, and that was only the beginning of his success. Early works, which, until this point, had enjoyed only a limited circulation, were quickly reprinted; subsequent titles, notably *Surveiller et punir* (1975), further garnered their author an international reputation; translations into the major European languages began to appear; and, last but not least, the commentaries quickly multiplied.[1] Rodríguez, on the other hand, would remain a relatively unknown figure, even following the publication of *La norma literaria* (1984) and notwithstanding his continuing productivity across three decades; translations would be few and belated and to date, as already observed, his work has been the object of only one full-length commentary.[2]

What could possibly account for such contrasting fortunes? How could two bodies of work that seemingly shared so much in common be received so differently? Undoubtedly, as in all such situations, circumstantial factors would play their part: to write in cosmopolitan Paris, with outlets into the global academy, was not to write in provincial Granada, on the margins of Europe. That said, the key to the disparities between Foucault and Rodríguez, we suggest, is to be found in their shared point of origin, namely the work of Althusser and, specifically, the *epistemological break*. The notion, to remind us, was one that Althusser borrowed originally from Gaston Bachelard and Georges Canguil-

---

1   E.g. Sheridan 1980, Smart 1983, 1985.
2   Caamaño 2008.

hem, but that he redefined crucially in terms of the opposition between science and ideology. In the philosopher's own words, the process of theoretical transformation 'establishes a science by detaching it from the ideology of its past and by revealing this past as ideological',[3] even as science must thereafter continually struggle to free itself from the ideology which 'occupies it, haunts it, or lies in wait for it'.[4] While Foucault will not be concerned with the ideology/science opposition in itself, the epistemological 'break' is a concept that will prove central to his work, and it is to that work that we now turn.

1   Making the 'Break'

The second part of Foucault's *Maladie mentale et personalité* (1954), Sheridan records,[5] situates mental illness in its social and historical context, in a straightforwardly Marxist manner, and, along with *Histoire de la Folie* (1961), shared enough in common with the Althusserian project to earn its progenitor's repeated plaudits. Principally, they attached the same importance to the notion of an epistemological rupture or break, of which Foucault discovered a classic instance in the radical shift in attitudes to madness that suddenly manifests itself at the end of the Middle Ages.[6] Methodologically, Foucault measures his distance from the historical continuities upon which traditional historicism insists. Over a relatively brief period, we learn, madness is transposed from an externality into an inner experience,[7] a process symptomatic of which was the abrupt appearance of the Fool and Madman at the centre of the theatrical stage.

Let us note, with an eye to our discussion below, the singular difficulty that Foucault experiences in ceasing to view Don Quixote through the prism of 'madness by romantic identification'.[8] The tenacity of the Romantic image is perfectly understandable: for generations scholars had contrasted Don Quixote, as the quintessence of the 'imaginary', to Sancho Panza, as the embodiment of the 'real'. Nor is it at all surprising that Foucault should project the figure of the knight in universalist terms: Don Quixote, we are informed, is immor-

---

3   Althusser 1990a, p. 168.
4   Ibid., p. 170.
5   Sheridan 1980, p. 5.
6   Foucault 1971, p. 13.
7   Ibid., p. 16.
8   Ibid., p. 28.

talised through his insanity.[9] Such a position, after all, had long been a commonplace among traditional critics. But this is a legacy difficult to square with
Foucault's alternative project to locate the knight at a point of rupture between
the 'Renaissance' and the eighteenth century, when '[t]he classical experience
of madness is born'.[10] Difficult to square, by the same token, with the relativist
notion that one set of values could be challenged and overturned, and in a relatively brief period of time. The watershed, allegedly, is 1656, the year in which
a decree was passed that founded the General Hospital in Paris and the process of confinement began. 'Behold [madness] moored now, made fast among
things and men'.[11]

That there is much in all of this to support the Althusserian programme
cannot be denied. Foucault views history as a process without a subject. The
sciences dealing with 'sanity' are determined in their development by discursive structures, otherwise by internal rules and restrictions that cannot be
thought within the category *subject*. Already discernible, then, are the outlines
of what will become a discursive unconsciousness of a systemic kind. At the
same time, however, Foucault appears to be reducing discourse to social institutions and the economic forces that provide its material conditions of existence.
'Throughout Europe, confinement had the same meaning, at least if we consider its origin. It constituted one of the answers the seventeenth century gave
to an economic crisis that affected the entire Western world'.[12] The insane, we
are assured, were locked away in hospitals for the same reason as were the
poor, the vagabonds and the unemployed, from whom they were barely distinguished. 'In the classical age, for the first time, madness was perceived through
a condemnation of idleness and in a social immanence guaranteed by the community of labour'.[13] In a word, they were perceived as a source of cheap labour.

One understands, then, the enthusiasm with which Althusser greeted the
appearance of Foucault's work.[14] But whether this enthusiasm is entirely justified is another matter entirely. Where is the evidence for the 'complex cultural
formations' and 'over-determination' that the master believes he discerns in the
work of his former pupil? Where the evidence for the alleged attempt to theorise 'the more general context of the economic, political, legal and ideological
structures of the time'? Seemingly, nowhere to be found. Althusser is guilty, we

---

9   Ibid., p. 32.
10   Ibid., p. 35.
11   Ibid.
12   Ibid., p. 49.
13   Ibid., p. 58.
14   Althusser and Balibar 1970, p. 45.

deduce, of projecting onto his former student his own notion of a social formation, with its distinct instances. The ideological instance, for sure, is conspicuous by its absence, which further alerts us to a more encompassing omission,
namely that of social theory in general. For practical purposes, Foucault 'makes
do' with what happens to be available, such as, for example, the 'Middle Ages',
'Renaissance', and 'Enlightenment' or 'Classicism', period concepts of the kind
that litter conventional historiography. That these now happen to be separated
by epistemic breaks was likely to prove a minor inconvenience to bourgeois
scholarship. The latter, after all, readily accepted the notion of radical transformations within an overarching Moving Spirit.

Similar observations apply to Foucault's next work, *The Birth of the Clinic*
(1963), which again deals with the discursive re-configurations of psychiatry
and medicine, but this time focused upon a relatively brief period at the end of
the eighteenth and beginning of the nineteenth century. Perforce, political considerations press for consideration: Foucault is dealing, after all, with the years
preceding and immediately following the Revolution, in which social institutions were radically reconstructed. Attention focuses on the radical change
in the ways in which, at an unconscious level, doctors viewed their object:
'The gaze is no longer reductive, it is, rather, that which establishes the individual in his irreducible quality'.[15] Integral to such change is the structural
relocation of medicine from the public to the private sphere of the family:
the hospital doctor, we learn, sees diseases only in a distorted, altered guise;
whereas the family doctor acquires true experience based on the natural phenomena.[16]

At this stage, Althusser remains firm in his support,[17] and understandably
so: as much as its predecessor, *The Birth of the Clinic* promotes the notion of
history without a subject, even as it captures every nuance of the relevant epistemological break. But if the commonality vis-à-vis Althusser survives, so too
does the discontinuity: as in his earlier work, Foucault lives by the illusion that
his historical investigations can make do without theory, at least in the strong
sense of the term. And, as in the case of all illusions, the consequences prove
serious. By discarding the Althusserian notion of structural causality, Foucault
has deprived himself of the means of theorising the relationship between discourse and society, hence his inability to explain the 'deeply rooted convergence' between political ideology and medical technology or the 'profound law'

15   Foucault 1973, p. xiv.
16   Ibid., p. 17.
17   Althusser and Balibar 1970, p. 45.

that binds medical and poetic experience together.[18] For an alternative perspective on such theoretical shortfalls and for a possible way of making up for them, let us turn to the work of Rodríguez.

2   Theorising the Ideological Unconscious

Compared to Foucault's early texts, Rodríguez's *Theory of Ideological Production* exhibits a much closer allegiance to the Althussserian legacy, not least of all with respect to the notion of an epistemological break. Of the latter, the Spaniard's actual research programme provides a particularly vivid instance: quite literally, after becoming acquainted with the work of Althusser, he throws his prior scholarly efforts into the street.[19] And when it came to theorising the transition from feudalism to capitalism, similarly dismissed are such period concepts as the 'Middle Ages' and the 'Renaissance',[20] to be replaced by 'social formations', 'modes of production' and related concepts. From the outset, everything is made to turn on the notion of the ideological unconscious: 'The notion of the subject (and the whole problematic within which it is inscribed) is radically historical because [...] it derives directly (and exclusively) from the very matrix of the bourgeois ideological unconscious: the "serf" can never be a "subject", etc.'[21] As we have already had cause to observe, the respective matrices form the basis of their corresponding ideologies, *substantialism* or *organicism*, in the case of the still dominant feudalism; *animism*, in the case of an emergent mercantile capitalism. These ideologies interlock inextricably during the Transition and the political struggle to control the newly created Absolutist State. To illustrate – also to be in a better position to draw a comparison with Foucault – let us see how Rodríguez handles Cervantes's *Don Quixote* (1605, 1615) with respect to the subject of madness.

Foucault, we have seen, was unable to detach himself from a Romantic tradition that saw in the knight and his squire, Sancho Panza, representatives respectively of the transcendental, ideal subject and its empirical, worldly counterpart. Rodríguez, by way of contrast, experiences no such difficulty: the worst way to read such a classic as the *Quixote*, he argues, confessedly taking his cue from Althusser's *Reading Capital*, is to identify it with one's own

---

18   Foucault 1973, pp. 38, 198.
19   Rodríguez 2002a, pp. 32–3.
20   Ibid., pp. 104 ff.
21   Ibid., p. 21.

unconscious categories.[22] A total change of critical terrain is called for. Objectively speaking, Don Quixote is the perfect example of a character torn between
conflicting ideologies, namely substantialism and animism. On the one hand,
he is a relic of a substantialist mode and hence compelled to read the world
as a book; on the other hand, he exemplifies qualities associated with the
proto-subject or beautiful soul promoted by animism. To construct for himself, in this latter capacity, a new identity, on the basis of his inalienable freedom, was necessarily to run terrible risks, not least of all in the context of a
Counter-Reformation Spain. These risks included being stigmatised as a madman, which explains why, towards the end of Part One of the novel, the knight
errant came to find himself confined within a cage and, subsequently, within
the walls of his home.

   Don Quixote's crime, if so it be – and we need to be very clear on this point –
is not that he believes in the world of chivalry – most of the people he comes
across in his adventures also believe in it. Rather, it is simply that, for these
same people, the chivalrous code has become an anachronism; which explains
why Don Quixote's original persecutors, namely the priest and the barber, are
content to re-insert the knight into the dominant ideological system, which
perforce is that of substantialism. The same cannot be said of the learned San-
son Carrasco, who, during the course of Part Two of the novel, will pursue the
unfortunate knight with an anger and murderous intent that, by a curious inversion, itself frankly borders on the insane. The internal, unconscious logic of the
narrative, as Rodríguez persuasively argues,[23] is unforgiving, and not simply
with respect to Carrasco: if Don Quixote is mad to consider himself a 'knight',
then equally mad are all those courtiers who believe themselves to be nobles
based on their 'blood' and lineage. The implications of which, ideologically
speaking, are potentially world-shattering, as becomes obvious at the Court of
the Duke and Duchess, within whose confines Don Quixote and Sancho are
forced to undertake what can only be described as a journey into madness.[24]

   Seemingly – and we are still following Rodríguez closely – there is no limit
to the sadism that the aristocratic owners of the chivalrous code show to others. And how otherwise than in terms of sadism can one describe the dangers
to which they expose their victims, dangers that are both physical – as when a
horde of wild cats is set loose upon Don Quixote – and psychological – as when
the Duchess casts doubts over the existence of Don Quixote's Lady Dulcinea.
Rodríguez elaborates in his commentary:

---

22   Rodríguez 2003a, pp. 69–70, 74n3.
23   Ibid., p. 258.
24   Ibid., p. 330.

And perhaps for this reason it is important to understand the logic of the Duke and Duchess as involving not a pale, nebulous power (after the fashion of the late Foucault), but as something real and concrete, as happens in any dominant class with respect to the oppressed. A power whose only limits are those that the dominant groups decide upon between themselves. And in the present case the situation is somewhat absurd insofar as the law and code of the nobles allows them to consider themselves as absolute *masters* and *lords* of their vassals.[25]

The perversion even extends to the otherwise defenceless Teresa, Sancho's wife, whom the Duchess does not hesitate to draw into the palace intrigue. Only Sancho, among her victims, offers any real resistance: 'Let nobody dare to amuse themselves at my expense, because we are what we are'.[26] At which point, according to Rodríguez, Cervantes is again seen to be walking an ideological tightrope, an activity made doubly precarious when he proceeds to portray the Duchess, in her own substantialist terms, as literally ulcerous and physically rotten.

Such, *in nuce*, is Rodríguez theory and history of ideological production, cashed out in the context of Don Quixote's madness. Its superiority over its Foucauldian equivalent, I suggest, is unquestionable. Except that Foucault's treatment of discursive structures in his early works was hardly his last word on the topic. Indeed, in the late 1960s, he undertook to spell out the theoretical basis of his research programme or, as he chose to call it, *archaeology*.

3   Theorising the Discursive Unconscious

In his next work, *The Order of Things* (1966), Foucault continued to hold fast to some of his earlier formulations, notably the notion of the epistemological break, instances of which he now located more precisely in 1650, which allegedly marked the beginning of the Classical age, and 1800, which witnessed the onset of modernity. In other respects, however, the new work heralds a methodological break of its own, internal to Foucault's own research programme. The social institutions and non-discursive forces to which, in his earlier work, discourses were seemingly reducible, were now displaced by a

25   Ibid., pp. 346–7.
26   Quoted at ibid, p. 354.

series of 'epistemes', understood as rules of formation or codes of discursive rationality. The result is an enhanced awareness of the 'unconscious of science', otherwise the unformulated thematics, the implicit philosophies, the unseen obstacles that *positively* condition the development of disciplines: 'What was common to the natural history, the economics, and the grammar of the Classical period was certainly not present to the consciousness of the scientist; or that part of it that was conscious was superficial, limited, and almost fanciful'.[27]

Foucault distinguishes between four epistemic epochs vis-à-vis the human sciences: the Renaissance, the Classical Age, the Modern Age, and the 'post-Modern' age. He chooses to preface his discussion, in the main body of his text, with illustrations drawn from Hispanic culture, in the form of a passage taken from the work of the Argentinian writer, Jorge Luis Borges, a picture, *Las Meninas*, and, once more, Cervantes's *Don Quixote*. We will return to Borges below. At the present juncture, let us consider the other two examples, by way of further elucidating Foucault's notion of the discursive unconscious.

Las Meninas, as is well known, is a painting by Diego Velázquez that undertakes to represent representation itself, by virtue of an intricate play of mirrors, reflections, imitations, and portraits. The aspect to which Foucault attaches particular importance is the invisibility of the person seeing, whose position corresponds with that of King Philip IV and his wife in the hidden foreground of the painting. That said, it is less to the absence of these figures in themselves, that is, these figures understood as independent subjects, that Foucault wishes to draw our attention but, more obscurely, to that of being in itself, insofar as this being correlates – the pictorial instance notwithstanding – with the order of language. While clearly modelled upon Hegel's *Geist* or Moving Spirit, being as language departs from this Spirit in one crucial respect: it will always remain remote and unmoved, rather more in the image of a systemic space that 'con-forms' empirical reality from without, by prioritising a particular epistemic figure.

Foucault explains the significance of *Don Quixote* along the lines already mapped out in *Madness and Civilisation*, by situating the text at the boundary between two epistemes. These correlate with the Renaissance, which prioritises the *resemblances* between things, and with Classicism, which prioritises an *order* based on the existence of *differences*. Don Quixote wanders through the world in quest of *resemblances*, insofar as these resemblances manifest themselves in the form of language. The knight's whole being, Fou-

---

27   Foucault 1970, p. xi.

cault's argument runs, consists of language – he is comparable quite literally to a sign or letter or graphism. Hence his frustration at the wiles of the magicians who, at every turn, contrive to disturb the relationship between words and things, and so between things and their appearances. Don Quixote's problem, broadly posed, is that, by the beginning of the seventeenth century, under the onslaught of Cartesian rationalism, language had broken off its former kinship with things. While Descartes, it is true, sought to transcend scepticism and so rest knowledge upon firm foundations, his *cogito* necessarily gave rise to the Unthought, and increasingly so. In Foucault's own words: 'The modern *cogito* does not reduce the whole being of things to thought without ramifying the being of thought right down to the inert network of what does not think'.[28]

Amidst all the talk about 'life', 'work', and 'language', one detail can easily pass unnoticed, namely the fact that, for Foucault, it is language itself that crucially determines the cultural space. By implication, life and work only enter into the equation through their capacity as *discourses*, discourses on life and work. On this basis, Foucault will proceed to argue that each episteme consists of an interpretation or diverse modality of language; that the successive transitions from one episteme to another presuppose at a deeper level a process of purification; and that through this process language progressively relinquishes its hold on a sensible world in order to assume the plenitude of its being in modernity. This plenitude, the argument concludes, is best captured by two specific disciplines: psychoanalysis and ethnology. 'It was quite inevitable', Foucault explains, 'that they should both be sciences of the unconscious: not because they reach down to what is below consciousness in man, but because they are directed towards that which, outside of man, makes it possible to know, with a positive knowledge, that which is given to or eludes his consciousness'.[29]

To so privilege the psychoanalytic unconscious is, inevitably, to fall victim to Bhaskar's *epistemic fallacy*, otherwise the subsumption of ontology under epistemology, to which, through underplaying the 'real object', Althusser himself arguably succumbed. Was this one respect in which Foucault remained indebted to his master? Bhaskar implies as much: 'I think in Foucault's work ... the failure to coherently thematise ontology and thematise the different ontologies that we know, the ontology of science, the ontology of the social world, results ultimately in an ontology of chance, of contingency, of accident'.[30] If so,

---

28   Ibid., p. 324.
29   Ibid., p. 378.
30   Bhaskar 2002b, p. 63.

we need to allow for the existence in Foucault of a discursive variant of the basic fallacy, in which a deep ontology is ceded to epistemology, under the guise of language.[31]

Since ontology is in fact irreducible to epistemology, the epistemic fallacy entails the generation of an implicit ontology or, as Bhaskar refers to it, *actualism*, which equates the real with empirical reality. Accompanying the epistemic fallacy, then, like a ghostly shadow, is its counterpart, the *ontic fallacy*, which entails the collapsing of the transitive dimension into its intransitive counterpart.[32] Symptomatically, the contradictions multiply: Foucault is undecided as to whether to talk in terms of *surfaces*, the domain of a flat ontology, or *depths*, the realm of discursive profundity. Archaeology, as a discipline, is to be emphatically distinguished from a phenomenological approach that prioritises a transcendental consciousness[33] and from a psychoanalytic tradition that reaches down 'to what is below consciousness in man', while, at the same time, we are alerted as to the 'immense density' of scientific discourse and to a reality so 'complex' that it needs to be approached 'at different levels'.[34]

4   Mirrors and Souls

In Spain, the bourgeois revolution was effectively blocked and reversed, as a consequence of which its Age of Reason proved to be a relatively muted affair, led by enlightened clerics.[35] Which raises the question as to why Foucault should choose to preface *The Order of Things* with a series of illustrations drawn from Hispanic culture. Their value, we suggest, is to be traced directly to Spain's prolonged transition from the 'Renaissance' to 'Modernity', in the context of which the production of cultural artefacts was played out, as it were, in slow motion, thereby affording instructive insights into the mechanisms involved. That said, the insights to be gained from Foucault's illustrations are limited precisely by the absence of their relevant cultural context. That absence is further compounded by Foucault's failure to take account of the research of Spanish scholars.

---

31   Bhaskar himself allows for the existence of a distinctively *linguistic* fallacy (Bhaskar 2002b, p. 72).
32   Bhaskar 1993, p. 237.
33   Foucault 1970, p. xiv.
34   Ibid., pp. 378, xiii, xiv.
35   For further details, see Read 1990 and 1992.

These Spanish scholars, it should come as no surprise to discover, have a rather different take on their national culture. For them, the radical historicity of the latter is a force to be reckoned with. Nor are they permitted the privilege of institutional blindness, of the kind that scholars in the First World routinely exhibit towards their Second or Third World equivalents.[36] Rodríguez, certainly, scrutinises Foucault closely on the subject of *Las Meninas*. He also bridles at evidence of what he describes as a 'vacuous obsession' with being,[37] preferring, by way of contrast, to focus upon the mirror that figures within the picture's scenario:

> *Las Meninas* fascinates, we are saying, as a mirror that reveals the vampiric undercurrent to the whole ideology of the private sphere, the ideology that sustains the bourgeois image of the picture – or the poem – from the 16th century onwards. As a concrete abstraction of this image of painting, the mirror does not provide a self-portrait – ... necessarily an exercise in coarseness – but materialises the invisible – and impossible – structure that underlies the whole process. He who possesses the secret of limitless form – the artist – can never appear himself as a concrete form, without revealing the whole secret of his dark, hidden art: the secret, which is no secret, of the reflection in the mirror: the secret of the ideological unconscious that actually determines it: the construction of the space of limitless form.[38]

There is much here that needs to be unpacked. Count Dracula, his castle and feudal trappings notwithstanding, is no rebellious lord but a rebellious son, or so Rodríguez will argue, reconstituted within the private space of the bourgeois family. His correlate, therefore, is the image of Christ, except that Christ is a soul incarnate, who thereby reflects the Lord's divinity. The vampire, by way of contrast, *serves* nobody, least of all the Lord, with the result that its body, unlimited by form, actually 'dis-incarnates', with the further, paradoxical result that it cannot be reflected in a mirror. Rodríguez is insistent: *Las Meninas* is the portrait of a body that is not there, that can be glimpsed only through the image of another image, namely that of the duchess, the dwarf, and other surrounding figures. The self-portrait, we are assured, is that of a body that simply

---

36   For further discussion, see Bartolovich and Lazarus 2002, pp. 10–14.
37   Rodríguez 2008b, p. 348.
38   Ibid., p. 349.

'gets in the way'. Rodríguez elaborates: 'The Christian tradition does not repress the flesh, it rather produces it; it does not repress sex but engenders it. And to repeat, it was not necessary for Foucault to remind us of the fact, as if he had made a great discovery'.[39] To further elucidate which, let us return to the *Quixote*.

According to Rodríguez, Cervantes poses a fundamental problem in the novel's opening words: 'In a certain village in La Mancha, which I do not wish to name, there lived not long ago a gentleman ...'.[40] The authorial subject makes the briefest of appearances, only quickly to be overwhelmed by an editorial apparatus of manuscripts, discovered in strange circumstances, and of translators that mysteriously materialise out of nowhere. The continuity vis-a-vis the substantialist Book is too obvious to require elaboration. For the novel to appear – and we are again following Rodríguez's analysis closely – two conditions are required, namely the discovery of daily life and the emergence of a 'free subject'.[41] Both are lacking in the 'baroque', which Rodríguez equates with the cultural manifestation of a resurgent feudalism. The still dominant feudal mode, which, we saw above, secretes unconsciously an opposition between the serf/servant and a lord/Lord, knows only the dual, analogical text, whose literal message demands that it be 'read' or decoded. The animist text, by way of contrast, discovers a new literalism – 'It happened that ...' – and equips itself with a version of the free subject that, however embryonic, still dares to make its presence felt.

To tease out some further implications of Rodríguez's reading, let us briefly set the novel in motion. In his first adventure, to remind ourselves, Don Quixote is as yet unaccompanied.

> He had not gone far when from a thicket on the right he heard a faint voice, raised, so it seemed to him, in complaint ...[42]

The voice, it transpires, is that of a boy, who is being beaten by his master for his alleged negligence in guarding a flock of sheep. Don Quixote's ideological unconscious is such that he is compelled to *read* the scene before him, and in *dual* terms. Hence, the literalism of the peasant, his mare, and his shepherd's staff is immediately transposed:

---

39   Ibid., p. 351.
40   Cervantes Saavedra 1950, p. 31.
41   Rodríguez 2003a, p. 74 ff.
42   Cervantes Saavedra 1950, p. 47.

> 'Discourteous knight, it is unseemly to attack a defenceless person. Mount
> your steed, and take your lance' – for the other also had a lance leaning
> against the oak to which his mare was tied ...[43]

Just as importantly, by virtue of his status as a knight, he is compelled to act
upon his reading, in other words, to 'prove' his worth.

Now it is easy to go wrong at this point. Incorrigible Kantian that s/he is, the
modern reader identifies the knight as a (free) subject, who fails to *see* what he
has in front of him. According to Rodríguez, Foucault is such a reader. Viewed
in such terms, Don Quixote is simply unable to match words with the things he
sees. Rodríguez begs to differ.

> The way resemblance actually works in the text is not as Foucault portrays
> it. The similarity between signatures is, admittedly, the key to a feudal
> world that imagines itself as written by the finger of God. But what this
> thereby implied is not a correlation between words and things (which
> would presuppose a prior distance between them) but rather a correla-
> tion between the writing of the book and the writing of the world.[44]

Cervantes, the argument runs, elaborates a substantialist or organicist text,
in other words, the 'Book of Chivalry', in order to annul it. The mare/horse,
peasant/knight, staff/lance, along with the windmills/giants, flocks/armies,
basin/helmet, etc. that proliferate throughout his novel serve to expose the hidden mechanism of the substantialist narrative from a literal, which to say from
an animist, standpoint.

Cervantes, then, is obliged, like any other author at the time, to locate himself
and his hero in organicist terms, except that, in his case, these are being 'corroded from within' by a new narrative literalism. This process perforce raises
a fundamental difficulty: who or what legitimates the law once the Lord/lord
has been displaced? And it is raised with particular urgency in the case of
the boy who is being so brutally manhandled. The boy, at least, knows a literal truth when he sees one: his master is emphatically not a knight errant
but Juan Haldubo, 'the rich man'; by the same token, he understands perfectly
how the new 'disorder' works and, more importantly, how its law is applied.
His master's promise to 'settle accounts' can mean only one thing. Don Quixote, by way of contrast, struggles hopelessly to resolve the financial transactions

---

43   Ibid.
44   Rodríguez 2003a, pp. 431–32.

between master and servant, and necessarily so: his only law is the code of chivalry, which has nothing to say about money. Predictably, he is dismissive of the boy's suspicions regarding what his master plans to do once the knight's back is turned. '"He will do no such thing" replied Don Quixote, "I have only to lay my command on him, and he will respect it"'.[45] His logic is impeccable, by chivalrous norms: the Lord is watching, and His law will prevail.

And so Don Quixote continues on his way until, on coming to a fork in the road, he loosens the reins and allows his nag the free exercise of its will,[46] which, needless to say, is to return to its stable. This seemingly trivial incident is deeply charged, ideologically speaking. A dominant organicist norm dictates that history is always *pre*-figured in the sense of pre-ordained, both individually and collectively, hence excludes the possibility of *chance* events. That Don Quixote should, at this moment, break with this tradition demonstrates practically what it means for substantialism to be subverted by an emergent animist norm. From the standpoint of the latter, history is not already *written*; on the contrary, it responds to the initiative of the free individual, even when that individual happens to be a horse!

5   A Borgesian Interlude: the Chinese Encyclopaedia

Jorge Luis Borges, we saw above, was the third Hispanic source upon which Foucault drew, after Velázquez and Cervantes, through which to illustrate the workings of his discursive unconsciousness. The text in question is an essay by Borges entitled 'El idioma analítico de John Wilkins', contained in *Otras Inquisiciones* (1953). Foucault famously began his preface to *The Order of Things* with the following extract that addresses the existence of a Chinese Encyclopaedia:

> [In its remote pages] it is written that animals are divided into (a) belonging to the Emperor, (b) embalmed, (c) tame (d) sucking pigs (e) sirens, (f) fabulous, (g) stray dogs, (h) included in the present classification, (i) frenzied, (j) innumerable, (k) drawn with a very fine camelhair brush, (l) *et cetera*, (m) having just broken the water pitcher, (n) that from a long way off look like flies.[47]

45   Cervantes Saavedra 1950, p. 48.
46   Ibid., p. 50.
47   Foucault 1972, p. xv.

To Foucault's intense amusement, the classification subverted the notions of *order* and *difference* upon which the whole Classical episteme rested. As is his habit, he makes no attempt to contextualise the statement, either historically, with respect to Hispanic culture, or, at a more local level, with respect to Borges' own individual trajectory.

Rodríguez, who, in this respect as in others, continued to read Foucault's work closely, predictably took exception to the neglect of history or, as he phrased it, 'the dust that time deposits'.[48] Unsurprisingly, therefore, the Spaniard will proceed to locate not only Borges's essay but Borges himself within a delicate play of intertexuality that embraces Locke, Hume, Berkeley, Kant, Hegel, and Nietzsche, among many others,[49] before coming to focus upon the details of Borges's own trajectory. By the early years of the twentieth century, the narrative runs, animism had assumed the guise of a distinctively *petty-bourgeois* ideology, otherwise, neo-idealism, mediated through Croce,[50] in which form it is re-absorbed by those avant-garde Hispanic movements currently in vogue, notably 'ultraism', in which Borges actively participated throughout the 1920s. The consequent need, felt by artists, to promote writing as a product of *personal expression* combines curiously with the disappearance of the notion of the author, provoked, Rodríguez argues, by the second industrial revolution. And so to the appearance of the several collections of Borges's classic stories and the essays contained in *Otras Inquisiciones*. To put these claims to the test, let us consider one of Borges's short stories taken from *Ficciones* (1941), namely 'Tlön, Uqbar, Orbis Tertius'.

The story, as is widely known, narrates how, on the occasion of a late-night supper, Borges and Bioy Casares share in the discovery of a fictional world, Tlön, traceable, it transpires, to an entry in an obscure encyclopaedia. As the story proceeds, the fiction gradually takes over and absorbs material reality. Only particular details need concern us. Firstly, the fact that, in the author's own words: 'I owe the discovery of Uqbar to the conjunction of a mirror and an encyclopedia. The mirror troubled the far end of a hallway in a large country house on Calle Gaona, in Ramos Mejía'.[51] Symptomatically, the 'ashen' editor-in-chief, Herbert Ashe, quickly fades away, together, incidentally, with the narrator himself: 'I began to leaf through [the encyclopedia] and suddenly I experienced a slight, astonished sense of dizziness that I shall not describe, since this is the

---

48   Rodríguez 2002b, p. 297.
49   Ibid., pp. 351ff.
50   Ibid., p. 352.
51   Borges 1999, p. 68.

story not of my emotions but of Uqbar and Tlön and Orbis Tertius'.[52] Significant details are the vampiric mirror, the lateness of the hour – 'Guess who's coming to supper?'[53] – and the process by which the narrator is drawn into an ideal world:

> The nations of that planet are, congenitally, idealistic. Their language and those things derived from their language – religion, literature, metaphysics – presuppose idealism. For the people of Tlön, the world is not an amalgam of *objects* in space; it is a heterogeneous series of independent *acts* – the world is successive, temporal, but not spatial. There are no nouns in the conjectural *Ursprache* of Tlön, from which its 'present-day' language and dialects derive: there are impersonal verbs, modified by monosyllabic suffixes (or prefixes) functioning as adverbs. For example, there is no noun that corresponds to our word 'moon', but there is a verb which in English would be 'to moonate' or 'to enmoon'. 'The moon rose above the river' is *'hlör u fang axaxaxas mlö'*, or, as Xul Solar succinctly translates: *Upward, behind the onstreaming it mooned.*[54]

The parallels with the Chinese encyclopaedia should not be lost, or the significance of the mirror. The latter's very existence threatens the author with dissolution, particularly one precariously positioned within a transitional ideology. Rodríguez draws a comparison with Montaigne, whose favoured medium was the essay, a genre to which, significantly, Borges was also attracted. The goal in each case was the same: the search for a non-fragmented subject. Rodríguez explains: 'The principal enigma of Borges, then, is his writing on the subject of non-transparency, in other words, on the problem of individuation, the problem of not being able to say "I am" other than through the mediation of the reflexion of the other, of one's double or the enemy'.[55] It is a thematic the Argentinian writer will rehearse again and again, through a series of agonic conflicts, between, for example, Red Scharlach and Lönnrot, Aureliano and Juan de Panonia, Emma Zunz and Loewenthal, Otto Dietrich sur Linde and David Jerusalem, and, above all, between himself and his alter ego: 'It's Borges, the other one, that things happen to. I walk through Buenos Aires and I pause – mechanically now, perhaps – to gaze at the arch of an entryway and its inner door; news of Borges

---

52   Ibid., p. 71.
53   Rodríguez 2008b, p. 340.
54   Borges 1999, pp. 72–3.
55   Rodríguez 2002b, p. 298.

reaches me by mail, or I see his name on a list of academics or in some bio-graphical dictionary'.[56] In Lacanian terms, one might say, Borges is stuck at the 'mirror stage'.

How, Rodríguez finally asks, is one to understand the sudden Parisian pre-dilection for an Argentinian writer who had, until the late '60s, led a relat-ively obscure existence? Against the backdrop, he replies, of a reaction, on the part of the Parisian Left, to a prevailing, rather crude realism. But that is only part of the picture. 'Borges fixes on the objectification of the "I" – in this way his texts realise their full modernity, wherein [...] perhaps lies the reason for their overwhelming success'.[57] The implication is clear: by some curious historical optic, a still embryonic 'subject' finds itself overlapping with the fragmented subject of late capitalism; or, alternatively framed, a marginal-ised culture, by virtue of its belated entry into modernity, finds itself speak-ing to the condition of a First World that is entering upon post-modernity. More recently, Rodríguez has further argued that the 'death of man', as pro-moted by Foucault, was itself rooted 'in the residue of a seigneurial, feudal-ising reaction of Protestant ideologues to the order of bourgeois classicism'.[58] To pursue these issues in more detail, let us return to Foucault's texts them-selves.

6   Empowering Discursive Unconsciousness

As early as the appearance of the English translation of *For Marx* (1969), to which he contributed a 'Letter to the Translator', Althusser was already meas-uring his distance from Foucault: while 'something' of his own ideas had passed into his former student, 'under his pen and in his thought even the meanings he gives to formulations he has borrowed from me are transformed into another, quite different meaning than my own'.[59] Just how close the ideas and how dif-ferent the meanings became clearer when Foucault came further to expand upon the conceptual basis of his work in *The Archaeology of Knowledge*. Let us elaborate.

In addition to the notion of an epistemological break, which continues to enjoy a methodological pre-eminence in the new work, there exist several other parallels between key Foucauldian concepts, on the one hand, and their ori-

---

56   Borges 1999, p. 324.
57   Rodríguez 2002b, p. 337.
58   Rodríguez 2015, p. 266.
59   Althusser 1990a, p. 257.

ginal, Althusserian counterparts, on the other. To be more specific, between the Foucauldian 'general history' and the Althusserian 'differential history'; between the Foucauldian critique of a unified spirit or world-view and the Althusserian critique of a Hegelian expressive causality; between the Foucauldian 'object of discourse' and the Althusserian 'object of thought'; between Foucault's distinct, relatively autonomous social 'levels' and Althusser's 'instances'; between the complexities that 'traverse' Foucault's 'discursive formation' and the matrix effect of the Althusserian social formation; and between Foucault's 'discursive unconsciousness' and Althusser's ideological unconsciousness. The final impression is that of a writer who has set out systematically to 'out-Althusser Althusser'.[60]

On the existence of a discursive unconsciousness Foucault is particularly forthcoming. The need for concessions is accepted at the outset. By his own estimate, the sheer pervasiveness of cultural conditioning would doubtless come as a very unpleasant shock to a bourgeois society that takes for granted the existence of a self-possessed, fully responsible subject, and it is to be anticipated that some will inevitably take offence.

> I understand the unease of all such people. They have probably found it difficult enough to recognise that their history, their economics, their social practices, the language (*langue*) that they speak, the mythology of their ancestors, even the stories that they were told in their childhood, are governed by rules that are not all given to their consciousness; they can hardly agree to being dispossessed in addition of that discourse in which they wish to be able to say immediately and directly what they think, believe, or imagine; they prefer to deny that discourse is a complex, differentiated practice, governed by analysable rules and transformations, rather than be deprived of that tender, consoling certainty of being able to change, if not the world, if not life, at least their 'meaning' ...[61]

And it was doubtless to offend such people as little as possible that the archaeologist chose to speak of 'discourse', as opposed to 'ideology', which he deploys only in a specialised context, notably when he is directly cribbing from Althusser with respect to ideology's unconscious hold over science.[62] That said, there was no gainsaying the fact that discursive unconsciousness, like its ideological counterpart, effectively marginalises the knowing subject or psycholo-

---

60   Resch 1992, p. 241.
61   Foucault 1972, pp. 210–11.
62   Ibid., p. 185.

gical individual. Which raises the puzzling question as to how Foucault was able to reconcile this same unconsciousness with a humanist Left that was scandalised by Althusser's 'anti-humanism'.

Crucial, clearly, was the decision to locate unconsciousness in 'discourse' or, to be more exact, in sets of discursive rules and codes at a level between the 'thoughts of men' and that of institutions or social and economic relations. 'These systems' Foucault emphasised, 'reside in discourse itself; or rather (since we are concerned not with its interiority and what it may contain, but with its specific existence and with its conditions) on its frontier, at that limit at which specific rules that enable it to exist as such are defined'.[63] By-passed in the wink of an eye were the key Althusserian notions of 'social formation', 'modes of production', 'relations of production' and so on. Understandably, the bourgeois academy was deeply appreciative, and seemed not always to notice that a high price was being paid in exchange for the exclusive focus upon discursive systems. These systems can certainly be qualified as 'prediscursive', Foucault allows, 'but only if one admits that this prediscursive is still discursive, that is, that they do not specify a thought, or a consciousness'.[64] Which is precisely what Bhaskar meant when, as we saw above, he talked of a linguistic variation on his epistemic fallacy.

Perforce, the compromise proved difficult to sustain, on both sides. Until this moment, the free, richly internalised, private subject had always been indispensable to the capitalist system – without it, and therefore without the freedom to exploit and to be exploited, this system simply collapses. Similarly, when he came to unpack his notions a little further, Foucault found himself plagued by certain fundamental ambiguities built into his formulations. Specifically, as in his earlier work, he struggles to reconcile an emphasis upon externalities, otherwise the systems and codes that operate 'at the most "superficial" level (at a level of discourse'),[65] with the notion of discrete levels of events, 'within the very density of discourse'.[66] One understands his dilemma: even as he emphasises the autonomy of discourse and its specificity, extra-discursive processes and social relations press for consideration, and it was to cater for these that the archaeologist turned to address the question of institutional power.

As was often the case, the change came about partly in response to developments within Althusserianism, which Foucault obsessively shadowed. From

---

63　Ibid., p. 74.
64　Ibid., p. 76.
65　Ibid., p. 62.
66　Ibid., p. 171.

an initial position that emphasised the unconsciousness of ideology, Althusser shifted in the late '60s towards an investigation of the way in which the subject was 'interpellated'. In the process, he transferred his focus of attention from the social formation, envisaged as a complex unity, to the Ideological State Apparatus.[67] In response to such manoeuvres and to meet what he perceived as a challenge, Foucault abruptly changed tack in his next work, *Discipline and Punish*, from a preoccupation with the dominating character of discourses, with respect to their internal organisation, to an emphasis upon their social nature and, even more specifically, upon their respective apparatuses and institutions. The notion of a systemic unconsciousness underwent corresponding changes: no longer identified with codes and systems of classification, it now assumes the trappings of a Power that pervades social apparatuses:

> It is rather a multiplicity of often minor processes, of different origin and scattered location, which overlap, repeat, or imitate one another, support one another, distinguish themselves from one another according to their domain of application, converge and gradually produce the blueprint of a general method. They were at work in secondary education at a very early date, later in primary schools; they slowly invested the space of the hospital; and in a few decades, they restructured the military organisation.[68]

Not only is disciplinary power imposed from *above* but also, perhaps principally, filters *upwards*, with the result that, as in the case of ideology, 'it leaves no zone of shade', even to the extent that it 'constantly supervises the very individuals who are entrusted with the task of supervising'.[69]

Foucault seemingly pushes beyond his master's theory of interpellation by displacing the focus of attention from a socially inflected ideology onto the more basic, trans-historical level of Power: 'The individual', Foucault is careful to argue, 'is no doubt the fictitious atom of an "ideological" representation of society; but he is also a reality fabricated by this specific technology of power that I have called "discipline"'.[70] Carried over, wholesale, from Althusser is the recognition of the individual as a social product. We are talking, in other words, of techniques for constituting individuals through exposure to the pressure exerted by knowledge and power or, more simply, a knowledge/power. While individuals may believe themselves to be in control of its operations, they are

67   Althusser 1971, pp. 127–86.
68   Foucault 1979, p. 138.
69   Ibid., p. 177.
70   Ibid., p. 194.

in fact their resultant. '[I]t is not that the beautiful totality of the individual is amputated, repressed, altered by our social order, it is rather that the individual is carefully fabricated in it, according to a whole technique of forces and bodies'.[71]

At first glance, Power thus conceived might seem to possess greater explanatory capacity than the traditional Marxist concept of exploitation. Crucially, Power regulates the body itself and not just the working day. What might seem a progressive step, however, when carefully considered, proves to be nothing of the kind. Power, it transpires, operates in the manner of a primal, telluric force that *precedes* society and, as such, resists explanation. Moreover, it functions as the protagonist of a narrative that, in broad outline, closely resembles its liberal counterpart, except that the story that unfolds tells not of the advance of civilisation but of the individual's increasing subjection to disciplinary control. The process is one of 'ascending individualisation', which it behoves the individual to resist. Unsurprisingly, Foucault's analysis calls a halt just at the point where more precision is called for. Thus, when it comes to disentangling the 'microphysics of power', we find these ambiguously located somewhere between, on the one hand, the great apparatuses and institutions and, on the other, 'bodies themselves with their materiality and their forces'.[72] In the absence of any causal nexus between the two, Foucault is excused from having to proceed further.

The liberal narrative, we deduce, has not been abandoned so much as inverted, which explains how it came about that, in the transformed circumstances of the late 1970s and 1980s, Foucault's disciplinary unconsciousness gradually relinquishes its grip upon the individual, to be replaced by what became an 'aesthetics of experience'.[73] The conjuncture was certainly one favourable to the kind of culturalist constructivism that this aesthetics promoted. In the heady climate of postmodernism, biology itself was ceding to discourse, notably with respect to women, blacks, and gays, at the same time that the last links between cultural products and economic structures were being severed. In Foucault's hands, history itself was loosening its moorings in the real: 'I am well aware that I have never written anything but fictions'.[74] Such confessions only confirm one's suspicion that, while there is no gainsaying the brilliance and breadth of his diverse histories, Foucault had never finally broken with the fundamental bourgeois allegiance to the subject / system dichotomy, nor, by

---

71   Ibid., p. 217.
72   Ibid., p. 26.
73   Foucault 1988.
74   Foucault 1980, p. 193.

same token, had he ever been able to detach his discursive unconsciousness from individual consciousness and hence from individual subjectivity.

7   Staging the State Apparatus

Although Foucault reacted immediately to Althusser's dramatic shift of focus towards the institutions, Rodríguez, by way of contrast, discerned in the mechanisms of interpellation a covert regression to the notion of a trans-historical subject. To begin with, he argued, it presupposed in the Subject who interpellates the subject a consistency that is belied by the contradictions rampant throughout the social formation. Moreover, he elaborated, the very example with which the philosopher undertook to illustrate the relevant mechanism, namely the encounter between Yahweh and Moses, was flawed. Yahweh, after all, was no Subject but a Lord and Moses no subject but a servant (of his lord). But most damaging of all, in the Spaniard's view, was the implication that an individuality existed prior to its subjection. 'Something that logically presupposes an error of the gravest kind when it comes to conceptualising the notion of what could be called the *ideological unconscious*'.[75] How, then, was the role of the State Apparatus to be accommodated?

In *Theory and History* Rodríguez had already responded forcefully to those Althusserians, notably Renée Balibar, Pierre Macherey, and France Vernier, who, by prioritising the role of the school as a major ideological apparatus, had succumbed to a mechanistic 'institutional sociologism'. From which it followed, according to the Spaniard, that the ideological function of literature was improperly framed. For example, the importance that was attached to the experience of social frustration in Camus' *The Stranger* was conducive to a 'vital experientialism' that covertly re-asserted the centrality of the bourgeois subject. 'The key to Camus' text', Rodríguez argued, 'does not lie here but rather in the following question: from the standpoint of which ideological unconscious is the experience of frustration assumed, lived and later "expressed" in a novel?'.[76] The basic objection to such experientialism can be posed in the form of another question: Who educates the Educators? Behind which lurks a presupposition: 'it is not the school that "creates" ideology, notwithstanding its function as a State Apparatus; the school only materialises and reproduces this ideology'.[77]

75   Rodríguez 2008a, p. 768.
76   Rodríguez 2002a, p. 30.
77   Ibid., p. 30.

Rodríguez's emphasis upon the material base failed to immunise him against the de-ontologisation in evidence in Althusser, to judge at least from his refusal to accept that competing theories of Literature shared objects in common.[78] To argue, furthermore, as the Spaniard does, that Marx's concepts of 'proletariat', 'surplus value' and 'social classes' are totally different from their bourgeois counterparts, that the two parties are addressing different 'real objects', is to raise insurmountable problems of incompatibility and, arguably, to succumb to an *ideological fallacy* every bit as damaging as its linguistic or discursive equivalent.[79] Such fallacies, we have seen, are invariably stalked by their inversion, namely the ontic fallacy, which collapses the subject into the object. It should come as no surprise, therefore, to find Rodríguez asserting that ideological notions need first to be 'produced' before they can be said to exist.[80] To conflate thus the mechanisms or laws that generate events with events themselves is necessarily to court an actualism that differs little from Foucault's positivism.

That said, Rodríguez's insistence upon the role of the relations of production does arguably provide a materialist ballast that protected him against a full regression to the subject/object opposition. Such becomes apparent when he turns, in *State, Stage, Language,* to address further the role of the State Apparatus. The theorisation of an ideological unconscious peculiar to a social system, his argument runs, involves a circular process whereby an ideological unconscious greases the social formation from below, through an effectivity exercised by the relations of production, before pervading the social formation institutionally from above.[81] Such was the framework within which the Spaniard would proceed to theorise the role of the State. By way of illustration, let us consider his essay on the relationship between the state/stage.

Rodríguez will pose this relationship in terms of (i) the opposition between the nobility and the bourgeoisie and (ii) in terms of struggles internal to the ideology of the latter. Feudal relations, we saw above, do not, of themselves, secrete a theatre, and for one simple reason: given the absence of a public/private distinction, the notion of a (public) stage was strictly inconceivable under feudalism. The rise of Absolutism, to remind us, preludes the formulation of the sixteenth-century theatre along public lines: the works of Calderón, like those of Shakespeare, consist of the public display of a public, which is to say, political, thematic. Particularly to be emphasised is the fundamental contradiction upon which the classical theatre rests: while being, like the Abso-

---

78   Ibid., p. 126.
79   See Read 2015a, pp. 477–8.
80   Rodríguez 2002a, p. 123.
81   Rodríguez 2008b, p. 11.

lutist State itself, the result of pressure exerted by the bourgeoisie or, more strictly, by bourgeois relations, the stage, *qua* public space, will continue to be dominated, in Spain at least, by feudal notions of 'blood', 'lineage', and 'honour'.

In the eighteenth century, things change dramatically, or so at least Rodríguez argues. 'What happens is that *with the triumph of bourgeois relations the public realm will be conceived as a "direct transcription" of the private*'.[82] With inevitable consequences: the public space of the classical stage will be reduced to the three walls of the bourgeois drawing room, from which are excluded all matters relating directly to politics and, by extension, to religion. The process parallels the changes taking place in other state apparatuses, legal and otherwise, in the transition from absolutism to the liberal state. The logic that explains the shift from the classical theatre to the family drama, in evidence in the plays of Diderot in France and in those of Moratín in Spain, also explains, as Rodríguez duly observes,[83] why, at the time of the French Revolution, patients begin to be transferred from state hospitals to the private domain of the family.[84] That said, it is with the matrix effect of the social formations, insofar as this impacts the theatre, that the Spaniard is principally concerned and it is to this 'scene' that he returns to theorise further the mechanisms of the ideological unconscious.

Even as, like any practising Althusserian, he accepts the relative autonomy of the different social instances (economic, political, and ideological), Rodríguez lingers on the causal connections, mediated through the social formation, between the liberal state and the bourgeois stage. With respect to the former, it bears recalling, signatories to the social contract can identify with the operations of the state precisely on the grounds that nothing existed *prior to* the state. In other words, liberal theory in effect presupposes the contrast between 'nature' and 'artifice'. The same logic, according to Rodríguez, dictates that the theatre audience can identity with events on the stage.[85] The only qualification to this logic concerns, in both cases, the nature of the relationship involved, which, while it should be *direct*, should also respect the illusion of distance. In other words, citizens should feel that their political leaders *represent* them, even while they accept the basic autonomy of the state; just as, in the same way, an audience must be able to identify with actors on the stage, even as its members recognise that they are separated from the latter by a 'pit'. The same

---

82   Rodríguez 2008b, p. 117.
83   Ibid., 118.
84   For details of this second process, Rodríguez acknowledges the contribution of Foucault's *The Birth of the Clinic*.
85   Rodríguez 2008b, p. 120 ff.

principle even determined acting styles: to act the part of a poor individual, for example, was not to behave as that individual might behave *in reality*: 'private truth, represented by the subjects entering into a contract, is not exactly equivalent to its public representation in the state or in the theatre'.[86] In sum, at all points the same standard prevailed: the illusion of proximity but never to the point of transparency.

Qualifications are in order when, still following Rodríguez, we turn to the theatre of the 'passions', which existed throughout the Enlightenment alongside the dominant family drama. In contrast to the latter, which was rooted in the classic bourgeois ideologies of rationalism and empiricism, this alternative theatrical tradition is secreted by the residual ideologies of the transition, notably, a substantialism now stripped of its sacralised elements and a re-emergent animism that was in the process of mutating into a recognizably petty-bourgeois ideology. I refer the reader to the relevant pages of *State, Stage, Subject* for more detail.[87] For our present purposes, it suffices to note the important respects in which this alternative theatrical tradition differs from its liberal counterpart. Principally, it demands of actors that they *identify* as much as possible with the parts they play, in defiance of a liberal tradition that, we have seen, insists on maintaining a certain distance. Dimly discernible are the outlines of an alternative theory of state, one that presupposes the existence of a natural, pre-social identity, from which the social individual is *alienated*.[88]

To all of which, Rodríguez would add one important proviso: the theatre of the passions constitutes a development internal to the bourgeois tradition, in other words, is appropriately conceived not as a challenge to the Enlightenment but, on the contrary, as 'the full revelation of the truth of rationalist order'.[89]

8   The Revenge of History

Althusser's notion of the unconsciousness of ideology proved to be a problematic legacy, particularly when combined with his materialist thesis of the specificity of thought and the process of thought with respect to the real. It was doubtless his former master's under-theorisation of the latter that encouraged Foucault to detach his concept of a discursive unconsciousness from the

---

86   Ibid., p. 121.
87   Ibid., pp. 123–31.
88   Ibid., p. 140.
89   Ibid., p. 127.

domain of the extra-discursive, a manoeuvre that the break from an archaeology of knowledge to a genealogy of power did little to rectify. Once Althusser's
general framework of relatively autonomous social practices had been jet-
tisoned, the impact of the real *on* language largely disappears in favour of the
power of language to name, classify and order the real. The theorisation of
Power effectively allowed Foucault to shift the focus from the rules of discourse
to practices and institutions, whereby to capture the mechanics of a domination that circulates unconsciously throughout social formations. That said,
insofar as power was always already present as a pre-social force, it did not lend
itself to distinguishing between different practices – economic, political, and
ideological. And that was not least of its drawbacks: power also proved to be an
unstable basis on which to construct an effective politics of resistance, which
explains, among other things, the reason for Foucault's final absorption into a
neo-liberal conformity.

Rodríguez, by way of contrast, was forced to watch from the margins of
an academic culture increasingly hostile to Marxism, whilst what he understood as the 'ideological unconscious' affirmed its hold under the umbrella
of a globalising financial capitalism. Capitalism's great success, he continued
to iterate, was that it had been able to disguise the reality of an 'infrastructure of exploitation', to the point at which the mechanisms of this exploitation
had become invisible. Without our realising it, we had come to accept, unconsciously, that 'we are born free'. The process was one that Rodríguez charged
Foucault with having facilitated, in conjunction with a 'Cultural Studies' that
would increasingly promote his texts. Obsessively he charted the spread of
archaeology and disciplinarity,[90] and when in 2008 the neo-liberal doctrines
that Foucault had finally come to embrace entered into crisis, he attacked with
a vengeance. 'Where are they now?' he asked, 'All those more or less phant-
asmagorical ramblings about social well-being, the rights of Man, full democracy and trans-national citizenship?'[91] Had he lived, the mockery ran, Foucault, for one, would have needed to do some serious re-thinking. 'How come
that nobody saw exactly what it meant to surrender oneself to a capitalism
whose hands had been freed?'[92] And doubtless, had he himself lived to witness
the recent turn of historical events – he died in 2016 – Rodríguez would have
further expatiated on the connection between Foucault's confessedly 'fictional'
narratives and the various exponents of 'fake' news.

---

90   E.g., Rodríguez 2002b, p. 79 ff.
91   Rodríguez 2013, p. 340.
92   Ibid., p. 340.

CHAPTER 7

Educating the Educators: The Critical Realists

The concept of the ideological unconscious, I argued in Chapter 2, raises major problems for critical realism, given the importance that this tradition attaches to 'intentional consciousness', which sits uncomfortably alongside the notion of the unconscious, whether libidinal or ideological. To further substantiate my claims, I need to persuade critical realists to take an interest in two areas which, to date, they have largely ignored, namely literature and literary theory, and history. Indeed, three of the weakest entries in the *Dictionary of Critical Realism* are those that deal respectively with 'aesthetics', 'historiography' and 'literary theory'.[1] The lack of interest in aesthetics is explained, if not justified, on the grounds of its roots in idealism,[2] whereas literary critics 'must emphasise [...] that texts simultaneously transcend and yet are grounded in contexts and reality'.[3] The reference to transcendence does not augur well for historiography, at least in its materialist guise. The critical realist contribution thereto, it comes as no surprise to discover, hinges largely on the form a critical realism-based narrative *would* take.[4] To add to our concerns, Roy Bhaskar himself, usually an enthusiastic promoter of holistic causality, appears to mark off the literary realm from any contaminating truck with the economy: 'Many of the Marxist critiques of capitalism as a hegemonic totality have viewed it expressively, as explaining what goes on in music and art as much as in the sphere of production. I do not want to go along with that kind of reductionism or expressivism'.[5] Disappointingly, he shares the traditional emphasis, eagerly embraced by generations of bourgeois critics, upon literature's crippled capacity to refer to the objective world.[6] Structural Marxism is no more interested in reductionism and expressivism than is critical realism – indeed, the *relative autonomy* of social instances or levels is central to its concerns – but it will resist tenaciously any attempt to insulate literature and the arts against the matrix effect of the social formation, seen as a totality. For the rest, suffice it to say that the Althusserian

---

1 Hartwig, ed., 2007. The respective entries are those of Tobin Nellhaus, Günter Minnerup and Philip Tew.
2 Ibid., p. 16.
3 Ibid., p. 281.
4 Ibid., p. 236.
5 Bhaskar with Hartwig 2010, p. 99.
6 Bhaskar 1991, p. 123.

focus upon the generative mechanisms that *produce* historical texts accords closely with the basic principles of critical realism, as will quickly become apparent in what follows.

But our first task must be to flesh out the concept of the ideological unconscious, as understood by Althusser.

1   Althusserian Unconsciousness Re-Visited

'Marxism', according to Bhaskar, 'never came to terms with the role of consciousness, ideas and intentionality, the defining characteristics of human agency, as foundational features of social life'.[7] Althusser's position on Marxism, by way of contrast, is best defined by simply reproducing the above comment but substituting 'unconsciousness' for 'consciousness, ideas and intentionality'. As we have seen, ideology for the French philosopher had very little to do with 'consciousness': people become conscious of their place in the world from within an ideological unconsciousness, the role of the latter being to facilitate social intercourse and to grease the workings of society in general. This emphasis upon unconsciousness would survive Althusser's shift of focus to ideological interpellation and his subsequent auto-critiques, indeed, would be positively enhanced when, subsequently, he became far less confident in the capacity of science to keep ideological influences at bay. These influences were generated, according to *Philosophy and the Spontaneous Philosophy of the Scientists*, within scientific practice and introduced from without, in the form of, for example, religious beliefs, political convictions, etc. Consider the following, in which Althusser assesses the reach of ideology within teaching:

> For intellectuals, nothing could be more difficult than perceiving the ideology conveyed by education, and by its curriculum, its forms and its practices. This applies to the sciences as well as the arts. Intellectuals live in culture, just as fish live in water; but fish cannot see the water in which they swim. Everything about them militates against their having any accurate perception of the social position of the culture in which they are steeped, of the teaching which dispenses it, or of the disciplines they practise – to say nothing of the positions they occupy in this society as intellectuals, academic or research workers. Everything militates against it ... Their practice, which they carry out in a framework defined

---

7   Bhaskar 2002a, p. 188n15.

by laws that they do not control, thus spontaneously produces an ideology which they live without having any reason to break out of it. But matters do not end there. Their own ideology, the spontaneous ideology of their practice (their ideology of science or the arts) does not depend solely on their practice: it depends mainly and in the last instance on the dominant ideological system of the society in which they live. Ultimately, it is this ideological system especially that governs the very forms of their ideology of science and of the arts. Whatever seems to happen before their eyes happens, in reality, *behind their backs*.[8]

In his earlier work, to recall, Althusser had deployed the metaphor of 'secretion' through which to theorise the overdetermination of any contradiction and of any constitutive element of society. Ideologies, he explained, 'have sufficient of their own consistency *to survive beyond their immediate life context*, even to recreate, to "secrete" substitute conditions of existence temporarily'.[9] By the time of *Philosophy and Spontaneous Philosophy*, he was thinking rather in terms of a 'cement', of Gramscian extraction, whilst still attempting to preserve the liquidity of the earlier image.

It should be noticed that, while insistent on the *unconscious* workings of ideology, at no point does Althusser speak of an 'ideological unconscious' as such, and the recent publication of previously unedited texts gives some indication as to why. Specifically, in his 'Three Notes on the Theory of Discourses', in which he grapples with Lacan and the libidinal unconscious, Althusser cedes the term 'unconscious' to psychoanalysis. Thus: 'The unconscious is the theoretical object (or object of knowledge) of psychoanalytic theory'.[10] By the same token, he reserves the 'subject' for historical materialism, which allows him to argue that the discourse of the unconscious 'is produced in and through ideological discourse'.[11] The solution is a neat one: it undoubtedly enables the Marxist to respect the autonomy of regional theories, while at the same time continuing to castigate the likes of Lévi-Strauss, who allegedly lacks any notion of a social formation or mode of production and is compelled, accordingly, to prioritise the notion of the subject *qua* 'human spirit' or 'brain'.[12] That said, it unfortunately has the further effect of precluding the notion of a distinctively 'ideological unconscious'. To consider how this concept is developed in Rodríg-

8   Althusser 1990b, p. 95.
9   Althusser 1990a, pp. 115–16.
10   Althusser 2003, p. 38.
11   Ibid., p. 60.
12   Ibid., p. 26.

uez, let us resume his discussion of the break between feudal *substantialism*, the dominant ideology of feudalism, and *animism*, the first form of bourgeois ideology.

2   Extracting the Concept

We take as our point of departure Andrew Collier's *Scientific Realism and Socialist Thought* (1989), as an early and superior popular presentation of critical realism, focusing specifically on a couple of pages that deal with the concept of 'extraction', as used by Althusser to characterise empiricism. Summarising Althusser's argument, Collier highlights the importance attributed to Galileo's promotion of the metaphor of the world as a book, which the Italian proposes as a model to those who, alternatively, would turn to the books of Aristotle, the latter viewed as a quasi-religious doctrine of 'vision' in which nature is transparent to our gaze. Collier supports the Althusserian reference with a comparable one to Bacon, which he correctly relates to the Protestant turn from scholastic theology to the Bible. The tactic is to connect this early opposition to scholastic doctrine, evinced by Galileo and Bacon, to Althusser's subsequent critique of empiricism, on the basis that both promote the notion of the transparent gaze.[13]

Collier's explanation is not as clear as it might be and only too brief, a symptom no doubt of the philosopher's impatience with the nitty-gritty of historical detail and the hurried conflation of centuries of scholarship and cultural history. The command to 'read the world as a book', we wish to argue, means different things to different social formations and, particularly during the complex transition from feudalism to capitalism, needs to be treated with particular care. To illustrate, let us first consider the slogan as it operates in its purest form, namely within substantialism, the heartland of feudal ideology. I take as my example a text of the medieval monk, Gonzalo de Berceo (ca. 1195–after 1262).

In the introduction to his *Milagros de nuestra señora* (*The Miracles of Our Lady*), Berceo describes the experience of a pilgrim who, during a long journey, takes refuge in a wonderful meadow, surrounded by all the glories of nature – flowers, streams, trees, fruit, birds, and so on. Just when the twenty-first-century reader is poised, unconsciously, to read the passage for its transparent literalness, however, the medieval bard calls a halt to proceedings:

---

13   Collier 1989, pp. 2–5.

Sennores e amigos,   lo que dicho avemos
palavra es oscura,   esponerla queremos:
tolgamos la corteza,   al meollo entremos,
prendamos lo de dentro,   lo de fuerza dessemos.[14]

(Friends and lords, what we have said / is a dark word; we wish to expose
it. / Let us remove the shells; let us enter the marrow. / Let us take what is
within, let us reject what is without.)

He then proceeds to *read* each of the wonders enumerated for their hidden,
allegorical meaning.

We need to pause and to carefully consider the scriptural framework that
sustains this and other such *dual* texts. The latter, it is important to realise, are not the 'works' of 'authors' who, as free subjects, 'express' what lies
within the privacy of their personal thoughts, but *'commentaries'* upon the
only book known to feudalism, the book of the Lord, be it the world or the
Bible. By the same token, the objects of *this* world (as opposed to the next)
are not *free* objects, but God's *signatures*, bearing the imprint of God's voice,
obscured by the Fall and now accessible only to those who know how to
read them, hermeneutically. And the reader of the feudal text is anything
but a *free* reader, but someone subject to the controlling apparatus of the
church hierarchy, which mediated all access to the sacred texts: reading, it
bears recalling, could be an occupation hazardous to life and limb. Protestant
claims to have *direct* access to a transparent text mark a radical break with
this normative process and were understood by contemporaries to be such.
From our standpoint, they signify the impact upon religion of a new ideology, that of the ascendant bourgeoisie, an ideology that was going to insti-
tute a radically new scriptural framework, based on the transparency of the
text and the 'free subject', free, in the last instance, to sell his or her labour
in the 'free' market. In this changed context, 'reading the world' will have a
radically different meaning, to understand which let us return to Collier's argument.[15]

Althusser, we are informed, identifies empiricism with a particular variant
of the notion of the transparency of the text, based on a process of 'abstrac-

---

14   Berceo 2011, p. 20.
15   For further detail on the relations between animism and religion, readers are referred to
      Theory and History of Ideological Production, specifically to the section on Christian anim-
      ism (Rodríguez 2002a, pp. 189–222).

tion', whereby 'the essence is abstracted from the real objects in the sense of an *extraction*, as one might say that gold is *extracted* (or abstracted, i.e. separated) from the dross of earth and sand in which it is held and contained'.[16] Collier feels a little uncomfortable with the extent to which Althusser is prepared to press this metaphor, but that is not the substance of his criticism, which is that '[n]o empiricist, so far as I know, has ever used this metaphor, yet Althusser says it was "*avowed* by the eighteenth century [*sic*] from Locke to Condillac"'.[17] The only historical reference he gives is to 'the aesthetics of Michelangelo'.[18] Collier concedes that the metaphor could be an attempt to describe Locke's distinction between primary and secondary qualities but believes that, if so, it is a misleading one.

One has to feel a little sorry for Althusser, famously savaged by E.P. Thompson in *The Poverty of Theory* and here given a rap over the knuckles for not knowing that Locke lived only four years of his life in the eighteenth century. Those writing on the Left need particularly to take note: they are being watched and had better get their 'facts' right. But we are not here to argue over the facts but over the importance attached to them, as the unconscious expression of an empiricist *literalism* that, Collier's doubts notwithstanding, found their classic thematisation in Locke and a cultural antecedent in Michelangelo. We will leave the Enlightenment until later. Taking our cue from Rodríguez, let us return to the reference to Michelangelo, somewhat summarily dismissed by Collier, to explore the ramifications of the idea of 'extraction', as mediated through the tradition of Petrarchan poetry and, in turn, through the early sixteenth-century Spanish poet, Garcilaso de la Vega.

> De aquella vista pura y excelente
> salen espirtus vivos y encendidos,
> y siendo por mis ojos recibidos,
> me pasan hasta donde el mal se siente;
>   éntranse en el camino fácilmente
> por do los míos como perdidos,
> llamados d'aquel bien que 'stá presente.
>   Ausente, en la memoria la imagino;
> mis espirtus, pensando que la vian,
> se mueven y se entienden sin medida;
>   mas no hallando fácil el camino,

---

16   Collier 1989, p. 2. Collier is citing Althusser and Balibar 1970, p. 36.
17   Ibid., p. 3. Collier is citing Althusser and Balibar 1970, p. 38.
18   Ibid.

que los suyos entrando derretían,
revientan por salir do no hay salida.[19]

(From that pure and excellent countenance / issue living and burning spirits that / being received by my eyes / pass within to where the hurt is felt. / On the way, they freely mingle with my spirits and moved by the same flame / sally forth, as if lost / attracted by that goal that is present. / When she is absent, I remember her; / my spirits, thinking that they see her, / are stirred and kindled to ecstasy; / but finding their path blocked / melt on contact with her spirits / and struggle to issue forth where no issue can be.)

Rodríguez picks up the thread of the Althusserian reference to Michelangelo or, to be more specific, two lines of a poem by Michelangelo,[20] through which to explore the process of abstraction as exemplified by Garcilaso. But before following him, we need to clarify some basic aspects of the sonnet form, which, through their sheer obviousness, are in danger of being passed over. Firstly, as we have already discussed, the Garcilasan text is separated from the feudal 'book' by a 'break', of the kind theorised by Althusser, through its capacity to foreground the literal (albeit frustrated) exchange between the eyes of the lover and his beloved. The eyes ('being received by my eyes') betray the presence not of serfs but of *beautiful souls* or proto-subjects, who view the world from their own particular, unique standpoint or *perspective*. But let us get back to the details of the Garcilasan text and the baring of the idea.

The conceptual nucleus of the sonnet stands opposed to what is superfluous or contingent in the soul, from which it is extracted in the same way that a 'form' is sculptured from the marble, etc. The baring, in both cases, presupposes a process of labour, otherwise the labour of reduction and condensation, of which, in the case of the 'sonnet', the text is the outcome. The capacity to carry out this operation is the unique, distinctive hallmark of the 'beautiful soul', to be distinguished from the common rump of mankind, not by his 'blood' or 'lineage' but by his sensitivity to the force of love, the Soul of the World, that permeates the whole of *this* world as much as the *next*.

It is in this sense, then, that the Petrarchan 'I' can be said to be the result of extraction or abstraction. It is immaterial whether the 'lady' extracts the beau-

---

19   Garcilaso 1989, pp. 54–5.
20   'Non ha l'ottimo partista alcun concetto / che un marmor solo in sé non circonscriva' (The best artist does not have any concept that is not circumscribed within the marble itself) (Rodríguez 2002a, p. 74).

tiful soul from the interior of the poet or whether the poet extracts it from his 'lady': the process of paring or baring the concept is the same.[21] In the words of Rodríguez:

> The problematic of 'extraction', it follows, always requires that, within this Neoplatonic context, all ideological production (specifically poetic) be conceived as nothing other than the process of constitution of the notion of the beautiful soul, either as an idea (or 'essential nucleus') shaped in the sonnet, or as the presentation of the sculpturing in itself (of its successes or its failures).[22]

While this is no place to enter into larger social issues relating to sixteenth-century Spain, to fail to see the struggle between substantialism and animism as part of a broader, class-based struggle between a dominant aristocracy and an emergent bourgeoisie is to understand nothing about the contradictions internal to the Spanish Absolutist State. The task that faced the bourgeoisie was to replace a social hierarchy founded upon seigneurial notions of lineage with one founded upon the spiritual qualities of the beautiful soul. 'Whence it transpires', writes León Hebreo in his classic animist text, *Diálogos de amor* (1535),

> That the inferior person not only loves with reason and desires to be joined to their superior, but also that the superior person loves and desires to be joined to their inferior, so that each should be as perfect as their station allows, and so that the universe should be united and bound tightly together, through the ligature of the love that connects the corporeal world to the spiritual, and the inferior to the superior.[23]

For a moment, under the rule of the new Emperor, Charles, it appeared that such notions might prove triumphant. Yet within a generation, the major exponents of animism, sometimes known as humanists, either prudently left the country, like Juan de Valdés, or, alternatively, like Juan de Vergara, found themselves rotting in the gaols of the Inquisition. The latter institution refused, in typically substantialist manner, to draw any distinction between the public and private spheres, a distinction indispensable not only to the workings of cap-

---

21   Indeed, it is immaterial whether the 'other' is a man or a woman. Garcilaso's sonnet XXXV is dedicated to the Florentine poet and friend, Mario Galeota.
22   Rodríguez 2002a, p. 75.
23   Hebreo [1535] 1947, p. 147.

italism but to the survival of animism. Ideologically, the consequences were enormous, including, among other things, the substantialist take-over of major animist genres – the sonnet, the picaresque novel, the stage-play – the latter destined to be filled with substantialist content. We return to aspects of this counter-revolution below, but for the moment let us pause to elaborate on the theoretical basis implicit in the above.

3   Causal Dynamics

In the classic Althusserian fashion, Rodríguez, we have seen, argues in the introduction to *Theory and History of Ideological Production* that every mode of production consists of three levels or instances: the economic, political, and ideological. While each level exerts its own influence, which allows it to be abstracted for analytic purposes, it is vital to envisage the determinate processes of the relatively autonomous levels as operating simultaneously, if unequally, at the level of the structured whole. We will be constantly misled in our reading of the Spaniard's work if we fail to hold in focus this key notion of complex unity, understood as involving the ongoing interaction of social elements caught in a constant interplay of reciprocal movements.

The forms of 'individuality', Rodríguez further argues, are distinct in each mode of production, so that there can be no individuality that is prior to its ideological constitution. We are faced rather with the construction of historical subjectivities from birth, a notion that forms the basis of Rodríguez's distinctive notion of an *ideological matrix*, according to which each mode is characterised by its own distinctive relation between exploiter and exploited. In the slave mode and under feudalism, the distinction between exploiter and exploited is clear, as is the nature of the exploitative process through which the former extracts the social surplus from the latter. Under capitalism, by way of contrast, the two elements of the matrix appear equal – a fair day's work for a fair day's pay – masking thereby the exploitative nature of the extractive process. The effect of these matrices is to annul the traditional base / superstructure relation in favour of a completely new problematic and to further displace the focus of attention from the subject, as the alleged source of ideology, to the systematics of each mode. In no sense can ideology be understood as a combination of political or philosophical ideas. It is rather constituted as a level, as real and material as any other. In sum:

> [I]n the construction of the image of the subject, the battle against the feudal ideology of servitude represents only one factor: the other factor

(the other face of the coin) is rooted in the actual construction of the bourgeois matrix, a matrix that requires that the articulation between different classes (dominant and dominated) always be conceived from the standpoint of the image of all men as free subjects, equal among themselves, in possession of their own inner truth. Without this basic image such a system cannot function. In other words, if the logic of the subject can only exist on the basis of certain objective conditions inscribed in a particular ideological matrix, if the 'subject' is an invention of this 'matrix', it will be pointless searching for such a logic within, for example, a 'slavery' ideology or the feudal ideology of 'service'.[24]

A certain amount of uncertainty has arisen in Marxism as to the precise mechanisms involved in these social relations. With respect to the operations of ground rent and landed property, Marx himself talked in terms of a 'general illumination which bathes all the other colours and modifies their particularity'. He elaborates: 'It is a particular ether which determines the specific gravity of every being which has materialised within it'.[25] Strange to say, his followers have failed to pick up on the potential fertility of such metaphors. Althusser, we saw above, opts for the notion of 'secretion', on the basis of which, presumably, Rodríguez proceeded to envisage 'serf' and 'subject' as 'mere secretions' of their respective ideological matrices.[26] That said, 'secretion' has provoked a certain amount of confusion and anxiety in translators and commentators,[27] and even Rodríguez appears to have his doubts, hence opting increasingly for 'the humus that sustains us or, rather, that pervades our every gesture',[28] as a way of capturing the influence of the ideological unconscious. Any remaining uncertainty in the case of the Spaniard doubtless stems from his desire to retain the notion of *fluidity*, through which to capture the extent to which an ideological unconscious 'soaks' or 'saturates' the literary text.[29]

Such semantic niceties are not without their importance. Superficially, they simply betray the attempts of theoreticians to grasp the complexities of psy-

---

24   Rodríguez 2002a, p. 18.
25   Marx 1973, p. 107.
26   Rodríguez 2002a, p. 23.
27   In a recent collection of essays on Althusser, we learn, among other things, that ideology 'generates or "secrets away" its systems of representations, ideas, beliefs' (Diefenbach at al. 2013, p. 289). Rodríguez's translator decides at one point to paraphrase the Spanish 'se segrega' with 'derives directly from' (Rodríguez 2002a, p. 30). For further discussion, see Read 2017.
28   Rodríguez 2008b, p. 22.
29   Rodríguez 2011a, pp. 34–5.

chic/social processes that cannot be observed directly. More profoundly, they raise the question of whether terms invented for one domain can be made serve effectively for others. At all events, of more concern in the present instance is the structural functioning of the ideological unconscious within the framework of the social formation.

Rodríguez, to reiterate, went to considerable lengths to argue, against his fellow Althusserians, that ideology is neither born in the individual nor in the school but, in the last instance, secreted from within 'the interior of the social relations themselves'.[30] After all, he asks, who educates the educators? The Spaniard's overt targets were Renée Balibar and Pierre Macherey, but in truth Althusser himself, in his classic essay 'Ideology and Ideological State Apparatuses', concedes only as an after-thought that the class struggle has its roots in the infrastructure.[31] Similarly, *Philosophy of the Encounter* succumbs to an institutionalist sociologism in the form of a preoccupation with factory buildings, machines and raw materials, at the expense of the exploitation that takes place in production.[32]

This difference of opinion over the location and functioning of ideology happily bridges the work of Rodríguez with that of Bhaskar. The latter, particularly in the works of the spiritual turn, is quick to promote the view that humankind's inalienable communist instincts are simply over-lain by non-communist elements. He concludes:

> So the project must be, in the immortal words of Marx's third thesis on Feuerbach, to educate the educators, the transformers of society, and this means, on the primacy of self-referentiality, their self-education, self-empowerment, that is, their shedding of everything that prevents them expressing their true nature which Marxism along with other secular projects must presuppose.[33]

Self-education requires that school pupils should free themselves from the chains of ideological unfreedom: 'Just go into the classroom, be empty, carry nothing in your mind'.[34] By this stage, we deduce, the philosopher has long since abandoned his self-perception as an *underlabourer* for the sciences and is now lecturing Marxists upon how they *must* constitute a utopian science,

---

30   Rodríguez 2002a, p. 30.
31   Althusser 1971, pp. 147–8.
32   Althusser 2006, p. 122.
33   Bhaskar 2002c. pp. 319–20.
34   Bhaskar 2002b, p. 335.

through a self-conscious process of *shedding*. This notion is one that the Spanish Marxist would view as remarkably naïve, but to understand more fully why, we need to sketch in some of the broader parameters of Bhaskar's work.

4   Reclaiming Reality

On more than one occasion, Bhaskar takes Althusser to task for, in *For Marx* and *Reading Capital*, leaving the criterion of scientificity completely intrinsic to science. The damage wrought by such epistemological autonomy allegedly proves devastating on several accounts: firstly, notwithstanding its status as a science of science, philosophy was left without a clear role; and, secondly, the *real object*, although ontologically prior to the *object of thought*, was reduced to the quasi-Kantian status of a limited concept.[35] While such criticism is to the point, Althusser, we know, conducted an auto-critique in his later works, as part of which philosophy was re-cast as an underlabourer charged with defending the category of science against the encroachments of ideology. Why, then, as Michael Sprinker reasonably asks, does Bhaskar continue to prioritise the early texts over those that issue from the auto-critique?[36]

Bhaskar's preference, I suggest, is to be explained by his equally strong attachment to the negative view of ideology that characterised Althusser's early work. As he had already explained in *Scientific Realism and Human Emancipation*: '[I]f emancipation is to be possible, well-grounded explanations of false consciousness and more generally ill-being must be capable of informing self-conscious transformative practice',[37] which directs us, in turn, to what is generally accepted as a particularly significant section of *The Possibility of Naturalism*:

> Society is both the ever-present *condition* (material cause) and the continually reproduced *outcome* of human agency. And praxis is both work, that is, conscious *production*, and (normally unconscious) *reproduction* of the conditions of production, that is society [...]. The conception I am proposing is that people, in their conscious activity, for the most part unconsciously reproduce (and occasionally transform) the structures governing their substantive activities of production. Thus people do not marry to reproduce the nuclear family or work to sustain the capitalist economy.

---

35   Bhaskar 1989b, p. 143.
36   Sprinker 1992, p. 131.
37   Bhaskar 1986, p. 242.

Yet it is nevertheless the unintended consequence (and inexorable result) of, as it is also a necessary condition for, their activity. Moreover, when social forms change, the explanation will not normally lie in the desires of agents to change them that way, though as a very important theoretical and political limit it *may* do so.[38]

Crucial in the present context is the opposition between 'conscious' and 'unconscious'. Critical realism is interested in ideology but less so in the unconscious, which, when mentioned in its texts, usually refers unambiguously to the libidinal or Freudian unconscious.[39] Quickly following upon this opposition is another, namely the ontological hiatus between people and society: 'I want to distinguish sharply, then, between the genesis of human actions, lying in the reasons, intentions and plans of people, on the one hand, and the structures governing the reproduction and transformation of social activities, on the other; and hence between the domain of psychological and the social sciences'.[40]

The problem with Bhaskar's argument is that, while it appears to allow for social forces that 'condition' agency, there is little or no sense in which an Althusserian 'ideological unconscious', secreted at the level of social relations, could conceivably pervade or marinate agency. The result is to leave the agent looking decidedly 'free' and sprightly and in full control of his/her intentions (to get married). The 'individual'/'society' opposition, I am saying, leaves the former remarkably insulated against the effects of the latter.[41]

Not surprisingly, the hiatus between people and societies was eagerly seized upon by Bhaskar's followers. Collier, for example, encourages us to imagine a situation in which, while all fundamental relations of production remain the same, two-thirds of the population of Britain are converted to Buddhism or Catholicism. While people's cultural habits, such as those associated with eating and drinking, may undergo a substantial change, the philosopher spec-

---

38   Bhaskar [1979] 1989a, pp. 34–5.
39   There is no entry for the unconscious in *Dictionary of Critical Realism*, and when the Freudian unconscious is mentioned, it usually takes second place to the ego, on the basis of Freud's protestations that 'Where id was, there ego shall be'. Symptomatically, Collier will reject the Lacanian reading of Freud that not only privileges the id but also – a major barrier to its reception within the ambit of the British academy – sins against the liberal preference for the 'plain style', which is to say for transparency. Bhaskar's attitude to psychoanalysis can at best be described as lukewarm. It is debatable, he typically explains (2002a, p. 156), whether it is the best way of getting rid of repressed residues.
40   Bhaskar 1989a, p. 35.
41   Kathryn Dean makes the same point (Dean et al. 2006, p. 161).

ulates, the inhabitants would still be living in a capitalist society.[42] What is notable about this experiment is not its result but the ease with which Collier can imagine a situation in which a capitalist society does not perforce secrete its own ideological superstructure; also with which he happily combines radically dissonant ideologies, seemingly detached from the economy.[43] In point of fact, there is no need of such thought experiments, since we have the historical evidence of what happens in the transition from feudalism to capitalism. One thing to notice, if not the first, is that the transition coincides with a carefully orchestrated, ideological shift in people's eating habits.[44]

It is true, of course, that Bhaskar's work did not stand still, and that he subsequently moved on to a dialectical stage, at which he explored many other levels of an increasingly structured and differential totality. It would be unreasonable, therefore, to hold him to the letter of *The Possibility of Naturalism*. That said, we subsequently find him still vigorously promoting the existence of 'well-grounded and causally efficacious reasons',[45] which combines, following his spiritual turn, with an even more insistent prioritising of self-change over social change.[46] Man, it is important to recognise, after Rousseau, is 'essentially free, but everywhere in chains',[47] chains that it is well within our capacity to '*shed*', should we be prepared to set our minds to it. Of course, it continues to be a fact that social structures, notably of a capitalist kind, are not just *out there*, but *in here*,[48] but not to the extent that the causal efficacy of ideas is in any way compromised: 'the moment you change yourself you are in the first instance immediately making society better'.[49]

I think we are now in a much better position to understand the puzzle that Sprinker raised with respect to Bhaskar's preference for the early as opposed to the late Althusser. What Bhaskar finds intolerable in the latter is the enormous causal efficacy attributed to ideology, at the expense of science, and the extent

---

42 Collier 1989, p. 97.
43 Somewhat surprisingly, Collier critiques Althusser for misplaced concreteness in distinguishing separate practices as ideological or scientific, rather than separate aspects of the same practice (Collier 1989, pp. 27–8), a claim that hardly squares with the positions outlined in *Philosophy and the Spontaneous Philosophy of the Scientists*.
44 The classic text on the refinement of social manners is Baldassare Castiglione's *Book of the Courtier* (1528). Reformation of Spanish eating habits had begun much earlier, in D. Enrique de Villena's *El arte cisoria* (1412).
45 Bhaskar 1993, p. 276.
46 Bhaskar 2002b, p. 44.
47 Bhaskar 2002b, p. 127.
48 Bhaskar 2002a, p. 151.
49 Bhaskar 2002c, p. 326.

to which it permeates the transitive dimensions, to the detriment of the 'free subject'. To defend these claims, I propose to return to the question, first raised, albeit in abstract, philosophical terms, in *The Possibility of Naturalism*, as to what it is to choose to get married, except that I will now be taking seriously the radical historicity of culture.

5   Love, Money, and Marriage

The plot of Moratín's *El sí de las niñas* (*The Maidens' Consent*) (1806) may be briefly summarised. Doña Francisca belongs to a family that, following the death of her father, has 'come down in the world'. The ambition of her mother, Doña Irene, is to marry her off to Don Diego, a wealthy older man who has taken a fancy to the young girl. Unfortunately for Don Diego, Doña Francisca, although a model of obedience (after having been 'well educated' in a convent), has fallen in love with Don Carlos, a young military man and cousin to Don Diego. After considerable intrigue, through which Doña Francisca's secret attachment is discovered, Don Diego cedes to the young girl's wishes and allows her to marry the man of her choice. The following section is from scene 11 of the first act:

DA IRENE	She is an obedient girl and will always do what her mother tells her.
D. DIEGO	That is true, but ...
DA IRENE	She is of good blood, chaste in thought, and will behave as she should, with honour.
D. DIEGO	Yes, I realise that; but without sacrificing her honour or her blood, could she not ...?
DA FRANCISCA	Shall I go, mama? (She gets up from her chair, then sits down again.)
DA IRENE	Certainly not, sir. She's been well brought up, the daughter of respectable parents, and cannot avoid behaving on all occasions as is fit and proper. The girl, as you see her now, is the very image of her grandmother.

After Doña Irene has declaimed, at inordinate length, on the aristocratic lineage of her family, the dialogue continues:

DA FRANCISCA	Shall I go, mama?
DA IRENE	Very well, off you go! Dear me! Why the rush?

DA FRANCISCA	Do you want me to do a French curtsy, Don Diego? (She gets up and curtsies graciously towards Don Diego, kisses Doña Irene, and goes off to the latter's room.)
D. DIEGO	Yes, my daughter. Please do!
DA FRANCISCA	Look!
D. DIEGO	Beautifully done! Three cheers for Paquita!
DA FRANCISCA	For you a curtsy, for mama a kiss.

Doña Irene and Don Diego then converse:

DA IRENE	She's an impish little thing, and pretty with it.
D. DIEGO	She has a certain natural flair that's fetching.
DA IRENE	What do you expect? Brought up without worldly artifice or trickeries, happy to find herself at her mother's side again.
D. DIEGO	My only wish is that she should talk more freely about our projected union and ...
DA IRENE	You'd hear the same from her.
D. DIEGO	No doubt I would; but I know that she finds me agreeable, and to hear it from that lovely little mouth of hers would be for me a joy indeed.
DA IRENE	You can rest assured in that respect; but bear in mind that it is not proper for a young lady to express openly what she feels ...

Doña Irene explains how ill-advised it is for fathers to marry off their teenage daughters to men who are hardly any older:

| DA IRENE | ... Who will be the one to run the home? Who the one to teach and correct the children? Because, sad to say, these young scatterbrains soon have a horde of children. |
| D. DIEGO | It's certainly sad to see surrounded by children many of those who lack either the talent, the experience or the virtue necessary to rear them properly.[50] |

The aim of a scientific analysis, from an Althusserian standpoint, would be to reveal the structural mechanisms that make such a text possible, in other

---

50   Moratín 1968, pp. 179–85.

words, to be 'symptomatic' in the sense of identifying the text's problematic.[51] A play, like a novel or poem, is not constituted by its 'manifest' content, its overt propositions or even the intentions of its author, still less by what the characters in the play understand by their words and actions. It is constituted by the 'latent structures' that determine the production of the script or text. A useful analogy would be to imagine a series of threads attached to each word of the above, which, if we were to tug away at them sufficiently, would gradually drag into view the totality of the social formation, otherwise visible only in its textual effects.

A symptomatic analysis of the scenes from *The Maidens' Consent* would quickly lock onto the 'good blood' or 'honour' valued by a decadent aristocratic family, in opposition to the 'talent' and 'sincerity' embraced by a dominant (within the context of the play) bourgeois liberalism. Rodríguez sees 'blood' and 'honour' as two of the major *ideologemes* that characterise the residual feudal ideology of substantialism or organicism, secreted by an ideological matrix that binds the 'serf' or 'servant' to his or her lord/Lord. 'Talent' and 'sincerity', by way of contrast, sustain the increasingly dominant ideology of liberalism, itself a continuation of animism, the first ideology of an emergent bourgeoisie, which we saw in operation in the Renaissance lyric. The 'beautiful soul', defined in Platonic terms, was a proto-form of the subject that has now assumed its full status as a 'free subject', to which even women (!) may aspire. Hence the title of Moratín's work and Don Diego's singular insistence, his patriarchal status notwithstanding, that Doña Francisca 'explain herself to me with absolute freedom'.[52]

The drama that unfolds is driven by the fraught opposition between the realms of the transcendental and empirical or, more specifically, between 'love' and 'money', the major ideologemes that drive the action of Moratín's play. How is the tension between them to be resolved? Naturally enough, the young lovers are those most resistant to the importance attached to money: 'What do I care about all the riches of the world?' questions Doña Francisca, rhetorically. Her only ambition is 'to love and to be loved'.[53] 'I bet he's very rich', speculates Don Carlos about his elder competitor, before giving vent to his discontent: 'Money be damned! The origin of so many disorders!'.[54] Of course, the mature characters, Doña Irene and Don Diego, are far more sensitive to the need to economise – Don Diego literally controls the financial affairs of his nephew.

---

51   Althusser and Balibar 1970, pp. 28–30.
52   Moratín 1968, p. 173.
53   Ibid., p. 222.
54   Ibid., p. 226.

While demonstrative of their allegiances, none of the characters embraces any particular ideological position unambiguously. Thus, Don Diego is fully prepared to pick up on Doña Irene's deployment of 'blood' and 'honour', although he 'belongs' to another ideology and is thereby constrained to employ the substantialist concepts as extraneous elements. The ideological ambiguity extends to institutions, such as the army in which Don Carlos is an officer: originally a feudal apparatus, in which the soldier took an oath of allegiance to a feudal lord, it had become, within the context of the Absolutist State, a salaried profession under the control of a centralised monarchy.

The reference to the State is a reminder of the theatre's role as an ideological state apparatus, whose function it was to thematise and legitimise the dominant ideology. This ideology finds expression, in the first instance, in the stage itself or, more strictly, the scenic apparatus, which, the script of *The Maidens' Consent* is careful to indicate, consists of 'the lounge of a boarding house with doors of four rooms leading off it'.[55] The transformation that these details materialise cannot be emphasised enough: the public space of the Golden Age theatre, otherwise the Court, has been replaced by the private space of the bourgeoisie. No less important than the physical locale is the information that 'the action begins at seven o'clock in the evening and finishes at five o'clock the following day', the unity of time contributing as it does to a 'realistic' break that, in the new drama, also sees prose replace poetry as the medium of discourse. The new realism extends to acting styles that are to combine 'nature' with a certain degree of 'artifice', a dichotomy whose roots are buried deep in contemporary culture:

> D. DIEGO   But you look so worried when you say that, and ...
> DA IRENE   It's only natural, sir. Don't you see that ...
> D. DIEGO   Say no more, Doña Irene. Don't try to tell me what is natural ... What is natural is that ...[56]

When the cultural horizon is extended in this way, what finally comes into view is not just the scenic props, with their total illusion of naturalness, but the state itself, and understandably so, for as Rodríguez reminds us, the principles that rule the stage are the very ones that, through a complex process of structural causality, determine the liberal state:

---

55   Ibid., p. 164.
56   Ibid., p. 211.

The aim is always to ensure that the spectator should identify with the stage (in the same way that the individual citizen should identify with the state) or, in other words, that the public should identify with the private truth represented on the stage. To achieve this, it is necessary to devise certain processes of representation that are conducive to the identifying attitude on the part of the public.[57]

The consequences are far reaching. Specifically, a whole new stage craft is developed to ensure that the spectator is 'enclosed' by what are essentially *family* trappings, with certain qualifications, as Rodríguez explains: such elements should be represented not only as a model for the arrangement not only of domestic life (hence, the 'drawing room') but also of society at large, through the extraction of relevant norms, laws and, ultimately, the barely visible meaning that, unconsciously, determines our behaviour.[58] Which returns us to the notion of *extraction*, disparaged above by Collier but now articulated within the context of Spanish bourgeois culture, albeit of a belated, strictly embryonic kind. The target is the extraction of art from nature, along the lines of the classic French theatre of the Enlightenment.

[T]he actor [...] should not prefer the 'merely natural instinct to the limitless study of art'. It is not the man who is beside himself with rage who captivates us: such a 'privilege' is 'reserved for the man who dominates himself' [...] The exact portrayal of a mean man, says Diderot, by way of example, prevents us recognising him as such [...]. Bare truth, he adds, would be miserly on the stage for which reason the modelling is indispensable.[59]

While Moratín participated in the polemic surrounding the Shakespearean theatre,[60] it was clearly the French influence upon him that was paramount. Rodríguez elaborates:

[W]hile the theatrical stage should be based on nature, a performance, even though it accords with the natural model, should not be exactly the

---

57   Rodríguez 2008b, p. 122.
58   Ibid., p. 128.
59   Ibid., pp. 133–4.
60   Rodríguez has reproduced a facsimile edition of Moratín's translation of *Hamlet* (1798)
      (Rodríguez 1991). See also the same text for details of Moratín's sojourns through England
      (pp. 51–5).

same as nature. Similarly with respect to the actor, who, while needing to seek inspiration in daily life or in 'naturalised' reality (to use the contemporary term), should nevertheless interpret his part in a 'modelled' or 'sublimated' manner, so as to allow the spectator in turn to identify with – to recognise him/herself in – what is represented. In a word, just as the state should reflect everyone, should function as a liberal model for every one of its citizens who would identify with it, similarly, within the theatrical setting a 'distance' should be established between the stage and the public, only to be immediately negated through the ideology of identification.[61]

Our aim, needless to say, is not to collapse stage-craft into state-craft. Rather we have tried to hammer home the shift, in evidence in Rodríguez's work, from treating cause as a thing to treating it as a relation or, more exactly, as an over-determined displacement effected unevenly and contradictorily by a structure or structures upon its/their elements. Thus do we arrive at the notion of a decision, to get married, that is determined in the last instance by an ideological unconscious understood as the matrix effect of a whole mode of production. In the words of Rodríguez:

> Through its determination by the network of family relations, the stage naturally condenses a whole series of contradictions that were latent within the new bourgeois societies, which would explain why, for example, Moratín's *El sí de las niñas* is clearly characterised by a logic that operates without being named in the text; the logic, in other words, of a pre-existent, autonomous and superior value of the private spirit of the *subject*. On this basis, the true drama that unfolds in Moratín's text is sustained by a conflict – typical of the new ideology – between the interior individual and social relations. More specifically, certainly in the case of Moratín, prevailing social relations embody values that derive from feudalism and others that are simply 'exterior' to the individual (riches, social convention, nobility). The latter will end up being diluted, just as the patriarchs or *viejos* will themselves recognise that the young should not be made to do something that is alien to the truth of their spirit. Moratín has yet to reach the stage of the Romantics, who sing the all-powerful virtues of love. Rather he counterposes private, individual truth to the exterior norms that are integral to both bourgeois wealth and feudal priv-

---

61   Ibid., p. 134.

ilege. Thus, the girl will not marry the rich old gentleman but the young man chosen because of the truth of her heart, except that, from our standpoint, the important point is that the girl should have to get married; that, from start to finish, family relations – in other words marriage – determine the whole development of the action, whatever the concrete content of the scene at each moment and irrespective of the focus of our attention (upon the man or his young counterpart, upon exterior norms or truth itself).[62]

The following conclusion seems unavoidable: the pressures of patriarchy notwithstanding, the young girl experiences herself as *free*, to say 'yes' or 'no' to her prospective suitors, and doubtless, for very ideological reasons, does not wish to know otherwise. At the same time, however, *we* know, scientifically, that, while not (pre)determined in any regulatory sense, her decision is ubiquitously overdetermined by a causal network that extends, in the last instance, to the limits of the social formation.

6 Deprocessualising History

Notwithstanding his assertion of the materiality of all existence, also of the primacy of the 'real object' over the 'object of knowledge', Althusser, we saw earlier, has frequently been chastised for egregiously undertheorising the intransitive dimension in knowledge production, and not least of all by Bhaskar. 'It does not follow from the fact that we can only know in knowledge that we can only know knowledge!'.[63] Not surprisingly, given his allegiance to his former master, Rodríguez has also proved vulnerable to the same charge.[64] That said, it is important to get the balance exactly right. Althusser is the first to concede the relation between *thought*-about-the-real and this *real*; he wishes merely to insist that 'it is a relation of *knowledge*, a relation of adequacy or inadequacy of knowledge, not a real relation, meaning by this a relation inscribed in *that real* of which the thought is the (adequate or inadequate) knowledge'.[65] Also to be taken into account is the fact that, in the words of Michael Sprinker, '[i]f Althusser has comparatively little to say about the "real-concrete", this is just because he (perhaps wrongly) conceived that to be the exclusive prerogative of

---

62   Ibid., pp. 152–3.
63   Bhaskar 1989b, p. 188.
64   Read 2010, pp. 22–3.
65   Althusser and Balibar 1970, p. 87.

the sciences';[66] and that, if he further failed to clearly articulate the concept of structural causality, as has also been claimed, that was because he considered such tasks to be 'an entirely empirical matter'.[67]

Having established this much, let us consider whether Bhaskar's own realist pretensions can be cashed in, practically speaking, at least as far as historiography is concerned:

> Modernity and its philosophical discourses, and the ideologies and social practices which underlie it, replaced the semi-enchanted world of the classical philosophical discourses of religion. A concatenated sequence of breaks, the reaffirmation, the rise of Galilean and Newtonian science, the genesis of capitalism, the growth of the metropolitan cities at the expense of the countryside and colonies, the rise of new forms of political association, the development of new theories of perspective, and above all the Cartesian revolution in philosophy generated a new discourse: the philosophical discourse of modernity.[68]

I cite this passage, taken from a late essay on 'The Nous of Perception and Re-Enchantment of the Tree of Life', to illustrate the shift, noted above, from the early phase of critical realism, in which Bhaskar envisaged philosophy as the underlabourer of the sciences, to one in which, through a dialectical shift and subsequent spiritual turn, he begins to enlist the resources of the sciences, in this case historiography, to underlabour for critical realism. His aim, in this case, is to chart the course of historical development through the series of breaks coincident with the rise of bourgeois individualism, from the English revolutions of 1640–60 to the collapse of the actually existing socialist block in 1989, followed by the emergence of the possibility of a new way of being human.

What might look to some awfully like a traditional history of (free-floating) ideas has not discouraged his followers from presenting Bhaskar as supportive of a contextualised 'thrownness' of thinking in a geo-historic context.[69] The

---

66   Sprinker 1992, p. 130.
67   Sprinker 1992, p. 134. Althusser, it should be said, confesses to having neglected the 'extremely important question' of empirical knowledge, which had led to 'a few (troubling) *silences* or even *ambiguities*', and to having unnecessarily antagonised historians and sociologists, 'who spend their time and their lives […] producing empirical knowledge' (Althusser 2003, p. 13).
68   Bhaskar 2002c, p. 285.
69   Norrie 2010, p. 74.

same thrownness, in its critical realist guise, is further recommended as the antidote to an Anglo-American philosophy that 'discards history in favour of a logic-driven analysis of concepts' and whose inexcusable crime is to take our present concepts as *natural*: 'Lacking a sense of the (dialectical) relationship between (analytical) concepts and (constellating) history, [such philosophy] cannot see beyond the current state of the world and the concepts it has produced'.[70] Except that, as is immediately obvious from the ensuing passage in Alan Norrie's work, there is one seemingly trans-historical concept that critical realism refuses to relinquish and which, on the contrary, it wishes to prioritise above all others, namely the philosophical / ideological concept of the free subject, which, while admittedly affected by causes that are 'prior and external' to it, is nevertheless left in a condition of 'underdetermination'.[71]

As we have seen from our discussion of medieval texts, the concept of the free subject is far from being trans-historical. True, this is not something that Bhaskar himself is likely to register – 'I am not an expert on medieval times' –[72] any more than are his critical realist supporters, content as they are to leap from Plato and Aristotle to Locke and Hume in a twinkling of an eye, without attaching too much importance to the realities of slave, feudal, or capitalist modes of production. But there are consequences, the most obvious one being a rapid descent into pop psychology based on a struggle between ideas: 'Because if we are all set against each other then obviously we must wish to possess or control instrumentally each other so that the old ideas of community, loving and sharing and giving ... go'.[73] Those old ideas, as we have seen, were based on the reading of the world as a book, a perspective that Bhaskar, since he thinks unconsciously within the boundaries of bourgeois ideology, is forced to relate to individualist perspectivism: 'This perceiving is also a reading of the world as a text and your readings will inform your action'.[74]

Of course, once he turns to the re-enchantment of life that drives his philosophy of meta-Reality, Bhaskar senses that what he is presenting as a 'break' is actually something in the nature of a return: 'This is very different from the way in which the world was conceived by the discourses of modernity, something much more in common with the organic world views prior to the bourgeois/Cartesian revolution'.[75] With one proviso: lacking the necessary the-

---

70   Norrie 2010, p. 75.

71   Ibid., p. 142.

72   Bhaskar 2002a, p. 114.

73   Bhaskar 2002c, p. 295.

74   Ibid., p. 295.

75   Ibid., p. 298.

oretical tools and historical awareness, he is driven, in the tradition of classical bourgeois ideologues from Hume onwards, to collapse bourgeois animism into feudal substantialism (to use Rodríguez's terms) and then to project the ensuing organicism trans-historically: 'And the whole thrust of the theory of the philosophy of meta-Reality has been to bring to the fore the essential reflexivity of the process of perception and action and of awareness-in-action; the irreducible and primitive character of the notions of "I see it", "I get it", etc.'[76]

The new primitivism shares something with its feudal counterpart – it remains a way of reading the world – but, strange to say, continues for the rest to be a thinly disguised form of the bourgeois *I/eye*, itself sometimes masquerading behind a collective 'we', that *sees* the *thing*. Thus, perception, it transpires, 'is the immediate way in which we read the world',[77] located in the isolated individual who sees his or her neighbour as a beggar or member of the working class or whatever, 'out of the myriad other ways in which we could immediately identify or read him'.[78] Pitched at such a high level of abstraction, the relevant concepts, such as those of the 'master' and the 'slave', function as universals and, as such, offer little purchase upon the real, structural mechanisms that explain historical conflict and therefore upon the motor of historical change. Such mechanisms, we should know, count for little when juxtaposed with the 'irreducibility of intentionality, its meaningful character', 'the irreducibility of agency', etc., for after all, '[t]he primacy of the first-person standpoint only makes the obvious point that you can only act through yourself'.[79]

It goes without saying that, within Bhaskar's scenario, ideology has ceased to perform any theoretical function, displaced as it is by the notion of 'pre-understandings' and an 'unexamined level of awareness';[80] that, furthermore, once the notion of the Althusserian break or *rupture* has been relinquished for that of the Foucauldian *episteme*, nothing stands in the way of a recognition of the truth of post-structuralism and postmodernism and an acceptance of the linguistic turn as 'an important moment in the development of the discourse of modernity'.[81]

---

76   Ibid., p. 299. On the claim regarding Hume and bourgeois ideologues, see Rodríguez 2002a, p. 297.
77   Bhaskar 2002c, p. 299.
78   Ibid., p. 300.
79   Ibid., p. 301.
80   Ibid., p. 304.
81   Ibid.

7   On Radical Historicity

Now I am going to ask critical realists to consider that what in 'The Nous of Perception' can look like wisdom may in fact be the very essence of bourgeois ideology and, to this end, ask them, once again, to descend from the giddy heights of abstraction to consider a historical object in all its immediacy, by resuming our earlier considerations on the birth of the sonnet.

In the opening pages of *Theory and History of Ideological Production*, Rodríguez explains:

> We take the term 'history' very seriously, for which reason we are not interested in any patched-up job. It is not simply a question of adding that old stand-by the historical 'context' or some other sociological context to the literary work in order to explain it from the 'outside' (whilst others explain the strictly literary element of the work, what lies within, its 'in itself').[82]

To be relinquished, if we, the readers, are to take the full measure of a 'radical historicity', are the notions, firstly, of an 'author', in the sense of an individual possessed of a 'mind' and 'reason', the single, uniquely responsible source of 'his' or 'her' ideas, judgements, tastes, etc.; secondly, of a subject who 'expresses' an interior truth, quintessentially in the form of *literature*; and, thirdly, of a human (poetic) spirit that is always immovable, in some sense always identical to itself, always prior to the objective production of the work. For what such notions presuppose is that literature and the subject that sustains it are universal categories, that Homer, Garcilaso and Mallarmé 'do not strictly "make" anything',[83] that the poet, stereotypically in the case of the Romantic, acts as a simple, passive conduit for transcendental forces from the beyond, when the reality is that the subject/poet is a historically localised notion directly – and uniquely – secreted by the bourgeois ideological matrix.

But if traditional critics, in asking whether Garcilaso truly loved his 'lady', are engaged (as Rodríguez suggests they are) in a fundamentally ideological exercise, the question remains: What, then, constitutes a specifically scientific approach to literary production? It is not a question that Rodríguez ducks: 'Our assumption is that all poetic processes (and literary processes in general) are perfectly *objective* insofar as they are always determined in the last instance by

---

82   Rodríguez 2002a, pp. 17–18.
83   Ibid., p. 131.

ideological relations (by which they are secreted and to which they belong). In turn these relations are determined by a specific matrix'.[84] That said, while ideological relations are the determining force (as opposed, presumably, to authorial intentions, inner spirits, etc.) in the poetic process, they are in no sense 'prior to' their literary production, as something awaiting its 'expression', but need themselves to be materially 'produced'. 'Only those people who want to ignore this fact', Rodríguez observes, a little unfairly, for those of us mired in bourgeois ideology, 'will find it at all abstruse'.[85]

Let us explore this matter further by returning to the question of the gaze and focusing on one of the classic episodes of *Don Quixote* (1605), by the time of whose publication animism had been defeated, as an independent movement, and Spain had assumed all the trappings of a 'police state'.

> At that moment they caught sight of some thirty or forty windmills, which stand on that plain, and as soon as Don Quixote saw them he said to his squire: 'Fortune is guiding our affairs better than we could have wished. Look over there, friend Sancho Panza, where more than thirty monstrous giants appear. I intend to do battle with them and take their lives. With their spoils we will begin to get rich, for this is a fair war, and it is a great service to God to wipe such a wicked brood from the face of the earth.'
>
> 'What giants?' asked Sancho Panza.
>
> 'Those you see there', replied his master, 'with their long arms. Some giants have them about six miles long.'
>
> 'Take care, your worship', said Sancho; 'those things over there are not giants but windmills, and what seem to be their arms are the sails, which are whirled round in the wind and make the millstone turn.'
>
> 'It is quite clear', replied Don Quixote, 'that you are not experienced in this matter of adventures. They are giants, and if you are afraid, go away and say your prayers, while I advance and engage them in fierce and unequal battle'.[86]

Faced by this episode, bourgeois critics have interpreted it as they were bound to do, from a positivist, phenomenological standpoint, as an instance in which a Kantian subject confronts a series of objects that he 'sees' as giants. In a word, Don Quixote is 'mad', happily so according to some critics, less happily, accord-

---

84   Ibid., p. 123.
85   Ibid.
86   Cervantes Saavedra 1950, p. 68.

ing to others. Attending rigorously to the historical determinations of the text, however, Don Quixote is nothing of the kind: he is a servant in the service of his Lord. Nor, for the same reasons, is the object he perceives a free object, marked by a literal *sign*, but, in true feudal style, a 'signature', inhabited by the voice of God, that demands, not that it be 'seen', but that it be heard or 'read'. Don Quixote assuredly *sees* that he is dealing with windmills, but that is not the point: he *reads* them as giants.[87]

So, is what we have here a substantialist text, in the true feudal mould, exemplified earlier by Berceo? Unfortunately, as Rodríguez continues to explain, things are not quite so straightforward. If *Don Quixote* were a genuinely substantialist narrative, he reminds us, our hero would be equipped with a *substance*, and his task in life would be to *prove* that substance, by overcoming what would be a series of *tests*. Of course, the hero/heroine may not always be *aware* of his or her true essence: the princess reared in a peasant community may not *know* she is a princess, but in the end, as the saying goes, blood will out. Moreover, if Cervantes's were a substantialist text, it would be a fundamentally *dual* text, which we, as readers, would be called upon to *read*, through a process of inversion, by which to extract its allegorical message. In other words, we would be asked to proceed very much in the manner of Don Quixote when confronted by the windmills. But none of this is true of *Don Quixote*: while a servant of his Lord, the eponymous hero is also a proto-free subject, exposed to the vagaries of chance, embarking upon a series of 'adventures' that are not in any way 'prefigured', as in the feudal narrative. Don Quixote's future, we are saying, is in no sense *already written*; rather it is something he will create, through his own individual initiative. True, in matters of morality, for example, the knight's norms remain resolutely feudal: moral imperatives will be obeyed because his Lord is watching. But as every secular character he comes across in his adventures knows, the world is no longer run in accordance with such norms, which must be created and legitimised anew.

Don Quixote's substantialist ideology, then, is undermined at every turn, thematically, by the secular characters he comes across during his travels. But we will miss a crucial aspect of the novel if we fail to look beyond this ideological struggle and register the actual literalism that underscores Cervantes' own writing. In the words of Rodríguez: 'Everything that happens and everything that Don Quixote reads is inscribed in his *dual* gaze upon the world, whilst at the same time it is all related to us by Cervantes (or by the narration) exactly

---

87   Rodríguez 2001b, p. 324.

as it happens: *literally*.[88] It is as if the substantialist elements of the narrative were subverted from within by the very form of writing. The Spanish Marxist draws his final conclusions:

> [I]n practice the *I* does not exist: as Freud indicated, it is all a question of a few frustrations and desires that try to rear their heads under the grammatical form of the personal pronoun or subject ... So that the nebulous 'I' is *trans-historical*: men and women have always dreamed. But in daily practice, in our vital, social, and subjective reality, what really exists (even in dreams) are the ideological forms of the radical historicity of the 'I-am'.[89]

8   British Marxism at Its Limits

Symptomatic of the inability of British Marxists to think outside the framework of the subject/object dichotomy, we have suggested earlier, was the notorious exchange between Thompson, Anderson, and Tom Nairn, with additions from Christopher Hill, on the question as to whether the British bourgeoisie possessed its own ideology. For Thompson, to remind ourselves, ideology is constituted by a conjunction of *ideas* (political, religious, or scientific), whereas for Anderson and Nairn, ideology was a question of the 'self-consciousness' of a subject, understood as the 'contents' of human reason. Rodríguez took exception to both positions:

> The debate, we are saying, is a false debate, since all the polemicists are in agreement as regards its basic terms: capitalism 'is' the 'capitalist spirit' (or at least, capitalism, as a material phenomenon, would not have been able to exist without *psychological motivation*, a motivation that will lead to more and more 'action', more and more 'capitalism').[90]

In other words, there is an 'unconscious' agreement over the 'economy/ psychology' relation typical of empiricism, that opposes a subjective, interiorised subject ('human psychology') to a material 'exterior', the latter impinging upon the former in the form of 'impressions'. It is this basic agreement that the

---

88   Rodríguez 2003a, p. 119.
89   Rodríguez 2003a, p. 118.
90   Rodríguez 2002a, p. 301.

Althusserian contests, further to suggesting the need to reconfigure the horizon of the debate in terms of the *objectivity* of bourgeois social relations and of
their corresponding ideological unconscious.[91] To elucidate how this argument
impinges upon the work of Bhaskar, let us turn to *Critical Realism and Marxism* and, more specifically, to the final essay in the volume by John Michael
Roberts.[92]

As was to be expected, given his Marxist framework, Roberts wastes no time
in taking Bhaskar to task for exploring the concepts of 'freedom' and 'emancipation' at too high a level of abstraction 'to be meaningful for political action'.[93]
Freedom from what? Emancipation to what end? The point is well made,
although Roberts falls short of full ideological critique. After all, its abstraction had not prevented the effective deployment of 'freedom' throughout the
history of the bourgeoisie. One's suspicions are further aroused when Roberts
himself enlists the concept for allegedly *scientific* purposes, through its association with consciousness. Thus: 'Unlike natural science [...], social science cannot afford to ignore human consciousness but must include ideas, beliefs, etc.
which individuals act upon when they interact with society and social structures'.[94] What is not clear is how 'consciousness' squares with the emphasis
upon social structures. And that is the least of it: 'species being' arrives in the
wake of consciousness to bolster the voluntarist inflection, hence further to
undercut the structural determination which Roberts otherwise wishes to promote.[95] True, the structuralist argument is pressed further: Bhaskar, allegedly,
'has no *ground* in which to say how freedom is constrained by a specific set of
ideological social relations such as a mode of production'.[96] But the final effect
is far from convincing.

Robert's difficulties, we suggest, are to be explained in terms of an unresolved tension between Structuralist Marxism and a British tradition unable
to detach itself from the subject/object binary, hence from bourgeois ideology.
The same tension is in evidence in other contributors to *Critical Realism and
Marxism*. Symptomatically, in their prefatory essay, the volume's editors take
for granted what has become the accepted wisdom of both critical realism
and British Marxism, namely, that '[u]ltimately Althusserian Marxism failed to
uphold successfully a mind-independent reality, fallibly knowable by human

---

91   Ibid., p. 301.
92   Brown et al 2002.
93   Ibid., p. 236.
94   Ibid., p. 237.
95   Ibid., p. 241.
96   Ibid., p. 243.

agents endowed with free will'.[97] Just as pertinently, in his own personal contribution to the volume, Jonathan Joseph critiques Althusser for prioritising the
relations of production at the expense of people, the 'true subjects of history'.
E.P. Thompson, as well as many other Western and 'classical' Marxists, Joseph
elaborates, 'rightly insists on bringing back the human subject'.[98] Except that
what British Marxists want to bring back is not the human subject *per se* but
the subject / object opposition, as the framework in which to think and from
which to defend the 'freedom' of the individual. For their part, Althusserians
were equally emphatic on the need to displace the focus of attention from 'concrete individuals' to the relations of production and political and ideological
relations, on the grounds that these relations simply cannot be thought within
the category of the subject; freedom, yes, but freedom from exploitation.

9   Conclusion

One of the very reasonable demands made by critical realism of any ideology-
critique is that it show a theory not just to be false or misleading, but to be the
necessary product of the social relations that generate it. The ideology of animism, we have argued throughout, was secreted by a historically localised set of
bourgeois relations, during the early stages of capitalism, facilitating their co-
existence with their feudal counterpart. We conclude by briefly foregrounding
what will have already struck the observant reader, namely the arresting similarities between the love-drenched cosmos that unfolds in Bhaskar's later texts
on meta-Reality and the central motifs of Platonic animism. Whether those
similarities can be said to rest upon subterranean connections is something I
will leave for another occasion, except to suggest that any relevant study might
do well to start with the concluding part of Rodríguez's *Theory and History of
Ideological Production*, which deals with the 'prolongation of animist poetics in
England'. Suffice it to note, with respect to critical realism, its provenance in a
petty-bourgeois class fraction determined to resist the arrogant, ruthless forms
assumed by the more Darwinist layers of the professional middle class.

    Against critical realism I have marshalled the resources of an Althusserian
tradition that prove far more serviceable to the scientific study and history of
ideological production. While this Althusserian tradition accepts that social
agents have intentions and take decisions within open-ended systems, it also

---

97   Ibid., pp. 19–20.
98   Ibid., p. 32.

insists that our understanding of these agents is advanced very little by the notion of 'free will'. By the same token, it also argues that the political defence of the majority is severely limited when restricted to concepts of rights and justice, because, in the words of Robert Resch, these 'signify, at best, half-hearted, ineffectual efforts to protect a vast majority possessing formal rather than substantive freedom from a small minority who actually exercise power and who actually are free'.[99] Rodríguez is even more guarded with respect to the celebration of a broadly conceived 'freedom', insofar as this celebration easily slips into the essentialist view of individuals as alienated from their true nature. His emphasis is clear: resistance to capitalism is most effectively focused on the one freedom that capitalists refuse to surrender, the freedom to exploit. Still to be considered is whether his theory of the all-pervasive reach of the ideological unconscious was itself determined, in the last instance, by the fortunes of a Spanish Communist Party. The latter, as we will be investigating below, emerged as the major voice of the opposition in post-Franco Spain only to lose the ideological battle over what constitutes 'freedom' and 'liberty' and to sink, as a result, into political irrelevance. And all within a matter of years.

---

99   Resch 1992, p. 31.

CHAPTER 8

Psychoanalytic Paradox and Capitalist Exploitation: Slavoj Žižek

The obstacles to establishing some kind of symbiotic relation between psycho-analysis and Marxism have long proved seemingly insurmountable, at least on the evidence of past efforts to overcome them.[1] On the one side, a funda-mentally introspective and universalising psychoanalysis, on the other, a rad-ically historicising and objectifying Marxism, and ne'er the twain shall meet, except to confess their irreconcilability. Nor does it make any difference when the focus is narrowed to the regional variations: Warren Montag, for example, refers, to the 'impossible encounter' between Althusserian Marxism and Lacan-ian psychoanalysis;[2] and at first blush Slavoj Žižek and Juan Carlos Rodríguez, who will be the focus of the present study, hardly constitute exceptions: the former castigates Marxists for their eagerness to over-historicise, whereas the latter chastises psychoanalysts for their ahistoricism. What, then, could pos-sibly be gained from pondering such oppositions further?

Our conviction is that Žižek and Rodríguez have each, independently, ex-plored aspects of ideology that the other needs to take on board. By any meas-ure, Žižek's work amounts to a powerful reformulation of the process of subject formation, specifically as this process relates to the subject's hidden depend-ence upon libidinal investments. Equally, Rodríguez has argued persuasively for the existence of a distinctively ideological unconscious, to be located not in the psychic depths of the individual but in the over-determined complex-ities of the social formation. We further believe that the two scholars' shared dependence upon Althusser offers a potential bridge between them at the same time as it throws into relief what fundamentally divides them; which explains why this dependence will be the first topic to be addressed below. But before then, let us briefly chart, in broad terms, the path that we intend to fol-low.

When in recent decades scholars have approached the controversy between Marxism and psychoanalysis, they have habitually done so on the basis of a number of presuppositions. Firstly, they have taken for granted the existence

---

1 For perhaps the best review of these efforts, see Wolfenstein 1993. For a critique of Wolfen-stein, see Caamaño 2008, p. 34.
2 Montag 1984.

of an 'ideology' and the 'unconscious' as substantive identities. Secondly, and as a consequence, their attention has switched to the 'subject', as the focal point of the ensuing debate. Thus, for Montag, 'the subject is not merely an element common to both ideology and the unconscious but actually marks the area in which the fields marked out by these concepts intersect'.[3] The key question then becomes: how can this common element be theorised so as effectively to *suture* both domains? With further consequences: principally, the subject is deployed as a trans-historical category, somewhat surreptitiously it has to be said, and to the obvious advantage of psychoanalysis.

Our own solution to this dilemma will be to reconstitute the ideology/unconscious dichotomy in the form of an opposition between the libidinal and the ideological unconscious. The libidinal variant, clearly, will be one already familiar enough. Indeed, practically speaking, Freudian scholarship may be said to enjoy a virtual monopoly of the 'unconscious'. As regards Žižek, it will take the form of a radically non-historical 'real kernel', which returns as the force of desire and, drawing its energy from the death drive, will proceed to subvert the discursive structures of language and to propel the subject into an endless quest for a forbidden maternal object; with the inevitable result that individual praxis is cast as the genetic origin of social structures and the main dynamic in the transformation of society. For Rodríguez, as we have seen throughout, ideology is secreted, *unconsciously*, by the social relations of production, 'before' being formally legitimised within the State Apparatus. The aim of the present chapter will be to put the libidinal unconscious and the ideological unconscious, understood as theoretical concepts, to the test of their objects, otherwise a number of texts located at strategic points in the transition from feudalism to capitalism.

1   Towards a Philosophical Anthropology

It is a decidedly 'curious accident', according to Žižek,[4] that Althusser's name is not mentioned once in *Der philosophische Diskurs der Moderne* (1985), even as its author, Jürgen Habermas, obsessively debates his differences vis-à-vis Foucault. Most curious indeed! The eclipse of the Althusserian school was not, allegedly, a consequence of any theoretical defeat; rather, it can be traced back to a 'traumatic kernel' that needed to be quickly forgotten and 'repressed'

---

3   Montag 1984, p. 70.
4   Žižek 1989, p. 1.

insofar as intolerable to academic sensibilities. The kernel in question, we learn, is the threat to the existence of an 'all-round' personality, a concept that both Habermas and Foucault in fact share, which suggests that the much-trumpeted opposition between the two scholars is of limited consequence. The more far-reaching encounter, Žižek concludes, is that between Althusser and Lacan.

So much is clear. But the reader who now expects Žižek to unfurl the basic concepts of Althusser – the 'social formation', the 'mode of production', the 'instances' ('economic', 'political' and 'ideological'), 'determination in the last instance', 'dominance', 'over-determination', and so on – is in for a surprise: the relevant dynamics, it transpires, are those of 'alienation' in the sense in which the subject is alienated from his or her essence, existentially speaking. Inevitably, this same reader will be led to protest: wherein precisely lies the difference between alienation, as Žižek conceives it, and the kind of trans-historical subjectivity for which Foucault and Habermas stand condemned? More importantly, how is the Lacanian's embrace of 'alienation' to be squared with Althusser's rejection of the very same concept, together with that of its counterpart, 'human nature'?[5] A rejection, incidentally, that remained a constant throughout Althusser's career, his self-criticisms notwithstanding. The Althusserian logic was unforgiving: any notion of a 'species being', understood as some primal lack, was incompatible with the emphasis, characteristic of the mature Marx, upon the constitutive role of social relations.

The puzzle is that Žižek knows all of this, accepts the reality of Althusser's opposition (albeit parenthetically), and yet continues to press the case for alienation. One can only assume that, even at this stage, the more important task was to reconfigure Althusserianism along Hegelian lines. Any aspects of Althusserianism that resisted absorption within the Hegelian notion of Man were simply to be ignored. 'In this perspective, the "death drive", this dimension of radical negativity, cannot be reduced to an expression of alienated social conditions, it defines *la condition humaine* as such: there is no solution, no escape from it; the thing to do is not to "overcome", to "abolish" it, but to come to terms with it, to learn to recognise it'.[6] Slowly but surely, a space is cleared in which to locate Man, understood as the immanent subject of all process, *outside* history and society. Žižek's next task is to unfold an overview of ideology, based upon the Hegelian distinction between three moments, corresponding, broadly speaking, to ideology understood 'in itself', 'for itself' and 'reflected

---

5   Althusser 1990a, pp. 44–8, 239–41.
6   Žižek 1989, p. 5.

in itself'; more specifically, to ideology understood as a 'complex of ideas'; as materialised in the Althusserian Ideological State Apparatuses; and, somewhat more elusively, as spontaneously at work at the heart of social 'reality'.[7]

The third category, while serving conveniently to 'cement' the entire social edifice together, ultimately proves to be something of an inconvenience, and it is easy to see why. Whereas the first two categories can be painlessly reconciled to the notion of the subject – as the source of ideas, of their institutional legitimation and formulation – ideology as a 'cement' suggests the impersonal operations of a structural, even unconscious kind:

> Today, in late capitalism, when the expansion of the new mass media in principle, at least, enables ideology effectively to penetrate every pore of the social body, the weight of ideology as such is diminished: individuals do not act as they do primarily on account of their beliefs or ideological convictions – that is to say, the system, for the most part, bypasses ideology in its reproduction and relies on economic coercion, legal and state regulations, and so on.[8]

Restated: we find ourselves 'knee-deep' in an obscure domain that is indistinguishable from ideology while being, at the same time, in the grip of a system that somehow manages to circumvent ideology, that takes the form, to elaborate, of an 'elusive network of implicit, quasi-"spontaneous" presuppositions and attitudes that form an irreducible moment of the reproduction of "non-ideological" (economic, legal, political, sexual ...) practices'.[9] Clearly, by hook or by crook, this laminated network, otherwise the social formation, with its multiple levels and contradictory causal processes, needed to be spirited away, if, that is, the focus of attention was to be transferred to the Lacanian subject and, by the same token, to a space reserved exclusively for the libidinal unconscious.

Žižek faces a dilemma whose full extent will become apparent if we pause to trace those 'spontaneous presuppositions and attitudes' to their Althusserian source in the notion of the unconsciousness of ideology.[10] But that is only the first of Žižek's problems: ideology, according to Althusser, not only functions unconsciously, it is also secreted elsewhere, in the social relations, which is to say, is born outside the subject. Suddenly the centrality of the latter is

---

7   Žižek 1994a, pp. 10–14.
8   Ibid., p. 14.
9   Ibid., p. 15.
10   Althusser 1990a, p. 233.

seriously under threat, and psychoanalysis with it, from an ideology that exercises a deeply pervasive influence over the social totality. Otherwise stated, the focus of attention is being transferred from the subject/object opposition to the 'structure in dominance' of the social formation.

To extricate himself from these entanglements, Žižek begins to pare back where he can. Ideology 'in itself', he decides on further reflexion, can be equated with mythological consciousness and, as such, is 'not yet ideology'. This leaves only the second and third moments, namely ideology insofar as it dominates and regulates the life of individuals 'from above', through the mediation of the Ideological State Apparatus, and ideology insofar as it is secreted spontaneously 'from below', through the process of commodity fetishism.[11] The 'elusive social network', it should be noted, has suddenly shrunk alarmingly – it is now confined to the realm of commodification. This is important because Žižek can then proceed to eliminate the third moment of ideology on the basis that, quite simply, Marx never characterised commodity fetishism as a form of ideology. For the progenitors of Marxism, the state was the first ideological force.[12] And even for Althusser, following his self-critical turn and the introduction of the concept of the ISA, 'ideology is always-already regulated by the externality of the State and its Ideological Apparatuses' (p. 19); which, conveniently enough from a Lacanian standpoint, leaves the subject detached within the pre-symbolic, from where to undermine and oppose an ideology restricted to the symbolic realm.

Marxists are unlikely to be convinced. As they are bound to point out, Marx had very little to say on the subject of ideology – except for *The German Ideology, a problematic text that was famously abandoned to the gnawing criticism of the mice* – and even less on the state, which somewhat detracts from the importance that, in this context, Žižek attributes to him. Similar qualifications are in order with respect to Althusser in that, while his interests undeniably shift from the spontaneous generation of ideology, in evidence in *For Marx* and *Reading Capital*, to the interpellation of the subject, explored in *Lenin and Other Essays*, it is debatable, to say the least, whether he ever *broke* with his earlier emphasis on the all-pervasive nature of ideology. Ideologies, he was well aware, were not born in the ISAs but from the social classes at grips in the class struggle.

Not that such a response would be likely to incommode Žižek to any extent, insofar as, having effectively confined ideology to the State Apparatus, he immediately proceeds to promote 'class struggle' as the perfect example of

---

11   Ibid., pp. 17–18.
12   Ibid., p. 19.

a spectral apparition, of the kind that 'fills up the hole in the real'.[13] Such a definition, it should be obvious, was perfectly calculated to rip the heart out of historical materialism and thereby to open up a hole of its own that, happily, psychoanalysis, was only too willing and able to fill: 'If it is to play this crucial role, the concept of the unconscious is to be conceived in the strictly Freudian sense'.[14]

We will be resuming our discussion of these matters below, but before then, let us turn to a scholar who, in contrast, to Žižek, departs not from the subject but from the social formation and, specifically, from the Althusserian notion of the unconsciousness of ideology.

2 The Dog That Didn't Bark

The 'curious accident' regarding Althusser, to which we saw Žižek allude above, refers obliquely to the 'curious incident' of the 'dog that didn't bark' in Conan Doyle's *Silver Blaze*. Curiously, Juan Carlos Rodríguez makes use of the same reference to derive some bitter satisfaction, in the post-script to the second edition of *Theory and History of Ideological Production*, from the non-reception of his work: '... sometimes the most significant thing about what happens is that *nothing happens*'.[15] The reasons for this non-reception, we have speculated, were varied and multiple, but principal among them, in the context of our present concerns, is Rodríguez's displacement of focus, along Althusserian lines, from the subject/object opposition to the social formation. Let us elaborate.

Rodríguez's first target, predictably enough, is the notion of 'Man' as the basis of a human condition: '... as can easily be shown, what is really conceived of as "ahistorical" [...] is the very notion of the "subject" (the same subject, for example, in the "medieval" and in the "modern" world) and of "man" or whatever he might be called'.[16] The Spaniard, it transpires parenthetically, will not be addressing the polemic ('boring for being so confused') either in favour or against Althusser. His primary concern is to distinguish between the physical reality of human beings and the object of his own critique, namely the 'notion' of 'Man'. 'The notion of the subject (and the whole problematic within which it is inscribed) is radically historical because ... it derives directly (and exclus-

---

13 Žižek 1994a, p. 21.
14 Ibid., p. 33n36.
15 Rodríguez 2002a, p. 33.
16 Rodríguez 2002a, p. 21.

ively) from the very matrix of the bourgeois ideological unconscious: the "serf" can never be a "subject", etc.'[17] Almost surreptitiously, the 'ideological unconscious' makes its entry. Why so surreptitiously?

The answer is complex and requires, *pace* Rodríguez, that we address the relevance of Althusser. Notwithstanding his emphasis upon ideological unconsciousness, the philosopher was curiously reticent when he came to the existence of an ideological unconscious *per se*. 'I believe that [it] is not possible to speak of an ideological unconscious', he wrote, unambiguously, in a private letter to René Diatkine. Except that a lingering doubt remained: 'In any event, that "unconscious" (which I would call by a different name, but never mind) exists, and *it should not be confused with the psychoanalytic unconscious*'.[18] At this point, Althusser appears to be at the limit of his thinking. It is not simply that for him (as for Žižek) the substantive concept of the unconscious has already been taken over by psychoanalysis but also that he has his doubts concerning its application to ideology.

The master's vacillations doubtless infected his students at the *Rue d'Ulm*; if so, this at least would explain Rodríguez's failure to grasp in full measure the nature of his 'ideological unconscious'. Of what does it consist? Whence does it arise? The Spaniard, seemingly, never pauses to reflect on such issues, even as he proceeds to theorise the relevant mechanism, which consists, allegedly, of the imposition of various '*matrices*' on 'their' social formation. He elaborates:

> ... each ideological matrix announces itself via certain key notions, to which it grants the status of essential and unalterable elements of reality. But it does so only to immediately camouflage its own status qua 'ideology' by sheltering and hiding behind the notions that it has already been able to establish as the truth about life.[19]

To be inscribed under feudal relations is automatically to imagine oneself to be a *serf* or *servant* of the Lord; more restrictively, to imagine oneself to be *bound* to a local lord. By the same token, all individuals under bourgeois social relations conceive of themselves as 'subjects' – quite simply they cannot think of themselves outside these limits. The focus of Rodríguez's attention is upon the transition from the fourteenth to the sixteenth century, when the medieval Hispanic kingdoms were in the process of transforming themselves into an Absolutist State. The motor of change can be located with some precision:

---

17   Ibid., p. 21.
18   Althusser 1966, p. 52.
19   Rodríguez 2002a, p. 22.

for the capitalist market to function successfully, indeed, at all, the bond that attached the serf to the earth and to the blood of their Lord needed to be broken.

Theory and History takes for granted a broad allegiance to the Althusserian problematic, hence the notion of a mode of production, made up of distinct levels or 'instances' – the economic, political, and ideological. Within the horizon of the transition from feudalism to capitalism, Rodríguez will be concerned with two antagonistic sets of social relations, namely servile relations and mercantile or manufacturing relations. Unsurprisingly, literary texts produced within the transition are inescapably fractured and contradictory, torn apart by conflicting ideological demands. We will be teasing out the details of this analysis below. Suffice it to note at this point one immediate consequence of the emphasis upon productive relations, namely the prioritising of the base over the ISA. Rodríguez explains: '... the dialectic inscribed in the literary texts (that which produces them as such, their internal logic) is what shapes an ideological unconscious'.[20] The priority that some have accorded to the ISA allegedly smacks of an 'institutionalist sociologism' that 'naturally brings in its train a parallel view of ideology – half mechanistic, half naïve – as a simple excrescence of material fact'.[21] Rodríguez has in mind certain fellow Althusserians, together with Max Weber, but his criticism would also apply to Žižek.

What may seem at first glance a mere nuance in fact marks a crucial distinction between mechanical and dialectical materialism. It is one that forms the basis of a more detailed critique of Althusser himself and that will extend, specifically, to the philosopher's notion of interpellation.[22] The nub of Rodríguez's objection to the latter may be briefly stated and is germane to the present discussion: Althusser's choice of Yahweh and Moses, as an example of the process of interpellation, is ill chosen insofar as it opposes not a subject to the Subject, as is claimed, but a servant to his Lord; equally calamitous is the implication that Moses existed in some sense before being interpellated, and that, more broadly, the historical individual exists as a subject prior to his or her subjection. The truth, namely that the subject is 'always already' constructed, was something that Althusser intuited but that he often let slip, as in his biblical illustration. 'Something that logically presupposes an error of the gravest kind when it comes to conceptualising the notion of what could be called the *ideological unconscious*'.[23] In sum, in contrast to Žižek, who, we saw above, prioritised

---

20   Ibid., p. 30.
21   Ibid.
22   Rodríguez 2008a.
23   Rodríguez 2008a, p. 768.

the shift in Althusser toward the investigation of interpellation, Rodríguez took his cue from the unconscious secretion of ideology, as theorised by the early Althusser.

Where did this leave the Spaniard with respect to the libidinal unconscious? Symptomatically, in *Theory and History*, he will insist on the possibility of accounting for cultural phenomena 'without the help of psychoanalytic or pietistic disquisitions', at least with respect to the phenomenon of Spanish mysticism, which, he insists, can quite adequately be explained in terms of the impact upon religious discourse of the emergent animist dynamic.[24] In the introduction to its English translation, it is true, he will concede the existence of two forms of the unconscious, ideological and libidinal, derived respectively from Marx and Freud. Except that he remains resolute in refusing the existence of a human nature, outside of 'a bundle of frustrations and desires' that, confessedly, 'rears its head in the grammatical form of the personal or subject pronoun'.[25] The effect is radically to restrict the role of the libidinal unconscious. 'So that although this nebulous "I" is "trans-historical" – all men and women have always dreamed –, at the daily level, which is that of our vital social and subjective reality, what actually exists (even in our dreams) are the ideological forms of "I am", which are radically historical'.[26] Again, the contrast with Žižek's ahistoricism could not be greater. To test the claims of both parties, let us turn to some specific examples, beginning with the first Spanish poet to be known by name, Gonzalo de Berceo.

3   Fetishism and Commodity Fetishism

Fallaron enna casa   del raví más onrado
un grand cuerpo de cera   como omne formado,
como don Christo sovo,   sedié crucifigado,
con grandes clavos preso,   grand plaga al costado.[27]

(They found in the home of the most honourable rabbi / a large wax figurine in the form of a man; / as Christ was, he was crucified, / fixed by large nails and a long wound in his side.)

---

24   Rodríguez 2002a, p. 200.
25   Ibid., p. 15.
26   Ibid.
27   Berceo 1989, verse 427.

Wrenching quotations out of context is a precarious operation, one that, no-toriously, lends itself to every kind of abuse. Texts are vulnerable entities, with which it is tempting to 'have one's way'. That said, the 'literal' context of the above verse from Berceo can be briefly summarised. *Milagros XVIII* records how, midway through a mass held to celebrate the Virgin Mother, the voice of La Gloriosa [the Glorious one] herself speaks forth from the heavens to inform a packed congregation that 'false and treacherous' Jews, who already bear the blame for the original crucifixion of Christ, are at that precise moment again subjecting her son to the same torment; upon hearing which, the officiating archbishop leads the Christian population into the Jewish quarter where, in the manner described above, they surprise a Jewish Rabbi and fellow conspirators re-enacting the first crucifixion on a wax effigy; these Christians then proceed to impose the severest penalty upon the Jewish coterie, namely death.

The fetishistic practices in evidence in the *Milagros*, of which the above is an instance, are not limited to the black arts. 'Good' objects are likewise cap-able of exerting a magical force, notably in the case of the Virgin's shawl that attaches itself tenaciously to a church thief (v. 719); having said which, there is no gainsaying the fact that Berceo associates the black arts characteristically with Jews, as in the case of the accomplice to Don Teófilo, who 'savié encan-tamientos e muchos maleficios' (v. 767) (knew charms and many spells). Even more strictly confined to Jews is the fetishistic attachment to money, displayed in 'El mercader fiado' (The Indebted Merchant) and throughout the *Milagros*.

From Žižek's perspective, the ideological figure of the 'Jew' or of its role as a 'fantasy object *a*' serves to 'stich up' the inconsistency of an ideological sys-tem,[28] so as to displace the social antagonism internal to the social body onto the Jew as a force of corruption. This displacement, we learn, is made possible by the association of Jews with financial dealings: the source of exploitation and of class antagonism is located not in the basic relation between working and ruling classes but in the relation between the organisers of production and the merchants who exploit them; in the light of which, Žižek is quick to con-figure the relevant scenario on the level of a trans-historical human condition and to condemn as over-hasty the Marxist and feminist attempts to historicise the Freudian Oedipus.[29] Berceo's anti-Semitism, at first blush, might seem to lend such claims support, but appearances quickly prove to be deceptive.

Objectively speaking, one is quickly struck by the prominence accorded to *servile* relations: 'Esto es summum bonum, servir atal Sennora, / que save a sus

---

28   Žižek 1989, pp. 48–9.
29   Ibid., p. 50.

siervos acorrer en tal ora' (v. 304) (This is the greatest good, to serve such a Lady, / who knows how to succour her servants at such an hour). And it is not simply the references to 'service' that litter the texts; equally oppressive in their presence are the key 'notions' that grease the servile relations – 'reward' (for services performed), 'honour', 'sinner', 'treachery' (committed by the 'vassal' vis-à-vis his 'lord'), and so on. Individuals equate with their 'substance', the latter defined in terms of 'blood', whether 'clean' or 'sullied', and of 'lineage', the mark of which is the existence of a facial 'aura' or, in the case of those who labour ('labradores'), the fact of its absence.

Collectively, these and other such ideologemes constitute the framework of the dominant ideology of feudalism, namely *substantialism* or *organicism*, itself structured on the basis of a split between a terrestrial world, which Berceo refers to as 'this world' or 'here', and a celestial world, otherwise 'the other world' or 'above'. This same duality is habitually reproduced within the feudal text, whose 'literal' reading is liable to capsise at any moment into its allegorical equivalent. That point occurs quite early on in the *Milagros*: 'tolgamos la corteza, al meollo entremos, / prendamos lo de dentro, lo de fuera dessemos' (v. 16) (Let us remove the shell, let us seize the marrow / let us grasp the inside, reject the outside). The implications are far-reaching. If the feudal serf/servant was by definition also *bound* to a lord, similarly, the object was never 'free' to be contemplated as a literal 'thing', but something to be *read*. And when it came to reading, there was only one book, that of the World or the Bible – the difference was immaterial; from which it followed that there could be only one author, the Lord, as opposed to the hordes of 'commentators' whose function was simply to decipher the Lord's text.

Such, then, in broad outline, was the nature of a substantialist ideology that, Rodríguez would remind us, functioned to grease the mechanisms through which feudal lords extracted the social surplus from an oppressed peasantry. In the case of Berceo and comparable ideologues, it should be added, the social surplus took the form of tithes paid to the Catholic Church. The next question is: what relevance does the Lacanian notion of a 'human condition' have to this ideological scenario?

At first glance, one is bound to answer, precious little. After all, the basic split in Berceo, we have seen, was between this world and the next, which is far removed from that between the libidinal unconscious and consciousness. True, there exists some kind of interiorised cut in Berceo's texts between an 'inside' and 'outside', but one that is emphatically embryonic and, moreover, quickly cashed out in terms of the *organic*: 'quessóse don Estevan bien entro el bientre: / nol primiren tenazas de fierro mas fuertmientre' (v. 242) (Don Esteban suffered within; iron pincers would not have grasped more strongly); 'plorando de sus ojos quanto podién plorar' (v. 389) (crying from his eyes as much they could), and so on. And while the potential for a family romance certainly exists, it is one that needed to be conducted in cosmic terms, through the juxtaposition of the Virgin *qua* 'mother' to Christ, *qua* 'son', both subservient to the Father, although He, it must be said, figures primarily as the 'Lord'. As for the 'unconscious', any claimant to that category would need to be similarly cosmic. Two possibilities suggest themselves: the Lord Himself, always suitably hidden and inscrutable, or the Devil, who exerts a constant, insidious influence upon sinners.

Yet it would be unwise to dismiss the psychoanalytic concepts too hastily. The Name-of-the-Father, we are reminded, functions to protect the child against its desire for the mother and the mother's desire *per se*. 'The mother's role is her desire', Lacan warns, 'That is of capital importance. Her desire is not something you can bear easily, as if it were a matter of indifference to you. It always leads to problems. The mother is a big crocodile, and you find yourself in her mouth'.[30] One of Berceo's characters who would doubtless agree is the canon who, in 'The Marriage and the Virgin', loved the Virgin more than most and, more importantly, was loved deeply by her: 'Assaz eras varón bien casado conmigo' (v. 341) (You were a man firmly married to me), to such an extent that he absconds on his wedding night, in obedience to the law of the Virgin ('no lo consintió ella que fuesse corrompido' (v. 348) (she did not consent that he should be corrupted).

Now while all of this is doubtless perfectly harmless stuff, the sexual resonances, from a moral standpoint, are decidedly unambiguous, and confirm the significance placed at the outset on the Virgin's name, 'La Gloriosa'.

> No es nomne alguno   que bien derecho no venga
> que en alguna guisa   con ella no se avenga;
> y no ha tal que raíz   en ella no la tenga:
> nin Sancho nin Domingo,   nin Sancha nin Dominga. (v. 38)

(There is no name that is more fitting / that in some way does not agree with her / that is not rooted in her: / neither Sancho nor Domingo, nor Sancha nor Dominga.)

An obvious logic suggests itself: while 'La Gloriosa', as an appellation, compares to the Name-of-the-Father, by virtue of its bearer's phallic attributes –

---

30   Quoted from Fink 1997, p. 56.

the staff of Moses (v. 40) and the rod of Aaron (v. 41) – her virginity and purity are unavoidably contaminated by liquid association with the maternal / material: 'Yo soy Sancta María / madre de Jesu Christo que mamó leche mía' (v. 109) (I am Saint Mary, mother of Christ, who drank my milk). The Virgin Mary, it would follow, functions as a fantasy object that shields us from getting too close to the maternal. Except that, by her very nature, as the *Mother* of Christ, she is singularly ineffective in annulling the mother-child unity, which doubtless explains why the feudal symbolic should prove vulnerable to the porous effect of the Thing. Notable in this respect is *Milagro xxv*, whose narrative literally gets *bogged down* in dirt and stench: 'Yo, mesquino fediondo, que fiedo más que can / can que yace podrido ...' (I, a stinking miser, who stink more than a dog, / a dog that lies rotten ...), 'soy suzio y falso' (I am dirty and false), 'todos feos y suzios' (everyone ugly and dirty), 'Don Suçio, don malillo' (Don Dirt, Don Evil), 'es logar fediondo, fedionda confradría' (it is a stinking place, a stinking company) (v. 796 ff.). Medieval sinners, we are reminded, appear before their lord, who is also their judge, only to confess their guilt; they are constitutionally rotten with sin. Not without reason, Jean-Joseph Goux characterises feudalism as distinctively *anal* in its cultural predilections.[31]

The outlines of a provisional hypothesis gradually take shape: the fetishism, as it manifests itself in Berceo, is but a means of clinging to the (maternal) Real, the latter figuring as a material residue from a primitive mode in which the signifier continued to constitute the double of the thing. The names of the Virgin, to pursue the same logic, could be seen as characteristic of a subsequent, distinctive mode of feudalism, whose symbols or signatures, while they continue to be loaded and over-invested with meaning, are partially occluded and, in consequence, stand in need of decipherment. To conclude the argument, the references to 'price', 'worth', 'value', and so on, scattered throughout the text of the *Milagros*, would then register the emergence of a distinctively 'phallic', mercantilist mode, characterised by its relative abstract signs. An attractive hypothesis, no doubt, that would find ample support in Goux, but one that raises a major theoretical problem: precisely what kind of causality determines the relation between the distinctive modes of production, the dominant signifying practices, and the various libidinal stages?

---

31   Goux 1990, pp. 78–9.

4   'Structural Causality' and 'Homologies'

Unsurprisingly, given the notoriously *recherché* language in which it is couched, Lacan's theory of the subject lends itself to a number of 'takes'. For Robert Resch, the Lacanian subject should be conceived as a high-level, interconnected neural network, none of whose registers – Real, Symbolic, or Imaginary – can function independently, as subjects in their own right.[32] Similarly, for Bice Benvenuto and Roger Kennedy, whatever permanence and stability can be found within a subjectivity of unstable tensions is an illusory feature of the ego. They further elaborate that, in contrast to Freud, who imagined the psychic apparatus to be arranged in the form of strata, leading from the surface to a depth, Lacan's registers are better thought of as shifting force fields of indeterminate hierarchy.[33]

For Žižek, the situation is radically different: the Lacanian Real is not only a subject in its own right but also the 'true' subject, located at the limit of symbolisation, to be constructed retroactively, through its effects upon the Symbolic. In this way, one paradox follows quickly upon another: the Lacanian subject should be imagined as a *void*, which returns in the guise of spectral apparitions in the gap 'that forever separates reality from the real'.[34] Of such apparitions, we have already seen, 'class struggle' was the classic instance. Class struggle, to remind ourselves, exists not as a positive entity but as an absence whose sole function is to efface its traces. 'What we have here is the structural-dialectical paradox of *an effect that exists only in order to efface the causes of its existence, an effect that in a way resists its own cause*'.[35] The concept of an absent cause is drawn straight from Althusser, except that it has undergone a radical transformation, to understand which we need to review the details of the Althusserian argument.

For Althusser, 'the whole existence of the structure consists of its effects', because present only in and through the reciprocal effectivity of its elements.[36] Sustaining such a claim is a notion of *structural causality*, which conceptualises the social whole as a parallelogram of forces each bearing within itself the imprint of the social whole. Independently of the matrix effect of the totality, each of the social instances exercises its own effectivity, of a transitive vari-

---

32   Resch 1999, p. 92.
33   Benvenuto and Kennedy 1986, pp. 80–1.
34   Žižek 1994a, p. 21.
35   Žižek 1994a, p. 22.
36   Althusser and Balibar 1970, pp. 188–9.

ety. Structural causality is to be distinguished from an expressive causality, of Hegelian extraction, that views all the phenomena of any one period – whether economic, political, or ideological – as an externalisation of a shared internal principle.[37] A cross section at any moment in historical time would reveal, from the Hegelian perspective, a totality consisting of various parts, each of which expresses the essence of the totality. To complicate matters still further, Althusser will insist that the on-going historical process consists of a series of 'conjunctures', to be understood as individual moments that collectively constitute the same process; and that while each of the social instances bears the imprint of the 'plenary time' of the totality, it also functions in accordance with its own unevenly developed 'differential history'.

Now there may appear to be little about this Althusserian scenario with which Žižek would necessarily disagree. His central claim, for example, that the class struggle 'is the unfathomable limit that cannot be objectivised'[38] arguably departs little from the norms of most forms of scientific realism, for which the *real* structures of society exist only in the form of their *actual* effects.[39] That said, on closer inspection, it transpires that the class struggle is being pressed beyond conceptualisation altogether, in accordance not with the requirements of an epistemological relativism, of realist extraction, but with those of a psychoanalytic paradox that denies the subject direct access to the lost (maternal) Thing.[40] This does not augur well for a dialectics that aspires to being materialist.

Revealingly, at this stage, Žižek prefers to confine his discussion of causality to the existence of 'homologies', specifically to the 'fundamental homology between the interpretive procedure of Freud and Marx'.[41] True, he will sometimes slip in the odd, surreptitious reference to structural causality. Thus, the paradox of the Lacanian Real is that it 'exercises a certain structural causality', to the extent that it 'can produce a series of effects in the symbolic reality of subjects'.[42] That said, the Lacanian is clearly anxious to contain reality within the domain of subjectivity. Hence, presumably, his preference for 'homology', which further serves to contain discussion within the horizon of language, which is to say, within the realm of the Symbolic. Structural causality and its

---

37   Ibid., pp. 186–7.
38   Žižek 1994a, p. 22.
39   See Bhaskar 1978.
40   See Resch 1999, 93; 2001, pp. 14–16.
41   Žižek 1989, p. 11.
42   Ibid., p. 163.

modus operandi, we surmise, always threatened to draw Žižek ineluctably into a wider debate over the complex unity of the 'social formation', which, to reiterate, he was most anxious to avoid.[43]

The slippage from a Lacanian materialism to Žižek's Lacanian idealism needs to be carefully charted, specifically insofar as idealism does not lack for warranty in Lacanian theory. The latter's symbolic, it bears recalling, may be said to *create* 'reality', in the extreme sense that what cannot be said in language does not *exist*, strictly speaking. 'In Lacan's terminology, existence is a product of language: language brings things into existence (makes them part of human reality), things which had no *existence* prior to being ciphered, symbolised, or put into words'.[44] Žižek's deep homologies must be understood accordingly. Crucially, they license the collapse of Althusser's structural instances into a single generative mechanism, along the lines of a Hegelian expressive totality; alternatively expressed, the social formation is stripped of its ontological complexity, to contain it within the horizon of an individual praxis. As might be guessed, a drastic reduction of this kind is not without its consequences, to illustrate which let us turn to a problem that both Lacanian psychoanalysis and structural Marxism address, each in its own idiosyncratic manner: the existence of multiple interpretations of a single literary work.

Žižek dismisses at the outset the assumption that there exists a 'true meaning' to a text, in the light of which one might assess various mutually exclusive readings of it. Quite simply, he argues, we don't know what *Antigone* meant for Sophocles or, in Hegelian terms, what *Antigone* means *in itself*; all that is accessible to us are the distorted reflections, from contrasting subjective standpoints, across the ages. To this, we concede, only the most dogmatic of rationalists could possibly object. But then comes a false step: allegedly, the 'true meaning' of *Antigone*, what Sophocles wanted to say, is constituted *afterwards* or, as Žižek would have it, retroactively, which in effect reduces the past to statements made about it and, in the process, commits the Lacanian to an ontological irrealism, to which any materialist worthy of the name must certainly object.[45]

The contrast with Structural Marxism could not be greater. The Althusserian can readily agree that a literary work is not best envisaged as expressive of a

43 Homology is also privileged by Jean-Joseph Goux (Goux 1990), as by other structuralists, and for the same reason, namely to avoid the discussion of *causal* relations. For an interesting discussion of homology, analogy and isomorphism, see (Rossi-Landi 1975, pp. 72–8).

44 Fink 1995, p. 25.

45 Žižek 1989, pp. 213–14. Here, it could be argued, Žižek is guilty of Bhaskar's 'epistemic fallacy'.

particular author. But neither will he allow it to be collapsed into the reader's response, even less into the response of a reader who is located in the present. The literary work, from the Althusserian perspective, is appropriately envisaged as the determinate ideological *product* of a determinate historical matrix. The reader's response, whether in the past or in the present, is to be configured along the same lines. The hermeneutic notion of an 'on-going totalisation', mimicked by Žižek, 'denies the objectivity of both the past and the text', as does a poststructuralist criticism that, by basing itself on the infinite multiplicity of the text, 'collapses writing into reading and abolishes even the memory of production'.[46] But to substantiate this and related claims still further, we must resume the thread of our historical analysis.

5   The 'Look' versus the 'Gaze'

A quick perusal of 'Courtly Love as Anamorphosis'[47] is sufficient to lend substance to Peter Dews' claim that Lacan 'returns psychoanalysis to a historical and political vacuum'.[48] For while certainly the outline of a long chivalrous tradition takes shape, from its beginnings in the eleventh century until its incorporation into a contemporary erotics, it does so somewhat haltingly and leaves us none the wiser as to why courtly love should have appeared 'at a certain moment in the history of poetry',[49] or why it should have undergone the transformations it did during its long 'forward march'.[50] And unsurprisingly so, insofar as Lacan is only ever concerned with the subject and language *as such*, which is to say, in the case of courtly love, with an art form that, stripped down to its basics, always involves a trans-historical encircling of the Thing.[51]

Similarly, while Žižek's commentary on Lacan recognises the relevance of the relation between the 'bondsman' or 'vassal' and his 'feudal Master-Sovereign',[52] these components of the social relation are free-floating elements, unencumbered by history. Within this trans-historical horizon, Žižek foregrounds the Lacanian concept of *anamorphosis*, otherwise the obtrusive detail on the canvas of a picture that, paradoxically, is only meaningful when viewed

---

46   Resch 1992, pp. 277, 278.
47   Lacan 2008.
48   Dews 1987, p. 108.
49   Lacan 2008, p. 175.
50   Ibid., p. 183.
51   Ibid., p. 174.
52   Žižek 1999.

obliquely. To look at it directly, the logic runs, would reveal nothing, would in fact destroy the illusion. The same logic explains why the Lady must remain forever inaccessible and devoid of real substance. Metaphorically speaking, she is compared to a 'black hole' around which desire circles or, alternatively, to the surface of a mirror. The effect in both cases is to place her pretender in an impossible position: he wants to sleep with her but fears to fall into her and to be consumed.

One key aspect of Žižek's essay needs to be emphasised. Allegedly, we can only grasp the libidinal economy of courtly love *now*,[53] following the emergence of the masochistic couple, towards the end of the nineteenth century; historical considerations, it follows, can be weighed only to the extent that they are read retroactively, with inevitable consequences: specifically, the historical-objective conditions that explain the transformation of courtly love are effectively erased. The logic is the same as we saw Žižek apply to 'class struggle': just as, in psychoanalytic terms, my past remains inaccessible to me, repressed beyond recall, so also is history located beyond the reach of objective knowledge. With obvious epistemic ramifications: in effect, the intransitive dimension of knowledge is being systematically collapsed into its transitive equivalent.

In respect to such issues, the position of Structural Marxism contrasts sharply with that of Lacanian analysis. Whereas the Althusserian accepts that knowledge is internally related to, or causally interdependent with, the social structures that constitute its object, he refuses to conflate the transitive and intransitive moments. From the standpoint of his realism, one can only appropriate what exists independently of the act of appropriation, which is another way of denying that the real object exists as a simple function of thought. To elucidate this position further, we propose to take our cue from Žižek and to focus upon the specific question of the *gaze*, although, needless to say, from a rather different perspective.

Within Rodríguez's theoretical framework, to recall, there were no 'subjects' under feudalism, only ever 'serfs/servants' and their lord/Lord. We will search in vain, amidst the paratactic blocks that form the feudal narrative, for evidence of an organising, authorial subjectivity. Perforce, given the Lord's dominance, it was His eye-view that prevailed. Servants of their lord never literally *look* at all, ideologically speaking; rather, they only ever *read*, and to command them to do otherwise amounted to a gesture in futility. Exactly how futile Galileo was to discover when he asked his critics to *look* through his telescope for evidence of celestial decay: from the standpoint of the Scholastics, the heavens were only

---

53   Ibid., p. 150.

ever there to be *deciphered*.[54] Before free objects could be contemplated in their literality, it was necessary to await the arrival of a new, distinctively secular ideology, referred to by Rodríguez as *animism*, secreted by a new set of social relations, namely those of mercantile capitalism.

In Spain, the relevant ideological 'break', as it occurred in the opening decades of the sixteenth century, is most visible in the form it took in the work of the great lyric poet, Garcilaso de la Vega (1501–36).[55] The following sonnet captures perfectly its consequences for the *gaze*.

> En tanto que de rosa d'azucena
> se muestra la color en vuestro gesto,
> y que vuestro mirar ardiente, honesto,
> con clara luz la tempestad serena;
>   y en tanto qu'el cabello, que'n la vena
> del oro s'escogio, con vuelo presto
> por el hermoso cuello blanco, enhiesto,
> el viento mueve, esparce y desordena:
>   coged de vuestra alegre primavera
> el dulce fruto, antes que'l tiempo airado
> cubra de nieve la hermosa cumbre.
>   Marchitará la rosa el viento helado,
> todo lo mudará la edad ligera
> por no hacer mudanza en su costumbre.[56]

(Whilst the colours of the rose and the lily / show themselves in your face, / and whilst your burning, chaste gaze / with clear light calms the tempest; / and while the wind stirs, scatters and disarrays your hair / that was mined from a vein of gold, / as it blows around your lovely white, straight neck; / gather the sweet fruit of your happy Spring, / before an angry clime / covers the beautiful summits with snow. / The icy wind will wither the rose, / fleeting time changes everything, / so as not to alter its ways.)

No better example could be found of what it means for a free individual or proto-subject or, as Rodríguez would have it, *'beautiful soul'* to contemplate *for the first time* – in a novel literary genre – an object that, equally, is no longer

---

54   Rodríguez 2002a, p. 136.
55   Rodríguez 2002a, p. 141 ff.
56   Vega 1989, p. 66.

traced by the *signature* of the Lord. The fleetingness of the moment (no longer subsumed under the eternity of the 'next world'), the sense of movement (no longer towards the stasis of the 'natural place'), the faded rose (to be contrasted with the death's head) – all of this is unthinkable within the framework of substantialism.

At this point, the Althusserian notions of structural causality and of the *relative autonomy* of the related instances of the social formation prove crucial. While the exchange between the two beautiful souls, condensed within the sonnet form, is determined by an emergent set of mercantile relations, it is so determined only *in the last instance*. The qualification is crucial. The primacy of the economy does not explain the ideological or cultural instance in the sense that the latter can simply be read off from the structure of the mode of production; it is never a question of one component impacting directly upon another, in accordance with a *linear* criterion. Like the sonnet, the literary 'dialogue', of the kind that proliferate in the sixteenth century, should not be envisaged as a direct reflex of the mercantile exchange.[57] But nor, by the same token, is the relation between two varieties of exchange to be understood *homologically*, which is to say, within the framework of a Hegelian, *expressive* causality. The relevant mechanism is the matrix effect of the social formation, whose mediated effectivities and laminated structures explain why the lonely hour of the last instance never comes.

Does psychoanalysis have anything to contribute to this debate? Very little, Rodríguez would seem to imply, if, that is, it is going to persist in reducing courtly rhetoric – the 'snow', 'ice', 'fire', 'light', 'fury', 'sympathy', and so on – to the supposedly ineffable 'eternal themes' of love and death.[58] A subject the beautiful soul may well be, but of a notably embryonic variety, equipped only to facilitate the co-existence of transitional ideologies. The theoretician of radical historicity is emphatic: it makes little sense to inquire into the nature of the 'real' relationship between Garcilaso and Isabel Freyre, as if it were an instance of 'romantic love', of the kind that bound José de Espronceda (1808–42) to Teresa Mancha.

Yet it would be premature, in our view, to dismiss the possibility of Lacanian input to the Althusserian analysis. To explain exactly why let us consider one more of Garcilaso's sonnets.

---

57   An ideological 'break' separates the 'dialogue' from its predecessor, the medieval 'dispute'. Other examples of novel literary genre include the picaresque novel and the Spanish 'comedia'.

58   Rodríguez 2002a, p. 143.

Con ansia estrema de mirar qué tiene
vuestro pecho escondido allá en su centro,
y ver si a lo de fuera lo de dentro
en su aparencia y ser igual conviene,
    en él puse la vista; mas detiene
de vuestra hermosura el duro encuentro
mis ojos, y no pasan tan adentro
que miren lo qu'el en sí contiene.
    Y así se quedan tristes en la puerta
hecha, por mi dolor, con esa mano,
que aun a su mismo pecho no perdona;
    donde vi claro mi esperanza muerta
y el golpe, que en vos hizo amor en vano,
non esservi passato otra la gonna.[59]

(While desperate to know / what lies hidden deep within your bosom, / and to see if its outside looks like / and corresponds to its inside, / I fixed my gaze upon it; but this is blocked / by the barrier that is your beauty, / so that my eyes cannot pass within, / to see what your soul contained. / And thus they linger sadly at the door, / closed to my pain by the hand / that pardons not even its own breast; / and there I saw clearly that my hope had died, / and that the blow that love struck in vain / had not passed beyond the surface of your gown.)

Clearly confirmed is the novelty of the literal gaze: 'I fixed my gaze', 'my eyes', 'I saw clearly'; also of the split between the 'inside'/ 'outside' characteristic of the embryonic bourgeois subject. But what the Althusserian analysis fails to explain is the persistence, in this sonnet as in others, of the barrier that blocks the lover's access to the object. Lacanian theory, we have seen, labours under no such restriction and offers valuable insight into the relevant specular process. The beautiful soul, it would explain, is the ego that sees itself reflected in its ideal ego, that is driven to alienate itself in its imaginary, specular other; in contrast to the servant of his/her lord, who identifies him/herself with a signifying trait in the big Other or ego ideal and who is, accordingly, constituted at the very place *from where* s/he is being observed, which is that occupied by the Lord.

An analysis prosecuted along these lines would doubtless have other things to add. If, for example, Goux was right to align feudalism with anality and

---

59   Vega 1989, p. 65.

the 'obsessive' attention to ritual, then he is further justified in associating an emergent capitalism with the 'phallic' stage and 'paranoiac' attachment to the perspective of the isolated individual.[60] Our only qualification would be that, from the strictly Althusserian standpoint, it would still make relatively little sense to view such obsessive and paranoiac behaviour as an instance of individual neurosis. The beautiful soul, it cannot be emphasised enough, remains a *proto*-subject, with all the limitations that this implies. We will need to await some time before the inside/outside division assumes an additional dimension, whereby the 'inside' component is further split into a division between the (libidinal) unconscious and consciousness.

6   The Paradoxes of Democracy

Given their theoretical deficiencies over matters relating to the libidinal unconscious, some Marxists, including those heretofore indifferent or hostile to the fate of Althusserianism, may understandably view with enthusiasm a Lacanian reformulation of an Althusserian theory of interpellation that only the sceptics among them could possibly refuse to accept as other than richly suggestive. And that is only the beginning: the reputation that Žižek has managed to garner for himself as a theoretician both of psychoanalysis *and* of Marxism may well even encourage the sceptics to pass over the evidence in his writings of what amounts to an astounding indifference to Marxist theory. Yet if past experience is anything to go by, such theoretical indulgence may well prove costly, perhaps doubly so in the case of a theoretician who, from the outset, has made no secret of his intent to target what in many respects constitutes the jewel in the crown of historical materialism, namely its concept of surplus value. Let us consider the details.

To state the Lacanian argument in its most brutal, succinct form: notwithstanding the importance it attaches to the extraction of surplus value, Marxism signally fails to take account of the leftover of the Real that eluded symbolisation.[61] Žižek appeals by way of support to the 'decisive formula' contained in the first volume of *Capital*, according to which 'the limit of capital is capital itself, i.e., the capitalist mode of production'. There are, the Lacanian suggests, two ways in which this formulation can be taken. The first is the familiar sense in which the forces of production outgrow the relations of production and

---

60   Goux 1990, 99, pp. 132–3.
61   Žižek 1989, p. 50.

thereby become an obstacle to these relations' further development. Alternatively, it can be argued that the moment of crisis will never in fact occur, for
the simple reason that, in contrast to earlier modes, capitalism is driven constantly to develop its means of production, in the quest to generate surplus
value. By extension, the same logic is deemed to apply to the extraction of
surplus-enjoyment: 'If we subtract the surplus we lose enjoyment itself, just
as capitalism, which can survive only by incessantly revolutionising its own
material conditions, ceases to exist if it "stays the same"'.[62] The homological
principle has never been used to greater economic effect: from the material
basis in surplus labour-time we pass over smoothly to the libidinal investments
in the formation of social subjectivity.

Even the more indulgent of Marxists are bound to contest such a premature
conflation of economics with psychoanalysis. The connection between the surplus value and surplus enjoyment, they will argue, while interesting in itself,
needs to be much more mediated, at least if the latter is not to be collapsed into
the former. Among other things, they will elaborate, the Lacanian focus enables
Žižek conveniently to bypass a whole body of Marxist theory on the dynamics of capitalism.[63] But that is not our main concern here. More troubling is
the series of textual manoeuvres required to support the Lacanian analysis. To
begin with, as Žižek is the first to confess,[64] the 'simplistic' model that accords
priority to the productive forces was far from being Marx's last word on the
subject, an inconvenient fact that the Lacanian attempts to veil through his
appeal, by way of textual support, to *Capital*, as opposed to the earlier *Preface
to the Critique of Political Economy*. The only problem with this argument is that
Capital notoriously inverts the earlier theoretical model to foreground the relations of production, at the expense of the productive forces, an inconvenience
that Žižek attempts to mask through citational subterfuge and by directing the
reader's attention to another dichotomy, namely that between the formal and
real subsumption of the process of production.

This is all very devious, but it is easy to see in which direction Žižek is headed:
by reducing Marxism to a crude economism, centred upon the productive
forces, a space is being cleared in which to insert the pre-symbolic kernel of
the Real, to be contrasted with the Symbolic itself. Žižek is quick to disqualify
any move to configure this contrast in terms of that between the private and
public spheres, the effect of which, he realises, would be to lock the Lacanian
distinction into a particular (capitalist) set of social relations. 'The real impasse

---

62   Ibid., p. 52.
63   For a useful condensation of this theory, see David Harvey 2014.
64   Žižek 1989, p. 51.

runs in the opposite direction – the very social law [...] is always already penetrated by an obscene, "pathological", surplus enjoyment'.[65] According to this argument, the real precedes the social sphere and divisions internal to it; it is a trans-historical void that is 'too hot' to be approached too closely, a vortex around which the drives endlessly circulate.

The political implications of this scenario are quite devastating: the historical dynamic, we are assured, consists of a succession of failed attempts to grasp, conceive, and specify a strange kernel. Targeted for specific censure is the Marxist conviction that it is possible to 'unmask' formal democracy. We are advised rather to follow the postmodern path and assume the constitutive paradox of democracy: *'I know very well* (that democratic form is just a form spoiled by stains of "pathological" imbalance), *but just the same* (I act as if democracy were possible)'.[66] To conclude: at any moment love for one's neighbour can capsise into a destructive hatred.

Rodríguez's Marxism is of a very different kind. It is less the failings of liberal democracy that most concern him but the fact that capitalism, as a mode of production, is based upon *exploitation*. Unsurprisingly, as we have seen, he takes as his starting point precisely the core of *Capital* that is repressed in Žižek. To remind ourselves:

> The specific economic form in which unpaid surplus labour is pumped out of the direct producers determines the relationship of domination and servitude, as this grows directly out of production itself and reacts back on it in turn as a determinant. On this is based the entire configuration of the economic community arising from the actual relations of production, and hence also its specific political form.

It is within the relations of production, not the forces of production, that, according to this logic, is to be found 'the innermost secret, the hidden basis of the entire social edifice'.[67] And such is the basis upon which Rodríguez constructs his model of the ideological unconscious, with radical consequences for his interpretation of Marx.

The Althusserian's first target is precisely the alleged existence of a transhistorical 'human nature', of which Žižek's 'human condition' is but a variation: *'Human nature* as opposed to the despotism of the nobility and as opposed

---

65 Žižek 1991, p. 159.
66 Ibid., p. 168.
67 Marx 1981, p. 927.

to the superstition of the Church'.[68] Every historical mode of production, the argument proceeds, has justified its own particular form of exploitation on the basis of a 'natural order', consisting of those born to slave, those born to serve, and, more recently, after four centuries of struggle against a dominant, then residual feudalism, those born free to be exploited. Relative to other modes, capitalism is distinguished by its capacity to mask the process through which the social surplus or, specifically in the case of capitalism, the surplus value, is extracted: 'Exploitation, the causes thereof, cannot be seen, but their effects are overwhelming',[69] for which reason Marx's earlier attempts to explain its hidden dynamics fell some way short of adequacy, as Rodríguez sets out to explain with respect to the *Manifesto*.

The Spaniard's point of departure is the question that Marx was the first to pose in his classic text: when and where does the bourgeoisie arise? There can be only one answer: in the first cities of late feudalism. So far so good! But then comes a more difficult question: *how* did this class arise? In the *Manifesto*, according to Marx, from the market. 'And that is absolutely false'.[70] Unfortunately, it was only the first false step. The bourgeois revolution, Marx's argument runs, is a product of a situation in which feudal relations of production were overthrown by a new set of productive forces. Even worse, it is implied that the productive forces create new sets of social relations, in short, create the bourgeoisie. Rodríguez is perfectly frank: 'This is not true and this is not Marxism (at most this is a Marxism that still has to discover the secret of surplus value and the fact that labour power is tantamount to the sale of life)'.[71] The reality is that we are dealing with a struggle between two social systems, namely feudalism and capitalism.

To illustrate the damaging consequences that result from Marx's preoccupation with the forces of production, Rodríguez takes the example of the so-called 'revolution' in Information Technology. If technological developments are the key to everything, the Spaniard asks, where does that leave class exploitation? He might well have put the same question to a marxisant Lacanianism that, we have seen, similarly accords primacy to the productive forces, as part of its programme to de-ontologise the class struggle. Except that, at most, the Lacanian would be only mildly inconvenienced. Exploitation, after all, was the least of his concerns. His objection is less to the respective claims of the relations and forces of production than to the Marxist concentration upon the productive

---

68   Rodríguez 2013, p. 136.
69   Ibid., p. 138.
70   Ibid.
71   Ibid., p. 140.

process as a whole, which, he believes, comes at a price, namely the writing out of the *id* from social relations and Marxism's consequent inability to explain the 'restlessness' of the subject within every discursive structure. To put both research programmes to one final test, let us consider how they cope respectively with that most characteristic of modernist literary genres, the detective novel.

7 The Private Eye: Traversing the Fantasy

To theorise crime fiction, Rodríguez returns to the circumstances that account for the appearance of the 'private eye' in the second half of the nineteenth century. In his first incarnation – Sherlock Holmes is obviously the classic instance – the private investigator emerges as both wealthy and intelligent, in which respect he contrasts with his public equivalent, namely the policeman, who is always portrayed as obtuse and dysfunctional.[72] The British detective, Rodríguez elaborates, occupies a medial position between his American and Continental equivalents: the former of these equivalents believes in civil society but distrusts the State, however minimalist, and, as a consequence, lacks a political language; whereas the latter, by way of contrast, sees no difference between civil society and the State and, as a consequence, readily enters into political debate.

Rodríguez concentrates upon American society and specifically upon the novels of Raymond Chandler. In these, as in their British equivalent, the public official not only fails but also fails miserably, which allegedly explains the appearance of the 'private eye', classically in the person of Marlowe. Intelligent and well educated, Marlowe only trusts individuality when it comes embodied in the symbolic form of the judge and the attorney; beyond these, the only law he recognises is that of the market, which accounts for the fact that, in contrast to his British counterpart, the American private eye is always armed.[73] And the rest follows: Marlowe sees the world from the outside, as a narrative without meaning, for which reason he knows the miseries of the world for what they are, namely the 'shit of the henhouse'; his subjectivity, accordingly, is not that of the empirical, 'psychological' individual but that of an individuality secreted by a specific set of class relations, relations that, unconsciously, need to construct a 'private eye'.

---

72   Rodríguez 2008b, p. 298.
73   Ibid., pp. 299–300.

There are two things, Rodríguez further clarifies, which Marlowe will not accept: his exploitation in the hands of others and the exploitation of those closest to him.[74] The break with Conan Doyle and Agatha Christie is, in this respect, absolutely fundamental: whereas these authors see only the immediate causes, Chandler sees the whole invisible, social network, of which the criminality that he confronts on a daily basis is but the empirical or actual expression. How does all of this compare to the Lacanian approach to the same tradition?

The modern novel, Žižek avers by way of an opening gambit, explores the impossibility of locating the individual's fate in a 'meaningful, historical' context.[75] His tactic will be to transfer the relevant dynamics to the detective novel: the plot of the latter, it transpires, is motivated by the struggle to integrate an act of murder into the Symbolic. The logic is already familiar from the above discussion of phallic anamorphosis: the detective initially confronts a spot that 'sticks out', a detail that is odd, queer and wrong and that introduces him into a dreamlike world in which he can never be certain as to who is playing the game; the task is then to reconstruct retroactively the process that lends meaning to this detail and to all those stemming from it. A preoccupation with meaning, let us note parenthetically, has marginalised any concern with historical context.

Once enclosed within the psychoanalytic space, the figure that is thrown into relief is that of the *femme fatale*. She it is who condenses the deceitful character of the universe, who incarnates the fantasy figure that fills out the void, and who must be resisted at all costs. To be drawn into her embrace is necessarily to experience, firstly, the phenomenon of *fading* or 'aphanisis', as one approaches the object of desire, to be followed, secondly, by the catastrophic extinction of desire and even by death. Desire can only exist, the argument runs, if the subject can endlessly pursue its object, endlessly insofar as it can thereby postpone its encounter with the original (maternal) object of the death drive. The subject, finally, faces an unenviable choice: to 'get what it *really* wants', which would spell its annihilation, or the living death of the Symbolic. To see how these claims pan out, in comparison to those of Rodríguez, let us turn, by way of illustration, to *Los mares del sur* (*Seas of the South*) (1979) by Manuel Vázquez Montalbán.

The very title of the novel encapsulates what the Lacanian would be the first to recognise as a fantasy object *a*, namely the utopian image of a Pacific paradise. Initially, the incomprehensible detail to which this image is attached takes

74   Ibid., pp. 308–9.
75   Žižek 1991, p. 49.

the form of a text discovered on the dead body of Stuart Pedrell: 'Nobody will now bear me to the south'. Understandably, the first task of the private eye, Pepe Carvalho, must be to reconstitute its literary context: 'He applied himself to [its] possible cabbalistic meaning'.[76] The reference to a feudal hermeneutic practice notwithstanding, the cosmic horizons of substantialism and a neo-Platonic animism, we should note, have shrunk to the inner world of the individual subject, which explains the temptation to re-configure the mystery of Pedrell's murder in terms of a case-study. 'He behaved schizophrenically. One thing was the world of business, another his intellectual life'.[77] That said, it is a temptation that the detective must resist.

Pepe Carvalho, it is important to realise from the outset, is, like Pedrell, the product not simply of Spain's long transition from feudalism to modernity – the detective himself points to the belatedness of his nation's industrial revolution[78] – but of its shorter equivalent, from the Franco dictatorship to democracy. Moreover, also like Pedrell, he is very much a *disenchanted* product insofar as, along with other Leftist intellectuals, he has been left high and dry by a Communist party busily entering into pacts with former fascist politicians; which explains the fact that, in contrast to his American counterpart, the Spanish detective remains very much a *political* outsider: 'This society, I'm telling you, is rotten. It believes in nothing'.[79] And if, in accordance with available models, Pepe Carvalho deals initially with an (incompetent) local police force, that force is itself, in contrast to the British and American precedents, deeply politicised: 'they have their eye on me' complains a young officer, 'for meddling in politics'.[80]

The so-called setting to *Seas of the South*, we conclude, is anything but incidental to the novel's plot motivation. Indeed, it is only by pondering its complexities that Carvalho can make that intuitive, indispensable leap from the literary context of a quotation to the real, material context of Pedrell's murder: 'His gaze travelled to the other side of the city. To the quarter of San Magín. A man dies of a knife wound and it occurs to his assassins to decontextualise him. He must be transferred to the other end of the city, but also to a framework in which the death might be meaningful, into an adequate human and urban landscape'.[81] San Magín, we learn, was the site of the speculative expansion masterminded

76   Vázquez-Montalbán 1996, p. 32.
77   Ibid., p. 39.
78   Ibid., p. 212.
79   Ibid., p. 13.
80   Ibid., p. 21.
81   Ibid., p. 106.

by a trio of entrepreneurs, of which Pedrell was one. The project was simple: the purchase of cheap land, cheap because run-down, lacking in proper social services and subject to flooding, to be occupied by an immigrant population; the only problem was that, for Pedrell, such a scheme constituted a moral dilemma, from which he wished to escape.

At this point, an Althusserian analysis may appear to throw most light upon *Seas of the South*. Equipped with his understanding of the relevant social mechanisms, Carvalho will proceed to unpick the mystery of Pedrell's assassination, which, in essence, consists of an honour killing, prosecuted by the brother of Pedrell's pregnant girlfriend, during the course of which the detective will be forced to confront the reality of his own relations of production and the contractual nature of his association with those who have hired his services. Except that at no point does Montalbán allow his reader to lose contact with the relevant, underlying psychic dynamics. Crucial in this respect is Pepe's relation to Pedrell's daughter, Yes, the novel's *femme fatale*. 'An Orphelia type, Carvalho thought, and he hesitated between shaking her up or feeling sorry for her';[82] wisely enough insofar as, her youthful naïveté notwithstanding, indeed, precisely on account of it, Yes is the very embodiment of the potentially lethal Thing.

Yes is, as Carvalho progressively discovers, not the only fantasy object to attract his attention. The maternal image that he confronts as he wanders the more poverty-stricken quarters of the city serves the same function. It is followed closely by the figure of Jimmy Carter, with whom Pepe identifies in his imaginary dealings with actress Faye Dunaway. And, of course, there is always the political fantasy of the revolution that would see Barcelona transformed into a utopia, although its charms prove eminently resistible to the tired, cynical Pepe, as do those of Yes' mother, the last incarnation of the *femme fatale*. The only people the detective really cares about are those in his immediate vicinity, namely Biscuter, his assistant, Charo, his prostitute girlfriend, and, of course, his dog, the discovery of whose slaughtered corpse closes the novel.

8   Conclusion

Such, in broad outline, are the contrasting attempts to theorise two forms of the unconscious, one libidinal and one ideological. Žižek, we have seen, set out to theorise a perceived homology between the structure of the psyche,

---

82   Ibid., p. 48.

on the one hand, and that of the social formation, on the other, to which end he reworks the opposition between the complex unity of the social formation and the subject in terms of the disjunction between the unconscious level of libidinal enjoyment and the conscious level of discursive meaning. Among the virtues of the key concept of 'homology' was that it contained discussion within the horizon of language and symbolisation and thereby eliminated the need to address issues relating to causality. Even more importantly, it allowed Žižek to eliminate the whole Althusserian edifice of a 'structure in dominance' in favour of a process of interpellation, to press Althusserianism back into the Hegelian box from which it had struggled to emerge, and, ultimately, to reset the debate in terms of the subject/object opposition central to bourgeois ideology.

For Rodríguez, by way of contrast, the enduring value of Althusser's work was to be located not in his theory of interpellation, which the Spaniard considered to be flawed, but in the philosopher's concept of contradiction, with respect to the complex diversity of competing ideologies and, by extension, the structured unity of the social formation. The matrix effect of the latter helped explain the pervasive, unconscious reach of ideology throughout every social level or instance. To depart from any other standpoint was, for the Althusserian, to sink the Marxist problematic and to invite its re-absorption within its idealist competitors. Presupposed throughout is a theory of the historical forms of existence of individuality, in accordance with which the concrete uniqueness of each individual is only to be reached via a long detour through the social formation. His successes notwithstanding, the Althusserian failed adequately to address desire, men and women, the law, and the forbidden object. The intellectual means to rectify such deficiencies are available but will require that the individual psyche be theorised as a *composite* component that is every bit as complex and structured as the social formation.

CHAPTER 9

The Rise of Podemos: Ernesto Laclau and Chantal Mouffe

'Death and the Compass', one of several stories by Jorge Luis Borges to have attracted the attention of Juan Carlos Rodríguez, offers a convenient vantage point from which to survey the latter's work. In appearance, the narrative in question is a typical example of crime fiction, consisting as it does of a series of mysterious deaths or, seemingly, assassinations, beginning with that of Doctor Yarmolinksi, whose solution falls to the lot of the appropriate law-enforcing agencies.[1] Each crime is accompanied by a set of clues, of a learned, literary nature, to the puzzlement of the police chief, Treviranus, and, initially, of the private detective Erik Lönnrot. After spending a hundred days poring over the relevant details, Lönnrot quite suddenly announces that he has solved the mystery, confessing to his shame that it took him so long to crack what turned out to be a clear-cut case. At this point, Treviranus receives a sealed envelope that contains a map of the city and a letter. The letter announces that there will be no more assassinations, while elucidating, with reference to an accompanying map, that the three assassinations occurred in the north, in the west and finally in the east; a red line joins these compass points so as to trace the form of an equilateral triangle. All these details, Lönnrot reassures Treviranus, confirm his conviction that the case is indeed closed. The detective then catches a train that, travelling south, bears him through endless suburbs to an abandoned estate containing a half-empty, oddly symmetrical mansion. Climbing up to the belvedere, Lönnrot is overwhelmed by two men, who hand him over to their leader, Red Scharlach. From Scharlach Lönnrot learns that, while he correctly intuited that the triangle was in fact a rhombus and that a fourth death was duly being prepared, he yet failed to realise that the death in question would be his own; and that, in other words, he has walked into a carefully laid trap, prepared, the detective is further informed, in revenge for an earlier confrontation between himself and Red Scharlach, from which the latter had emerged the loser.

Rodríguez's interest in Borges's story lies in the allegorical use to which it lends itself by way of explaining the eclipse of Marxism during the transition

---

1   Borges 1999, pp. 147–56.

in Spain from the dictatorship of Franco to social democracy in the 1970s. The four points of the compass, allegedly, are the key: the first case was the assault in the west upon the unions and workers' movement, engineered by Margaret Thatcher and Ronald Reagan; the second, the disappearance of Marxism in the north, otherwise in the Scandinavian countries and in Germany, thanks to the Marshall Plan; the third, the horror of the eclipse of Marxism in the east under Stalin; and, finally and crucially, came the fourth act of disappearance, which took place in southern Europe in the form of the implosion of the commun- ist parties of France, Italy, and Spain. Fittingly, this fourth death corresponds, at the level of detail, to its equivalent in Borges's story, which, to recall, was something of a 'sham' or 'simulacrum', staged by Red Scharlach himself.[2] Work- ing the analogy, Rodríguez asks what it was that the Spanish Left, like Lönnrot, failed to see.

The answer, it transpires, is global capitalism, otherwise, the elephant in the room: so large and conspicuous, yet so easily ignored, or so Rodríguez reas- ons. While the inequalities of exchange within capitalism had always been effectively disguised, the routine extraction of surplus value became virtually invisible following the eclipse of Marxism (as an explanatory paradigm) and the rise of the digital economy. Retrospectively, as far as Spain is concerned, the logic of the unfolding plot is clear: after forty years in exile, forty years of struggle against a Francoist autarky, the Spanish Communist Party walked into a trap, after the fashion of Lönnrot. Quite simply, to elaborate, the Party failed to see that the lemma 'Spain is different', like that of 'socialism in one country', was no longer functional; that, more specifically, the debate over Franco had been surpassed by a more encompassing neo-liberal thematic, 'the freedom of the individual'. The situation, Rodríguez continues, grew desperate. Anxious to be legitimised, the SCP even donned a 'euro' disguise, but with catastrophic results: '... everything degenerated into political verbosity, a crude politicking'.[3] Cast in a minor role on a global stage, the Party found itself marginalised and, within a relatively brief period, eliminated as a political force.

While the above analysis is intriguing as a 'take' on the eclipse of the various Marxisms, the allegorical application of Borges's story does not, in my opin- ion, figure among Rodríguez's best efforts. It is, quite simply, too abstract, too arbitrary, which is to say, insufficiently grounded in textual detail. To transform it productively, in the desired direction, I propose to introduce the battle of narratives that forms the nucleus of Borges's own story, but that Rodríguez's reading effectively bypasses.

---

2 Rodríguez 2013, pp. 22–32.
3 Rodríguez 2013, p. 27.

As events are played out, the literal account of Yarmolinsky's murder, narrated by the police commissioner, Treviranus, is surpassed by that of the private detective, Lönnrot, which dispensed with the actual details of the crimes in order to reveal their secret design. Lönnrot's more abstract narrative, however, is encompassed in turn by that of Red Scharlach, which makes use of an actual murder to fabricate a totally transcendental fiction. Played out against the backdrop of this scenario, Rodríguez's analysis assumes an added urgency: the literal narrative of 'socialism in one country', promoted by the Communist Party, was eclipsed by that of social democracy, based on the 'freedom of the individual'. The details fit the case: in practice, the PSOE paid only lip-service to the socialist tradition before accommodating to the forces of neo-liberalism, to devastating effect in Spain, which, by virtue of its delayed transition from feudalism, was still open to revolutionary change. To give the narrative one final twist: Marxism itself was, at the time, being threatened with absorption, similarly from within, by a post-Marxism intent upon a radical reconfiguration of the classical tradition. And it is to this reconfiguration that we now turn.

1   Ernesto Laclau: Goodbye to All That

Notwithstanding their focus upon methodological as opposed to epistemological issues, the temptation to interpret Althusser's texts along epistemological lines, we argued above, would prove irresistible, particularly during the period of neo-liberal ascendancy. In the case of many Leftist scholars, this temptation took the form of a gradual dismantling of the Althusserian social formation and its re-inscription within the dialectic of consciousness, as a prelude to an ultimate exit from Marxism. Archetypical in this respect was the work of Ernesto Laclau.

Initially at least there was little about Laclau's work to indicate the direction it would subsequently take. Indeed, the Argentinian's first major contribution to academic debate (1971) took the form of a Marxist critique of André Gunter Frank's theory of colonial underdevelopment, extended in a post-script (1977) to include the 'world system' theory of Immanuel Wallerstein. The problem with the Frank-Wallerstein approach, Laclau argued, was that it addressed issues relating exclusively to commodity exchange, which, although pitched at the level of the global economic system, presupposed a gross simplification of the capitalist mode of production and, specifically, a neglect of the relations of production. Obscured thereby was the fact that the relations of production prevailing throughout colonial Latin America were essentially pre-capitalist; and that, moreover, European mercantilists, with an eye to maximising their profits, had a vested interest in ensuring that these relations remained suitably under-developed.[4] In sum, far from weakening and disintegrating pre-capitalist relations, integration of the Latin-American economies into the world market actually served to bolster them.

The logic of Laclau's argument seems incontestable: so focused was Frank upon commercial profit that he had missed the structural complexity of a global system that functioned on the basis of multiple modes of production; which makes it rather strange that by the time Laclau came to add a postscript to his original article, within the framework of his *Politics and Ideology in Marxist Theory* (1977), the seeds of an anti-Marxism appear to have been sown. If Wallerstein was paying insufficient attention to the political and ideological instances, Laclau wondered, did the fault lie with Wallerstein or with Marxism and the conceptual shortcomings thereof? With the latter, it transpires: Laclau now concedes to the critics of Marxism and, specifically, to critics of Althusserianism that the concept of the mode of production was damagingly abstract.[5]

The next chapter in the same volume, 'The Specificity of the Political', follows much the same pattern as the first. It begins with a defence of Althusserianism, as articulated by Nicos Poulantzas in his exchange with Ralph Miliband. Miliband, we are informed, is excessively preoccupied with empirical data;[6] more fundamentally, he operates within the subject/object problematic, which in effect reduces social classes to *interpersonal relations*.[7] Laclau, then, has perfectly grasped the differences between the two scholars: one takes as his point of departure the *motivations of conduct* of the individual actors, as the origin of *social action*, the other the notion of an objective social formation. The negative consequences of the subjectivist intervention, the argument proceeds, are profound: by diverting attention from the objective structures and laws of the system onto the personal motivations of agents, Miliband has succumbed to the insidious influence of empiricism, with its epistemological obsessions, and thereby jeopardised the whole Marxist enterprise.

Everything, then, seems perfectly straightforward, until, that is, Laclau begins to critique Poulantzas's position, also in the severest terms. The Greek Marxist's taxonomy, it transpires, is indeed pitched at too high a level of abstraction, as Miliband had reasonably argued, to the extent that it succumbs finally to a species of *formalism*.[8] At such altitudes, it becomes impossible to establish

---

4   Laclau 1979, p. 33.
5   Ibid., p. 48.
6   Ibid., p. 52.
7   Ibid., p. 53.
8   Ibid., p. 70.

logical relations between concepts.[9] The fault, Laclau further argues, lies not so much with Poulantzas as with the conceptual system upon which he is dependent, namely Althusserianism. Carefully considered, the latter raises a whole series of questions. Why is it concerned with only three instances? What is one to make of the distinction between 'determinant' and 'dominant' instances? Also, of 'determination in the last instance'? Very soon, the posing of questions becomes a way of stating objections. Are not Althusser's concepts but a series of metaphors, carrying little in the way theoretical content, and devised solely to solve an artificial problem created by the metaphysic of instances?[10] How is it possible for transitive causality and structural causality to operate conjointly? By implication, it is not. What happens in different modes of production? Althusserianism, seemingly, has no answer.

Now it is true that Althusser is largely concerned with theory in the abstract. But even so, within these limits, there were obvious responses to the problems that Laclau poses. Take, for example, the number of instances into which Althusser organises the social formation, namely economic, political, and ideological. Why these and only these? The selection appears to Laclau somewhat arbitrary and closed. And yet it must be clear, to anyone familiar with the Althusserian canon, that the philosopher has focused upon functions that might reasonably be taken as indispensable to social existence; that the number of instances is open rather than closed; and that, by the same token, the specification of distinct practices simply serves a heuristic purpose.[11] Moreover, if Althusser was sometimes short of specificities, it was because he assumed their provision to be the task of the separate sciences; on perfectly justifiable grounds, to judge by subsequent developments and the Althusserian contributions to the social sciences.[12] Laclau totally ignores the existence of such work because, like so many of Althusser's critics, he was primarily concerned to disqualify the Althusserian problematic *in toto*, for purely ideological reasons, not to resolve difficulties internal to it.

Unsurprisingly, Laclau sometimes misconstrues Althusser's text to the point of perversity. For example, in the chapter on 'Fascism and Ideology' he confesses to being puzzled by Poulantzas's alleged failure to retain what is, arguably, the most important of Althusser's contributions to Marxism, namely the theory of ideological production and, specifically, the interpellation of the

---

9   Ibid., p. 73.
10   Ibid., p. 77.
11   Resch 1992, p. 36.
12   See Resch 1992, p. 105 ff.

'subject' through discourse.[13] Yet one wonders why Laclau should be so mystified. Had not he himself, in his earlier essay, justified Poulantzas' tenacious resistance to the subject/object problematic? Viewed from the standpoint of his *Political Power and Social Classes*, there could be nothing very strange about Poulantzas' indifference to the concept of interpellation. Nothing so very strange, that is, except for somebody like Laclau, who is seeking not only to reinstate the subject in its former centrality but also to contain it within the realm of discourse: '[W]hat constitutes the unifying principle of an ideological discourse is the "subject" interpellated and thus constituted through this discourse'.[14] From such a position as this, the royal road to post-Marxism stood open.

What is perhaps most surprising about Laclau's text is its failure to engage the research conducted in Hispanic scholarship, which, beyond question, was the site of the most productive application of Althusserian concepts, and to the contested field of ideology to boot. Conspicuous by its absence was any reference to Rodríguez and the research activity emanating from Granada. Perhaps, as a scholar anxious to carve out a place for himself within the European academy, the Argentinian wished to avoid, for eminently professional reasons, the disparagement routinely meted out to students of Hispanic culture by metropolitan-based scholars. Whatever the reasons, as we will see below, a considerable price was to be paid, not least of all by those Spanish 'politólogos' and experts in public relations who have recently rushed to enlist under the banner of Laclau's post-Marxism.

2   The State/Stage under Absolutism

Notwithstanding the charge of 'structural abstractionism', levelled against Althusserian Marxism, Poulantzas at least was alert to the dangers of deducing knowledge from general concepts, hence of detaching the general theory from concrete research. '[W]e do not yet have enough systematic regional theories of the political in the different modes of production', he warned, 'nor enough particular systematic theories of the different modes of production'.[15] Explicitly in response to Poulantzas' work,[16] Rodríguez soon began to rectify this situation with respect to Spain and the development of its Absolutist State. In broad

---

13   Ibid., p. 100.
14   Ibid., p. 101.
15   Poulantzas 1973, p. 24.
16   Rodríguez 2002a, p. 36n4.

outline, he argued, a clear distinction between the public and private sectors had been established by the opening years of the sixteenth century. 'A struggle, then, develops in the interior of the "public" sphere, at both the ideological and political levels, between the bourgeoisie and the nobility, compounded by an attempt to constitute itself on the part of the Absolutist State'.[17] 'Bourgeoisie' and 'nobility' are deployed with a proviso: to talk in such terms, Rodríguez concedes, courts an obvious danger, that of subsuming sets of social relations under 'subjects', within the framework of the bourgeois subject/object opposition. By way of response, the Althusserian undertook to displace the theoretical focus to the causal efficacy exercised intransitively by the social formation conceived as a whole. The tactic would prove richly rewarding with respect to the dialectical relations between the Spanish state and the Spanish stage and, pace Laclau, explains the dominance exercised by the political instance.

Like its counterpart within the English and French theatrical traditions, the relatively sudden appearance of the Spanish *comedia* in the sixteenth century constitutes a response to the pressure of emergent bourgeois relations upon a dominant feudalism. To exist, the new theatre required a literal division between an audience (that paid to enter) and the stage. Rodríguez elaborates: '... *the stage is not simply the effect of the appearance of ideology as a public phenomenon; it is also the representation of* res publica, *that is, of the political'.*[18] While the nobility is unable to prevent the appearance of the public/private split, which is essential to the functioning of a capitalist economy, it is still dominant enough at the political level to fill the public sphere with its own substantialist thematics. To narrow our focus still further, let us turn to a play by Lope de Vega to which Rodríguez refers only in passing but that perfectly illustrates his central theoretical claims.

The plot of *El villano en su rincón* (*The Villein in his Corner*) (1611) may be briefly summarised. While Juan Labrador, a rich peasant, is perfectly willing, indeed eager, to acknowledge his servility to the King and his Court, he feels no compulsion to go and *see* his lord, even when the latter happens to be in his vicinity. When the King is apprised of the fact, he is suitably outraged and arranges to confront Juan Labrador. The action throughout is leavened by the amorous interchanges between the King's courtiers and the local peasant women, that will eventuate in appropriately arranged marriages. As for Juan Labrador, he will be 'rewarded' with a permanent position at Court and thereby forced to 'enjoy' the presence of his monarch on a daily basis. Let us unpack the action with an eye to its underlying ideological tensions.

---

17   Ibid., p. 37.
18   Ibid., p. 46.

Lope, it should be clear at the outset, is basically an ideologue of the nobility, concerned to alert his monarch to the dangers of becoming too detached from his 'súbditos', hence to the need to lock the peasantry back into a dominant pattern of feudal relations. Perforce, the relevant categories are substantialist: the 'vassal' 'serves' his 'lord', who in turn conceives of himself as a representative of *his* lord in *this* world; equally substantialist are the social ties that bind one party to the other: the serf/servant was made in the image of his lord/Lord. To threaten the specular relation was to threaten both the social and cosmic orders:

> Vasallo que no se mira
> en el Rey, esté muy cierto
> que sin concierto ha vivido,
> y que vive descompuesto.[19]

(A vassal that does not see himself / in the image of the King needs to be aware / that he has lived a life without order / and that he lives ill composed.)

In the case of Juan Labrador, it was to further court the charge of treason: 'Yo tengo en este rincón / no sé qué de rey también' (lines 1669–70) (In this corner of mine, / I am also something of a king). But within carefully specified limits: the peasant who boasts of his independence and autonomy is careful throughout to underline his economic allegiance to the King.

> REY   ¿Dio el dinero?
> OTÓN   En famosas coronas de oro puro;
>   y, sin este dinero, te presenta
>   doce acémilas ... (lines 2283–86)

(KING: Did he pay up? / OTÓN: In famous crowns of pure gold; / and, in addition to this money, he presents you with twelve mules ...)

As long as taxes are paid, in money and in kind, it suffices to impose a strictly ideological penalty, namely that of compulsory attendance at Court – a perfect example, let us note in passing, of the immediate effect exercised transitively by the economic instance on its political and ideological counterparts.

---

19   Vega 2010, lines 2902–5.

The Villein, we conclude, confirms Rodríguez's claim that, certainly by the early seventeenth century, the Spanish nobility had been able to impose its authority and its value-system at the political level, to block economic development in Spain and hence to condemn the country to a prolonged transition from feudal to capitalist relations. Symptomatically, the challenge to the state staged in Lope's play emanates from the peasantry, not from an emergent bourgeoisie: by no stretch of the imagination can Juan Labrador be said to qualify as a beautiful soul. That said, there could be no question of negotiating a regression from transitional to feudal relations in their pure form. The appearance of the theatre, as a generic form was, like the sonnet and the novel, a measure of the pressure of bourgeois relations, evidence also that, while it may have been able to control the public sphere, the nobility had been forced to *live with* the public/private distinction. Even a royalist ideologue as committed as Lope was forced into acts of compromise, not least of all at the level of the *comedia*'s thematics, as *The Villein* illustrates only too clearly. Let us consider, by way of example, the importance attached to niceties of dress.

Clothing, within an organicist context, was quite literally substantial: it marked a person's essential being. Yet from the outset of Lope's play, it is clear, the thematic has undergone a radical transformation along animist lines. Specifically, the plot turns upon the possibility of assuming a *disguise*, in other words, of the possibility that a character can *become another* merely by changing his or her attire. Hence, the very opening scene of the play turns on the fact that Lisarda, a peasant girl, appears 'en hábito de dama' (dressed as a lady). The attendant courtiers are appropriately deceived, but only temporarily: delegated to follow Lisarda to her home, Marín, a servant, witnesses the lady's transformation back into a peasant girl, of a suitably elevated kind, to be sure – she is, after all, the daughter of Juan Labrador – but a peasant girl nevertheless (lines 263–4). While the ensuing social mobility works both ways – the king will make the acquaintance of Juan Labrador while disguised: 'en hábito disfrazado. / Ser cazador me he fingido' (lines 1982–3) ('in disguise. / I have pretended to be a huntsman'), attention focuses upon the changes undergone by the peasantry in their transition from a rural to a courtly setting. Thus, Feliciano emphasises the transformation in evidence in his sister: 'tienes nuevo ser' (line 2685) (you have a new being), before leaving her to ensure that the other family members are similarly attired, so as adequately to reflect his own elevated status.

By way of contrast to the thematic of dress, where the impact of animism is immediate and obvious, *The Villein* appears, at least at first sight, to leave substantialist ideology unchallenged in matters relating to marriage. Perforce, peasant girls aspire to a marriage through which to *serve* their husbands: 'Yo no puedo serviros sin casarme' (I cannot serve you without being married to you), protests Lisarda to the courtier, Otón (line 1323). And it is through the control over nubile women that the patriarch asserts his power: 'mi voluntad en público declaro' (line 1527) (I declare my will in public), asserts Juan Labrador, confident in the financial power that he exerts through the payment of a dowry. But even here, within the sphere of personal relations, once the focus of attention is displaced from marriage to love, an ideological clash proves unavoidable. Quite simply, the substantialist norm of *servility* cannot be squared with the animist promotion of *freedom*, at least when it comes to selecting one's partner. As Lisarda explains to her cousin:

> Yo no nací, mi Belisa,
> para labrador por dueño;
> para mí su estilo es sueño
> y su condición es risa.
> Yo me tengo de casar,
> por mi gusto y por mi mano,
> con un hombre cortesano,
> y no en mi propio lugar. (lines 659–66)

(I was not born, my Belisa, / to be owned by a peasant; / for me his style is absurd / and his condition a laughing matter. / I aim to marry, / according to my taste and by my own hand, / a courtly man, / and not from my village.)

Constanza, Lisarda's companion, similarly seeks to promote the force of love, which, according to her, has the capacity, like that of music (with which it is closely connected), to bring about harmony and equality between those who are separated socially: 'El amor tiene poder / de concertar voluntades' (lines 1162–3) (Love has the power / to join wills together). Love is the gateway into the *private sphere* of the garden, the preferred location for the lovers' tryst, where, according to Lisarda, the socially unequal may come together and individuals can break free of the bonds that, in the public realm, hold them in check (lines 1350–7).

Alarmingly, love sometimes threatens to know no bounds. Hence, even as the Infanta discourses with the King regarding 'service' and 'blood', Otón mutters subversively: 'Mas, ¿cuando amor tuvo ley? / Porque con ley no es amor' (lines 2560–1) (But since when was love lawful? / Because if it is lawful it is not love). But note, only mutters and, crucially, out of hearing: passion, substantially speaking, only ever figures marginally; and love, under absolutist rule, hesitates openly to speak its name. And with reason – the patriarch still has the capacity to bite back, and with a vengeance. Particularly instructive in this respect is the scene in Lope's play in which the King, having inserted himself by devious means into the private household of Juan Labrador, finds himself, unexpectedly, in the bedchamber of his host's daughter. His reaction is immediate, namely to assert his sense of ownership, which clearly extends to her body; also, in the circumstances, predictable: from a substantialist standpoint, the king is ill disposed to recognise the existence of a private sphere. Equally immediate and predictable is Lisarda's reaction:

> Suelte; que el Diablo me lleve,
> si no le dé un mojicón.
> ¡A villana en su rincón
> desa manera se atreve! (lines 1921–4)

> (Let go; the Devil take me, / if I don't punch you. / To a villein in her own home / you dare to behave in this way!)

The classic stage will eventually replace the public Court with the private drawing-room, but it will be some time before even bourgeois dramatists gain access to the boudoir.

3   Chantal Mouffe: Reductionism Inverted

None of the above was of the slightest interest to Laclau, who, we have seen, was content to assert dogmatically that the Althusserian schema of modes of production, of determination in the last instance, of (political) dominance, etc. was simply unworkable and unproductive. He was undoubtedly strengthened in his convictions after joining forces with Chantal Mouffe, who, to judge from a recent interview with Íñigo Errejón – one of the leaders of the newly constituted Spanish political party, Podemos – had been charting a parallel course throughout the 1970s. In the interview in question, Mouffe speaks of her transition from a fairly orthodox Althusserianism, during a period spent in Colombia, to one broadly aligned with Gramsci.[20] She does not elaborate upon the reasons for her realignment, although one guesses from an essay published in the late 1970s[21] that it had much to do with the Althusserian attachment to

---

20   Errejón and Mouffe 2015, p. 72.
21   Mouffe 1979.

the 'social formation', thence to economics 'in the last instance'. Such concepts would prove difficult to reconcile with the primacy Mouffe wished to accord to politics and thence to subjectivity. Let us consider the details.

'The central problem of contemporary Marxism', Mouffe asserts at the outset, 'lies in the elaboration of a non-reductionist theory of ideology and of politics which will account for determination in the last instance by the economic'.[22] What such a non-reductionist theory will require, it immediately transpires, is a shift of focus from the Marxist concept of a social formation to the 'irruption of a *subjective* principle into *objective* historical processes' (italics added), in other words, to the familiar subject/object paradigm fundamental to bourgeois ideology. The only problem was how such a shift was to be negotiated given the seemingly insurmountable obstacle that Althusserian theory posed to it. As an initial move, Mouffe side-steps any consideration of the early Althusser, together with the unconsciousness of ideology, in order to focus upon the philosopher's famous essay on the Ideological State Apparatuses, which, while continuing to exclude consciousness as an originating source, at least had the virtue, from Chantal's perspective, of concentrating attention upon the subject and its interpellation, hence upon the 'subjective principles of identity'. Pressing the logic of the argument, the one-time Althusserian proceeds to strip down the social formation to a multiplicity of 'social agents', each hailed in terms of sex, family, social class, nationality, race, and so on. She imposes a further condition: none of these categories is to be prioritised over the others, thereby leaving a problem to be solved, namely that of 'determining the *objective* relation between these subjective principles or ideological elements'.[23]

Structural Marxism, we are reminded, had gone to some lengths to theorise the causal processes functional to social formation. While recognising the existence of individual structures (economic, political, and ideological) and of their transitive effectivities, it yet insists upon the matrix effect of the whole, through which to explain, among other things, economic determination in the last instance. The strength of Althusserianism lay in its ability to hold the relevant causalities and conflictual forces in productive tension. But Mouffe is interested in none of this or in historical complexities. As will quickly transpire, her thinking is restricted to the rise of liberal democracy, which is to say, contained within the horizon of bourgeois ideology. Predictably enough, her focus is upon the interrelationship between diverse social elements, a focus that she justifies along the following lines: 'In a reductionist perspective each of these

---

22   Mouffe 1979, p. 171.
23   Ibid., p. 171.

[elements] has a necessary class-belonging. But if, on the contrary, we accept the principle of over-determination, we must conclude that there can exist no necessary relation between them, and that it is consequently impossible to attribute a necessary class-belonging to them'.[24]

The syntactic convolutions that Mouffe's text sometimes exhibits are symptomatic, we suggest, of the effort required to negotiate the transition from the problematic of Structural Marxism to its bourgeois equivalent, more specifically, to reconfigure the structural relations characteristic of the former in terms of the 'human relations' (and centrality of the subject) characteristic of the latter. The following is typical:

> To stress determination in the last instance by the economic is equivalent to saying determination in the last instance by the social classes inasmuch as we define classes as constituting antagonistic poles in the dominant relations of production. This brings us, therefore, to the following assertion: if the ideological elements referred to do not *express* social classes, but if nevertheless classes do in the last instance, determine ideology, then we must thereby conclude that this determination can only be the result of the establishing of an articulating principle of these ideological elements, one which must result in actually *conferring upon them* a class character.[25]

What Mouffe has done is replace the notion of economic, political, and ideological relations, understood as a play of structural forces relating to prices, exchanges, wages, profits, rents, etc., with 'social classes', understood as 'subjects', hence as forms of 'class consciousness'. With the reversion to bourgeois ideology came a whole new series of problems to be resolved, relating to the dynamics of subjectivity, which explains the sudden enthusiasm for Gramsci. 'According to him hegemony involves the creation of a *higher synthesis*, so that all its elements fuse in a "collective will" which becomes the new protagonist of political action which will function as the protagonist of political action during that hegemony's entire duration'.[26]

By this point, we are located emphatically within a free-floating superstructure. All contact with the other elements of the complex unity of the social formation has been severed, not because they have been shown to be theoret-

---

24   Ibid.
25   Mouffe 1979, pp. 171–2.
26   Ibid., p. 184.

ically unnecessary but because they constitute a constraint upon the exercise of political will. These elements will be recuperated as 'background' or 'context', when it is necessary to lend some flesh to the bare discursive bones, but strictly in terms of a subjective 'world view'. In effect, having eliminated objective reality outside discourse, the social formation has been reduced to its political instance, itself reconfigured as a struggle for power between diverse social groups. Left behind is not simply Althusserianism but Marxism as well. What Robert Resch has argued with respect to those other post-Marxists, Barry Hindess and Paul Hirst, also applies to Laclau and Mouffe: unable to provide either a compelling critique or theoretically interesting alternative to structural Marxism, 'their particular current of post-Marxism flows smoothly into the larger stream of postmodernism'.[27]

Perforce, the spectre of idealism rears its head in the form of social relations that have become, by anyone's reckoning, dangerously disembodied and formalised. A re-materialising impulse eventuates by way of response. 'Another very new aspect of the Gramscian problematic of ideology is the importance which he attributes to the *material and institutional nature of ideological practice*'.[28] From which it follows that schools, churches, the media, etc. figure as the source of ideology. 'This ensemble of apparatuses is termed the *ideological structure* of a dominant class by Gramsci, and the level of the superstructure where ideology is produced and diffused is called *civil society*'.[29] Since, within this problematic, the apparatuses in question have been despoiled of their structural outworks, the Althusserian 'last instance' proves to be an irrelevance insofar as totally unable to resolve 'the most serious problem of [the] marxist theory of ideology'.[30] The only task that remained was to displace the theoretical focus from 'class' consciousness to the 'group' consciousness.

Rodríguez has a rather different take upon the rise of liberal democracy and the struggle for political ascendancy; different, not least of all, in the sheer concreteness of his analyses.

4   The Eighteenth-Century Drama: from Public to Private

Rodríguez begins his analysis of the 'Age' or 'Century' of the 'Enlightenment' by measuring his distance between the Hegelian historicism implicit in these

---

27   Resch 1992, p. 105.
28   Ibid., p. 187.
29   Ibid.
30   Ibid., p. 199.

concepts and the Althusserian 'social formation'. Integral to the former is the notion of expressive causality, according to which the phenomena of any one period – relating to its economy, law, philosophy, etc. – are viewed as externalisations of a single internal principle. Rodríguez, by way of contrast, takes as his point of departure a social formation that caters for the co-existence of different modes of production and their associated, contradictory ideologies. Broadly speaking, within a European context, the ideologies in question consist of a dominant liberalism and rationalism, of bourgeois derivation, and the various feudal residues that constitute their counterpart. '[A]ny interpretative approach to the 18th century that views it as a *homogeneous, linear entity*', the Althusserian warns, 'is destined to fail'.[31]

Contradictions, disorder, imbalances, it follows, will constitute the norm, hence more than justify the need for a 'differential history', through which to theorise the distinct, uneven rhythms of development characteristic of the relatively autonomous instances. Such rhythms were particularly in evidence in Spain where, as we saw above, the resurgence of feudal relations had delayed the transition to capitalism. 'In Spain the bourgeoisie will never carry through its political and ideological revolution, which is not to imply that it did not carry through a revolution at the economic level (sheltering – for a variety of reasons – under another, non-bourgeois ideology)'.[32] The 'other' ideology in question draws its sustenance from the first stage of the transition; crucially, it accounts for the muted and belated impact of bourgeois rationalism and liberalism in Spain, which is not to say, to reiterate, that this country failed to register the impact of Enlightenment thinking: '[A] whole new literature is being promoted, a whole new expressive and mental universe, a new way (different when not antagonistic to the one that preceded it) of conceiving the world and human relations in general'.[33] Nowhere is the ensuing disorder more apparent than in the theatre.

The theatre of the sixteenth and seventeenth centuries, we saw above, was thematically contained within the political, which is to say, within the public sphere. In the eighteenth century, with the triumph of the bourgeoisie, this situation changes completely: politics is displaced in favour of the private sphere, the exploration of which pertains to a newly conceived *drama*. Broadly speaking, the distant, sacralised space of the Court gives way to the more proximate, bourgeois drawing room. Henceforth, the audience can *identify* with what it

---

31   Rodríguez 2008b, p. 110.
32   Ibid., p. 108.
33   Ibid., pp. 110–11.

sees before it. The rationale behind the move is identical to that which explains the liberalisation of the state: displaced is the notion of Truth, as an expression of the divine, in favour of a truth that is merely conventional, contractual, and human. The distance between the public and the stage corresponds to that between the public and the state. In the latter case, parliamentary procedures ensure that the bourgeois subject is able to identify with the state. Each person signs a social contract, which ensures that he is effectively *represented*. Such is the stuff out of which revolutions are made: 'What happens is that *with the triumph of bourgeois relations the public realm will be conceived as a "direct transcription" of the* private'.[34] To elaborate Rodríguez's argument, let us consider Moratín's *La comedia nueva* or *The New Drama* (1792).

In effect, the title says it all: Moratín's play not only provides a perfect example of the new bourgeois theatre but also comments upon its structure metacritically. The action centres upon the circumstances of a playwright who anxiously awaits the outcome of the first night of his play. As part of what is manifestly a collective, commercial enterprise, Don Eleuterio, the playwright in question, employs his family, notably his wife, Doña Angustias and sister-in-law, Doña Mariquita, for secretarial assistance. It is his misfortune to be an exponent of the traditional courtly theatre, who must yet survive in a new world order in which a theatre-going *public* that pays increasingly adjudicates and dictates the terms of success. Don Hermógenes, pretender to the hand of Doña Mariquita, performs the role of an aristocratic pedant, now reduced to penury. The critical role falls to Don Pedro, the rational proponent of the new, rule-based theatre, whose sad task it is simply to remind Deon Eleuterio of the realities of the new order. Those realities include Don Pedro's own marginalised role: in contrast to his predecessor, the traditional patron of aristocratic extraction, he is limited to *private* interventions in the public sector and to offering practical advice and assistance to Don Eleuterio when the latter's play inevitably flops.

The setting of the action throughout is a café, which, together with the bourgeois drawing room, the other preferred location of the new drama, bridges the private to the public sphere. Within its confines, the different characters, now instantly recognizable as 'characters', can meet, mingle, and converse socially. In the opening scene, the waiter, Pipí, questions a gentleman customer, Don Antonio, as to the exact nature of the theatrical 'laws' or 'rules' that, he has heard, govern the new drama. 'My dear fellow, it's difficult to explain', responds Don Antonio, 'Rules are things that foreigners make use of, particularly the

---

34   Ibid., p. 117.

French'.[35] A contrast is implied between the new, ruled-based drama and Don Eleuterio's play, which, it quickly transpires, constitutes a degenerate continuation of the earlier theatre – symptomatically, it is replete with references to 'vassals', 'emperors', 'traitors', 'court', and other ideologemes redolent of another age.

While emphatically an example of the new man of 'reason', Don Pedro is himself, to reiterate, something of a 'transitional figure'. Rich, generous, and, above all, 'honourable', after the manner of his predecessor, the aristocratic patron, he yet boasts a considerable 'talent', otherwise the distinguishing feature of the 'worthy gentleman' ('hombre de bien') of bourgeois derivation. His favoured terrain, it cannot be sufficiently emphasised, is that which separates the public from the private sphere.

> I am the first to appear in the spectacles, in the parades, in the public pageants; I combine such pleasures with study; the few friends I have are close friends, to whom I am indebted for the happiest moments of my life. If I am the odd man out at private functions, that is something I regret; but what is one to do? I do not wish to lie, am unable to dissemble, and believe that telling the truth, frankly, is the worthiest attribute a gentleman can have.[36]

The balance is clearly a delicate one, between retreating into the domain of privacy, the preferred choice of a future generation of Romantics, and what Don Pedro categorises as 'preaching', an activity reserved for members of the nobility, politicians, and other figures of authority. It is not that the newly configured gentleman wants for ambition – he certainly aims to control the public sphere, but only *obliquely*, from his location in the private. His intervention in the case of Don Eleuterio is paradigmatic in this regard.

Don Eleuterio's status is similarly of an intermediate kind. Undoubtedly, he shares something in common with Don Hermógenes: both are relics of an earlier mode, struggling to survive in a new world order. But there the similarity ends, for whereas Don Hermógenes is manifestly an aristocrat fallen upon hard times, Don Eleuterio is a petty-bourgeois artisan, whose misfortunate it is to practice in a theatrical profession that is rapidly undergoing capitalisation. Their fates vary accordingly, for whereas the absurd Don Hermógenes promptly disappears once the promised dowry fails to materialise, Don Eleu-

---

35   Moratín 1968, p. 67.
36   Ibid., p. 73.

terio is deemed worthy of rescue, which is where Don Pedro enters into the equation. 'I have a fair number of businesses near Madrid', he boasts, 'In fact, I have just offered a position to a young fellow of merit who understands how they are run'.[37] Not only will he provide Don Eleuterio with a 'useful' job of a suitably pedestrian kind, he will also ensure that Doña Agustina and Doña Mariquita return to the private sphere, the former to resume her domestic duties, the latter to await the arrival of an appropriate suitor. Don Pedro's primary responsibility, we are left to conclude, is that of stabilising of the bourgeois family structure.

So much, then, is clear: on the one hand, we have modern adaptations of an earlier theatre, on the other the new *drama*. And yet, as indicated above, things are not quite so straightforward as this may suggest. Rodríguez, whose focus happens to be upon the French tradition, distinguishes between two kinds of eighteenth-century drama, on the one hand, the classically bourgeois, 'family' drama of Diderot (represented in Spain by Moratín), and, on the other, the 'drama of passion' of Voltaire. Originating in the animist ideology of the early bourgeoisie, this second tradition would become, by the eighteenth century, the distinctive ideology of a *petty* bourgeoisie.[38] Hence the need to distinguish it from its classic equivalent. Rodríguez contrasts the social philosophies that sustain each kind of drama: for the classic bourgeoisie, there is nothing *prior to* the signing of the social contract by 'free subjects'; for the petty bourgeoisie, entry into society presupposes the *alienation* of a prior human essence; but always on the understanding that both traditions represent variations on a common bourgeois thematic: 'Passion', it follows, within the context of this second tradition, is to be conceived not as an emotion that is *opposed* to reason, but, on the contrary, as the full revelation of the truth of rationalist order.[39] Such is the guise in which it will impact upon the Romantic theatre. Let us briefly consider an example drawn from Spanish culture: *Don Álvaro o la fuerza del sino* or *Don Álvaro or the Force of Destiny* (1835) by Angel de Saavedra, Duque de Rivas.

Again, as in the case of *The New Drama*, the title says it all. Don Álvaro is determined *substantially*, which is to say, he is determined at the outset by his 'blood' and 'lineage'. To be sure, as the product of an 'illegitimate' marriage between a Spanish aristocrat and an Inca princess, he is himself ignorant as to his true essence, as indeed is everyone else: 'We only know that he arrived from the Indies two months ago, and that he brings with him two black men and a

---

37   Ibid., p. 131.
38   Rodríguez 2008b, p. 136.
39   Ibid., p. 127.

good deal of money ... but who is he?'.[40] All that is known for certain is that, sooner or later, in accordance with substantialist logic, 'blood' will out – hence the repeated references to the stars and to fate. From the outset, then, we are located in an emphatically feudal setting, dominated by concerns of 'honour', on the basis of which the Marquis of Calatrava is led to resist the pretensions of Don Álvaro, of such dubious extraction, to his daughter's hand. Such is the density of the feudal ideologemes that, initially, one might be tempted to think little has changed since the sixteenth and seventeenth centuries: '*hidalguía*', 'treachery', 'destiny', celestial influence, duels, honour killings, warfare, and so on, mediated through the animist claim that 'each man is the son of his deeds'.[41]

In this case, however, first appearances prove deceptive: this is a feudal world with a difference, notably for the sense of decay that attaches to the aristocratic figures and that leads them to become an object of mockery for the tavern revellers: 'These lords of Seville are vanity and poverty, all of a piece'.[42] The exactness of the portrayal is quickly confirmed: by the mid-eighteenth century, in which the play is set, the dynamics of a seigneurial lineage are recognisably those of the Oedipal, petty-bourgeois family. Passion is the dominating force that motivates the obsessively attentive patriarch, the controlling brothers, the emotional daughter, and the rebellious suitor. Against a subliminal backdrop of storms, thunder, and lightning, all are brought finally to their collective ruin, destroyed from within by the same unconscious drives that, in the form of a poetic violence, tear asunder the prosaic forms of Saavedra's text.

In such works the path of the ideological unconscious manifestly intersects with that of its libidinal counterpart, which explains why, in his parallel treatment of French family drama, Rodríguez feels called upon to explore further the relationship between the two forms. He is encouraged by the fact that Freud himself spoke in terms of the unconscious as a *scene*, thereby inviting comparison with the theatrical version of the same.[43] More encouragingly still, the comparison immediately yields parallels: just as the visible behaviour within the family consists of symptoms that are the psychic effects of hidden mechanisms, so the social formation consists of hidden causal processes that are visible only in their effects. In the Spaniard's own words: '... curiously, [Freud] will speak of the *unconscious* as a stage or objective space ruled by a set of invisible laws that the "actors" do not control but which they "support"'.[44]

---

40   Saavedra 1991, p. 55.
41   Ibid., p. 56.
42   Ibid., p. 54.
43   Rodríguez 2008b, p. 147.
44   Ibid.

Differences there were: the bourgeois drama explores the interaction between the public and private spheres, within a shared space; whereas psychoanalysis gains access internally to the boudoir, hence to the hidden reaches of the private. By the same token, the theatre boasts of its free, autonomous subjects, in the form of its 'characters' and 'protagonists'; whereas psychoanalysis dramatises the interactions between 'consciousness', 'reason', 'personality', and so on. But more striking are the similarities: 'The subject, it transpires, is an illusion, is never real; the character does not exist, nor does the protagonist, or autonomous consciousness, or psychology. All such unitary categories shatter into a thousand pieces before our very eyes, to be exposed for what they are, namely different effects of certain basic determinations that govern both scenarios'.[45] What Freud failed to detect, nay, was unable to detect, was that the determinations that dictate the constitution of the bourgeois family can be shown to resolve themselves ultimately into an 'ideology' that lends itself to objective analysis within the framework of the social formation.

5   From the Social to the Discursive Formation

Laclau and Mouffe combined in *Hegemony and Socialist Strategy* to continue a research programme that will see the social formation, understood as a structure in dominance, further stripped of its material complexity, as a prelude to its full integration into the subject/object paradigm. The first stage consisted of the dismantling of the classical Marxist legacy, to be achieved through conflation with the Marxism of the Second International. The latter, to remind ourselves, theorised the social formation in terms of the base/superstructure model, on the understanding that the superstructure functioned as a simple reflection of the economic base. Attributed to Marx, thereby, is the view of the economy as an autonomous, self-regulated universe that functioned strictly in accordance with its own endogenous laws; also, by extension, the view of the productive forces as neutral in their operations and unilinear in their development.[46]

We do not propose to enter into detail by way of refuting what constitutes, in the words of Ellen Meiksins Wood, a 'breath-taking misreading of Marx'.[47]

---

45   Ibid, p. 149.
46   Laclau and Mouffe 2014, pp. 67–71.
47   Wood 1986, p. 59.

Suffice it to say what even the most perfunctory reading of *Capital* will reveal, namely that Marx argued consistently and at length that the 'economic sphere' is permeated by relations of class exploitation, hence also by an ideology of resistance and struggle secreted at the level of the relations of production and formalised at the superstructural level.[48] One can only surmise, given the distortions to which they subjected Marx's texts, that the two post-Marxists, as was their habit, were less interested in exegetical accuracy than in clearing a theoretical space in which to detach ideology from its anchoring in the social formation and, by extension, in which to formulate their own political programme, uninhibited by the need to ground the latter in its objectively real conditions of existence.

Laclau and Mouffe looked to Gramsci to provide the necessary left-cover for the transferral of focus from base to superstructure, hence from the productive processes to those relating to cultural hegemony; also, for the necessary material ballast with which to stabilise what always threatened to be an unstable, top-heavy structure. While the materiality in question was strictly that of the mechanistic, hence sociological variety – typically, the Ideological State Apparatuses – it proved, from the perspective of Laclau and Mouffe, more than sufficient to allow them legitimately to dispense with the base/superstructure dichotomy. 'In fact, through the concepts of historic bloc and of ideology as organic cement, a new social category takes us beyond the old base/superstructure distinction'.[49] The aim was to detach the field of subjectivity from the economic base and hence undercut the case for a class-based politics, as traditionally understood: 'For Gramsci, political subjects are not – strictly speaking – classes, but complex "collective wills"; similarly, the ideological elements articulated by a hegemonic class do not have a necessary class-belonging'.[50]

Robert Resch has accused Laclau in his early work of failing to grasp the determinant role of the economic function, as theorised by Althusser and Poulantzas, hence of 'grossly misrepresenting the subtle indirect determination of the matrix effect'. Structural Marxism is culpable of reductionism, he further argues, only if one is seeking to defend a pluralist indeterminacy, of the kind embraced by Laclau.[51] The drift of such a critique is difficult to fault: throughout Laclau's work, and increasingly after joining forces with Mouffe, key Althusserian concepts are being eliminated as being inconvenient

---

48   For a full critique, I refer the reader to Wood 1986 and Geras 1990.
49   Ibid., p. 57.
50   Ibid.
51   Resch 1992, p. 386n2.

for a political voluntarism: 'In order to place ourselves firmly within the field of articulation, we must begin by renouncing the conception of "society" as [the] founding totality of its partial processes'.[52] That said, some qualifications are called for. On closer inspection, it transpires that Laclau and Mouffe are dispensing with the matrix effect only to recuperate it within a post-Marxist framework at the level of discursivity. They are unquestionably assisted in this manoeuvre by two points of vulnerability in the Althusserian problematic.

The first point was the weak ontological status of the Althusserian social structures that, to recall, were present only in their effects. Such a conflation of the real with the actual (in Bhaskarian terms) undoubtedly facilitated the containment of the social formation within the horizon of discursivity, thence its transformation into discursive formation. Once set in motion, there was no limit to the process of de-ontologisation.

> But this discursive formation can also be seen from the perspective of *regularity* in dispersion, and be thought, in that sense, as an ensemble of differential positions. This ensemble is not the expression of any under-lying principle external to itself – it cannot, for instance, be apprehended either by a hermeneutic reading or by a structuralist combinatory – but it constitutes a configuration, which in certain contexts of exteriority can be *signified* as a totality.[53]

What, may be asked, has happened to the referent? This brings us to a second point of Althusser's vulnerability, namely the distinction between the 'object of thought' and the 'real object'. Although understood by Althusser (as by Marx) to be a methodological strategy, this distinction, we have seen, lent itself to an epistemological reading, which left the object of thought dangerously detached from its real-concrete equivalent. Post-Marxists were quick to seize upon the opportunity thereby offered to further confine the object of thought to the realm of discourse and, in effect, to conflate non-discursive with discursive practices. Every object, Laclau and Mouffe proceed to argue, is constituted as an object of discourse, insofar as no object is imaginable beyond its discursive formulation; further to which, 'any distinction between what are usually called the linguistic and behavioural aspects of a social practice is either an incorrect distinction or ought to find its place as a differentiation within the social pro-duction of meaning'.[54] By this stage, the horizons of the social formation have

---

52   Laclau and Mouffe 2014, p. 82.
53   Ibid., p. 92, original italics.
54   Ibid., p. 93.

shrunk alarmingly: 'This was the moment when language invaded the universal problematic, the moment when, in the absence of a centre or origin, everything became discourse'.[55]

The notion of a structure without a centre or origin, clearly a derivative of Althusser's famous, if not infamous, anti-humanism, suggests that the post-Marxists benefited not only from the philosopher's vulnerabilities but also from his strengths. These included his insistence that, rather than the point of departure for an investigation, real men were the point of arrival, after the long detour through the social formation. Set against the notion of 'Man' was that of the subject as an historical construct, otherwise as the fragmented effect of social structures. All of which was grist to the post-Marxian mill: 'Far from considering that "Man" has the status of an essence – presumably a gift from heaven – such an analysis can show us the historical conditions of its emergence'.[56] But within limits, which the post-Marxists will proceed to spell out. Principally, the Althusserian notion of a social formation is dismissed as 'meaningless';[57] following which 'classes' and the 'class struggle' are marginalised; the petty-bourgeois concept of the 'people' is substituted for Marxist 'masses'; and the subject is restored to its former primacy. In sum, what remains of Marxism is re-inscribed within the subject/object paradigm.

How was it possible to sustain such a solipsistic framework? The answer is simple: it was not, and for one obvious reason: to dispense with the real by reducing everything to discourse makes it impossible to think of language as being *about* some thing or something, which is an absurdity. Hence, the rather sly reference to a reality beyond language, as when, for example, Laclau and Mouffe concede that 'the practice of articulation, as fixation/dislocation of a system of differences, cannot consist of purely linguistic phenomena; but must instead pierce the entire material density of the multifarious institutions, rituals and practices through which a discursive formation is structured'.[58] But if everything consists of discourse, how is it possible for linguistic practice to pierce anything?[59] And that is only the beginning: by what right do the post-Marxists refer throughout *Hegemony and Social Strategy* to the spread of capitalist relations of production, the logic of 'production for profit', the 'commodification' of social life, economic crises, unemployment, the disintegration of the family cell, bureaucratisation, the homogenisation of social life, and so

---

55   Ibid., p. 98.
56   Laclau and Mouffe 2014, p. 103.
57   Ibid., p. 130.
58   Ibid., p. 95.
59   For a discussion of this point and related issues, see Boucher 2008, pp. 93–7.

on? Are these not concepts that the post-Marxists have pillaged from another theory and from one that they have summarily dismissed?

To conclude: while every research programme is afflicted, marginally, by its own internal difficulties, which await resolution, indications are that it is the hard core of post-Marxian theory that is vulnerable to critique.

6   García Lorca: the Objectivity of the Text

On the face of it, few authors would seem less inviting to the Althusserian theoretician of ideology than García Lorca insofar as few authors constitute an experiential presence quite equal to that of the Granadine poet and dramatist, to judge at least from the veritable flood of critical works that have long threatened to drown his works: I knew Lorca, his family, his friends, have the anecdotes of colleagues, had access to the manuscripts, to inside information, etc. 'Almost like a wound that will never be healed'.[60] What greater challenge could there be to a critic who is determined to displace the focus of attention from the subject/object opposition to that of the impersonal social formation, understood as a structure in dominance? And yet that is precisely the challenge that Rodríguez set out to meet head-on in his *Lorca y el sentido* (*Lorca and Meaning*) (1994).

The first, key step was to envisage Lorca's texts less as a source of meaning and more as a *product* of a series of invisible relations that determine it. Such relations, we should know (and as Rodríguez hastens to remind us), are invisible in the sense, as explained by Althusser, that they are present only in their effects. 'Only one thing matters, then: not the realisation of the *subject/object* opposition (which always implies a phenomenological subjective identity) but the objectivity of the text on the margin of such a relation'.[61] The second step, possibly even more important than the first, was to draw a distinction between the object of thought and the real object: only the bourgeois critic, the Althusserian argument runs, fantasises *qua* subject about uniting with his/her object, about encountering the *real* García Lorca: 'There was no reason why the conceptualisation of Lorca had to be an echo of Lorca'.[62] To which end it was necessary to establish a critical distance between the Althusserian project and

---

60   Rodríguez 1994a, p. 11. An exception to critical practice is Juan Caamaño, whose analysis, like our own, follows Rodríguez in transferring the focus of attention from Lorca, the man, to the ideological unconscious that determines his texts (Caamaño 2008, pp. 121–56).

61   Ibid., pp. 9–10.

62   Ibid., p. 11.

the mass of bibliographical data that sustained the traditional critical approach to this particular author.

Once located on his own theoretical terrain, what precisely were the goals that Rodríguez set himself? In essence: to establish a contrast between such major works of Lorca as *Bodas de sangre* (*Blood Wedding*) (1932), *Yerma* (1934) and *La casa de Bernarda Alba* (*The House of Bernarda Alba*) (1936) and the 'unrepresentable' works *El público* (*The Public*) (1929–30) and *Comedia sin título* (*Play without a Title*) (1936); not, clearly, in terms of a developmental process but of two parallel trends. The first trend, according to Rodríguez, presupposes an opposition between 'lo dicho' (what is said) and 'lo no dicho' (what is not said), in other words, between a norm and what is repressed as a consequence of its imposition, modelled along the lines of the psychoanalytic split, internal to a single psyche, between consciousness and the unconscious. Rodríguez is prepared to concede the possible relevance of such distinctions in the case of Lorca, also the 'truth' of their associated concepts of *repression, frustration, alienation, marginality, homosexual fear,* etc., together with the importance for Lorca of the non-alienated medium of music. That said, he is, unsurprisingly, more drawn to the second trend, in evidence in the 'unrepresentable' texts, that opposes 'el dicible' (the sayable) to 'el no dicible' (the non-sayable), understood as two '*lateral*' worlds.

The notion of laterality is not easy to grasp. It combines with that of *historicity*, to be contrasted with the universality of a 'human nature', as theorised by bourgeois critics. Human nature, according to the Althusserian, was a concept through which bourgeois critics sought to deny, by rendering them *invisible*, the existence of class divisions and exploitation: '... if there is something that really characterises our world, it is its invisibility. Or rather invisibility as a spectacle. And on confusing, like any good positivist, reality with the relation between the eye and the thing, our world confuses what cannot be seen with what does not exist'.[63] Enlisted to sustain this view, it goes without saying, is the Althusserian rejection of the subject as an ontic category: individualities doubtless exist, but in the form of *slaves, serfs, subjects* and (postmodern) *fragments.* The consequences are far reaching: '... *if language "speaks us", it is impossible to choose between one language and another*; even more impossible if the *other language* has never existed. By which I mean that nobody can be repressed with respect to something that they have never had; or can be deprived of it. Neither homosexuals nor proletarians nor women (exploitation in general and in schools: marginalisation, etc.) have ever had their own language'.[64]

---

63   Ibid., p. 20.
64   Ibid., p. 80.

Rodríguez proceeds to elaborate his argument with respect to the internal logic of *The Public* and *Play without a Title*. What cannot be said, he argues, are the dramatic relations of production, although perforce the action turns on their objective forms: the characters, the prompter, the director, the public, the author, the spectator, the stagehand. The structure that determines these forms can never be described positively by its presence, *behind the scene*, but only negatively by its traces and effects. True, in *The Public*, something survives of the notion of otherness, *behind the masks*: 'But do you realise', protests student 4 to student 5, 'that the Juliet who was in the sepulchre was a youth in disguise, a trick of the scene Director, and that the real Juliet was muzzled under the seats?'[65] And even in *Play without a Title*, the Author remains convinced as to the 'reality' of the production: 'We are not in the theatre. Because they will come and knock down the doors. And all of us will be saved. Inside there exists a terrible air of lies, and the characters of plays only ever say what can be said in the presence of delicate young ladies, while hiding their true anguish'.[66] Except that reality is true/false in the same way as the ideology through which people 'live' their daily lives.

There is much about these 'unperformable plays', Rodríguez's argument runs, that appears to resemble the allegorical form of the feudal 'auto sacramental'. Effaced on both sides is the notion of *individuality*, understood as the constitutive essence of characters, as the perspectival centre from which the world is viewed. Except that, on closer inspection, any such similarity proves to be purely deceptive: the feudal figures that join in the dance of death are defined by their substantial identities: in Lorca's unperformable plays, by way of contrast, everything is fluid and in flux. As Man 1 says to the Director: 'Romeo can be a bird and Juliet can be a stone. Romeo can be a grain of salt and Juliet can be a map'.[67] As in *A Midsummer Night's Dream*, all forms are protean: 'Love is pure chance and Titania, queen of the sylphs, falls in love with an ass'.[68] The Magician encourages a resistant Director to indulge his creative fantasies: 'Construct a wire archway, with a curtain and a tree with fresh leaves, open and close the curtain in time and nobody will be surprised to find that the tree has turned into a serpent's egg'.[69]

In sum, we would add, the characters of Lorca's unperformable plays, like the figures in Cremonini's pictures, as theorised by Althusser, are haunted by

---

65   Lorca 2004, p. 107.
66   Lorca 2018, p. 79.
67   Lorca 2004, p. 72.
68   Ibid., p. 114.
69   Ibid.

an absence, 'that of the humanist function which is refused them',[70] to which extent the plays, like the pictures, serve to 'make *visible* (*donner à voir*), by establishing a distance from it, the reality of the existing ideology'.[71] Whether such were the intentions of the artist concerned is quite beside the point: 'At any rate, we know that "consciousness" is secondary, even when it *thinks*, in the principle of materialism, its derivative and conditioned response'.[72] Rodríguez would agree, except with a proviso: what Althusser characterises as a secondary consciousness is in fact a form of the ideological unconscious. Understood in the light of the latter, the subject assumes the status of a mask; more exactly, is the site where all masks are effaced, to be replaced by the 'final unveiling of the whole social structure':[73]

> AUTHOR   (*entering*) Here! Here! Tell the truth about the old sets. Stick
>   knives into the old thieves of oil and bread. Let the rain soak
>   the looms and erase the drop curtain.
> VOICE   Fire!
> VOICE   (*More distant*) Fire!
> AUTHOR   (*entering*) Fire![74]

Such is the revolutionary moment when the people invade the theatre, when the public occupy the pit, and when, correlatively, the distance between the citizens and the state is finally closed.

7   Podemos: Life in the Media

In 1976 Rodríguez managed to persuade Althusser to visit Granada. 'The Transformation of Philosophy' was delivered to an audience of over 5,000, including many inhabitants from the rural districts of La Vega who flooded into the city. And yet, as Rodríguez has described in a late essay, 'Pensar desde la explotación' (Thinking from the standpoint of exploitation), the Althusserian project was already in jeopardy in France, where a generation that had won the war against the Nazis and that believed it could carry through a revolution was

---

70   Althusser 1971, p. 239.
71   Ibid., pp. 241–2.
72   Ibid., p. 242.
73   Rodríguez 1994a, p. 95.
74   Lorca 2018, p. 95.

having to accept the reality of a Party afflicted by fatal weaknesses.[75] Even in Spain, the attempt by the Communist Party to enter into the democratic process, under the guise of Euro-communism, proved abortive, notwithstanding its strong presence in the unions: '*communist* was always the same damnable word, however much *Euro* was prefixed to it'.[76] The effects of external propaganda were real enough, but that was not the whole story: Party leaders and intellectuals also found themselves consistently outflanked, and in so many ways, by the changes and innovations of contemporary capitalism. And truth to say, according to Rodríguez, the Marxist presence within the universities was never what was claimed, either among lecturers or students: '… in general the debate centred more on the war against Franco or on the old historiography, rather than on Marx or Lenin, as applied to the concrete reality of the moment'.[77] The symptoms of apostasy were everywhere apparent and quite soon former supporters of the Left were figuring among the cheer-leaders of neo-liberalism.

The process of erosion continued over the ensuing decades to the extent that, by the time of the major crisis of 2008, Marxism and its associated vocabulary had fallen under erasure, as an obvious consequence of which capitalism itself had ceased to be a target of criticism. Of course, capitalism had only ever been visible in its effects; nor was there anything new about the attempt to legitimise it ideologically, through an appeal to 'freedom' and 'human rights'. But digitalisation had undoubtedly lent it a novel, vaguely illusory element, to devastating effect: the self-censorship that was formerly unconscious was now taking place consciously. It was best not to talk about capitalism, ran the constant refrain, notwithstanding the ravages it was currently wreaking, for the simple reason that capitalism now struck people as very distant from their concerns. As far as corrupt bankers, a shameless elite, and the despotic Merkel were concerned – yes, criticism was fine, 'but to accept that capitalism is in itself a corrosion of life … the thought cannot be entertained, since it would presuppose thinking or accepting that our own lives are also corrupt and corroded'.[78]

It was perhaps inevitable, given the circumstances, that, in the wake of the 2008 crisis, the political party that was to become the voice of a new generation in Spain, namely Podemos, should look for theoretical legitimation not to Marxism but to the post-Marxian tradition of Laclau and Mouffe. And that was only the beginning: with the eclipse of Marxism, it was now possible to

---

75   Rodríguez 2013, pp. 15–68.
76   Ibid., p. 43.
77   Ibid., p. 45.
78   Ibid., p. 9.

sever completely the ties that had tenuously bound Laclau and Mouffe to the
Marxist legacy. For Mouffe herself it was a logical development: '[W]e were
already thinking that theorisation in terms of class, after the Marxist fashion,
was inadequate', she confesses in an interview with Íñigo Errejón, one of the
major spokespersons for Podemos, 'because social classes are social subjects
that are constructed'.[79] By the same token, Gramsci's emphasis upon class as the
nucleus of hegemony could now be totally rejected: 'That was also something
that we abandoned'.[80] It only sufficed, allegedly, to tease out the further implications of the Italian's argument: what is considered a 'natural order' is, in effect,
only ever the result of hegemonic practices that, carefully considered, only exist
in a discursive form, a form totally without residue: 'It is never a manifestation
of a deeper objectivity, external to the practices that cause it. For this reason,
society should never be perceived as the unfolding of an outside logic, whatever
its source: the forces of production for Marx, the development of the Absolute
Spirit for Hegel or the laws of history for the various positivist currents'.[81] And
yet, strange to say, Mouffe continues to find incomprehensible the animosity
exhibited by Marxists towards the post-Marxist programme.

For his part, Errejón accepts the bulk of the post-Marxian baggage without
question. His central theoretical claim is that identities never exist *beforehand*,
in an essentialist form; rather, they are always 'produced through a discursive construction'.[82] From the outset, therefore, attention focuses upon words,
upon their meanings, and, tactically, upon the need to generate a popular
identity that can be politicised along electoral lines, through the deployment
of key oppositions, notably 'citizenship' versus 'cast', and 'democracy' versus
'oligarchy'. Having said which, more important than the oppositions to be cul-
tivated are those to be avoided, notably 'Left' and 'Right'. Quite simply, such
entities, however relevant elsewhere, do not correspond to the situation to be
found in Spain. Even 'populist', it transpires, needs to be treated circumspectly
insofar as 'we cannot use a term that the media have made devilish'. 'Nobody'
Errejón elaborates, 'with any pretension at all to one day winning [an election],
can accept a definition that for the collective imaginary immediately connotes
demagogy'.[83]

Now it is important to recognise that, within their limits, the spokespersons
for *Podemos* have identified serious problems for the Left. Undoubtedly, the

79   Errejón and Mouffe 2015, p. 17.
80   Ibid., p. 33.
81   Ibid., pp. 44–5.
82   Ibid., p. 100.
83   Ibid., p. 114.

Marxist language inherited from the past is that of the living dead and needs urgently to be revitalised through translation into a modern idiom. Moreover, while the Left was long ago alerted to the importance of modern media – one thinks automatically of Raymond Williams's *Communications* (1961) – *Podemos* has been right to insist on the qualitative changes that have accompanied the digital revolution. The key question, from an Althusserian perspective, is the extent to which it is possible to carry out the task of translation with respect to Marxism without trivialising the tradition's conceptual core. Doubtless the displacement of focus, engineered by Podemos, onto the 'Berlusconisation' of politics, eviction, precarity, etc. was effective enough,[84] but only in the short term and at a cosmetic level. Moreover, lost sight of is the fact that, in exchange for these limited gains, the battle over discourse has already been lost, through the exclusion of 'exploitation', 'surplus value', the 'rate of profit', 'class conflict', and so on.

In any event, far more important than such relatively minor semantic squabbles is the theory that sustains them. Laclau and Mouffe, we saw above, progressively negotiated an inversion of the base/superstructure model of the Second International to the point at which the superstructure, in the form of the discursive formation, is left suspended in mid-air. Podemos consciously models itself on this top-down inversion, in opposition to a social Left that insists on construction from the base upwards. After having been dematerialised, this superstructure is then rematerialised in the form of the state apparatuses, whereby to shield it against the charge of idealism. In the words of Pablo Iglesias, the leader of Podemos: 'Precisely because we come from where we come, we clearly understand that it is the institutions that transform society'.[85] Iglesias is presumably referring to 'our' location in the University. Allegedly opposed to this view was a version of Marxism associated with the Catalán Marxist, Manuel Sacristán, based on the lie ('mentira') that change begins at the microsocial level.[86] 'Lie'? The word merits closer scrutiny, not for its moral implications – cheap rhetoric of this kind is the political norm – but for what it tells us about Iglesias's ontological convictions. After all, he is not accusing Sacristán of being ideological but of *lying*, which involves both a knowledge of being incorrect and a desire to deceive others; more importantly, in the present context, it assumes the existence of an objective world. Now it is this assumption that lands Iglesias in the familiar post-Marxist bind: if everything

---

84   Iglesias 2015a, p. 35.
85   Iglesias 2015b, p. 106.
86   Ibid., p. 106.

is a product of discourse, if, in Iglesias's words, 'reality is created by the means of communication',[87] how exactly is one able to assess statements in terms of their truth value?

These are not minor considerations, as we have been at pains to insist throughout. How is it possible to square the view that objects have an essential relation to thought with the materialist assertion, seemingly indispensable to any form of Marxism, of the primacy of the real? Quite simply, it isn't. Sacrifices have to be made, and it comes as no surprise to find that it is Marxism that has to make them. While there is no gainsaying its excellence as a diagnostic tool, Marxism as a basis for a science of politics is, allegedly, a non-starter. 'Politics is not completely autonomous of social relations or of the economy; but to attempt to derive a science of politics or a theory of politics from social structures or from the development of historical forces tied to the productive processes is simply an idiocy'.[88] To lies are now added idiocies. These would be grave charges indeed if they were true, but of course they are not. Rather they betray an understanding of Marxism that, as in the case of Laclau and Mouffe, is arrested at the stage of the Second International, that is disengaged from the most recent developments in the philosophy of science, not to mention the Marxist legacy of political thinking, so glibly dismissed by Podemos.[89]

What the leaders of Podemos view as a democratic advance actually constitutes a regressive aberration, theoretically speaking, characterised, on the evidence of Iglesias's *Politics in a Time of Crisis*, by a strange combination of causalities, namely transitive causality with respect to the past and, specifically, to the history of Spain; an expressive, totalising causality with respect to the global present; and the autonomous practice of free-floating subjects with respect to the future. Much of the confusion appears to derive from the Gramscian legacy of voluntarism, although exacerbated in the circumstances of the present conjuncture. To the extent that one can make sense of it all, it would appear that, from the standpoint of a practical politics, Podemos overestimates the changes to be achieved through discursive means and, by extension, underestimates the political power of the capitalist state. The same theoretical weakness attaches to their cultural analyses, which have largely focused on a narrow selection of dominantly erotogenic films and the dynamics of

---

87   Ibid.

88   Ibid., p. 156.

89   In the words of Pablo Iglesias: 'I believe that a person over the age of 75 ought to be looking after his grand-children and enjoying retirement' (Iglesias 2013, p. 84). For an overview of Marxist political theory and its history, see Townshend 1996.

their reception, detached from any attempt at causal explanation.[90] In sum, while refreshingly responsive to changing cultural patterns under global capitalism and courageous in its condemnation of political corruption, Podemos has proved unable to transcend the limits of a libertarian voluntarism. Its claims to have passed through and beyond the problems inherited from classical Marxism are delusional and potentially damaging, not least of all to itself.

Faced by such developments in what passes for social theory, Rodríguez saw no reason to abandon, and every reason to reiterate, his conviction in the explanatory priority of social structures over human practice in history. Symptomatically, in a late essay, he took exception to the focus upon the autonomised level of capital, as a 'market', through which post-Marxists sought to re-affirm their leftist credentials and their continuing allegiance to the Marxist heritage. 'Exchange value' and 'use value', he reminded those scholars concerned, notably Slavoj Žižek, derived conceptually from the work of the classical economists and were not authentically Marxist. As an Althusserian, he preferred to locate the circulation of speculative capital not within a restricted domain, as a form of *bad* capitalism, the implication being that a *good* capitalism could well do without it, but within a broader structural framework, of exploitation *en bloc*.[91]

8   Borges Revisited

By way of conclusion, let us return to Borges's 'Death and the Compass' to ponder the implications of some of its seemingly unimportant details.

To recall, from the perspective of Treviranus, the policeman, there is little that needs to be explained: a robbery has been committed; somebody has been killed. No more, no less. And so it transpires: the first death, was indeed accidental: a theft of diamonds that went wrong. For the literalist, who is also an empiricist, the case is closed. Lönnrot, on the other hand, believes that there is more to the death than – a significant phrase – *meets the eye*, sufficiently so to arouse his interest. 'You will reply', he remarks to Treviranus, 'that reality has not the slightest obligation to be interesting. I will reply in turn that reality may get along without that obligation, but hypotheses may not'.[92] Reality, for the private detective, is one thing: the model constructed by the investigator is something entirely different. The detective's preference lies with the latter, and

---

90   See Iglesias 2014.
91   Rodríguez 2013, p. 60.
92   Borges 1999, 148.

rightly so. Except that unbeknown even to him, reality had already ceded to fiction at the outset, in a hotel where the spheres of the personal and impersonal intersect, on a foreshore, where land meets sea, in a northern location, where life drains away: fittingly, the first victim, Dr Marcelo Yarmolinsky was 'a man of gray beard and gray eyes';[93] to enter into fiction is to be de-materialised.

Red Scharlach, the writer *par excellence*, incorporates elements taken from both the empirical realist and metaphysical idealist. Fiction, he concedes, must take a real event as its point of departure; but nothing more: the skill of the author lies in using this contingency as a basis on which to construct a fictional edifice. Indicative of his superiority as a writer is Red Scharlach's capacity to incorporate the detective into his own narrative. In a manner of speaking, Red Scharlach is Lönnrot's creator; and like any storyteller, he is quite entitled to kill off his protagonist whenever he chooses.

Seemingly, there is no limit to the gambler's creative skills: not only does he cast his agonist as a fictional character but also turns him into a reader. It is a role that Lönnrot, for his part, enthusiastically embraces; and justifiably so – by any estimation, he is no mean literary critic. The clues left after each murder, the detective immediately recognises, constitute a text to be deciphered. His only error, which will cost him his life, is his failure to realise that, with each death, he is being drawn deeper and deeper, into a fantasy world, whose backdrop is 'the emptiest and most godforsaken of the echoing suburbs on the western outskirts of the capital'. Imperceptibly, material reality is relinquished – 'the city crumbled away; the sky expanded, and now houses held less and less importance'[94] – or, more exactly, assumes a faded, fictional status: 'They came to their miserable destination; a final alleyway lined with pink-colored walls that somehow seemed to reflect the rambunctious setting of the sun'.[95]

And thus does the idealist's scenario unfold: Liverpool House, site of the third murder, is a tavern owned by Black Finnegan, a former Irish criminal, otherwise the reincarnation of Borges's favourite philosopher, Bishop Berkeley; by the time of the fourth crime, Lönnrot is attached to empirical reality by the merest of threads. A train journey will lead him into the heartland of the idealism. 'Lönrrot considered the remote possibility that Scharlach was to be the fourth victim, but then rejected it ... He had virtually solved the problem; the mere circumstances, the reality (names, arrests, faces, the paperwork of trial and imprisonment), held very little interest for him now'.[96] All that is required

---

93   Ibid., p. 147.
94   Borges 1999, p. 149.
95   Ibid., pp. 149–50.
96   Ibid., pp. 152–3.

is to cross the final frontier: 'A rusty fence defined the irregular perimeter of the villa's grounds';[97] and to climb the dusty stairs, through circular chambers – suggestive of repetition – to the belvedere, where the narrative will end. Red Scharlach enlightens him as to the labour required to give birth to a transcendental fiction: 'Nine days and nine nights I lay between life and death ... I came to abominate my own body'.[98] And all that remains is for Lönnrot to assume his fictional identity completely, in death: 'He felt a chill, and an impersonal, almost anonymous sadness'.[99]

The two narrators, then, will battle it out. But not quite to the end, to judge at least by the 'circular chambers' and Red Scharlach's reference to a 'next time' and if we are to be guided by another of Borges's stories, 'The Circular Ruins'. In the latter, a 'taciturn' man from the South takes up his abode within a temple ring – again the circularity – devoured by an ancient holocaust. He too will 'dream a man', in other words, construct a fiction, unsuccessfully at first, because insufficiently detached from material reality; successfully when he surrenders entirely to his dream-world. The end of his meditations comes suddenly when his abode is threatened by fire.

> For a moment he thought of taking refuge in the water, but then realised that death would be a crown upon his age and absolve him from his labors. He walked into the tatters of flame, but they did not bite his flesh – they caressed him, bathed him without heat and without combustion. With relief, with humiliation, with terror, he realised that he, too, was but appearance, that another man was dreaming him.[100]

Trapped within their own creations, Borges's idealists are caught in an endless, upward spiral. At each level, the subject parades a god-like creativity only to discover his or her – remember Emma Zunz – own fictional status as an object of another's imaginings. Seemingly, there is no exit. Or is there? Borges explores the question in 'Pierre Menard, Author of the *Quixote*'.[101]

If Pierre Menard is successfully to re-inscribe the *Quixote*, he will need to surpass Lönnrot as a *reader* and Red Scharlach as a *writer*. An ambitious project, to be sure, but perfectly feasible in principle, at least from the standpoint of the phenomenologist, for whom a work cannot be said to exist without a

---

97   Ibid., p. 153.
98   Ibid., p. 154.
99   Ibid., p. 156.
100   Borges 1999, p. 100.
101   Ibid., pp. 88–95.

reader to re-inscribe it. Except that, as Rodríguez is the first to point out, with 'Pierre Menard' in mind,[102] the re-inscription of a text cannot finally be compared, phenomenologically speaking, to its production; the two activities are quite different; the reader operates from an elevated standpoint; the writer, by way of contrast, is directly determined by contemporary forces (social, historical, and material).

Matters come to a head in Borges's story in the form of two identical texts, one from Cervantes's *Quixote*, the other from Menard's re-creation, both of which, as Borges presentation makes perfectly clear, are to be interpreted quite differently, within their respective cultural contexts. Rodríguez explains: 'Borges cannot understand this radical materiality of the literary work other than by conceiving it from the point of view not of objective reality, but of the negation of any meaning prior to the intellectual work – the labor of the writer – and of the writing itself (of literature, in sum) in any society'.[103] In other words, like any good phenomenologist, Borges is constrained to think in terms of a disembodied content that *precedes* the onerous task of expression. Which raises a seemingly insurmountable problem, '[b]ecause this ideological horizon is not an outside vantage point from which the text can be seen (from which it can be read)'. To accept the objective reality of literature, and therefore the intrinsic materiality of the text, a change of theoretical terrain is called for: 'What we are talking about is something much more fundamental, namely the internal logic of each text. About what produces it and from where it is produced, and, in the last instance, about the radical historicity of literature'.[104] This is the historicity that a certain Marxist tradition, not to mention a bourgeois tradition of academic literary criticism, *unconsciously* does not wish to recognise.

---

102   Rodríguez 2008b, pp. 344–7.
103   Ibid., p. 345.
104   Ibid.

Conclusion

We began our discussion of Rodríguez with a paradox: a scholar who mounts a sustained critique of his contemporaries has failed, reciprocally, to attract from them the degree of attention that one might have expected, given the quality of his work. The essence of the critique may be briefly stated: any Marxism that takes on board unthinkingly the subject/object dichotomy or variations thereupon is bound to be drawn inexorably into the orbit of bourgeois ideology, of which this dichotomy is the linchpin; a Marxism worthy of its name, it further follows, must be able to 'change the terrain', so as to locate itself within the framework of its own problematic, based upon the notion of the mode of production. The price to be paid, in the absence of this relocation, is apparent from Roy Bhaskar's critical realism, which, notwithstanding important gains, takes the subject/object opposition as the basis on which to evaluate Marxism alongside select bourgeois models. The effect, more broadly, is to promote the negative view of ideology as a form of false consciousness, as opposed to an opaque unconsciousness, the further consequence of which is to slight the extent to which ideology penetrates knowledge production.

Along similar lines, Noam Chomsky conflates a transcendental subject, of confessedly Kantian extraction, with the linguistic system, from which basis he argues the existence in the mind of intrinsic structures, of the kind deemed necessary to process the amorphous, meaningless, elusive images furnished by sensation. Such innatism, following Chomsky's schema, contrasts with the empiricist focus upon the sensation, articulated by Locke along the lines of a 'double experience', which concedes to the mind a degree of interiority, and by Hume in terms of a single experience, generative of ideas that are either true or merely imaginative. Rodríguez's tactic, by way of response, is to reconfigure the rationalist/empiricist dichotomy in radically social, historical terms: the Kantian subject, his argument runs, is but a variation on the beautiful soul, of animist extraction, adapted to meet the requirements of a distinctively *petty* bourgeoisie; empiricism, by way of contrast, is secreted by capitalist relations in the classic phase of bourgeois development, from the late seventeenth century onwards. In other words, the Althusserian reconfigures historically, at the level of the social formation, the structures that Chomsky attributes to an individual 'psychology'.

Fred Jameson and Terry Eagleton raise a different set of issues, compared to the transformational grammarian, and constitute a greater challenge to Rodríguez in that both fall within the ambit of Marxism. Immediately arresting is the convergence between Jameson's 'political unconscious' and the Althusserian's 'ideological unconscious'. Asked, after a lecture delivered in Stony Brook, New York, in 1995, about the connection between the two, the Spaniard was brutally to the point: politics, as far as he was concerned, related to issues of decision-making, hence to the realm of consciousness. The obvious implication was that the term 'political unconscious' was something of a misnomer. Hegel, he briefly elaborated, was the key: Jameson continues to operate in terms of the subject, albeit one identified with the process of alienation without a subject. Elsewhere, in print, he has been more forthcoming. Jameson's concept of post-modernity, he argues, presupposes the operation of an 'expressive causality'. Applied to postmodernism, this Hegelian principle gives rise to a performative contradiction: the theoretician for whom the Spirit of the Age consumes everything, presumably including himself, yet manages to escape its influence. By the same token, and much more insidiously, social contradictions in general are effectively annulled and obliterated. Jameson stands accused on all accounts.

Compared to Jameson's, Eagleton's relation to Althusserianism was always more intimate and, for that very reason, more fraught. More intimate inso-far as he was exposed directly to the impact of Althusser, under the auspices of the New Left, and more fraught insofar as his academic context was per-force one deeply imbued by a native empiricism. An unconscious attachment to the subject/object opposition was unavoidable: quite simply, it exhausted the available conceptual resources. Initially, Raymond Williams's brand of cul-tural materialism afforded an intellectual space from which to mount a meas-ure of resistance, but it was not long before Eagleton was even kicking over these traces: viewed from an Althusserian standpoint, such materialism was guilty of prioritising the role of personal experience, with the inevitable result that it over-subjectivised the social formation. At this point, an Althusserian 'break' seemed unavoidable, indeed, in the making. But the promise held out was soon dashed when the notion of an embryonic ideological unconscious, originating in Althusser, is displaced in the direction of its Freudian counter-part and, predictably, in the process, re-inscribed within the framework of the subject/object dichotomy. Eagleton's only contribution to the debate, it tran-spires, had been to over-objectivise the social formation, through a process of inversion. Rodríguez's estimate is damning: Eagleton's work remains within the horizon of positivism.

Our discussion of Michel Foucault foregrounded the other half of the para-dox posed above, namely the 'silence' that has surrounded Rodríguez's work. The thematic of 'the dog that didn't bark' has been a constant throughout our discussion of Rodríguez but was brought sharply and unavoidably into focus with respect to Foucault. The disparities in reception are not easy to explain.

The telling factor was probably one to which Rodríguez himself alludes in another context, namely that Spain had failed, historically, to catch the capitalist train, with inevitable consequences: principally, the country's bourgeois culture was left cramped, confined, and isolated on the margins of Europe. But other factors should not be excluded, as we have been at pains to suggest. In the case of Foucault, also to be taken into account was the Althusserian factor: while both Foucault and Rodríguez were deeply indebted to their former master, Foucault betrays throughout only a veiled indebtedness to Althusser and Structural Marxism, whereas, from the outset, Rodríguez protested a fundamental allegiance to a scholar who, he repeatedly confessed, had 'changed his life'. With inevitable consequences: Foucault's anti-Althusserian bias would progressively mutate into a rather vulgar anti-Marxism, focused upon 'discourse' and 'power' and, eventually, into an aesthetics of the individual, whereas Rodríguez, nurtured under Francoist fascism, would continue to prioritise 'ideology' and 'exploitation', within a Marxist framework.

If Rodríguez stood in need of a few lessons in self-promotion, then Slavoj Žižek, a scholar similarly originating on the margins of Europe, was somebody to whom he might have applied for instruction. The Slovenian might also have seemed a useful touchstone in other ways, notably in his capacity as a Lacanian theorist: what better way to assess the claims of the ideological unconscious than through a comparison with its libidinal counterpart?[1] Yet the signs were also there that such logic was to be resisted. Rodríguez himself initially passed up the chance of a direct engagement with Freudianism and the promised book on Freud never appeared, which suggests that major difficulties had arisen.[2] Whatever these were, an encounter with Žižek could only have compounded them: the overt design of the Lacanian project was to return the Cartesian subject, in the guise of Kantian self-consciousness, to its position of eminence and, even worse, to raise it to the level of sublimity, at the expense of the radical historicity of culture upon which Marxists were tiresomely wont to insist. What is distinctive about Žižek's take upon the subject/object binary is the 'undecidable' ambiguity that, allegedly, characterises it, when approached from the standpoint of our 'experience'. And experience was something that Rodríguez, along with other Althusserians, only ever 'picked up with pincers'.

In a press interview in 2003, Rodríguez reflected upon his relation to Althusser. 'He and his wife read my first book and adopted me almost as a son. I

---

1   Juan Caamaño, at least, seems to have assumed so: the first chapter of his commentary on Rodríguez bears the title 'The Agency of Ideology: Freud and Marx'.

2   Rodríguez himself confirmed as much in private correspondence.

went to work with him in Paris'.[3] Anecdotally, he would recall the kindness of Althusser's wife, who appreciated the importance of the fact that, in contrast to so many Parisian intellectuals, a Spaniard knew what it was to struggle against a fascist dictator on a daily basis. Similarly, Rodríguez would evoke the circumstances of Althusser's famous lecture in Granada – the swish of pages as the audience, in unison, followed the script that had been circulated beforehand. Such details are worth recalling insofar as they are a reminder of the circumstances in which *Teoría e historia* (1974) made its appearance and are germane to an appreciation of some of its more idiosyncratic features. It is impossible, for example, to peruse its introduction without being struck by the extent to which its author takes for granted a workable knowledge of Althusserianism on the part of his reader. The assumption would prove costly when the work came to be received. With the benefit of hindsight, it is clear that Althusser's reputation was already seriously on the wane by the mid-1970s. As Rodríguez was again the first to recognise, with respect to the Granada conference, Althusser was guaranteed no comparable reception north of the Pyrenees, nor indeed in Madrid or Barcelona. Former students were already turning against him, while scholars who at one time counted themselves among his followers were making every attempt to distance themselves from him. Among the latter, none figured more prominently than Ernesto Laclau and Chantal Mouffe.

Laclau's innovation was to problematise the basis of ontology through questioning the difference between, in Althusserian terms, the real object and the object of thought. It was not that he refused to accept the existence of the former. Rather that, in his view, such an existence was discursively constructed. In other words, he concedes at one moment that the real object exists intransitively with respect to discourse, while drawing it back at the next moment to the level of the signifier and signified. As should be obvious, a scholar who formerly tipped his hat to Althusser, was in the process of relocating on the terrain of the subject/object opposition or, to be more exact, on the terrain of the subject. Such a focus translated politically, in particular in the hands of Chantal Mouffe, into a species of left populism, central to which was the creation of a stark division between an 'us' and a 'them', picked up and translated by the leaders of the political party, Podemos, into an attack upon an elite or '*la casta*', made up of corrupt politicians and bankers, who have conspired against the 'people' and who are held as responsible, among other things, for the crash of 2008 and the ensuing austerity programme. While conceding the need to refurbish the tired rhetoric of the Left, Rodríguez has continued to insist, in opposition to

---

3   Rodríguez 2016, p. 113.

such populists, that the opposition between the individual and society, and variations on the same, does not actually exist other than as an ideological support; specifically, as a support to a capitalist system that requires the existence of 'free subject', free in the sense of being the owner of labour power, hence to be exploited by a system dedicated to the pursuit, production, and extraction of surplus value.

Recognition of his place in Spanish intellectual life came late to Rodríguez, in the form of an honorary doctorate from the University of Almería and a celebratory volume, *La literatura no ha existido siempre: Para Juan Carlos Rodríguez* (2015). While the latter provides evidence of his final acceptance, at least in the Hispanic world, several of the contributors strangely interpret the absence of a recognisable 'school' in positive terms, as if there were some virtue to scholarly reticence.[4] We await a serious sociological analysis of academic life in provincial Granada: a discipline that attaches great importance to the relations of production needs to consider those prevailing in its own institution. For those not directly connected to the Spanish Academy, it would be interesting to learn, among other things, why it has failed to generate extended commentaries on *Teoría e historia*, a text that stood in real need of such, or on Rodríguez's work in general.

Such negative considerations apart, indications are that the research programme begun by Rodríguez is far from exhausted, at least if the work of Manuel del Pino Berenguel is anything to go by. This former student of Rodríguez has thrown important light upon one of the more neglected aspects of Marxism, upon which *Teoría e historia* touches with respect to the sixteenth century but only tangentially, namely the contribution of theoretical production to economic production. Althusser tends to portray science as liberating and positive in its influence. Science, to be sure, is liable to be corrupted by power, but power itself comes from elsewhere. Del Pino Berenguel finds it far from accidental that scientific theory – surplus knowledge – enters into the equation at the same time as, on the economic level, formal subsumption mutates into real subsumption, with an eye to the production of surplus value. Nor, by the same token, is it far from accidental that such a development occurs when the pre-capitalist state is similarly mutating into its absolutist equivalent and when, on the level of ideology, feudal serfs are becoming 'free subjects', free, that is, to dispose of their labour power.[5] Amongst other things, Del Pino's work promises to throw light upon the fraught relation between surplus value and surplus enjoyment or *jouissance*. But that awaits a future discussion.

---

4 See Read 2017.
5 See Del Pino Berenguel 2008, 2017.

Bibliography

Althusser, Louis 1971, *Lenin and Philosophy and Other Essays*, translated by Ben Brewster, New York: Monthly Review Press.

Althusser, Louis 1976, *Essays in Self-Criticism*, translated by Grahame Lock, London: NLB.

Althusser, Louis 1990a [1969, 1965], *For Marx*, translated by Ben Brewster, London: Verso.

Althusser, Louis 1990b, *Philosophy and the Spontaneous Philosophy of the Scientists and Other* Essays, translated by Ben Brewster, James H. Kavanagh, Thomas E. Lewis, Grahame Lock and Warren Montag, London: Verso.

Althusser, Louis 1996, *Writings on Psychoanalysis: Freud and Lacan*, translated by Jeffrey Mehlman, New York: Columbia University Press.

Althusser, Louis 2003, *The Humanist Controversy and Other Writings*, translated by G.M. Goshgarian, London: Verso.

Althusser, Louis 2006. *Philosophy of the Encounter. Later Writings, 1978–87*, translated by G.M. Goshgarian. London: Verso.

Althusser, Louis 2014, *On the Reproduction of Capitalism: Ideology and Ideological State Apparatuses*, translated by G.M. Goshgarian, London: Verso.

Althusser, Louis and Étienne Balibar 1970 [1968], *Reading Capital*, translated by Ben Brewster, London: NLB.

Anderson, Perry 1968, 'Components of the National Culture', *New Left Review*. 50, July/Aug: 3–58.

Anderson, Perry 1974, *Lineages of the Absolutist State*, London: Verso.

Anderson, Perry 1980, *Arguments within English Marxism*, London: NLB.

Anderson, Perry 2013 [1974], *Passages from Antiquity to Feudalism*, London: Verso.

Bartolovich, Crystal and Neil Lazarus (eds) 2002, *Marxism, Modernity, and Postcolonial Studies*, Cambridge: Cambridge University Press.

Benton, Ted 1984, *The Rise and Fall of Structural Marxism: Althusser and His Influence*, New York: St Martin's.

Benvenuto, Bice and Roger Kennedy 1986, *The Works of Jacques Lacan*, New York: St Martin's.

Berceo, Gonzalo de 1985, *Milagros de Nuestra Señora*, Madrid: Cátedra.

Bhaskar, Roy 1978, *A Realist Theory of Science*, 2nd ed., Hassocks, Sussex: Harvester.

Bhaskar, Roy 1986, *Scientific Realism and Human Emancipation*, London: Verso.

Bhaskar, Roy 1989a [1979], *The Possibility of Naturalism: A Philosophical Critique of the Contemporary Human Sciences*, 2nd ed., Hemel Hemstead: Harvester.

Bhaskar, Roy 1989b. *Reclaiming Reality: A Critical Introduction to Contemporary Philosophy*, London: Verso.

Bhaskar, Roy 1991, *Philosophy and the Idea of Freedom*, Oxford and Cambridge, MA: Blackwell.

Bhaskar, Roy 1993, *Dialectic: The Pulse of Freedom*, London: Verso.

Bhaskar, Roy 2002a, *Reflections on Meta-Reality: Transcendence, Emancipation and Everyday Life*, New Delhi and London: Thousand Oaks and Sage.

Bhaskar, Roy 2002b, *From Science to Emancipation: Alienation and the Actuality of Enlightenment*, New Delhi/Thousand Oaks/London: Sage.

Bhaskar, Roy 2002c, *Meta-Reality: Creativity, Love and Freedom*, New Delhi and London: Thousand Oaks and Sage.

Bhaskar, Roy with Mervyn Hartwig 2010, *The Formation of Critical Realism: A Personal Perspective*, London: Routledge.

Bottomore, Tom (ed.) 1983, *A Dictionary of Marxist Thought*, Oxford: Basil Blackwell.

Borges, Jorge Luis 1999, *Collected Fictions*, translated by Andrew Hurley, New York: Penguin Books.

Borges, Jorge Luis 2007 [1953], *Otras Inquisiciones*, Barcelona: Destino.

Boucher, Geoff 2008, *The Charmed Circle of Ideology: A Critique of Laclau and Mouffe, Butler and Žižek*, Melbourne: Re.press.

Bourdieu, Pierre and Terry Eagleton 1994, 'Doxa and Common Life: An Interview', see Žižek (ed.), 265–77.

Brontë, Emily, 2003 [1847], *Wuthering Heights*, London: Pan Macmillan (Collector's Library).

Brown, Norman O. 1968, *Life against Death: The Psychoanalytical Meaning of History*, London: Sphere.

Brown, Andrew, Steve Fleetwood and John Michael Roberts 2002, *Critical Realism and Marxism*, London: Routledge.

Buchanan, Ian, 2006 *Fredric Jameson: Live Theory*, London: Continuum.

Caamaño, Juan Manuel 2008, *The Literary Theory of Juan Carlos Rodríguez: Contemporary Spanish Cultural Critic*, Lewiston: Edwin Mellen.

Callari, Antonio and David F. Ruccio (ed.) 1996, *Postmodern Materialism and the Future of Marxist Theory: Essays in the Althusserian Tradition*, Hanover: Wesleyan University Press.

Callinicos, Alex 1976, *Althusser's Marxism*, London: Pluto.

Callinicos, Alex 1987, *Making History: Agency, Structure and Change in Social Theory*, Oxford: Basil Blackwell (Polity Press).

Callinicos, Alex 1989, *Against Postmodernism: A Marxist Critique*, Cambridge: Polity Press.

Callinicos, Alex 2006, *The Resources of Critique*, Cambridge (U.K.) and Malden, MA: Polity Press.

Callinicos, Alex 2014, *Deciphering Capital: Marx's Capital and its Destiny*, London: Bookmarks.

Carnoy, Martin 1984, *The State and Political Theory*, Princeton: Princeton University Press.

Cervantes Saavedra, Miguel de. 1950. *The Adventures of Don Quixote*, translated by J.M. Cohen. Harmondsworth: Penguin.

Chomsky, Noam 1966, *Cartesian Linguistics: A Chapter in the History of Rationalist Thought*, New York: Harper & Row.

Chomsky, Noam 1968, *Language and Mind*, New York: Harcourt.

Chomsky, Noam 1987, *The Chomsky Reader*, New York: Pantheon.

Claramonte, Manuel Breva 1983, *Sanctius' Theory of Language: A Contribution to the History of Renaissance Linguistics*, Amsterdam: John Benjamins.

Collier, Andrew 1989, *Scientific Realism and Socialist Thought*, Hemel Hempstead: Harvester Wheatsheaf.

Collier, Andrew 1994, *Critical Realism: An Introduction to Roy Bhaskar's Philosophy*, London: Verso.

Creaven, Sean 2007, *Emergentist Marxism: Dialectical Philosophy and Social Theory*, London: Routledge.

Creaven, Sean 2015, 'The "Two Marxisms" Revisited: Humanism, Structuralism and Realism in Marxist Social Theory', *Journal of Critical Realism*, 14, 1: 7–53.

Dean, Kathryn, Jonathan Joseph, John Michael Roberts and Colin Wight 2006, *Realism, Philosophy and Social Science*, Basingstoke: Palgrave MacMillan.

Del Pino Berenguel, Manuel 2008, 'Teorías y capital', *Laberinto*. 28, 3: 77–86.

Del Pino Berenguel, Manuel 2017, 'Marx y Juan Carlos Rodríguez', *Pensar desde abajo*, 6: 129–37.

Dews, Peter 1987, *Disintegration: Post-Structuralist Thought and the Claims of Critical Theory*, London: Verso.

Diefenbach, Katja, Sara R. Farris, Gal Kirn, and Peter D. Thomas (eds) 2013, *Encountering Althusser: Politics and Materialism in Contemporary Radical Thought*, London: Bloomsbury Academic.

Eagleton, Terry 1967, *Shakespeare and Society: Critical Studies in Shakespearean Drama*, London: Chatto & Windus.

Eagleton, Terry 1970, *The Body as Language: Outline of a 'New Left' Theology*, London and Sydney: Sheed and Ward.

Eagleton, Terry 1986, *Against the Grain*, London: Verso.

Eagleton, Terry 1991, *Ideology: An Introduction*, London: Verso.

Eagleton, Terry 1996 (1983), *Literary Theory: An Introduction*. 2nd ed., Oxford and Cambridge, Massachusetts: Blackwell.

Eagleton, Terry 2006 (1976), *Criticism and Ideology: A Study in Marxist Literary Theory*, London: Verso.

Eagleton, Terry 2012, *The Event of Literature*, New Haven and London: Yale University Press.

Eagleton, Terry and Matthew Beaumont 2009, *The Task of the Critic: Terry Eagleton in Dialogue*, London/New York: Verso.

Elliott, Gregory 1987, *Althusser: The Detour of Theory*, London/New York: Verso.

Errejón, Íñigo and Chantal Mouffe 2015, *Construir pueblo: hegemonía y radicalización de la democracia*, Barcelona: Icaria.

Fink, Bruce 1995, *The Lacanian Subject: Between Language and Jouissance*, Princeton, New Jersey: Princeton University Press.

Flieger, Jerry Aline 1982, 'The Prison-House of Ideology: Critic as Inmate', *Diacritics*, 12, 3: 47–56.

Foucault, Michel 1970 (1966), *The Order of Things: An Archaeology of the Human Sciences*. London: Tavistock.

Foucault, Michel 1971 (1961), *Madness and Civilisation: A History of Insanity in the Age of Reason*, translated by Richard Howard, London: Tavistock.

Foucault, Michel 1972 (1969), *The Archaeology of Knowledge*, translated by A.M. Sheridan Smith, London: Tavistock.

Foucault, Michel 1973 (1963), *The Birth of the Clinic: An Archaeology of Medical Perception*, translated by A.M. Sheridan, London: Tavistock.

Foucault, Michel 1979 (1975), *Discipline and Punish: The Birth of the Prison*, translated by Alan Sheridan, Harmondsworth: Penguin Books.

Foucault, Michel 1980, *Power/Knowledge: Selected Interviews and Other Writings: 1972–1977*, translated by Colin Gordon, Leo Marshall, John Mepham, Kate Soper, New York: Pantheon Books.

Foucault, Michel 1981 (1976), *The History of Sexuality: Volume 1: An Introduction*, translated by Robert Hurley, Harmondsworth: Penguin.

Foucault, Michel 1986 (1984), *The Care of the Self*, translated by Robert Hurley, New York: Vintage Books.

Geras, Norman 1986, *Literature and Revolution: Essays on Marx*, London: Verso.

Geras, Norman 1990, *Discourses of Extremity: Radical Ethics and Post-Marxist Extravagances*, London: Verso.

Goshgarian, G.M., 2013, 'The very essence of the object, the soul of Marxism and other singular things: Spinoza in Althusser 1959–67', in Diefenbach et al, 89–111.

Goux, Jean-Joseph 1990, *Symbolic Economies: After Marx and Freud*, translated by Jennifer Curtiss Gage. Ithaca, New York: Cornell University Press.

Gramsci, Antonio 1971, *Selections from the Prison Notebooks of Antonio Gramsci*, translated by Quintin Hoare and Geoffrey Nowell Smith, London: Lawrence and Wishart.

Groff, Ruth Porter et al. 2015, 'In Memoriam: Roy Bhaskar 1944–2014', *Journal of Critical Realism*, 14, 2: 119–36.

Hartwig, Mervyn (ed.) 2007. *Dictionary of Critical Realism*, London: Routledge.

Harvey, David 2014, *Seventeen Contradictions and the End of Capitalism*, London: Profile Books.

Hebreo, León 1947 [1535], *Diálogos de amor*, translated by Inca Garcilaso de la Vega, Buenos Aires: Espasa Calpe.

Helmling, Steven 2001, *The Success and Failure of Fredric Jameson: Writing, the Sublime, and the Dialectic of Critique*, Albany: State University of New York.

Huarte de San Juan, Juan 1977 [1575, 1594], *Examen de ingenios para las ciencias*, Madrid: Editora Nacional.

Iglesias, Pablo 2013, *Conversaciones entre Pablo Iglesias y Nega (LCDM)*, Barcelona: Icaria.

Iglesias, Pablo 2014, *Maquiavelo frente a la gran pantalla: cine y política*, Madrid: Akal.

Iglesias, Pablo 2015a, *Politics in a Time of Crisis: Podemos and the Future of European Democracy*, translated by Lorna Scott Fox, London: Verso.

Iglesias, Pablo 2015b, *Una nueva transición: materiales del año del cambio*, Madrid: Akal.

Isaacs, Jorge, 1988 [1867], *María*. México: Rei.

Jameson, Fredric 1971, *Marxism and Form: Twentieth-Century Dialectical Theories of Literature*, Princeton N.J.: Princeton University Press.

Jameson, Fredric 1972, *The Prison-House of Language: A Critical Account of Structuralism and Russian Formalism*, Princeton, N.J.: Princeton University Press.

Jameson, Fredric 1981, *The Political Unconscious: Narrative as a Socially Symbolic Act*, Ithaca, New York: Cornell University Press.

Jameson, Fredric 1984 [1961], *Sartre: The Origins of a Style*, New York: Columbia University Press.

Jameson, Fredric 1991, *Postmodernity or, The Cultural Logic of Late Capitalism*, London: Verso.

Jameson, Fredric 1994, *The Seeds of Time*, New York: Columbia University Press.

Jameson, Fredric 2002, *A Singular Modernity: Essay on the Ontology of the Present*. London and New York: Verso.

Jameson, Fredric 2010, *Valences of the Dialectic*, London: Verso.

Jameson, Fredric 2011, *Representing Capital: A Reading of Volume One*, London and New York: Verso.

Jessop, Bob 1985, *Nicos Poulantzas: Marxist Theory and Political Strategy*, New York: St. Martin's.

Kaplan, E. Ann and Michael Sprinker (eds) 1993, *The Althusserian Legacy*, London: Verso.

Lacan, Jacques 2008, 'Courtly Love as Anamorphosis', in *The Ethics of Psychoanalysis: 1959–60*, translated by Dennis Porter, London: Routledge, 171–90.

Laclau, Ernesto 1979 [1977], *Politics and Ideology in Marxist Theory*, London: Verso.

Laclau, Ernesto and Chantal Mouffe 2014 [1985], *Hegemony and Socialist Strategy: Towards a Radical Democratic Politics*, London: Verso.

Lazarillo de Tormes 1987, Mexico: Rei.

Lecourt, Dominique 1975, *Marxism and Epistemology: Bachelard, Canguilhem, Foucault*, translated by Ben Brewster, London: NLB.

Leff, Gordon 1958, *Medieval Thought: St Augustine to Ockham*, Harmondsworth: Penguin.

León, Fray Luis de 2015, *De los nombres de Cristo*, Madrid: Ediciones Q.

Lorca, García 2004, *El público, Teatro completo II*, Barcelona: Debolsillo.

Lorca, García 2018, *Comedia sin título*, Madrid: Cátedra.

Lukács, Georg 1971, *History and Class Consciousness: Studies in Marxist Dialectics*, translated by Rodney Livingstone, Cambridge, Massachusetts: MIT Press.

Lukács, Georg 1973 [1923], *History and Class Consciousness: Studies in Marxist Dialectics*, translated by Rodney Livingstone, London: Merlin Press.

Macherey, Pierre 1978, *Theory of Literary Production*, translated by Geoffrey Wall, London: Routledge and Kegan Paul.

Manuel, Don Juan 1974 [1327–32], *Libro de los estados*, Oxford: Clarendon Press.

Manuel, Don Juan 1981 [1342], *Libro de las armas*, in *Obras completas*, Madrid: Gredos, 117–40.

Manuel, Don Juan, 1982 [1330–5], *Libro de los enxiemplos del Conde Lucanor e de Patronio*, Madrid: Cátedra.

Marx. Karl 1973, *Grundrisse: Foundations of the Critique of Political Economy* (*Rough Draft*), translated by Martin Nicolaus, Harmondsworth/London: Penguin Books/ New Left Review.

Marx, Karl 1976, *Capital: A Critique of Political Economy*, volume I, translated by Ben Fowkes. London: Penguin Books/New Left Review.

Marx, Karl 1981, *Capital: A Critique of Political Economy*, volume III, translated by David Fernbach. London: Penguin Books/New Left Review.

Miliband, Ralph 1970, 'The Capitalist State: A Reply to Nicos Poulantzas', *New Left Review*, 59: 53–60.

Miliband, Ralph 1973, 'Poulantzas and the Capitalist State', *New Left Review*, 82: 83–92.

Montag, Warren 1984, 'Marxism and Psychoanalysis: The Impossible Encounter', *Minnesota Review* (New Series), 23: 70–85.

Montag, Warren 2003, *Louis Althusser*, Basingstoke, Hampshire, and New York: Palgrave Macmillan.

Montag, Warren 2013, *Althusser and His Contemporaries: Philosophy's Perpetual War*, Durham/London: Duke University Press.

Montengón, Pedro de, 1984 [1786], *Eusebio*. Madrid: Editora Nacional.

Moratín, Leandro Fernández de, 1968 [1792, 1806], *La comedia nueva. El sí de las niñas*, Madrid: Clásicos Castalia.

Mouffe, Chantel 1979, 'Hegemony and Ideology in Gramsci', in *Gramsci and Marxist Theory*, edited by Chantel Mouffe, London: Routledge, 168–204.

Moya Casas, Pablo César and Juan Varela-Portas de Orduña 1999, 'Entrevista a Juan Carlos Rodríguez', *Ferrán*, 17: 73–83.

Norrie, Alan 2010, *Dialectic and Difference: Dialectical Critical Realism and the Grounds of Justice*, London and New York: Routledge.

Norrie, Alan 2012, 'Who is "the Prince"? Hegel and Marx in Jameson and Bhaskar', *Historical Materialism* 20, 2: 75–104, http://dx.doi.org/10.1163/1569206X-12341234.

Otero, Carlos Peregrín 1970, *Introducción a la lingüística transformacional (retrospective de una confluencia)*, Mexico: Siglo XXI Editores.

Pereira Zazo, Oscar et al 1994, 'Subjectivity in Early Modern Spain', Special Issue, *Journal of Interdisciplinary Literary Studies*, 6.2.

Poema de Mio Cid 1977, Madrid: Cátedra.

Poulantzas, Nicos 1973, *Political Power and Social Classes*, translated by Timothy O'Hagan, London: NLB.

Poulantzas, Nicos 1976, 'The Capitalist State: A Reply to Miliband and Laclau', *New Left Review*, 95: 63–83.

Poulantzas, Nicos 1978, *State, Power, Socialism*, London/New York: Verso.

Read, Malcolm K. 1981, *Juan Huarte de San Juan*, Boston: Twayne.

Read, Malcolm K. 1983, *The Birth and Death of Language: Spanish Literature and Linguistics: 1300–1700*, Madrid: Turanzas.

Read, Malcolm K. 1990, *Visions in Exile: The Body in Spanish Literature and Linguistics: 1500–1800*, Amsterdam: John Benjamins.

Read, Malcolm K. 1992, *Language, Text, Subject: A Critique of Hispanism*, West Lafayette: Purdue University Press.

Read, Malcolm K. 1998, *Transitional Discourses: Culture and Society in Early Modern Spain*, Ottawa: Dovehouse.

Read, Malcolm K. 1998, 'The Ideological Transformations of Tirso's Don Juan: Laws of Change and Traces of Desire in Baroque Linguistics', in Read 1998, 51–90.

Read, Malcolm K. 1999, 'Cristóbal de Vallalón: Language, Education and the Absolutist State', in *Culture and the State in Spain (1550–1850)*, edited by T. Lewis and F.J. Sánchez, New York: Garland, 1–33.

Read, Malcolm K. 2003a, 'From Feudalism to Capitalism: Ideologies of Slavery in the Spanish American Empire', *Hispanic Research Journal*, 4, 2: 151–71.

Read, Malcolm K. 2003b, *Educating the Educators: Hispanism and its Institutions*, Newark: University of Delaware Press.

Read, Malcolm K. 2004a, 'Ideologies and the Spanish Transition Re-Visited: Juan Huarte de San Juan, Juan Carlos Rodríguez and Noam Chomsky', *Journal of Medieval and Early Modern Studies*, 34, 2: 309–43.

Read, Malcolm K. 2004b, 'Racism and Commodity Character Structure: The Case of Sab', *Journal of Iberian and Latin American Studies*, 10, 1: 61–84.

Read, Malcolm K. 2010, *The Matrix Effect: Hispanism and the Ideological Unconscious*, n.p.: CreateSpace.eBook.

Read, Malcolm K. 2015a, 'The Legacy of Althusser Revisited and Re-Discovered: Juan Carlos Rodríguez', in *La literatura no ha existido siempre*, edited by Miguel Ángel García, Ángela Olalla Real, Andrés Soria Olmedo, Granada: Editorial Universidad de Granada: 465–80.

Read, Malcolm K. 2015b, 'What We Talk About When We Talk About Marxism: Juan Carlos Rodríguez, Althusser and the Ideological Unconscious', *Mediations*, 29, 1: 69–100, available at www.mediationsjournal.org/articles/what-we-talk-

Read, Malcolm K. 2017, 'The Dog that didn't Bark: The Case of Juan Carlos Rodríguez', *Alabé* 16, July–Dec. available at www.revistaalabé.com.

Read, Malcolm K. 2019, *Latin American Colonial Studies: A Marxist Critique*, Cambridge Scholars Publishing.

Regan, Stephen (ed.) 1998, *The Eagleton Reader*. Oxford: Blackwell.

Resch, Robert Paul 1992, *Althusser and the Renewal of Marxist Social Theory*, Berkeley: University of California Press.

Resch, Robert Paul 1999, 'Running on Empty: Žižek's Concept of the Subject', *Journal for the Psychoanalysis of Culture and Society*, 4, 1: 92–98.

Resch, Robert Paul 2001, 'The Sound of Sci(l)ence: Žižek's Concept of Ideology-Critique', *Journal for the Psychanalysis of Culture and Society*, 6, 1: 6–20.

Roberts, Adam 2000, *Fredric Jameson*. London: Routledge.

Rodríguez, Juan Carlos 1990 [1974], *Teoría e historia de la producción ideológica: las primeras literaturas burguesas (siglo XVI)*, Madrid: Akal.

Rodríguez, Juan Carlos 1991, *Moratín o el Arte Nuevo de hacer Teatro*, Granada: Ediciones Anel.

Rodríguez, Juan Carlos 1994a, *Lorca y el sentido: un inconsciente para una historia*. Madrid: Akal.

Rodríguez, Juan Carlos 1994b, *La poesía, la música y el silencio (De Mallarmé a Wittgenstein)*, Seville: Renacimiento.

Rodríguez, Juan Carlos 1996 [1982], *Granada Tango*, 2nd. ed., Madrid: La Tertulia.

Rodríguez, Juan Carlos 1998a, 'Lecturas de nuestra vida: sueños y discursos objetivos (En torno a la explotación ideológica)', *Iralka*, 10: 5–12.

Rodríguez, Juan Carlos 1998b, *Brecht, siglo XX*, Granada: De guante blanco/ Comares.

Rodríguez, Juan Carlos 2001a, 'La literatura y la pesadilla del yo (Freud y los dos inconscientes)', in *Matrices del siglo XX: Signos precursores de la posmodernidad*, Madrid: Universidad Complutense, 393–425.

Rodríguez, Juan Carlos 2001b, *La literatura del pobre*, 2nd ed., Granada: De Guante Blanco/Comares.

Rodríguez, Juan Carlos 2001c [1984], *La norma literaria*, Madrid: Editorial Debate.

Rodríguez, Juan Carlos 2002a, *Theory and History of Ideological Production: The First Bourgeois Literatures (the 16th Century)*, translated by Malcolm K. Read. Newark: University of Delaware Press.

Rodríguez, Juan Carlos 2002b, *De qué hablamos cuando hablamos de literatura: Las formas del discurso*, Granada: De Guante Blanco / Comares.

Rodríguez, Juan Carlos 2002/3, *Althusser: Blow-Up (las líneas maestras de un pensamiento distinto)*, Granada: Asociación Investigación & Crítica de la ideología literaria en España.

Rodríguez, Juan Carlos 2003a, *El escritor que compró su propio libro: para leer el Quijote*, Barcelona: Debate.

Rodríguez, Juan Carlos 2003b, *Literatura, moda y erotismo: el deseo*, Granada: Icile.

Rodríguez, Juan Carlos 2005, *Pensar/leer históricamente (entre el cine y la literatura)*, Granada: Icile.

Rodríguez, Juan Carlos 2008a [2003], 'Althusser: Blowup (Lineaments of a Different Thought'), translated by Malcolm K. Read, *PMLA*. 123, 3: 762–79.

Rodríguez, Juan Carlos 2008b, *State, Stage, Language: The Production of the Subject*, translated by Malcolm K. Read, Newark: University of Delaware Press. (Title in Spanish: *La norma literaria*.)

Rodríguez, Juan Carlos 2011a, *Tras la muerte del aura (En contra y a favor de la Ilustración)*, Granada: Editorial Universidad de Granada.

Rodríguez, Juan Carlos 2011b, *Para una lectura de Heidegger*, Granada: Editorial Universidad de Granada.

Rodríguez, Juan Carlos 2012, *Formas de leer a Borges (o las trampas de la lectura)*, Almería: Editorial Universidad de Almería.

Rodríguez, Juan Carlos 2013, *De qué hablamos cuando hablamos de marxismo (Teoría, literatura y realidad histórica)*, Madrid: Akal.

Rodríguez, Juan Carlos 2015, *Para una teoría de la literatura (40 años de Historia)*, Madrid: Marcial Pons.

Rodríguez, Juan Carlos 2016, *Pensar la literatura: entrevistas y bibliografía (1961–2016)*, Granada: Asociación Icile.

Rodríguez, Juan Carlos and Álvaro Salvador 1987, *Introducción al estudio de la literatura hispanamericana: Las literaturas criollas de la independencia a la revolución*, Madrid: Akal.

Rossi-Landi, Ferruccio 1975, *Linguistics and Economics*, The Hague and Paris: Mouton.

Ruben, David-Hillel 1977, *Marxism and Materialism: A study in Marxist Theory of Knowledge*, Hassocks, Sussex: Harvester Press.

Saavedra (Duque de Rivas), Ángel de 1991 [1835], *Don Álvaro o la fuerza del sino*, Madrid: Cátedra.

Sheridan, Alan 1980, *Michel Foucault: The Will to Truth*, London: Tavistock.

Smart, Barry, 1985 [1983], *Foucault, Marxism and Critique*, London: Routledge and Kegan Paul.

Smart, Barry 1985, *Michel Foucault*, London: Routledge.

Sotiris, Panagiotis 2013, 'Rethinking aleatory materialism', in Diefenbach et al, 27–41.

Sprinker, Michael 1992, 'The Royal Road: Marxism and the Philosophy of Science', *New Left Review*, 191 (Jan-Feb): 122–44.

Thomas, Peter D. 2011, 'Conjuncture of the integral state? Poulantzas's reading of Gramsci.' In *Reading Poulantzas*, edited by Alexander Gallas, Lars Bretthauer, John Kannankulam and Ingo Stützle, Pontypool: Merlin Press, 277–92.

Thomas, Peter 2013, 'Althusser's last encounter: Gramsci', in Diefenbach et al, 137–51.

Thompson, E.P., 1995 [1978], *The Poverty of Theory or an Orrery of Errors*, London: Merlin Press.

Torre, Esteban 1977, *Ideas lingüísticas y literarias del doctor Huarte de San Juan*, Seville: Publicaciones de la Universidad de Sevilla.

Townshend, Jules 1996, *The Politics of Marxism: The Critical Debates*, London and New York: Leicester University Press.

Tucker, Robert C. (ed.) 1978, *The Marx-Engels Reader*, 2nd ed. London/New York: W.W. Norton & Co.

Vázquez Montalbán, Manuel 1996 [1979], *Los mares del sur*, Barcelona: Planeta.

Vega, Garcilaso de la 1989, *Poesías completas*, Madrid: Castalia.

Vega, Lope de 2010 [1611?], *El villano en su rincón*. Madrid: Castalia.

Villalón, C. De 1966 [c. 1550], *El scholástico*, Madrid: Consejo Superior de Investigaciones Científicas.

Williams, Raymond 1965, *The Long Revolution*, Harmondsworth: Penguin Books.

Wolfenstein, Eugene Victor 1993, *Psychoanalytic Marxism: Groundwork*, New York and London: Guilford Press.

Wood, Ellen Meiksins 1986, *The Retreat from Class: A New 'True' Socialism*, London: Verso.

Žižek, Slavoj, 1989 *The Sublime Object of Ideology*, London and New York: Verso.

Žižek, Slavoj 1991, *Looking Awry: An Introduction to Jacques Lacan through Popular Culture*, Cambridge, Massachusetts: MIT Press.

Žižek, Slavoj 1994a, 'The Spectre of Ideology', in *Mapping Ideology*, edited by Slavoj Žižek, London: Verso, 1–33.

Žižek, Slavoj (ed.) 1994b, *Mapping Ideology*, London: Verso.

Žižek, Slavoj 1999, 'Courtly Love, or Woman as the Thing', in *The Žižek Reader*, Edited by Elizabeth Wright and Edmond Wright, Oxford: Blackwell, 148–73.

Index of Names

Index of Subjects

www.ingramcontent.com/pod-product-compliance
Lightning Source LLC
Chambersburg PA
CBHW061601120626
46550CB00004B/1577